Statistics for Economists

Statistics for Economists

Linus Yamane
Pitzer College, USA

World Scientific

NEW JERSEY • LONDON • SINGAPORE • BEIJING • SHANGHAI • HONG KONG • TAIPEI • CHENNAI • TOKYO

Published by

World Scientific Publishing Co. Pte. Ltd.
5 Toh Tuck Link, Singapore 596224
USA office: 27 Warren Street, Suite 401-402, Hackensack, NJ 07601
UK office: 57 Shelton Street, Covent Garden, London WC2H 9HE

Library of Congress Cataloging-in-Publication Data
Names: Yamane, Linus, author.
Title: Statistics for economists / Linus Yamane, Pitzer College, USA.
Description: Hackensack, NJ : World Scientific, [2024] | Includes index.
Identifiers: LCCN 2023039668 | ISBN 9789811278723 (hardcover) |
ISBN 9789811287923 (paperback) | ISBN 9789811278815 (ebook for institutions) |
ISBN 9789811278822 (ebook for individuals)
Subjects: LCSH: Economics--Statistical methods.
Classification: LCC HB137 .Y34 2024 | DDC 330.01/5195--dc23/eng/20230925
LC record available at https://lccn.loc.gov/2023039668

British Library Cataloguing-in-Publication Data
A catalogue record for this book is available from the British Library.

For any available supplementary material, please visit
https://www.worldscientific.com/worldscibooks/10.1142/13483#t=suppl

Desk Editors: Sanjay Varadharajan/Pui Yee Lum

Typeset by Stallion Press
Email: enquiries@stallionpress.com

Preface

This first course in statistics is designed for bright undergraduates. There are dozens of statistics textbooks in the market. But most of these textbooks are either pitched too high or too low for my students at the Claremont Colleges. Many use calculus and are designed for graduate students in technical fields. Others provide black box formulas without any derivations. This textbook tries to derive everything from the first principles without using calculus or linear algebra. It is important for students to understand why they are doing what they are doing. Otherwise, students cannot distinguish meaningless results from significant results.

While my own education through New Jersey public schools, MIT, and Yale was primarily focused on mastering calculus, my academic career has focused on the use of statistics and econometrics. As an economist and as a human being, I use the concepts of probability and statistics every day. The concepts covered here are important for everyone to understand in order to make sound decisions in our daily lives.

This textbook is relatively short. It covers all the fundamental ideas in probability and statistics. It is primarily designed to prepare undergraduate economics majors for a course in econometrics or linear regression analysis. It will help all undergraduates learn to appreciate, understand, and undertake empirical research. It is based on over three decades of experience teaching undergraduate statistics. I hope you find it useful.

About the Author

Linus Yamane is a Professor of Economics and Asian American Studies at Pitzer College in Claremont, California. He earned his B.S. in Economics at M.I.T. and his Ph.D. in Economics at Yale University. He has been teaching statistics and econometrics for over 35 years. He has taught at Yale University, Harvard University, Wellesley College and Pitzer College. He has published a number of papers on Asian Americans and labor market discrimination. He has worked at AT&T Bell Laboratories, the World Bank, and the Japan Development Bank. He enjoys playing tennis and road biking.

Acknowledgements

Every single idea in this book was developed by other scholars. I am merely putting their ideas in one place. I am grateful for many excellent teachers over the years like Harold Freeman, Edwin Kuh, Randall Olsen, Jon Peck, David Pollard, Don Andrews, Gene Savin, Peter Phillips, and Gary Chamberlain. The work of people like Joshua Angrist, Christopher Dougherty, David Germany, Damodar Gujarati, Darrell Huff, Allen Paulos, Jörn-Steffen Pischke, Christian Rudder, Seth Stephens-Davidowitz, Richard Thaler, Henri Theil, Charles Wheelan and Jeffrey Wooldridge have made their way into these pages. All the errors here are my own.

I would like to thank several generations of Claremont College students for their insightful questions. I thank Nati Azmera, Stella Stringer, and Elijah Weiss for their careful reading. I thank Lucas Yan for his excellent comments, suggestions, questions, and corrections. And I thank Pitzer College for providing me with a sabbatical and Kwansei Gakuin University for providing me with a beautiful and peaceful campus to write.

This book is dedicated to Julie and Chaska, who make it all worthwhile, and to the memory of my parents, Tetsuo and Mitzi Yamane, who made me lucky.

Contents

Chapter 1

Why Statistics?

1.1 Introduction

Most college students take statistics. Every college student should take statistics. No matter what your major or your career or your life focus, you should understand the concepts discussed in statistics classes. While the entire math curriculum in the American educational system from pre-school through high school is designed to get you to understand calculus, this design is misdirected. The math curriculum should be designed to get all students to understand statistics. Very few adults use calculus on a regular basis. But all adults need to use the principles of probability and statistics to make decisions every day. Statistics should be the most useful course you take in college.

The general goal of this textbook is to help you become a wise human being. Over the last few decades, an enormous amount of research in behavioral economics has demonstrated that human beings systematically behave in inconsistent ways. We use heuristics, mental shortcuts, and rules of thumb. Our decisions are strongly influenced by how our risky options are framed. We are averse to loss. And we tend to favor the known over the unknown, including known risks over unknown risks. This course aims to teach you to think more clearly.

1.2 Goals

1.2.1 *Think more clearly*

We have four specific goals in this course. The first is to think more clearly. According to Mark Twain, Benjamin Disraeli said "there are three kinds of lies: lies, damned lies, and statistics." Since we are confronted with an enormous amount of information every day, we need to be able to properly judge the conflicting claims of politicians, advertisers, and others. We want to learn to interpret information correctly and not to read too much or too little from the data.

Suppose an automobile manufacturer says that "90% of all our cars sold in this country in the last 10 years are still on the road," suggesting that their cars are reliable and long-lasting. Would you draw a different conclusion if you were told that this company recently entered the U.S. market and that 90% of its cars were sold in the last 3 years?

Suppose that you are told that "3 out of 4 doctors surveyed prefer Tylenol to aspirin." Would you go out and buy some Tylenol the next time you have a headache? Would it make a difference if they had surveyed 4 doctors or 40 doctors or 4,000 doctors? Wouldn't you want to know?

Suppose a historian tells you that there was an epidemic of teenage pregnancies in the U.S. 50 years ago. "The proportion of infants whose mothers were teenagers rose, from 14% in 1960 to 18.9% in 1975, a dramatic rise of 35%." Does this mean that a larger percent of teenagers had babies in 1975 than in 1960? Is it possible that teenagers were no more likely to have a baby in 1975 than in 1960 and that older women were just having far fewer babies in 1975 than in 1960? Yes.

Suppose you are introduced to a 30-year-old American woman named Marion. You learn that she is very shy and withdrawn, invariably helpful but with little interest in people or the real world. A meek and tidy soul, she requires order and structure and has a passion for detail. Do you think Marion is more likely to be a salesperson or a librarian? Most people respond with a librarian. But there are 20 times more retail salespersons in the U.S. than librarians.

Marion may not be a very good salesperson, but she is much more likely to be a salesperson than a librarian.

1.2.2 *Understand uncertainty*

The second goal in this course is to learn to more accurately perceive risk and uncertainty. Benjamin Franklin once wrote that "in this world nothing can be said to be certain except death and taxes." This leaves a lot of uncertainty to examine with probability and statistics. Unfortunately, too many people are statistically illiterate. Most Americans seem unable to deal with the fundamental notions of numbers and chance. There are large gaps between popular perceptions of various risks and the reality of them (see Table 1.1).

In 2003, a 22-year-old was killed when the Big Thunder Mountain Railroad roller coaster at Disneyland derailed. Afterward, attendance at Disneyland dropped dramatically. Some 16–19 million people go to Disneyland each year. Very few of them actually get killed. There have been only a handful of deaths in the history of the park. But

Table 1.1. Causes of death.

Lifetime Odds of Dying in U.S. (2021)	
Heart disease	1/6
Cancer	1/7
Covid-19	1/10
Opioid overdose	1/58
Suicide	1/91
Car crash	1/93
Fall	1/98
Gun assault	1/208
Motorcycle	1/747
Drowning	1/1,006
Fire or smoke	1/1,287
Choking on food	1/2,659
Bicyclist	1/3,546
Sunstroke	1/4,655
Dog attack	1/53,843
Hornet, wasp and bee stings	1/54,516

Source: National Center for Health Statistics, National Safety Council. Permission to reprint/use granted by the National Safety Council © 2023.

about 3,000 people die each year in car accidents in the State of California. There are 39 million people in California. When you hear about someone getting killed in a car accident, do you stop driving to work?

When Americans are killed by terrorists abroad, do you cancel your summer European vacation? Thousands of Americans did just that after a handful of Americans were killed abroad in 2015 and 2016. But millions of Americans travel abroad every year. The odds of getting killed by a terrorist are minuscule. People overestimate these risks. You are much more likely to be killed driving to the airport.

The flip side of uncertainty is certainty. People seem to be much more certain about some things than they should be. They systematically underestimate some risks. There are persistently high rates of entrepreneurial entry, despite the frequency of entrepreneurial failure. There are high rates of mergers and acquisitions, despite the very high failure rate. There are very high rates of trading on the stock market despite the cost of trading. People are overly optimistic about their future success on the job market and underestimate the risk of failure.

People tend to underestimate risks they willingly take but overestimate risks in situations they cannot control. They do not hesitate to drive from Los Angeles to San Francisco but get nervous about flying from LA to SF. From major heart surgery to a course of minor drugs, people overestimate the benefits and underestimate the risks of a variety of medical procedures. People tend to overestimate the probability of positive events and underestimate the probability of negative events happening to them in the future. Do you really think you are going to win the state lottery? Most of us are not very realistic.

1.2.3 *Understand the world*

The third goal of the class is to learn how the world works. Academic research is a search for the "truth." We want to figure out what causes what. They teach us a lot of theories in our college classes. But how do we know if any of these theories help us to understand the real world? How do we evaluate whether these theories are useful or worthwhile?

In economics classes, we learn that federal budget deficits stimulate the economy. We learn that increasing the money supply will decrease the interest rate. We learn that higher taxes lead to deadweight loss. In other classes, you might learn about how smoking causes lung cancer or how greenhouse gases cause global warming. How do we know if any of these claims are true?

In this class, we will learn how to look at the data to test various theories about the world. We will learn how to discard some theories and to keep others. We will learn how to work toward a better and better understanding of how the world works through the examination of empirical data.

1.2.4 *Make decisions under uncertainty*

The fourth and final goal of this class is to learn how to make decisions under conditions of uncertainty. You have to make these kinds of decisions every day. Should I take this statistics class? What classes should I take this semester? What major should I choose? What career will bring me the most happiness? Whom should I marry? What car should I buy? How much should I save? Should I have kids? How should I allocate my savings between stocks, bonds, and real estate? How much insurance should I buy?

These are all personal decisions. When society faces similar questions, we call them policy questions. If we are in a recession, should we expand government spending, and if so, by how much? The answer depends on the size of the government spending multiplier which, in turn, depends on the size of the marginal propensity to consume. How big are these? How do we know? Should the Federal Reserve decrease interest rates? If so, by how much? Does it depend on the sensitivity of investment to interest rates? Does it depend on the sensitivity of exchange rates to interest rates? How does it depend? How do we know?

If you are running a company, you may want to maximize profits. But does this mean increasing the price or decreasing the price of your product? The answer depends on the elasticity of demand. What is your estimate of the elasticity of demand? How certain are you of this estimate?

When you increase advertising for your product, it may increase sales. But advertising is not free. You might increase your profits by increasing or decreasing your advertising expenditures. What should you do? How should you decide?

Should farmers use manure or compost as fertilizer? We can try both on separate fields and examine the resulting crop yields. But weather, irrigation, type of soil, etc. vary from one field to another from year to year. How do we control for all these things to figure out which is a better fertilizer?

1.3 Who Should I Marry?

Let us consider a specific example of decision-making under uncertainty. How do you decide whom to marry? Some people will decide with their heart. But what if you want to decide with your head? What should you do?

We might begin by creating a model of your dating life and decision-making. Suppose you will meet N potential spouses in your dating life. N may be a small number for some and large for people like Neymar or Maria Sharapova. You have to estimate N for yourself. We assume you can rank all the dates you meet in order of preference. You prefer Avery over Riley, and Riley over Casey. We assume your soulmate is equally likely to be any of the N potential spouses. We assume you meet your dates sequentially, and you only date one person at a time. If you reject a date, they are gone forever. If you choose to marry someone, you forgo all the dates who would have followed. Under these circumstances, how do you decide whom to marry?

The best policy decision here is known as the 37% rule. You should reject the first 37% of all the potential spouses and marry the first person afterward who is superior to all previous dates. If you follow this rule, you are more likely to end up with your soulmate than with any other policy rule. The probability of finding your soulmate with this policy is also 37% for large N. The proof uses the idea of conditional probability and a little calculus. But the results should make some intuitive sense. You generally do not want to marry the first person you go out with. You want to get some sense of the people out there. And then you want to marry the first person who is better than anyone else you have ever dated.

1.4 Is Statistics Hard?

Since everyone should learn statistics, this textbook is designed to explain statistics to all college students. All you will need to know to understand the statistics in this textbook is addition, subtraction, multiplication, division, and how to take logs. While knowledge of calculus is always useful, it is not necessary to understand this textbook. We will not use linear algebra either. We will just use basic algebra, take a few logs, and draw many graphs.

This does not mean that statistics is necessarily an easy subject. We are mostly learning how to think clearly, and thinking clearly is not always easy. But we can learn to think clearly with some practice. We will do many problems together, but you will need to do many more on your own if you are going to get good at statistics. It is like learning to play tennis. I can explain how to hold the racquet and how to hit the ball, but there is no way you are going to become a good player unless you get out on the court and hit a lot of tennis balls. Remember that if you spend 10,000 hours on anything, you can become an expert and write your own book.

This textbook is designed for undergraduate economics majors. All majors are welcome, but the examples will mostly be drawn from the field of economics. The specific topics in statistics we will cover are the ones most useful for economists. The textbook will prepare students to further their study of statistics, econometrics, or regression analysis. We will begin the textbook by learning about probability, then proceed to statistical inference, and then finish with regression analysis. We will use Excel which is the software available on almost every computer in the world.

There must be hundreds of college-level statistics textbooks on the market. While this is a very standard course in statistics, this textbook does not line up well with other textbooks. Some textbooks require the use of calculus and linear algebra and are appropriate for applied math majors and graduate students. Other textbooks keep the math simple but do not provide any derivations. They present formulas without explaining where those formulas come from. This textbook will derive almost all of the formulas from first principles without using calculus or linear algebra. Students will learn why we do what we do. We will avoid using these black boxes that students apply blindly. While a little more theoretical than other similar textbooks, you will develop a deeper understanding of the material.

1.5 Are Americans in Love?

We see the results of polls all the time. Here are the results of a Gallup poll on love. They randomly selected 1,002 Americans and asked them whether or not they were in love. This is what they found in a 1991 Gallup Poll (see Table 1.2).

What can we learn about Americans from this kind of poll? It seems like men are more likely to be "in love" than women. People from the West, rural areas, Republicans, the wealthy, and Protestants are more likely to be "in love". But this poll only asked 1,002 Americans whether or not they were in love. We learned something about these 1,002 Americans, but can the responses of 1,002 Americans tell us how all 333 million Americans are feeling?

1.6 Population

In general, we will be interested in the larger population. We may be thinking about all college students, all Americans, or all human beings. We might be thinking about all firms or all countries. We are generally thinking about the larger world out there. The population

Table 1.2. Love.

Gallup Poll (February 6–9, 1991)			
Male	76%	Republicans	77%
Female	65%	Democrats	61%
East	74%	Over $50,000	89%
West	67%	Under $20,000	46%
Rural Area	81%	Protestant	73%
Large City	70%	Catholic	70%
White	71%	College graduate	75%
Non-white	65%	Non-High School graduate	49%

might be finite (all Americans) or infinite (all real numbers). The population might be conceptual like the set of all possible hands in a game of poker or all possible lottery ticket numbers.

While we are generally interested in understanding something about the larger population, it is often impossible to gather information on every element in the population. If the population is infinite, it would be impossible to examine every element of the population. Even if the population is finite, it may be too costly to examine every element within it. No one wants to call all 333 million Americans to ask them about love. Thus, the best we can do is to gather data on a smaller subset of the entire population. We call this a sample.

1.7 Sample

We usually want a randomly selected sample from the larger population. We say a sample of size n is randomly selected if every possible sample of size n is equally likely to have been chosen. While some samples are created by the experimenter, most samples in economics are created by "nature." We know that any population that is not completely homogeneous can only be approximately represented by a sample. So, how do we generalize the characteristics of the sample to the entire population?

1.8 Goals

The Gallup poll did not survey every single American, only 1,002 Americans. But we can actually say something about all Americans from this very limited sample.

Statistical inference is the method by which we generalize the sample characteristics to the entire population. Statistical inference is the way we draw general conclusions about the phenomena under consideration, beyond the facts of the observed sample data. It allows us to make rational decisions from incomplete data and make wise decisions in the face of uncertainty. We can make informed statements about Americans in general and also test theories we might have about Americans.

In order to do this, we need some understanding of probability. For example, we need to understand the probability of Gallup surveying the particular 1,002 Americans that it did. How likely was this particular sample to be chosen as opposed to some other random sample of Americans? How likely is it for our sample data to look the way it does?

Suppose we have a theory that men are more likely to be "in love" than women. We can test this theory by asking a random sample of men and women. If our theory is true, our sample responses are likely to look a particular way. If our theory is not true, our sample responses are less likely to look that way. So if our survey responses are of the likely kind, then we have evidence to support our theory. If our survey responses are of the unlikely kind, it casts some doubt on our theory. But we need to understand probability to understand how likely or unlikely particular outcomes are.

Thus, this course will cover basic concepts in probability. Then we will move on to statistical inference, the process of learning something about the larger world from some sample data. And we will conclude with regression analysis, the process of learning about the relationships between two or more variables. But before we really begin, we still need to define what we mean by statistics.

1.9 Exercises

(1) Would you prefer to buy frozen yogurt which is 20% fat or frozen yogurt which is 80% fat-free? (same)

(2) We are preparing for an outbreak of the COVID delta variant which is expected to kill 600 people. Two possible programs are proposed. If Program A is adopted, 200 people will be saved. If Program B is adopted, there is a 1/3 probability that 600 people will be saved and 2/3 probability that no people will be saved. Which program would you choose?

Now suppose we are preparing for an outbreak of the COVID omicron variant which is expected to kill 600 people. Two possible programs are proposed. If the Program A is adopted, 400 people will die. If Program B is adopted, there is a 1/3 probability that no people will die and 2/3 probability that all 600 will die. Which program would you choose?

Did you choose the same program for both COVID variants?

(3) If you have prostate cancer, one treatment is to have a prostatectomy, removal of the prostate. Would you undertake this surgery if you had a 90% chance of surviving the operation? Would you undertake this surgery if you had a 10% chance of dying during the operation? (same)

(4) Suppose the iPhone SE sells for $500. If you had a coupon for $50 off, would you consider buying the phone? If you had a coupon for 10% off, would you consider buying the phone? Does one sound more attractive than the other?

(5) Would you be more willing to drive across town to save $10 on a $20 purchase than $10 on a $1,000 purchase even though the effort expended and the amount of money saved would be the same?

(6) Would you drive across town during a blizzard to see the Chicago Bulls play basketball if you already bought the non-refundable tickets? Would you drive across town during a blizzard if someone had given you the tickets for free?

(7) Consider two gambles. With gamble A, you win $1,500 with a probability of 33%, $1,400 with a probability of 66%, and $0 with a probability of 1%. With gamble B, you win $920 with certainty. Which gamble do you prefer? Why?

Chapter 2

Descriptive Statistics

2.1 Introduction

While it is easy to lie with statistics, it is even easier to lie without them.

—Frederick Mosteller

Statistics can be defined as the collection, organization, presentation, analysis, and interpretation of numerical facts and data. The goal of statistics is to gain appropriate information from data. The field of statistics is often separated into two different areas: descriptive statistics and inferential statistics.

2.2 Descriptive Statistics

Descriptive statistics describes the collection, organization, and presentation of data. It shows us how to summarize and describe a given dataset. We see descriptive statistics everywhere.

Every day we see the win/loss record of our favorite sports teams, or hear that the stock market has gone up, or that the cost of borrowing money has gone down. We hear about global temperatures going up or about college admission rates going down.

Every month the Bureau of Labor Statistics (BLS) generates the Employment Situation Summary which provides descriptive statistics about the labor force. The BLS also generates the Consumer Price Index every month describing the level of prices in the economy.

Every quarter all publicly traded companies generate a quarterly report about their sales, costs, operations, earnings, and dividends. They provide a numerical description of how their company is doing.

And every year most colleges generate an annual report describing their operating revenues, the operating expenditures, and their net operating income or loss. They will report on the number of faculty, staff, and students, their admissions and enrollment figures, their endowment, and comprehensive fees.

For many years, my favorite bedtime reading was the *US Statistical Abstract* which contained data on demography, labor force, production, international trade, prices, and incomes. Almost as fun was the data Appendix to the *World Development Report* published by the World Bank. All of these data are now readily available online. You can Google anything these days and bring up reams of data.

There are many methods of collecting data. Three of the most common methods are direct observation, experiments, and surveys. You can count the number of cars that drive through an intersection at various times during the day. You can run an experiment to see if children prefer to have one marshmallow immediately or will wait 10 minutes to have two marshmallows. You can conduct surveys through interviews or self-administered questionnaires to solicit information directly from people on whether they are happier now than they were 10 years ago.

Good measurement is essential to improving the human conditions. Ben Bernanke writes, "In many spheres of human endeavor, from science to business to education to economic policy, good decisions depend on good measurement."

While careful thought is required in the collection of data, we will not dwell on this topic here. Most economists will work with data which have been collected by others. Enormous amounts of data are collected by private firms (Amazon, Google, Microsoft, etc.), local and national governments (Bureau of Labor Statistics, Department of Commerce, Federal Reserve, etc.), and international organizations (World Bank, IMF, United Nations, etc.). The focus will be on how to analyze the data we have already collected.

2.3 Inferential Statistics

Inferential statistics describes the way we draw general conclusions about the phenomena under consideration, beyond the facts of the observed data. It is about rational decision-making from incomplete data. It is about wise decision-making in the face of uncertainty. We know very few things in this world with certainty. Do omega-3 fatty acids decrease the likelihood of heart disease? Maybe, but we may never know for sure. Nevertheless, we still need to make decisions like whether or not to eat more fish. How do we look at the data and make the best decisions possible?

2.4 Variables

A variable is a characteristic of any entity being studied that is capable of taking on different values across entities or time or place. This could be your age or whether you go to a public or private school. Variables can be **qualitative variables** or **quantitative variables**. The qualitative variables place entities into groups. We might be looking at the brand of a car, the marital status of an individual, the academic major of a student, or the political system of a country. Sometimes, qualitative variables are called categorical variables because we are putting entities into categories.

The quantitative variables take on numerical values. This could be the number of shoes you own or the years of education you have. Quantitative variables can be discrete or continuous variables. Discrete quantitative variables might be the number of children, or the number of games won, or the number of days the stock market goes up. These variables can be represented by some integer. Continuous quantitative variables might be annual income, or weight in pounds, or inches of snowfall. These variables can be represented by real numbers. A continuous variable can take any real value between two real numbers, but a discrete variable can only take on a countable number of possible values.

2.5 Describing Variables

Whenever we look at data, whether it is qualitative data or quantitative data, we will generally ask three questions. First, we want to know something about what is being measured by the data. Is it income or wealth? How are these quantities being measured? Is it real or nominal dollars at the individual or state or country level? And why are these quantities being measured? Are we interested in the standard of living or the market value of economic output? Depending on why we are interested in these data, real after-tax income might be better than GDP per capita.

Second, we will ask why all the data observations are not the same. Since there are 12 inches in every foot, we do not spend much time exploring how many inches there are in a foot. When you look at a variable like height, some people are 25 inches tall and others are 96 inches tall. We will ask what values this variable might take, and how often. Where are most of the observations? Why are some observations much larger than other observations? We will want to describe the data. How tall are most people? What is the center of the distribution? How much variation is there? What does the dispersion look like?

And third, we will want to eventually look at relationships. What is the relationship between this variable and other variables? Is there a relationship between height and weight? Is it a positive relationship or a negative relationship? Is it a linear relationship? Is it a strong relationship or a weak relationship? Is it a causal relationship? By understanding these relationships, we get a better understanding of how the world works.

We will begin by looking at each variable by itself and then look at its relationship with other variables. And when we are looking at a variable, we will begin by looking at graphs of the variable, because a picture is worth a thousand words, and then proceed to look at numerical summaries of the variable.

2.6 Graphing Data

The kind of graphs we use will depend on the kind of data we have. In general, qualitative data will call for different types of graphs than quantitative data.

2.6.1 *Pie charts and bar graphs*

With qualitative data or categorical data, we will typically use pie charts and bar graphs.

Pie charts will immediately give you an impression of the relative size or importance of each category. The bar graphs can represent the actual counts in each category or the percentage share in each category or both (see Figures 2.1–2.4).

And you can have many more categories. The limit will be the size of your page (see Figures 2.5–2.6).

The bars may be two-dimensional or three-dimensional. You should be careful whenever you see a three-dimensional bar chart. Three-dimensional bar charts can give you very misleading impressions about the relative importance of each category. They should be used and viewed with caution.

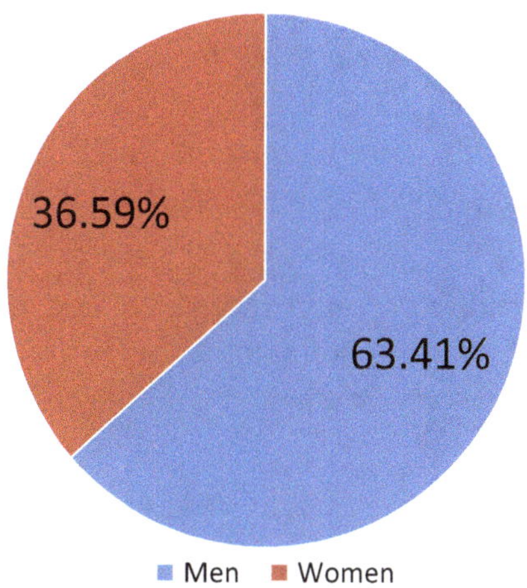

Fig. 2.1. Gender distribution pie chart.

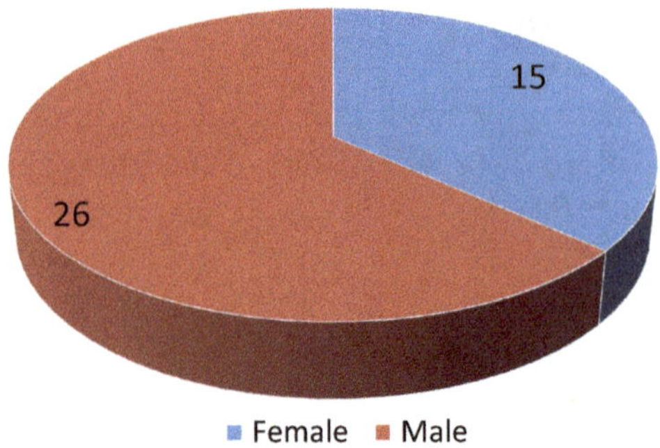

Fig. 2.2. 3D gender distribution pie chart.

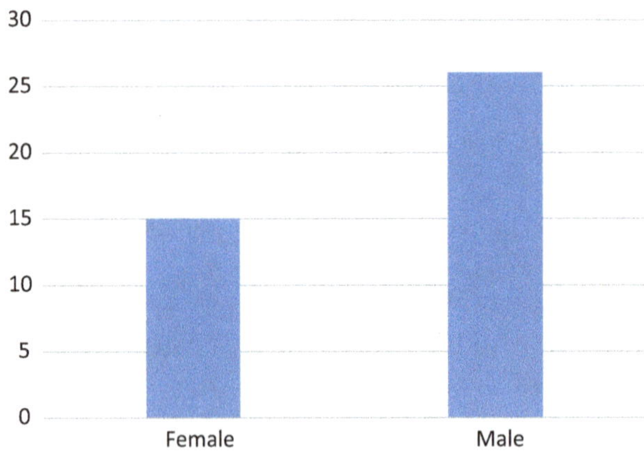

Fig. 2.3. Gender distribution bar chart.

The President earns twice as much as the Professor in Figure 2.7. But Figure 2.8 gives you the impression that the President earns about eight times more.

Excel is a spreadsheet program which can easily generate pie charts and bar graphs from your data.

2.6.2 *Stem plots*

With quantitative data, pie charts and bar graphs work less well. You can make them, but they are much less informative. For quantitative data, we begin with stem plots or stem and leaf diagrams. Stem

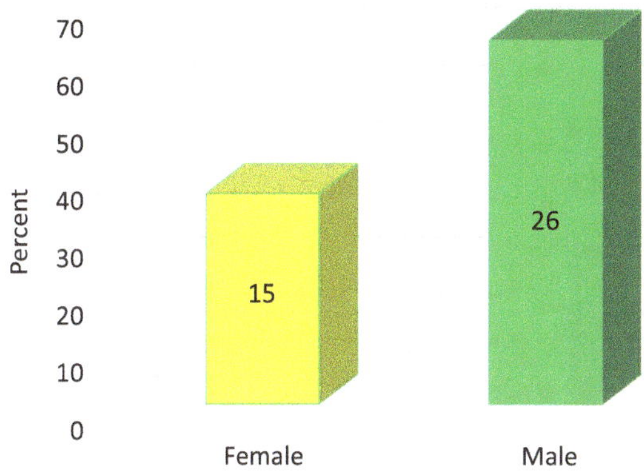

Fig. 2.4. 3D gender distribution bar chart.

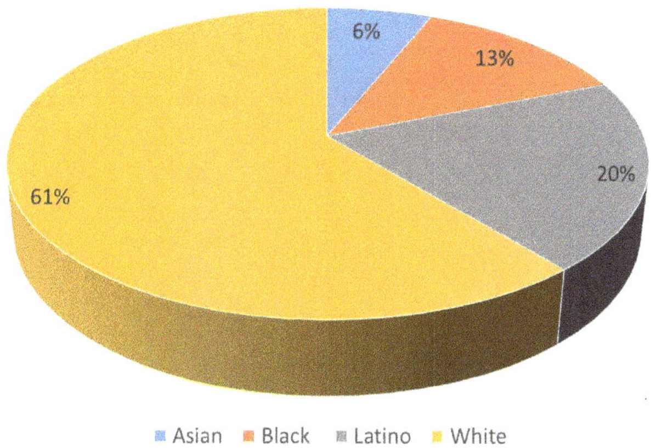

Fig. 2.5. Diversity pie chart.

plots are useful when you do not have too many observations, and the numerical values fall within a limited range of numbers such as 0–100 or 200–300.

On stem plots, the stem is defined as all but the last digit of your data points. The leaf is defined as the last digit of your data points. If a data point is 356, the stem is 35 and the leaf is 6. In order to create a stem and leaf diagram, begin by making a vertical column with all the integer numbers from the smallest stem to the largest stem. Put

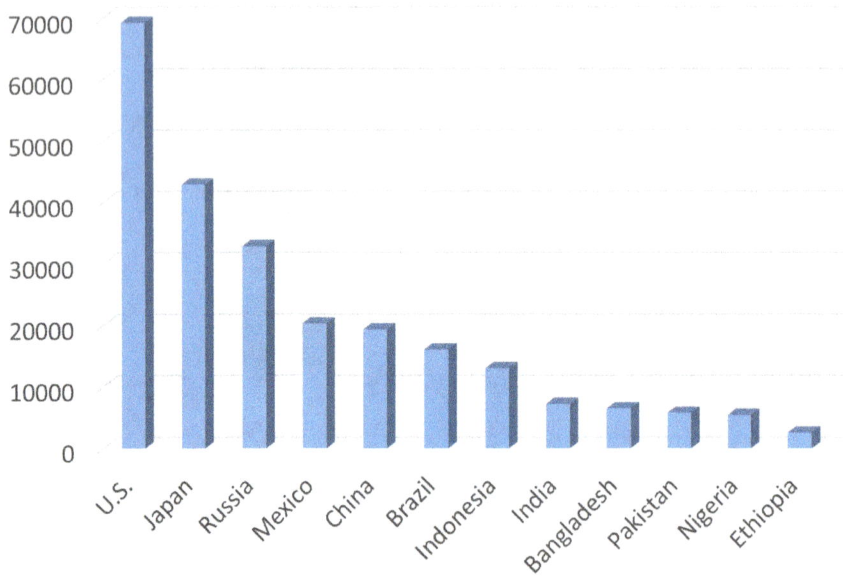

Fig. 2.6. GDP per capita.

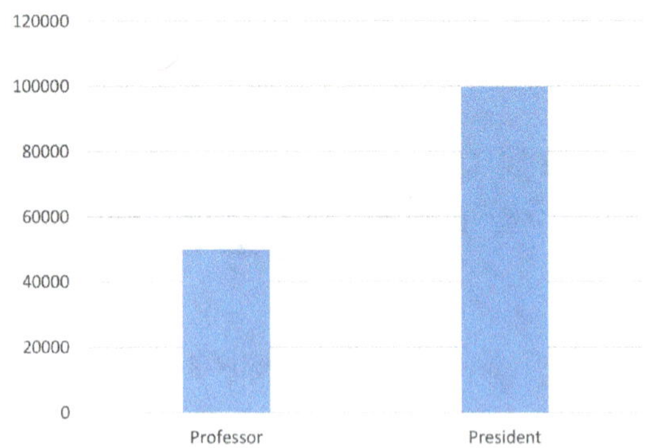

Fig. 2.7. Income inequality.

the largest stem on the top and the smallest stem on the bottom. Then, put each leaf in a row next to the appropriate stem. This is a stem and leaf diagram. Every single data point is represented on a stem and leaf diagram. By looking at a stem and leaf diagram, you can recreate all the observations in your dataset.

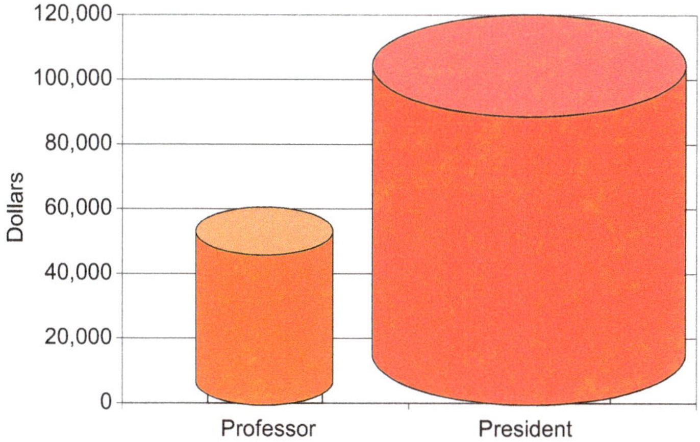

Fig. 2.8. 3D income inequality.

Suppose you have the following sample of male weights: 185, 175, 200, 178, 180, 165, 230, 185, 190, 170, 125, 205, and 175. We might first sort the data in order like the following: 230, 205, 200, 190, 185, 185, 180, 178, 175, 175, 170, 165, and 125. We note that the numbers range from 125 to 230. The first two digits of these numbers range from 12 to 23. Thus, we begin by creating a stem with all the numbers from 12 to 23. Then, we record the 3rd digit of every number next to the appropriate stem. We will get a stem plot which looks like this (see Table 2.1).

Once you have created a stem plot, you can examine the overall distribution of the data. Note the overall pattern and any striking deviations. What is the shape of the distribution, the center of the distribution, and the spread of the distribution? Are there any outliers which fall outside the overall pattern of the data? Does the distribution have one peak or several peaks? If it has only one peak, we say it is unimodal. If it has two peaks, we say it is bimodal. If it has more peaks, we say it is multimodal. Is the distribution symmetric or skewed? If it is skewed, is it skewed to the right (positively skewed) or skewed to the left (negatively skewed)? (See Figures 2.9–2.11).

Stem plots of some variables are not very interesting. For example, stem plots of the heights of the students in a class will probably be

Table 2.1. Stem and leaf diagram.

Stem	Leaf
24	
23	0
22	
21	
20	50
19	0
18	550
17	8550
16	5
15	
14	
13	
12	5
11	

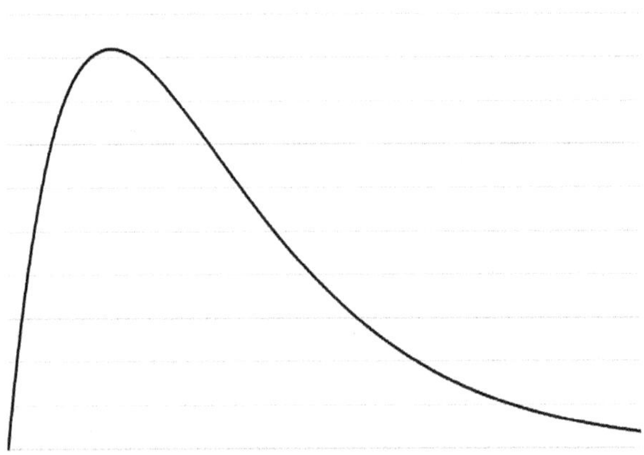

Fig. 2.9. Skewed right.

fairly uninformative. Most of the students will be between 60 and 69 inches tall, and a few students will be between 70 and 79 inches tall. So all the students may fall into one of these two cells. You will get no sense of the dispersion of heights within in the class.

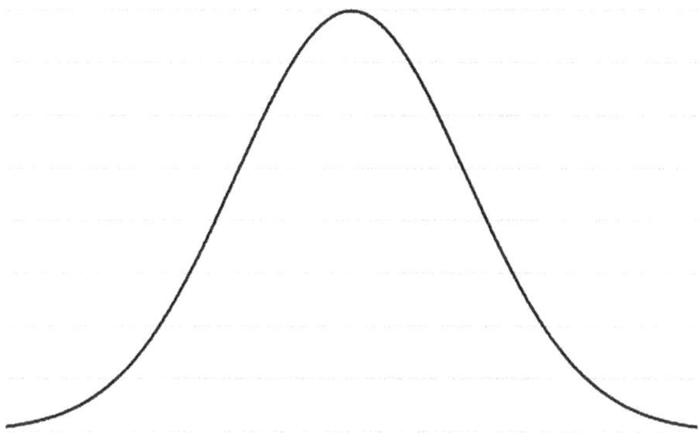

Fig. 2.10. Symmetric.

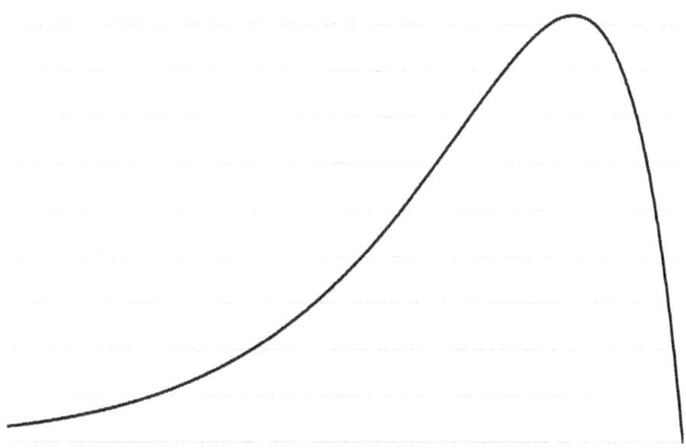

Fig. 2.11. Skewed left.

2.6.3 *Histograms*

With small datasets, stem plots can give you a quick way to visualize your data. But with larger datasets, stem plots quickly become unmanageable. If you take a stem plot and put it on its side, you have the beginnings of a histogram. In general, histograms can do everything a stem plot can do and more. Histograms are more powerful because you can choose the size of each cell rather than having the cells defined by the data. You can also have each cell represent the count of observations in the cell or the percent of all observations which fall in the cell.

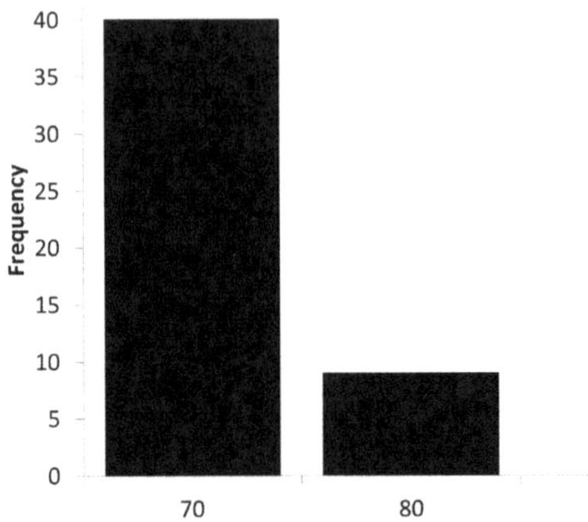

Fig. 2.12. Histogram with 10-inch cells.

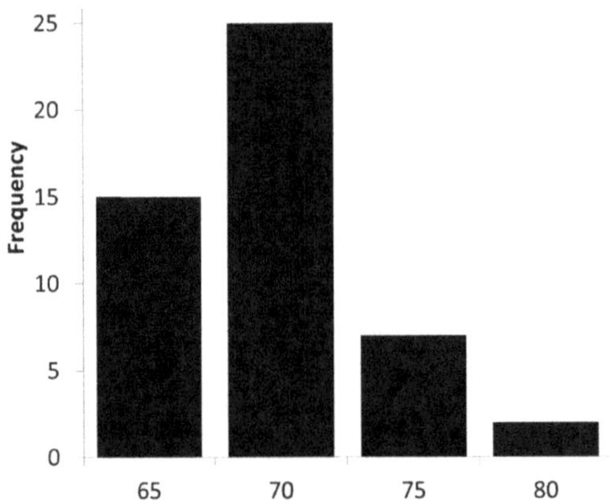

Fig. 2.13. Histogram with 5-inch cells.

Here, we have some histograms of the heights of a sample of students. The first histogram uses 10-inch bins (see Figure 2.12). Everyone who is 61–70 inches tall is in the first cell, and everyone from 71 to 80 inches tall is in the second cell. In the second histogram, we use 5-inch bins (see Figure 2.13). We have students 61–65, 66–70, 71–75, and 76–80 inches tall.

Here, we have histograms with 2-inch cells and half-inch cells (see Figures 2.14 and 2.15).

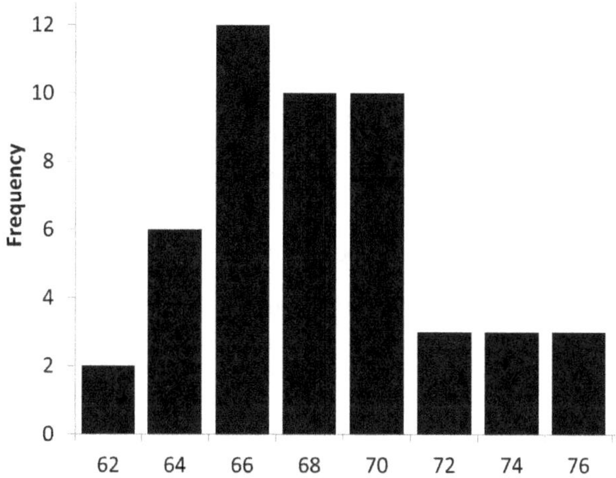

Fig. 2.14. Histogram with 2-inch cells.

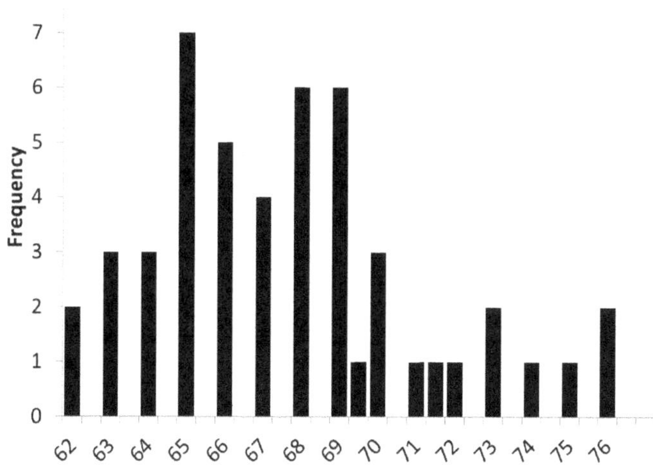

Fig. 2.15. Histogram with half-inch cells.

We observe that the size of the cells can give you different impressions about the distribution. As a producer of histograms, you can decide for yourself which cell size generates the most informative histograms. As a consumer of histograms, you should be aware that your impressions might be manipulated. Excel can generate histograms for your datasets.

2.6.4 *Time series plots*

If you have time series data, you will probably graph the data over time. A time series is a sequence of numerical data points in successive order. A time series tracks the movement of the chosen data, such as GDP or unemployment or inflation, over a specified period of time with data points recorded at regular intervals, usually annually, quarterly, monthly, or daily (see Figure 2.16).

When you look at a time series plot, observe any seasonal variations or repetition at regular intervals. GDP typically grows more slowly in the first quarter of the year than in the rest of the year. It is hard to produce goods and services in the snow. Are there any trends over time? Is there a persistent long-term rise or fall?

As with any graph, you should pay attention to scales being used on both the horizontal and the vertical axes of the graph. The vertical and horizontal scales on time series graphs can be manipulated to give you the impression that some variable is going up quickly or hardly going up at all.

Fig. 2.16. US real GDP per capita (2012$).

(a)

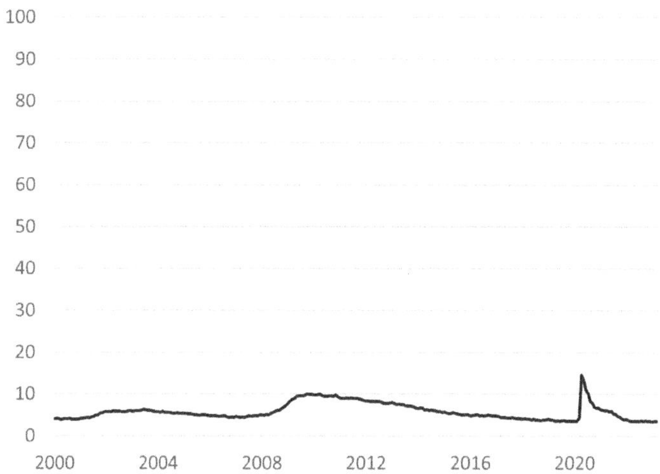

(b)

Fig. 2.17. Unemployment rate.

Figure 2.17a is a graph of the unemployment rate in the US from 2000 to 2020. In Figure 2.17b the unemployment numbers are exactly the same, but the left-hand scale is different. You can get a very different impression from the two graphs.

2.7 Numerical Summaries

After we have graphed our data and have a general sense of the data, we will look at some numerical summaries of the data. We want to use numbers to describe the shape of the distribution. We would like some measure of the center of the distribution and the spread or dispersion of the distribution. We might also want to know if the distribution is symmetrical or skewed either to the right or to the left. We might also want to know if the distribution has a single peak or a number of peaks. A graph will give us a sense of all these things with just a glance. But we may want a more precise measure of all these characteristics. Let's start with a measure of the center of the distribution.

2.7.1 *Center of a distribution*

To measure the center of a distribution, there are a number of measures we might consider. The first is the **mean** or the average value of the data. If there are n observations, we merely add up all the observations and divide the total by n. We use $\bar{X}$ (read as X bar) as our notation for the mean of the data.

$$\bar{X} = \frac{\sum X_i}{n} = \frac{X_1 + X_2 + \cdots + X_n}{n} \tag{2.1}$$

If our sample data are represented by the numbers 2, 5, 7, and 7, the sample mean is 5.25. The mean or average is a useful number. But we should be aware that it is sensitive to outliers. If Taylor Swift walks into our classroom, the average income of the people in our class with rise dramatically. This average number may tell us very little about the incomes of most of us in the classroom.

A second measure is the **median** or the middle value of the data. This is the midpoint of the distribution. Here, we arrange all the observations from smallest to largest, and the median is the middle value. There will be a middle value if we have an odd number of observations. If we have an even number of observations, we take the two middle values and their average. If our data are represented by the numbers 2, 5, 7, and 7, the median is 6, the average of 5 and 7.

A third measure is the **mode** or the most common value of the data. Which observation appears most frequently? This is the mode. If our data are represented by the numbers 2, 5, 7, and 7, the mode is 7. The mean and the median make no sense when you are dealing with qualitative data. If there are 12 women and 8 men in the room, what is the mean? This makes no sense. But since there are more women than men, the mode would be a woman.

The distribution of household incomes in the United States is skewed to the right or positively skewed. About 10% of households earn more than $180,000 a year. They pull the distribution to the right. Consequently, the mean household income is much higher than the median household income. The mean household income is $90,021, but the median household income is $63,179. A unimodal distribution is skewed right if the mean is greater than the median. It is skewed left if the mean is less than the median.

2.7.2 *Spread of a distribution*

Once we have some sense of the center of a dataset, we should look at some measures of the spread or dispersion in the data. You will often hear terms like 1st quartile, 2nd quartile, and 3rd quartile to give you a sense of the spread of the data. A quarter of the observations will fall below the 1st quartile, a half of the observations will fall below the 2nd quartile or median, and 75% of the observations will fall below the 3rd quartile. Consequently, a quarter of the observations will fall above the 3rd quartile, and 75% of the observations will fall above the 1st quartile.

We can generalize the concept of **quartiles** by defining the meaning of **percentiles**. A percentile indicates the value below which a given percentage of observations in a group of observations falls. So, 33% of the observations will fall below the 33rd percentile and 67% of the observations will fall below the 67th percentile. Thus, the 1st quartile is the same as the 25th percentile. The 2nd quartile is the same as the median or the 50th percentile. And the 3rd quartile is the same as the 75th percentile.

It turns out that finding a particular quartile or percentile in a set of data is not as straightforward as one might think. There is more than one way this can be done. We will calculate percentiles using the following procedure. We begin by using this formula to find the position of any percentile:

$$L_p = (n+1)\frac{P}{100} \tag{2.2}$$

where L_p is the position, n is the sample size, and P is the percentile. Remember that the 1st quartile is the 25th percentile, etc. So, we can use this formula to help determine quartiles and percentiles.

Suppose we are looking at the weights of some students in a class. The raw numbers are as follows: 135, 185, 120, 185, 140, 135, 138.6, 180, 153, 140, 135, 180, 175, 175, and 160 lbs. Note that we have 15 observations.

First, we should sort these numbers from smallest to largest: 120, 135, 135, 135, 138.6, 140, 140, 153, 160, 175, 175, 180, 180, 185, and 185.

To find the median or the 50th percentile, we would use the formula above as follows:

$$L_{50} = (15+1)\frac{50}{100} = 8$$

Thus, the median would be the 8th observation or 153 lbs.

To find the first quartile or the 25th percentile, we would use the formula above as follows:

$$L_{25} = (15+1)\frac{25}{100} = 4$$

Thus, the first quartile would be 4th observation or 135 lbs.

To find the 33rd percentile, we would use the formula above as follows:

$$L_{33} = (15+1)\frac{33}{100} = 5.28$$

The 33rd percentile is in the 5.28th position. What does this mean? It means the 33rd percentile is between the 5th position and the 6th position and is 28% of the way from the 5th position to the

6th position. We take the difference between those two values in these positions ($140 - 138.6 = 1.4$), multiply the difference by decimal number of the position, 0.28, ($0.28 \cdot 1.4 = 0.392$), and add that number to the smaller value ($138.6 + 0.392 = 138.992$) to give us 138.992 as the 33rd percentile.

There are a number of ways to get a sense of the dispersion in any dataset. The **range** is the distance between the minimum and the maximum observation. The range of our student weights is $185 - 120 = 65$ lbs. But the range is very sensitive to outliers. Again, if Konishiki (Hawaiian Japanese sumo wrestler) walks into our classroom, the range of weights will dramatically increase. An alternative to the range is the **interquartile range** (IQR), the distance from the 1st quartile to the 3rd quartile. This is a measure of dispersion which is not affected by changes in the tails of the distribution. Now, Konishiki can walk into the room, and the interquartile range in our weights will not change much. The IQR in this dataset is 45 lbs ($180 - 135 = 45$) whether the heaviest person in the room weights 185 lbs or 633 lbs.

We have used the term outlier without a formal definition. One rule of thumb is as follows: An observation is an **outlier** if it is more than $1.5 \cdot IQR$ above the 3rd quartile or below the 1st quartile. Using this criterion, there are no outliers in this dataset. But you should always use your best judgment. If an observation is a legitimate data point which has been generated in the same way as all the other data points, it need not be considered an outlier. But if an outlier is the result of an experimental error, you may want to exclude the observation from the dataset.

In order to describe the dispersion of a dataset, a common technique is to present the **five-number summary**. The five-number summary includes the minimum observation, the 1st quartile, the median (2nd quartile), the 3rd quartile, and the maximum observation. The same information is often presented as a box plot (see Figure 2.18). In a **box plot**, the central box spans the 1st and 3rd quartiles. The line through the box marks the median. Observations which are more than $1.5 \cdot IQR$ outside the box are individually plotted as possible outliers. And the lines extend from the box to the smallest and largest observations not suspected of being outliers.

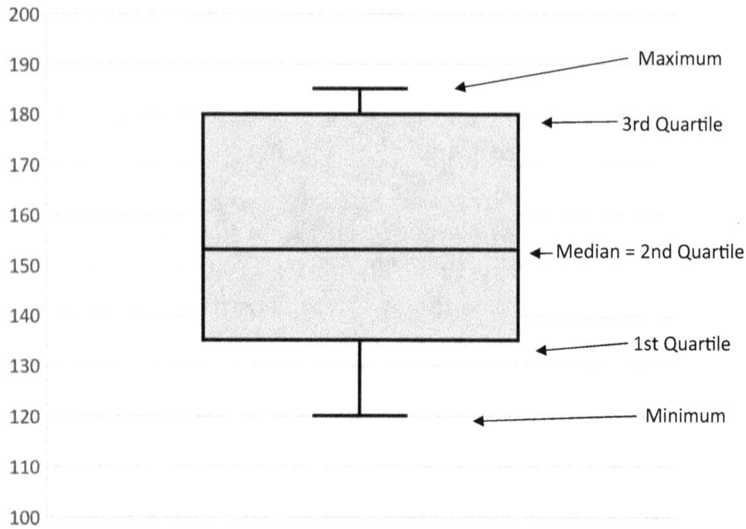

Fig. 2.18. Box plot of weights.

Box plots provide a nice way to illustrate the distribution of a single dataset or to compare the distributions of two datasets with just five numbers. But histograms and stem plots can provide more details of the distribution.

The most common measures of dispersion are the **sample variance** and the **sample standard deviation**, particularly with symmetric distributions. We can calculate the sample variance of a dataset with the following formula:

$$s^2 = \frac{(X_1 - \bar{X})^2 + (X_2 - \bar{X})^2 + \cdots + (X_n - \bar{X})^2}{n-1} = \frac{\sum (X_i - \bar{X})^2}{n-1} \quad (2.3)$$

Note that the variance will always be positive. The standard deviation is defined as the square root of the variance. The sample standard deviation is

$$s = \sqrt{s^2} = \sqrt{\frac{\sum (X_i - \bar{X})^2}{n-1}} \quad (2.4)$$

We use formulas (2.3) and (2.4) when working with sample data. We have observations on some, but not all, members of a population. If we have data on all the members of a population, then we would measure the population variance or the population standard deviation. If we have data on all the members of the population, we divide by n rather than $(n-1)$ because $\bar{X}$ will equal the true population mean.

Most of the observations in a dataset are either going to be above the mean or below the mean. The standard deviation tells us the typical distance from the mean for the points in the dataset. If the standard deviation is equal to zero, it means there is no variation in the data. All the observations are equal to each other and the mean. We probably think about the standard deviation more than the variance because the units make more sense. If we are looking at a dataset on student heights measured in inches, the standard deviation will also be measured in inches. The variance will be measured in inches squared. Thus, it is more natural to think about the standard deviation rather than the variance. Of course, if you know one, you know the other. $s = \sqrt{s^2}$.

Suppose again that our sample data are represented by the numbers 2, 5, 7, and 7. We have the sample mean $\bar{X} = 5.25$. To calculate the sample variance, we have

$$\begin{aligned} s_x^2 &= \frac{(2-5.25)^2 + (5-5.25)^2 + (7-5.25)^2 + (7-5.25)^2}{4-1} \\ &= \frac{10.5625 + 0.0625 + 3.0625 + 3.0625}{3} = 5.58333 \end{aligned}$$

And the sample standard deviation $s_x = \sqrt{s_x^2} = \sqrt{5.58333} = 2.3629$.

We note that the variance and the standard deviation are sensitive to outliers. Since the deviation from the mean is squared, large deviations from the mean have a big impact on the variance and standard deviation. Once Yao Ming, formerly of the NBA Houston Rockets, walks into the room, the variance and standard deviation of our heights will increase dramatically. Yao Ming is 7 foot 6 inches tall.

When you want to describe a dataset, should you report the five-number summary or the mean and standard deviation? We typically use the mean and standard deviation if we have data with a symmetric distribution. We prefer the five-number summary if we have data with a skewed distribution. Of course, you can always report both sets of summary statistics. And you can include a plot or graph to provide the best overall picture of a distribution.

What happens if we change the units of measure? What if we measure heights in centimeters rather than inches or the temperature in Celsius rather than Fahrenheit? What happens to the mean, variance, and standard deviation of your data? They will all change but in a straightforward manner.

2.8 Linear Transformations

Suppose Y is a linear transformation of X. For example, if X measures height in inches, and Y measures height in centimeters, we know that $Y = 2.54X$. And if X measures temperature in Fahrenheit, and Y measures temperature in Celsius, we know that $Y = \frac{5}{9}(X-32)$. Let $Y = aX + b$, where a and b are constants. If the mean of X is $\bar{X}$ and the variance of X is s_x^2, then the mean, standard deviation, and variance of Y are given by the following:

$$\bar{Y} = a\bar{X} + b \tag{2.5}$$

$$s_y = a(s_x) \tag{2.6}$$

$$s_y^2 = a^2(s_x^2) \tag{2.7}$$

Suppose the daily high temperature in Death Valley, CA, has a mean of 92.6 degrees Fahrenheit with a standard deviation of 19.5 degrees. The daily high temperature can range from 48 to 130 degrees. We can figure out the mean and variance of the temperature in Celsius as follows:

$$C = \frac{5}{9}(F - 32)$$

So,

$$\bar{C} = \frac{5}{9}(\bar{F} - 32) = \frac{5}{9}(92.6 - 32) = \frac{5}{9}(60.6) = 33.666$$

And the standard deviation in Celsius is

$$s_c = \frac{5}{9}s_f = \frac{5}{9}19.5 = 10.8333$$

And the variance in Celsius is

$$s_c^2 = 10.8333^2 = 117.36111$$

Given the mean and variance of X, we can figure out the mean and variance of Y. We will just assert these relationships now and demonstrate these later in the textbook.

To briefly recap the material here, we are talking about descriptive statistics. When you are first presented with a new dataset, you want to get some sense of the data. What does the data look like? You should first look at some pictures of the data. Plot your data with a stem plot or with a histogram. Look at the overall patterns, and note any outliers or striking deviations. Sometimes, we make mistakes cutting and pasting data from one source to another. These mistakes can show up as outliers in a graph of the data. After you have looked at the data, calculate some numerical summaries to describe the center and the spread of the distribution. Use the mean and variance and/or the five-number summary.

2.9 Relationships

After we have looked at each of our variables individually, we will typically want to look for relationships between variables. Is there a relationship between two variables X and Y? Is it a positive relationship or a negative relationship? Is it a strong relationship or a weak relationship? Is it an explanatory relationship? We ultimately want to learn about what drives what in this world.

2.10 Quantitative Data

If we have quantitative data, we will again begin with some graphical displays and then proceed to numerical summaries. If the patterns are regular, we can try to model the relationship. Perhaps there is a stochastic relationship between X and Y of the following form:

$$Y_i = a + bX_i + u_i \tag{2.8}$$

where a and b are constants and u_i is a random error term. Here, Y_i is called the dependent variable and is typically the response variable measuring the outcome of some experiment. And X_i is the independent variable which helps to explain the changes in the dependent variable. The X_i could be the number of cigarettes smoked, and Y_i could be the rate of lung cancer. This is a stochastic relationship because the exact value of Y_i depends on the value of X_i and the value of u_i, a stochastic (random) error term.

2.10.1 *Scatterplot of X and Y*

We start by illustrating the relationship between two quantitative variables on the same entity with a scatterplot. You should put the dependent or response variable Y on the vertical axis and the independent or explanatory variable X on the horizontal axis. You can look at the scatterplot and see if there is a positive relationship, a negative relationship, or no relationship. You can also get a sense of how strong these relationships might be (see Figure 2.19).

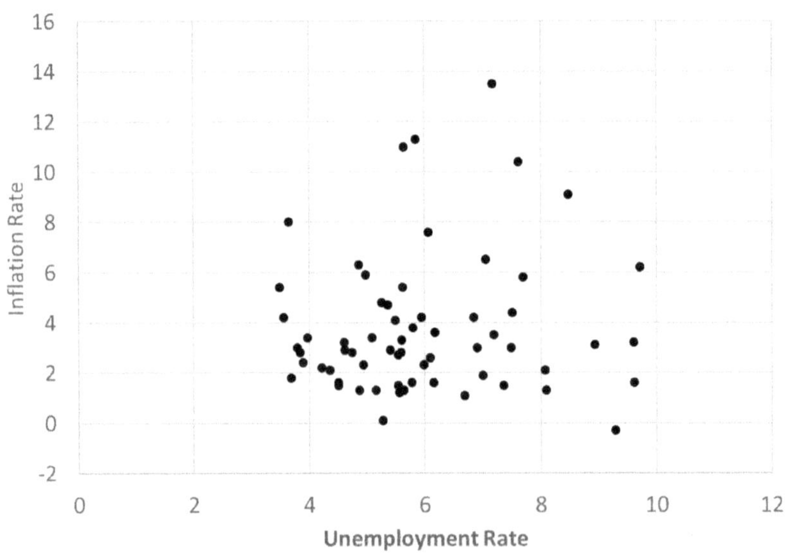

Fig. 2.19. Inflation and unemployment (1960–2021).

2.10.2 *Covariance*

After you have looked at the scatterplot, you will want a numerical summary measure of the relationship between the two quantitative variables. The first measure is the **sample covariance** between the two variables. The covariance is defined as follows:

$$\mathrm{cov}_{xy} = \frac{\sum_N (X_i - \bar{X})(Y_i - \bar{Y})}{N-1} \tag{2.9}$$

If the covariance is positive, it means that the two variables move together. When X goes up, Y tends to go up as well. If the covariance is negative, it means that the two variables move in opposite directions. When X goes up, Y tends to go down. And a covariance near 0 means that there is no linear relationship between the two variables. The size of the covariance (as opposed to the sign of the covariance) is hard to interpret because it depends on the units being used to measure both X and Y. Thus, a covariance equal to 0.56 for inflation and unemployment above does not tell us much of anything except that there is a positive relationship between the two variables.

2.10.3 *Correlation coefficient*

The covariance tells you nothing about the strength of the relationship between the two variables. Thus, we are usually more interested in the **correlation coefficient**. The correlation coefficient tells us about both the direction of the relationship and the strength of the relationship.

$$r_{xy} = \frac{\mathrm{cov}_{xy}}{s_x \cdot s_y} \tag{2.10}$$

where cov_{xy} is the covariance of X and Y, s_x is the standard deviation of X, and s_y is the standard deviation of Y. It can be shown that

$$-1 \leq r_{xy} \leq 1 \tag{2.11}$$

The correlation coefficient will always be between -1 and $+1$. If there is a perfect positive linear relationship between two variables, like the temperature in Celsius and the temperature in Fahrenheit, then the

Table 2.2. Data.

X	Y
1	2
2	2
3	5

correlation coefficient will be +1. If there is a perfect negative linear relationship between two variables, like the distance from the north pole and the distance from the south pole,[1] then the correlation coefficient will be −1. And if there is no linear relationship between the two variables, the correlation coefficient will be 0.

Let's work through a simple example. Suppose we have the following data on two variables X and Y (see Table 2.2).

We begin by calculating the mean and the variance of both X and Y. We have $\bar{X} = \frac{1+2+3}{3} = 2$ and $\bar{Y} = \frac{2+2+5}{3} = 3$. We also have $s_x^2 = \frac{(1-2)^2+(2-2)^2+(3-2)^2}{3-1} = 1$ and $s_y^2 = \frac{(2-3)^2+(2-3)^2+(5-3)^2}{3-1} = 3$.

The covariance between X and Y will be

$$\begin{aligned}
\text{cov}_{xy} &= \frac{\sum_N (X_i - \bar{X})(Y_i - \bar{Y})}{N-1} \\
&= \frac{(1-2)(2-3) + (2-2)(2-3) + (3-2)(5-3)}{3-1} \\
&= \frac{1+0+2}{2} = \frac{3}{2} = 1.5
\end{aligned}$$

And the correlation coefficient is

$$r_{xy} = \frac{\text{cov}_{xy}}{s_x \cdot s_y} = \frac{\text{cov}_{xy}}{\sqrt{s_x^2} \cdot \sqrt{s_y^2}} = \frac{1.5}{\sqrt{1} \cdot \sqrt{3}} = 0.866$$

The correlation coefficient between SAT scores and first-year college grades is 0.56. The correlation coefficient between high school grades and first-year college GPA is also 0.56 (see Figure 2.20). The correlation coefficient between inflation and unemployment above is 0.13.

[1]We are assuming we are on the surface of a spherical planet.

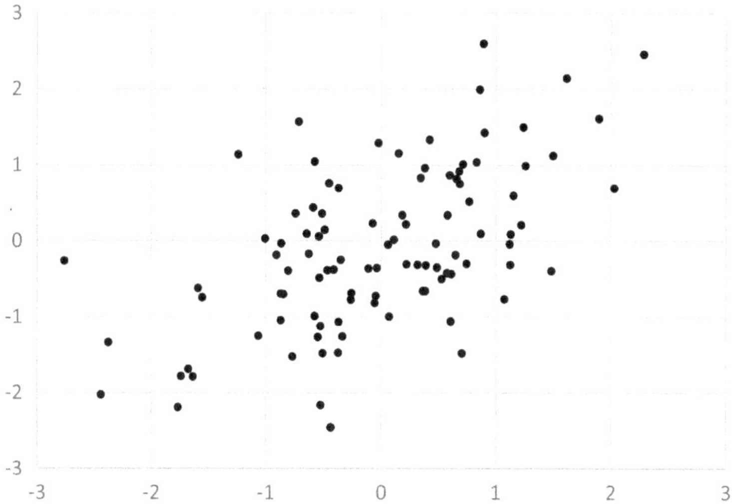

Fig. 2.20. Correlation coefficient = 0.56.

We will note here that these are measures of the linear relationship between two variables. If there is a nonlinear relationship between two variables, perhaps $Y = X^2$, the covariance or the correlation coefficient will not pick up this nonlinear relationship.

2.10.4 *Correlation ≠ causality*

We should also note that correlation is different from causality. If X causes Y, we expect X to be correlated with Y. Causality implies correlation, but correlation does not imply causality. When people buy lots of flashlights, strawberry Pop-Tarts, and beer at Walmart, a hurricane is likely to hit the area. And when women switch from regular lotion to unscented lotion and start to buy scent-free soap, big bags of cotton balls, hand sanitizer, and washcloths, they are likely to be pregnant. There is a lot of correlation here but not necessarily any causality.

2.11 Qualitative Data

With qualitative data, we look for relationships between variables differently. We look for relationships between variables by looking at cross tables, a two-way table consisting of rows and columns. The different categories of the first variable appear along rows, and the different categories of the second variable appear along the columns. You can present the count data in each of the cells or the percentages. The percentages can be of the row totals, the column totals, or the total sample size. If the percentages are roughly the same across the rows and across the columns, then there will appear to be no relationship between the two variables. Here, you can see that students in some parts of the world are more or less likely to choose particular majors (see Tables 2.3–2.6).

Once you have the count data from Table 2.3, you can create all the other tables. European students appear more likely to major in Engineering, and American students appear more likely to major in Social Sciences.

2.11.1 *Simpson's paradox*

One potential problem with cross tables is known as **Simpson's paradox**. Consider the following admissions data from U.C. Berkeley (see Table 2.7).

Table 2.3. Major and World Region.

	U.S.	Europe	Asia	Total
Engineering	61,941	158,931	280,772	501,644
Natural Science	111,158	140,126	242,879	494,163
Social Science	182,166	116,353	236,018	534,537
Total	355,265	415,410	759,669	1,530,344

Table 2.4. Major and World Region (%).

	U.S. (%)	Europe (%)	Asia (%)	Total (%)
Engineering	4.05	10.39	18.35	32.78
Natural Science	7.26	9.16	15.87	32.29
Social Science	11.90	7.60	15.42	34.93
Total	23.21	27.14	49.64	100.00

Table 2.5. Major by World Region.

	U.S. (%)	Europe (%)	Asia (%)
Engineering	17.44	38.26	36.96
Natural Science	31.29	33.73	31.97
Social Science	51.28	28.01	31.07
	100.00	100.00	100.00

Table 2.6. World Region by Major.

	U.S. (%)	Europe (%)	Asia (%)	Total (%)
Engineering	12.35	31.68	55.97	100.00
Natural Science	22.49	28.36	49.15	100.00
Social Science	34.08	21.77	44.15	100.00

Table 2.7. U.C. Berkeley Admissions.

	Admissions to U.C. Berkeley	
	Applicants	Percent Admitted (%)
Men	8,442	44
Women	4,321	35

When we look at the overall admission rates, it appears that U.C. Berkeley is discriminating against female applicants. Armed with these data, a lawsuit was filed against U.C. Berkeley for gender discrimination. In response, U.C. Berkeley disaggregated the data. Students who apply to Berkeley have to apply to particular programs. They presented the admission rates by program in Table 2.8.

Female applicants appear to be admitted into each program at roughly the same rates as male applicants. Since female applicants tend to apply to programs with lower admission rates, their overall admission rates are lower than for male applicants. The lawsuit was

Table 2.8. U.C. Berkeley Admissions by Program.

	Men		Women	
Program	Applicants	Admitted (%)	Applicants	Admitted (%)
A	825	62	108	82
B	560	63	25	68
C	325	37	593	34
D	417	33	375	35
E	191	28	393	24
F	272	6	341	7

consequently dismissed.[2] In this case, the aggregation of the data created a misleading picture of what was going on. Sometimes, it is important to disaggregate the data to see the real picture.

On the other hand, there are times when disaggregating the data can lead to a very misleading picture, and you need to aggregate to see what is going on. Consider the following statistics for two major league baseball players, David Justice and Derek Jeter, for the years 1995 through 1997.

Table 2.9 provides data on hits, at bats, and the season batting average. The batting average is the number of hits divided by the number of at bats. Every year David Justice had a higher batting average than Derek Jeter. But who has the higher batting average over the entire three-year period? Who was the better baseball batter over the three years?

Table 2.9. Batting Average by Year.

	1995		1996		1997	
Derek Jeter	12/48	0.250	183/582	0.314	190/654	0.295
David Justice	104/411	**0.253**	45/140	**0.321**	163/495	**0.329**

[2]One might wonder why there is more excess demand (lower admit rates) in the programs which are attractive to women. There might be discrimination in the allocation of resources.

Table 2.10. Batting Average over 3 Years.

	1995–1997	
Derek Jeter	385/1284	**0.300**
David Justice	312/1046	0.298

Over the three-year period, Derek Jeter actually had a higher batting average (see Table 2.10). This one goes under the heading of "you can't average averages." In this case, disaggregating the data into annual statistics gave us a misleading sense of the better baseball player. Simpson's paradox is a phenomenon in which a trend appears in several different groups of data but disappears or reverses when these groups are combined. Should you aggregate or disaggregate? Yes. You should do both to figure out what is really going on. Be careful when you take averages (see Figure 2.21).

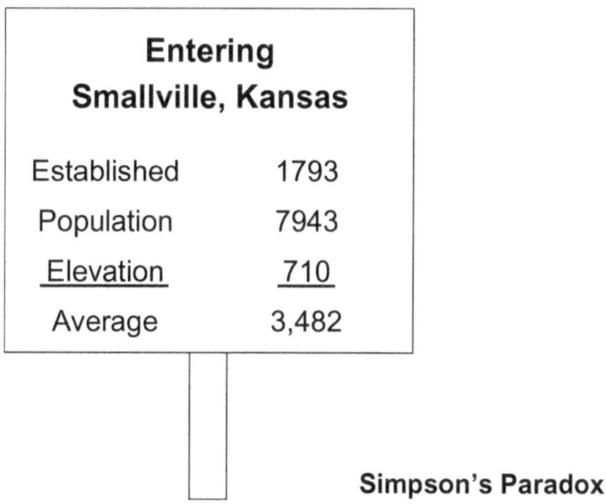

Fig. 2.21. Be careful when you take averages.

2.12 Exercises

(1) The median household income in the United States was \$67,521, while the average household income was \$97,026 in 2020. What does this say about the skewness of the income distribution? (skewed to the right)

(2) A study examined how long aircraft air conditioning units operated after being repaired. Here are the operating times (in hours) for one unit:

97	51	11	4	141	18	142	68	77
80	1	16	106	206	82	54	31	216
46	111	39	63	18	191	18	163	24

What are the mean, median, sample standard deviation, sample variance, first quartile, and third quartile?

$$(76.81,\ 63,\ 63.71,\ 4059.31,\ 18,\ 111)$$

(3) Suppose there are two possible treatments, A and B, for kidney stones. The following table presents the success rates for these treatments with small kidney stones and with large kidney stones.

	Treatment A	**Treatment B**
Small Stones	$81/87 = 93\%$	$234/270 = 87\%$
Large Stones	$192/263 = 73\%$	$55/80 = 69\%$
All Stones	$273/350 = 78\%$	$289/350 = 83\%$

Which treatment appears better for all kidney stones? If you had kidney stones, would you opt for treatment A or treatment B? Explain. (Treatment A)

(4) Suppose the Los Angeles Lakers scored the following points in their last nine games: 146, 120, 112, 110, 118, 111, 109, 110, and 108.

(a) Create a stem and leaf diagram of these data.
(b) Draw a box plot of these data.

(5) We have gathered data on height (inches) and weight (lbs) for a random sample of nine American men.

Weight	130	140	160	165	168	175	188	240	250
Height	68	67	70	71	73	74	67	67	73

Calculate the sample covariance and the correlation coefficient for height and weight.
(19.37, 0.164)

Chapter 3

Probability

3.1 Introduction

If there is a 50–50 chance that something can go wrong, then 9 times out of ten it will.

—Paul Harvey

Probability is the likelihood or chance of an event occurring. The Chinese were perhaps the earliest people to formalize odds and chance 3,000 years ago. The Greek philosophers discussed randomness at length but only in non-quantitative forms. It was only in the 16th century that Italian mathematicians began to formalize the odds associated with various games of chance. Around 1564, Gerolamo Cardano wrote his *Book of Games and Chance* which contains the first systematic treatment of probability. Cardano was an accomplished gambler and included a section on effective cheating methods in his book.

We can think about probability in a number of different ways. Here, we will discuss the three standard ways of thinking about probability. These are classical probability, frequentist probability, and subjective probability.

3.2 Classical Probability

In classical probability, we define the probability of one event occurring out of n possible events, when all n are equally likely, as $1/n$.

The probability of any one of m events occurring when there are n equally likely possible outcomes is m/n.

If you toss a fair coin, there are two possible outcomes, head or tails. Both of these outcomes are equally likely. So, the probability of a head is 1/2 and the probability of a tail is 1/2.

If you roll a six-sided die, there are six possible outcomes, all equally likely. So, the probability of any particular outcome is 1/6. The probability of rolling a 3 is 1/6.

Under classical probability, all you have to do is count the number of possible outcomes. Since they are all equally likely, the probability of any particular outcome is 1 over the number of possible outcomes.

But what if all the possible outcomes are not equally likely? Suppose you toss two coins. There are three possible outcomes. You might get two heads, you might get two tails, or you might get one head and one tail. Does each of these three outcomes have a 1/3 probability?

The answer is no. We are looking at the problem incorrectly and need to count the outcomes more carefully. It might help to use a probability tree to illustrate all the possible outcomes (see Figure 3.1).

With the first coin, you can get a head or a tail, and with the second coin, you can get a head or a tail.

There are four equally likely outcomes: Head Head, Head Tail, Tail Head, and Tail Tail. So, each of these possible outcomes has probability 1/4. The probability of getting two heads is 1/4. Two of these outcomes have a head and a tail. So, the probability of getting one head and one tail is $2/4 = 1/2$.

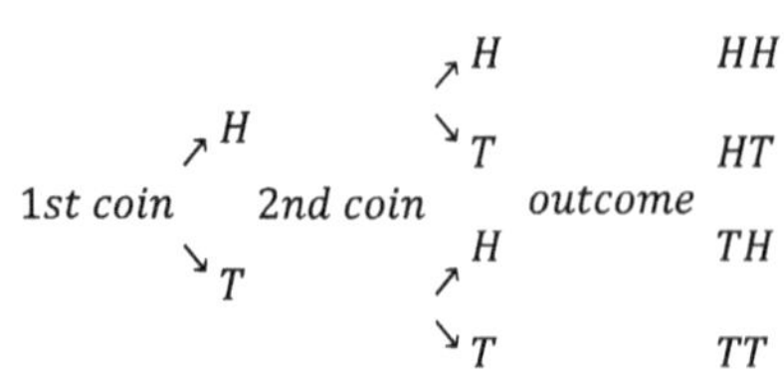

Fig. 3.1. Tossing two coins.

What if we have three coins? The first coin can be a head or tail. The second coin can be a head or tail. And the third coin can be a head or tail. Using a probability tree, we see that we have 8 possible outcomes. $2 \cdot 2 \cdot 2 = 8$. There is only one way to get three heads. So the probability of getting three heads is $1/8$.

Suppose there is a restaurant with a fixed-price menu serving three courses. For the appetizer, you must choose one appetizer from a list of 5 appetizers. For the main course, you must choose one main course from a list of 3 main course dishes. And for dessert, you must choose one dessert from a list of 4 desserts. If there are 50 of you at your dinner party, can you all have different dinners? Yes. How many different dinners can you have? The answer is $5 \cdot 3 \cdot 4 = 60$. And if there is a prize for ordering the chef's favorite dinner combination, the probability of winning would be $1/60$.

Suppose you randomly select a nuclear family with two children. You are then told that one of the children is a girl named Sue. What is the probability that Sue has a brother? Since you randomly selected a nuclear family with two children, there were four equally likely possibilities for the gender sequence of the children: boy boy, boy girl, girl boy, and girl girl. Since we subsequently learn that one of the children is named Sue, we know that we have a boy girl, girl boy, or girl girl, and all three of these sequences is equally likely. Sue has a brother in two of these sequences, and a sister in only one. Thus, the probability that Sue has a brother is $2/3$. If we are told that Sue is the older child, then the probability that Sue has a brother is $1/2$.

Consider a game with three cards. The first card is black on both sides. The second card is red on both sides. And the third card is black on one side and red on the other side. A card is randomly selected and placed on the table. If the side facing up is red, what is the probability that the other side of the card is also red?

Since one side of the card is red, this card cannot be the black/black card. Thus, it must either be the red/red card or the red/black card. Is the answer 50%?

Suppose your professor offers to bet you even money (you can win or lose the same amount of money) that this is the red/red card. Should you take the bet? If the visible side of the card is the red side of the red/black card, you will win. But it could also be either side of the red/red card. In either of these cases, the professor wins. There are two ways for the professor to win, and only one way for you to win. This is why she is the professor. This is a con game because you are misled into thinking that the event is which card was drawn. The event is actually which side of which card was drawn.

Here is the same problem stated in a different way. Suppose there are three bags with two coins in each bag. One bag has two silver coins, one bag has two gold coins, and one bag has a silver coin and a gold coin. You cannot look into the bags. You choose one of the bags at random. You reach your hand in and draw out a gold coin. What is the probability that the remaining coin in the bag is also gold? The answer is 2/3.

There is a famous problem called the Monty Hall problem. This problem evolved out of an American television game show called "Let's Make a Deal" which started in 1963 with host Monty Hall and ran on and off for several decades. There are three big doors on the stage. Let's call them door #1, door #2, and door #3. There is a grand prize like a car behind one of the doors, and there is a booby prize like a goat behind the other two doors. You are asked to pick one of the doors. Suppose you choose door #1. Monty Hall will then open one of the other doors, door #2 or door #3, to reveal a goat. You are now given the option of sticking with door #1, or switching to the other door Monty Hall did not open. What should you do? Should you switch or stick with door #1, or does it not make any difference?

To figure this out, we can list all the possible scenarios. Since each of these scenarios are equally likely, we can determine the optimal strategy. Without loss in generality, assume the grand prize is behind door #1.

If we follow the don't switch strategy, there are three possible outcomes. We can pick door #1, Monty Hall shows us door #2, and we stick with door #1. We win. We can pick door #2, Monty Hall shows us door #3, and we stick with door #2. We lose. Or we can pick door #3, Monty Hall shows us door #2, and we stick with door #3. We lose (see Table 3.1).

Table 3.1. Don't switch strategy.

	Door #1	Door #2	Door #3	Outcome
Pick door #1	Car	Goat	Goat	Win
Pick door #2	Car	Goat	Goat	Lose
Pick door #3	Car	Goat	Goat	Lose

If we follow the switch strategy, there are three possible outcomes. We can pick door #1, Monty Hall shows us door #2, and we switch to door #3. We lose. We can pick door #2, Monty Hall shows us door #3, and we switch to door #1. We win. Or we pick door #3, Monty Hall shows us door #2, and we switch to door #1. We win (see Table 3.2).

Table 3.2. Switch strategy.

	Door #1	Door #2	Door #3	Outcome
Pick door #1	Car ⟶	Goat	⟶ Goat	Lose
Pick door #2	Car ⟵	Goat	Goat	Win
Pick door #3	Car ⟵	Goat	⟵ Goat	Win

If we don't switch, we have a 1/3 chance of winning as we always did. But note that 2/3 of the time we lose. So "most of the time" the car is behind one of the other two doors. Monty Hall shows us a door which has a goat and thus you learn which door has the car "most of the time". So by switching, we can increase our chances of winning the car.

All we did here was to count all the possible outcomes, each of which is equally likely. And by counting all the possible outcomes, we find that switching is the better strategy.

The problem with the classical approach is that all possible outcomes are not always equally likely. They are equally likely with a fair coin or a fair die. But what about other kinds of events? What is the probability that you will get an A in a class? You will either get an A or not get an A. But these two events need not be equally likely.

What is the probability that there will be a 9th season of Game of Thrones? There may be or there may not be. But these two outcomes may not be equally likely. When you ask someone out, will they say yes or will they say no? Are the two events equally likely?

3.3 Frequentist Probability

With frequentist probability, we look at the frequency of a particular outcome in a large number of trials. To find the probability of getting a head when you toss a coin, you would toss the coin a large number of times and see how often it comes up heads. If it comes up heads 524 times out of 1,000 tosses, we would say the probability of heads is 524/1,000 = 52.4%.

If in a large number n of identical situations a certain event occurs m times, then its probability is m/n.

The spreadsheet software Excel has a few random number generators. Rand() will generate a random number between 0 and 1. Suppose we want to know the probability of rand() generating a number larger than 0.50. We could run rand() a large number of times and see what happens. I ran rand() 3,000 times, and it gave me a number larger than 0.5 exactly 1,478 times. Thus, the probability appears to be 1,478/3,000 = 49.27%.

Do you have any friends who are expecting a baby? Will the baby be a boy or a girl? Are these outcomes equally likely? In 2017, there were 3,855,500 babies born in the United States. Of these, 1,972,885 were boy babies, and 1,882,615 were girl babies. Thus, the probability of having a boy baby was 1,972,885/3,855,500 or 51.17%.

Suppose a life insurance company wants to offer a 60-year-old male a $100,000 term life insurance policy. If the individual passes away during the year, his estate will receive $100,000. If the individual does not pass away, he gets nothing. The life insurance company wants to know the probability that this individual will pass away. They might look at all 60-year-old males in the United States and see how many of them pass away during the year. If there are 1.95 million 60-year-old males, and 22,230 of them pass away during the year, then the probability of death would appear to be 22,230/1.95 million = 1.14%.

Fig. 3.2. Roulette wheel.

Roulette is a casino game involving a 32-inch wheel (see Figure 3.2). You spin the roulette wheel in one direction and roll a ball in the opposite direction. Eventually, the ball ends up in one of many colored and numbered slots along the side of the wheel. In Europe, there are 37 slots numbered from 0 to 36. In the U.S., there are 38 slots numbered from $00, 0, 1, 2, 3, \ldots, 36$. The slots numbered 0 or 00 are green and belong to the house. The slots numbered 1–36 are either black or red. Each of the slots is equally likely only if the wheel is perfectly fair, clean, and balanced. In the old days, this was usually not the case.

In 1881, Joseph Jaggers, an English engineer, went to Monte Carlo, France, and recorded the outcomes at the roulette table every day for an entire month with his son and nephew. Then, he bet heavily on the numbers that won most frequently the previous month. He ended up winning 1.5 million francs and broke the bank in Monte Carlo. This is about $10 million today.

Modern roulette wheels made by top brands like Cammegh are extremely precise and any bias would be minuscule compared to the house advantage.

But what if we don't have lots of repetitive data?

In 55 BC, Julius Caesar invaded Britain. Most historians believe that Caesar crossed the Thames River at Brentford. Suppose some historians tell you that there is a 30% chance that Caesar actually crossed the Thames River at East Tilbury. What does this mean?

Does this mean that if we were to replay history over and over and over, Caesar would cross the Thames at Brentford 70% of the time and at East Tilbury 30% of the time?

In U.S. history, we have had 19 Republican presidents, 14 Democratic presidents, and 11 presidents from other parties. So in the next Presidential election, do the Democrats have a $14/44 = 31.82\%$ chance of winning?

The 22 FIFA World Cup tournaments have been won by eight national teams. Brazil has won five times, and they are the only team to have played in every tournament. What is the probability that Brazil will win the next World Cup? Is it $5/22 = 22.73\%$?

These outcomes are clearly uncertain. But how can we quantify them? How do you quantify the uncertainty that surrounds fairly unique circumstances which cannot be repeated?

Will my professor give me an extension? Will I make the U.S. Olympic team? Who will win the World Series? Will I get into medical school? Will interest rates go up?

3.4 Subjective Probability

Reverend Thomas Bayes (1701–1761) was an English statistician who never published his most famous work in statistics. His approach was to weigh all the available evidence and logical arguments to come up with a personal subjective probability. Instead of the frequency of some phenomenon, Bayesian (subjective) probability is a reasonable expectation representing a personal state of knowledge or personal belief.

An event has a subjective probability of m/n of occurring if you are indifferent between a gamble hinging on this event and a gamble hinging on the draw of a red card from a deck in which a fraction m/n of the cards are red.

What is your subjective probability that it will snow tomorrow? I would have you choose between the following two gambles. In gamble A, you will win \$20 if it snows tomorrow. In gamble B, you will win \$20 if I draw a red card from a deck with 1 red card and 4 black cards. Depending on your decision, I will revise the number of red and black cards in the deck until you are indifferent between the two gambles. At that point, I will know what your subjective probability is that it will snow tomorrow. We should note that everyone will have their own subjective probability that it will snow tomorrow.

Suppose the betting odds are 7 to 1 that Brazil will win the next FIFA World Cup. This means that if Brazil wins, you get \$7, and if Brazil does not win, you pay \$1. This suggests that people think the probability Brazil will win the World Cup is 12.5%.[1] This is much lower than the frequency with which Brazil has won the World Cup in the past.

An objectivist, who asserts the validity of objective phenomena over subjective experience, might object to the Bayesian approach. They might say it is not scientific to pull probabilities out of the air.

For example, what if the event has already occurred? What is the probability that October 23, 1845, was a Tuesday? Since there are seven days in a week, a Bayesian would say $1/7 = 14.28\%$. But an objectivist would say the probability is 0. October 23, 1845, was a Thursday, and it always will be a Thursday. So, there is zero probability that it will ever be a Tuesday.

3.5 Back to Classical Probability

Let us return to our classical notion of probability. The probability of any one of m events occurring when there are n equally likely possible outcomes is m/n.

If you flip a fair coin, you can get a head or a tail. The probability of a head is $1/2 = 50\%$. If you roll a fair six-sided die, the probability of rolling a 5 is $1/6 = 16.67\%$. In these cases, it is fairly easy to count the number of possible outcomes. Beyond being careful, sometimes it can be difficult to count the number of all possible outcomes. We may need some tools to help us count the number of possible outcomes.

[1] We cover this on page 96.

For example, what is the probability of getting four of a kind in a poker hand? A four of a kind is a poker hand that contains four cards of one rank and one card of another rank. We need to be able to count all the different ways of getting four of a kind. We also need to be able to count all the possible poker hands that could be dealt with. We could use some tools to help us do this.

Here, we present some standard counting procedures in three steps.

3.5.1 *Ordering n distinct items*

How many different orderings are there for n distinct objects? Suppose you are directing Hermione, Ron, and Harry. When they are on the screen, one person needs to stand on the left, one in the middle, and one on the right. How many different ways are there to do this? We can list them all out here:

Hermione, Ron & Harry	Ron, Harry & Hermione
Hermione, Harry & Ron	Harry, Ron & Hermione
Ron, Hermione & Harry	Harry, Hermione & Ron

You can put any of the three people on the left, and then one of the two remaining people in the middle, and whoever is left must go to the right. Thus, there are $(3)(2)(1) = 6$ possible orderings.

You are interviewing candidates for the position of Economics advisor. Four people have applied. They are Carmen, Milton, Elinor, and Friedrich. You need to decide the order in which you interview them. How many different ways are there? You could interview any of these four people first, and then any of the remaining three people second, and then either of the two remaining people third, and whoever is left must be last. Thus, there are $(4)(3)(2)(1) = 24$ possible orderings.

In general, the number of different orderings of n distinct items is

$$n! = n(n-1)(n-2)\cdots 2 \cdot 1 \tag{3.1}$$

This is read as n factorial.

Consider a horse race with 10 horses and a prize for picking the exact finishing order of the 10 horses. How many possible orderings are there? The answer is 10 factorial.

$$10! = (10)(9)(8)(7)(6)(5)(4)(3)(2)(1) = 3{,}628{,}800$$

If all ten horses are evenly matched, the odds of picking the one winning order are 1/3,628,800.

3.5.2 *Permutations of x out of n distinct items*

What if we have n distinct items, but only want to choose x of them arranged in a particular order?

Consider a horse race with 10 horses ($n = 10$) and a prize for picking the first 3 places ($x = 3$) where order matters. All you care about is which horse comes in first, which horse comes in second, and which horse comes in third. This is known as a "trifecta." The order of the remaining 7 horses does not matter.

How many different orders of finish are there? Any of the 10 horses could come in first, any of the remaining 9 horses could come in second, and any of the remaining 8 horses could come in third. So, there are $(10)(9)(8) = 720$ possible 3-horse orderings.

In general, the number of different permutations of x out of n distinct items is

$$P_x^n = {}_nP_x = n(n-1)(n-2)\cdots(n-x+1) = \frac{n!}{(n-x)!} \tag{3.2}$$

Different books will use different notations to indicate permutations.

Suppose you are the coach of the Real Madrid soccer club. With a tie score at the end of overtime play in the Champions League Final, you are going to a penalty shoot-out. Of the eleven players on the field, you need to select five players to take the penalty kicks. You also have to choose the order in which these players take their kicks. How many different ways are there to do this? How many five-player sequences are there where order matters?

$$P_5^{11} = \frac{11!}{(11-5)!} = \frac{11 \cdot 10 \cdot 9 \cdots 2 \cdot 1}{6 \cdot 5 \cdots 2 \cdot 1} = 11 \cdot 10 \cdot 9 \cdot 8 \cdot 7 = 55{,}440$$

You have one minute to make a decision from all these options. Good coaches have probably thought about this question ahead of time.

3.5.3 *Combinations of x out of n distinct items*

With permutations, the order made a difference. It made a difference whether Eden Hazard of Real Madrid took the first penalty kick or the last. But suppose your job is just to pick the five players to take the penalty kicks, and you leave it up to the players to decide the actual order. How many different five-player combinations are there? We are not deciding on the order of the kicks now, just the five players to take the kicks.

Permutation counts include all possible sequences of the same 5 players. For every 5 players, there are $(5)(4)(3)(2)(1) = 120$ such ordered sequences. So, each 5-player combination was counted 120 times in the permutations above. To find the number of different 5-player combinations, we have

$$\frac{5{,}5440}{120} = 462$$

In general, with n players, and x to be selected, there are $\frac{n!}{(n-x)!}$ possible orderings. Since each combination of x players could be ordered in $x!$ different ways, then the total number of combinations is given by

$$C_x^n = {}_nC_x = \binom{n}{x} = \frac{n!}{x!\,(n-x)!} \tag{3.3}$$

This is the number of x-item combinations using n distinct items. The order is not important here. We are only counting the number of x-item combinations. Different books will use the three different notations above to indicate combinations of x out of n.

The number of possible 5-player combinations that the coach could choose is

$$C_5^{11} = \frac{11!}{5!\,(11-5)!} = \frac{11\cdot 10\cdot 9\cdot 8\cdot 7\cdot 6\cdot 5\cdot 4\cdot 3\cdot 2\cdot 1}{5\cdot 4\cdot 3\cdot 2\cdot 1\cdot 6\cdot 5\cdot 4\cdot 3\cdot 2\cdot 1} = 462$$

Please note that $0! = 1$ and $C_0^n = C_n^n = 1$. If we select 0 players or all n players, there is only one possible way to do this.

Fantasy 5 is a lottery game which is played in numerous states, though the rules are slightly different in every state. In Florida, you need to pick five numbers between 1 and 36. In Georgia, you need to pick five numbers between 1 and 42. Here, the order of the numbers does not matter. You just need to pick the five winning numbers. What is the probability of winning in Florida and in Georgia?

The total number of possible combinations in Florida is

$$C_5^{36} = \frac{36!}{5!\,(36-5)!} = \frac{36!}{5! \cdot 31!} = 376{,}992$$

So, the probability of winning in Florida is $1/376{,}992 = 0.0000026526$.

The total number of possible combinations in Georgia is

$$C_5^{42} = \frac{42!}{5!\,(42-5)!} = \frac{42!}{5! \cdot 37!} = 850{,}668$$

So, the probability of winning in Georgia is $1/850{,}668 = 0.0000011755$. You are more than twice as likely to win Fantasy 5 in Florida than in Georgia. Of course, the jackpots are likely to be smaller in Florida than in Georgia. Here, we are just talking about winning the top jackpot by matching all five numbers. There are actually smaller prizes for matching some, but not all, of the numbers.

The lottery game SuperLotto Plus in California is a little more complicated. In this game, you have to pick five lucky numbers from 1 to 47 and one MEGA number from 1 to 27. Again, the order of the numbers does not matter here. You just have to select the winning five numbers along with the winning MEGA number. How many different possibilities are there?

First, consider the five numbers from 1 to 47. How many combinations are there?

$$C_5^{47} = \frac{47!}{5!\,(47-5)!} = \frac{47!}{5! \cdot 42!} = 1{,}533{,}939$$

And with each of these combinations, you need to select a MEGA number between 1 and 27. So, the total number of possible winning numbers is $1{,}533{,}939 \cdot 27 = 41{,}416{,}353$. Thus, the probability of winning the SuperLotto Plus jackpot in California is $1/41{,}416{,}353$.

On average, you will lose money playing the lottery because all the money spent buying lottery tickets is not returned to the public in the form of winnings. But if you choose to play the lottery, please play responsibly. And you might think about the following. If two people pick the same winning numbers, they have to split the jackpot. So, if you win the jackpot, it is preferable to be the only winner. The odds of winning the jackpot with the numbers 1, 2, 3, 4, 5, and MEGA number 6 are just as good as with any other set of numbers. But no one else is likely to choose these particular numbers in sequence. Consequently, you are likely to win more money this way. People also frequently bet on their birthday or the birthday of family members. So, if you bet on numbers larger than 31, you are less likely to share any jackpot winnings with others.

The probability of winning the lottery is very, very, very small. How does it compare to getting a royal straight flush in a hand of poker? A deck of cards consists of 52 cards. There are four suits called clubs, diamonds, hearts, and spades. There are 13 cards in each suit ranging from Ace, 2, 3, 4, ... 10, Jack, Queen, and King. A royal straight flush is a five-card hand with an Ace, King, Queen, Jack, and 10 of the same suit. Since there are four suits, there are four royal straight flushes in a deck of 52 cards.

How many 5-card hands are there in a deck of 52 cards? Here, we are choosing 5 cards out of a deck of 52 cards, and the order is not important. We just need to have the right five cards. The sequence in which we receive these five cards does not matter. So, this is a combination problem.

$$C_5^{52} = \frac{52!}{5!\,(52-5)!} = \frac{52!}{5! \cdot 47!} = 2{,}598{,}960$$

Since there are 4 royal straight flushes in a deck, the probability of a royal straight flush[2] is going to be

$$P(\text{royal straight flush}) = 4/2{,}598{,}960 = 1/649{,}740$$

[2]This is the probability of having a royal straight flush after being dealt five cards at random, i.e., five-card stud poker. There are many other variants of poker, and the associated probabilities will vary.

You are 63.7 times more likely to get a royal straight flush than to win the SuperLotto Plus lottery.

What is the probability of a straight flush? A straight flush is five cards of sequential rank in the same suit. This could be A, 2, 3, 4, 5, or 2, 3, 4, 5, 6, or 3, 4, 5, 6, 7, ... or 10, J, Q, K, A. Note that the A (Ace) can be at the bottom or the top of the sequence. Since there are 10 straight flush hands in each suit, and there are 4 suits, there are 40 straight flushes in a deck of cards. We are counting a royal straight flush as a straight flush:

$$P(\text{straight flush}) = \frac{40}{2{,}598{,}960} = \frac{1}{64{,}974}$$

What is the probability of a four of a kind? In order to have a four of a kind, you need all four cards of the same rank along with a 5th card which can be any of the other remaining 48 cards. Since there are 13 ranks, there are $13 \cdot 48 = 624$ different five-card hands containing a four of a kind:

$$P(4 \text{ of a kind}) = \frac{13 \cdot 48}{2{,}598{,}960} = \frac{1}{4{,}165}$$

Let's think about some non-poker and non-lottery examples. Suppose you have 6 straight lines in a two-dimensional space. Assume no two lines are parallel, and no three lines cross at the same point. How many triangles are there? You might draw 6 straight lines and try to count all the triangles. But what if we generalize this problem? What if we have n straight lines in a two-dimensional space where $n \geq 3$? How many triangles are there? This is a challenging question until you realize that it is a combination problem. You observe that any three lines will create a triangle. So, how many different ways are there to choose three lines out of the n lines in this space?

$$C_3^n = \frac{n!}{3!\,(n-3)!}$$

If there are 6 lines, there will be

$$C_3^6 = \frac{6!}{3!\,(6-3)!} = \frac{6!}{3! \cdot 3!} = 20 \text{ triangles}$$

Suppose you have an urn with n balls, each a different color. You draw three balls. How many three color combinations are there? This is the same problem as above. You will have

$$C_3^n = \frac{n!}{3!\,(n-3)!}$$

3.6 Rules of Probability

Consider a random experiment where one and only one of several well-defined outcomes will occur with uncertainty as to which one.

Suppose there are 10 possible outcomes which are all equally likely. We might number these outcomes as $1, 2, 3, \ldots, 10$ (see Figure 3.3).

Let us represent these outcomes in a Venn diagram. Developed by mathematician John Venn (1834–1923), a Venn diagram shows all the possible logical relations between a finite collection of different sets. A Venn diagram can represent all the possible outcomes of an uncertain experiment.

Define event A as the set of basic outcomes 4, 5, and 6. We write this as $A = \{4, 5, 6\}$. We say that event A has occurred if the experiment gives rise to any of its basic outcomes, in this case, 4, 5, or 6 (see Figure 3.4).

Since there are 10 possible outcomes which are equally likely, and event A consists of three of these 10 outcomes, the probability of event A is 30%. We write this as follows:

$$P[A] = 3/10 = 0.30$$

We note that $0 \leq P[A] \leq 1$ because all probabilities must be between 0 and 1. And the sum of all the probabilities of the possible outcomes

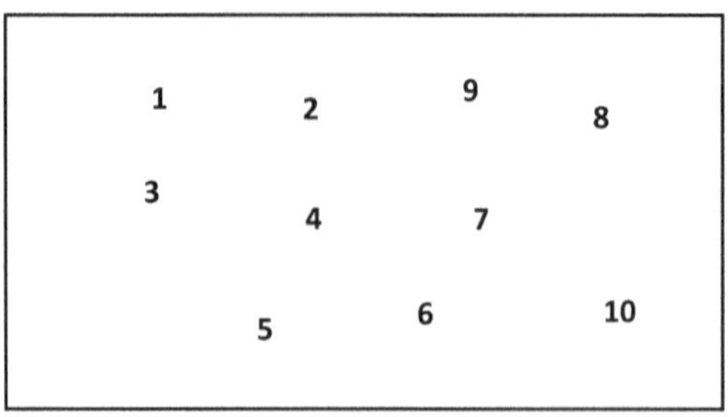

Fig. 3.3. Venn diagram 1.

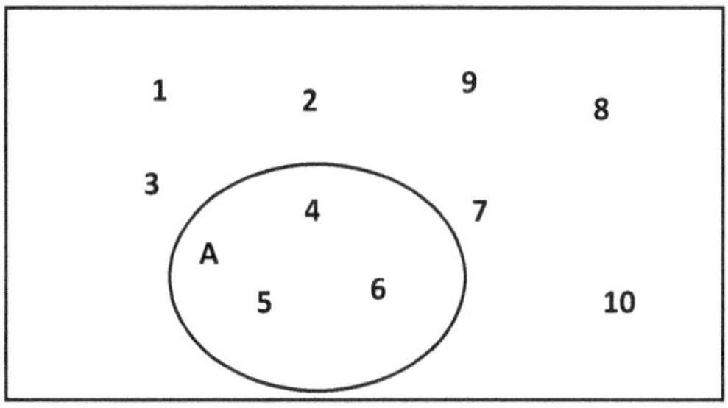

Fig. 3.4. Venn diagram 2.

must sum to 1, $\sum_1^{10} P[i] = 1$. One of the outcomes must happen. More generally, if there are n possible outcomes, $\sum_1^n P[i] = 1$. We also note that $P[\emptyset] = 0$ where $\emptyset$ is the empty set. If you ever calculate a probability and get a number less than 0 or greater than 1, you know you made a mistake somewhere.

3.6.1 *Conditional probability*

We often want to know the probability of something given that something else has occurred. We call this a conditional probability.

What is the probability of getting financial aid given that you are accepted to college? What is the probability of going to jail given that you are convicted of a crime? What is the probability of breaking your legs given that you are skiing?

We want to know $P[A]$ given that B has occurred. We write the conditional probability of A given that B has occurred as $P[A \mid B]$.

Suppose we roll a ten-sided die with equally likely outcomes $1, 2, 3, \ldots, 10$. Let us define the event A as all even numbers, and event B as numbers bigger than 7:

$$A = \{2, 4, 6, 8, 10\} \quad P[A] = \frac{5}{10} = \frac{1}{2}$$

$$B = \{8, 9, 10\} \qquad P[B] = \frac{3}{10}$$

$$P[A \mid B] = P[\text{even number} \mid \text{larger than } 7]$$

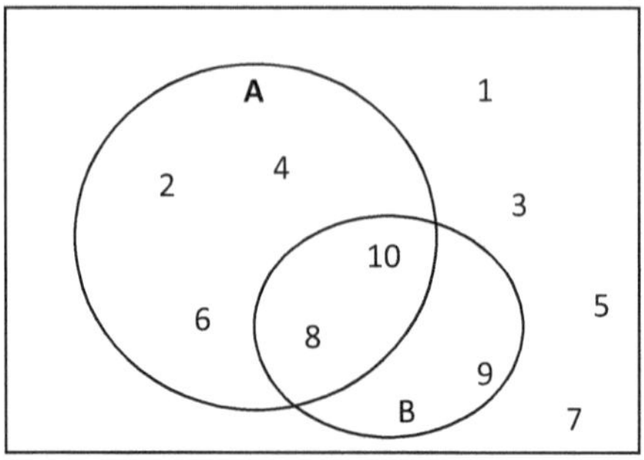

Fig. 3.5. Conditional probability.

If we roll a number larger than 7 (see Figure 3.5), what is the probability it is even? We have a possible outcome 8, 9, or 10. Two of these numbers are even. So, the probability is 2/3.

Before we get ahead of ourselves, let us define a few terms.

The **intersection** of A and B refers to all outcomes that belong to both A and B. The probability that both A and B happen is written as $P[A \text{ intersect } B] = P[A \text{ and } B] = P[A \cap B] = P[B \cap A]$.

The **union** of A and B refers to all outcomes that belong to either A or B or both. The probability that A or B happens is written as $P[A \text{ union } B] = P[A \text{ or } B] = P[A \cup B] = P[B \cup A]$.

When we determine the conditional probability

$$P[A \mid B] = P[\text{even number} \mid \text{larger than } 7]$$

we are interested in the probability of the intersection of A and B (even numbers larger than 7) relative to the probability of B (numbers larger than 7):

$$\begin{aligned} P[A \mid B] &= \frac{P[A \text{ intersect } B]}{P[B]} = \frac{P[A \text{ and } B]}{P[B]} = \frac{P[A \cap B]}{P[B]} \\ &= \frac{2/10}{3/10} = \frac{2}{3} \end{aligned}$$

We have $P[A \mid B]$ above. How about $P[B \mid A]$? This is the probability that the number is greater than 7 given that it is even.

By symmetry,

$$P[B \mid A] = \frac{P[A \cap B]}{P[A]} = \frac{2/10}{5/10} = \frac{2}{5}$$

We have

$$P[A \mid B] = \frac{P[A \cap B]}{P[B]} = \frac{P[B \cap A]}{P[B]} \tag{3.4}$$

$$P[B \mid A] = \frac{P[A \cap B]}{P[A]} = \frac{P[B \cap A]}{P[A]} \tag{3.5}$$

We note that $P[A \mid B] \neq P[B \mid A]$ above. These probabilities are usually not the same. $P[A \mid B]$ does not equal $P[B \mid A]$ unless $P[B] = P[A]$.

For example, $P[\text{American citizen} \mid \text{speak English}] \approx 20\%$. Lots of people speak English all over the world, particularly in the U.S., India, and Pakistan. Most of them are not U.S. citizens. But $P[\text{speak English} \mid \text{American citizen}] \approx 95\%$. Most American citizens speak English.

What is the probability that you have a King if we know you have a face card? A face card is a card with a King, Queen, or Jack on it. Face card $= \{\text{K}, \text{Q}, \text{J}\}$. $P[K \mid \text{face card}] = 1/3$. But what is the probability that you have a face card given that you have a King? $P[\text{face card} \mid K] = 1$. A King is a face card.

If you are a woman, what is the probability that you study at Scripps College, a women's college?

$$P[\text{student at Scripps} \mid \text{you are a woman}] = \text{low}.$$

But if you are a student at Scripps College, the probability is very high that you are a woman.

$$P[\text{you are a woman} \mid \text{student at Scripps}] = \text{high}.$$

Generally, $P[A \mid B]$ is different from $P[A]$. Straight probabilities are generally different from conditional probabilities. Above we saw that $P[A \mid B] = \frac{2}{3}$ while $P[A] = 1/2$ where $P[A \mid B] = P[\text{even number} \mid \text{larger than 7}]$. Consider the following probabilities. They are not going to be the same.

P[someone is over 250 pounds] vs P[over 250 lbs | over 6′5″tall]
P[going to jail] vs P[going to jail | convicted of a crime]
P[live to be 90 years old] vs P[live to be 90 | 88 years old]
P[graduate from college] vs P[graduate from college | senior in college]

But if A and B are **independent**, then $P[A \mid B] = P[A]$. This means the chances of A occurring are independent of what happens to B. And if $P[A \mid B] = P[A]$, then $P[B \mid A] = P[B]$, that is, if A is independent of B, then B is independent of A.

Here are some examples of events A and B which are independent:

A: Rolling an even number on a die
B: Tossing a head with a coin

A: Being born in the month of February
B: Being over 65 years old

A: Dodgers winning the World Series
B: Christine Lagarde winning the Nobel Peace Prize

Consider a deck of cards. Let event A be drawing a King. Let event B be drawing a Queen. When we draw cards from a deck of cards with replacements, events A and B will be independent. Replacement means that whenever we draw a card from the deck, we put the card back into the deck before drawing another card.

If we do not replace the cards, then these events will not be independent. The probabilities will change as the number of cards remaining in the deck change.

We have defined some probability terms. We will now consider three useful probability rules. They are known as the (1) addition rule, (2) multiplication rule, and (3) subtraction rule.

3.7 The Addition Rule

You are watching the evening news on Friday, and the weather forecaster says there is a 50% chance of rain on Saturday and a 50%

chance of rain on Sunday. What is the chance that it will rain sometime during the weekend? It is tempting to add the probabilities and say 100%. But can we be 100% sure it will rain during the weekend? Can we ever be 100% sure about anything in this world? Probably not.

Suppose we flip a fair coin twice? What is the probability of getting at least one head? You might get a head on the first coin flip or you might get a head on the second coin flip. This is the same problem as the weather forecast problem above. It might rain on Saturday or it might rain on Sunday. Can we just add 50% and 50%? No. We cannot be 100% sure that we will get at least one head.

When we add the $P[A]$ to the $P[B]$, we end up double counting the intersection of A and B. It might rain on Saturday AND on Sunday. You might get a head on the first coin AND the second coin. We need to count the joint events once and only once. Thus, we need to remove the intersection of A and B because it was double counted:

$$P[A \text{ or } B] = P[A \cup B] = P[A] + P[B] - P[A \cap B]$$

$$P[A \cup B] = P[A] + P[B] - P[A \cap B] \tag{3.6}$$

$$P[A \cup B] = \frac{1}{2} + \frac{1}{2} - \frac{1}{4} = \frac{3}{4}$$

Consider 10 people represented by this Venn diagram on Figure 3.6.

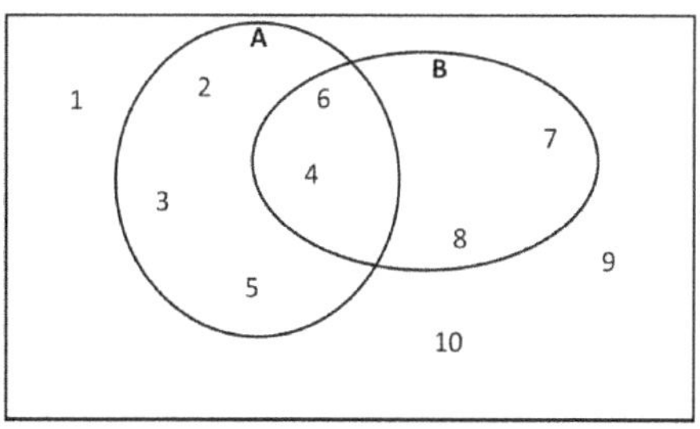

Fig. 3.6. Venn diagram 4.

Define sets A and B as follows:

A: People who are under 30 $= \{2, 3, 4, 5, 6\}$
B: Women $= \{4, 6, 7, 8\}$

If we select a chairperson at random, what is the probability of getting a woman or someone under 30?

$$P[A \cup B] = P[A] + P[B] - P[A \cap B]$$
$$[A \cup B] = \frac{5}{10} + \frac{4}{10} - \frac{2}{10} = \frac{7}{10}$$

What if no double counting problem exists? Then, we say that A and B are mutually exclusive. A and B are **mutually exclusive** if the intersection of A and B is the empty set or null set, if $A \cap B = \emptyset$. If A happens, B cannot happen, so $P[A \cap B] = P[\emptyset] = 0$ (see Figure 3.7).

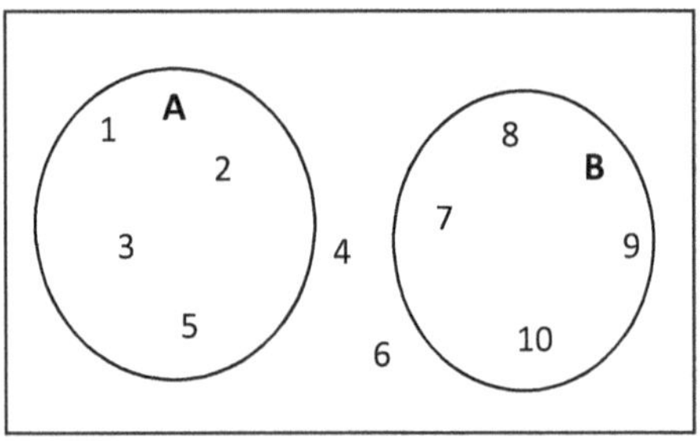

Fig. 3.7. Mutually exclusive.

Since $P[A \cap B] = 0$, $P[A \cup B] = P[A] + P[B]$ if A and B are mutually exclusive. Of course, it is still true that $P[A \cup B] = P[A] + P[B] - P[A \cap B]$. It just happens that $P[A \cap B] = 0$ when A and B are mutually exclusive.

3.7.1 *Example*

Suppose you run a business and have contracted everything out at fixed prices. If the Federal Reserve contracts the money supply, then interest rates rise and you have problems. Alternatively, if the

Federal Reserve expands the money supply, and this leads to inflation, you may also have problems.

If $P[\text{money supply contracts}] = 0.20$ and $P[\text{money supply expands}] = 0.10$, then the probability that your business is in trouble is

$$\begin{aligned} &P[\text{business trouble}] \\ &\quad = P[\text{money supply contract or money supply expands}] \\ &\quad = 0.20 + 0.10 = 0.30 \end{aligned}$$

The events "money supply contracts" and "money supply expands" are mutually exclusive. Money supply can contract, expand, or stay the same. If one happens, the other things are not happening.

3.8 The Multiplication Rule

What is the probability of both A and B occurring? What is the probability of $P[A \cap B]$?

From the definition of conditional probability, we have

$$P[B \mid A] = \frac{P[A \cap B]}{P[A]} \quad \text{and} \quad P[A \mid B] = \frac{P[A \cap B]}{P[B]}$$

Thus, it follows that

$$P[A \cap B] = P[A] \cdot P[B \mid A] = P[B] \cdot P[A \mid B] \tag{3.7}$$

This rule is easily extended:

$$\begin{aligned} P[A \cap B \cap C] &= P[(A \cap B) \cap C] = P[A \cap B] \cdot P[C \mid A \cap B] \\ &= P[A] \cdot P[B \mid A] \cdot P[C \mid A \cap B] \end{aligned} \tag{3.8}$$

We note the pattern, giving us

$$\begin{aligned} P[A \cap B \cap C \cap D] = P[A] \cdot P[B \mid A] \cdot P[C \mid A \cap B] \\ \cdot P[D \mid A \cap B \cap C] \end{aligned} \tag{3.9}$$

3.8.1 *Examples*

(1) Probability of drawing two aces in a row from a deck of cards with no replacement

A_1: Ace on first draw
A_2: Ace on second draw

$$P[A_1 \cap A_2] = P[A_1] \cdot P[A_2 \mid A_1]$$
$$P[A_1] = 4/52$$
$$P[A_2 \mid A_1] = 3/51$$
$$\text{so } P[A_1 \cap A_2] = (4/52) \cdot (3/51) = 1/221 = 0.0045$$

(2) Probability of drawing 4 aces in a row without replacement

$$\begin{aligned} &P[A_1 \cap A_2 \cap A_3 \cap A_4] \\ &\quad = P[A_1] \cdot P[A_2 \mid A_1] \cdot P[A_3 \mid A_1 \cap A_2] \\ &\qquad \cdot P[A_4 \mid A_1 \cap A_2 \cap A_3] \\ &\quad = \frac{4}{52} \cdot \frac{3}{51} \cdot \frac{2}{50} \cdot \frac{1}{49} = 0.0000037 \approx 4/1\,\text{million} \end{aligned}$$

Here we are sampling without replacement. The selected card is removed and cannot be selected again. This changes the number of aces remaining in the deck along with the number of cards remaining. Thus, the probability of the first ace is different from the probability of the second ace.

Sometimes we sample with replacement. With replacement, the selected card is put back into the deck and can be selected again. So, the number of aces in the deck along with the number of cards in the deck do not change. Now the probability of drawing an ace does not change.

With replacement, the probability of picking 4 straight aces is much higher:

$$\begin{aligned} P[A_1 \cap A_2 \cap A_3 \cap A_4] &= P[A_1] \cdot P[A_2] \cdot P[A_3] \cdot P[A_4] \\ &= \frac{4}{52} \cdot \frac{4}{52} \cdot \frac{4}{52} \cdot \frac{4}{52} = 0.000350 \approx 7/20{,}000 \end{aligned}$$

Note that if A and B are **independent**, then $P[A \cap B] = P[A] \cdot P[B]$. We always have $P[A \cap B] = P[A]\,P[B \mid A]$. But if A and B are independent, then $P[B \mid A] = P[B]$. So, $P[A \cap B] = P[A] \cdot P[B]$ if A and B are independent. QED.[3]

3.9 The Subtraction Rule

Though the multiplication rule is easily extended, the addition rule is not so easily extended.

Recall the addition rule with two sets of outcomes:

$$P[A \cup B] = P[A] + P[B] - P[A \cap B]$$

What happens when we have three sets of outcomes? What is $P[A \cup B \cup C]$?

$$\begin{aligned} P[A \cup B \cup C] &= P[A] + P[B] + P[C] \\ &-P[A \cap B] - P[A \cap C] - P[B \cap C] + P[A \cap B \cap C] \end{aligned} \tag{3.10}$$

But you do not want to memorize this. And the formula only gets more complicated with more outcomes. Do you really want to figure out $P[A \cup B \cup C \cup D]$? Trust me. You do not.

Instead of trying to learn these crazy formulas, we observe that it is often much easier to figure out the probability of something not happening than the probability of something happening.

The **complement** of an event A, denoted $\bar{A}$ or sometimes A^c or occasionally A', occurs whenever A does not occur. The notation depends on the textbook. We will use the notation $\bar{A}$ to denote the complement of A. Since event A happens or does not happen, we have the following:

$$P[A] + P[\bar{A}] = 1 \tag{3.11}$$

This gives us the **Subtraction Rule**:

$$P[A] = 1 - P[\textbf{not } A] = 1 - P[\bar{A}] \tag{3.12}$$

[3] "Quod Erat Demonstrandum" which loosely translated means "that which was to be demonstrated."

The probability of something occurring is equal to 1 minus the probability of something not occurring. Sometimes it is easier to find the probability of something **not** occurring than the probability of something occurring.

What is the probability of getting **at least** one Head with 3 coin flips?

$$P[\text{Head on 1st flip or Head on 2nd flip or Head on 3rd flip}]$$
$$= 1 - P[\text{no Heads}] = 1 - P[\text{3 Tails}] = 1 - \frac{1}{8} = \frac{7}{8}$$

3.10 Some Examples

At this point, we have learned some definitions, how to count (number of orderings, permutations, and combinations), and the three rules of probability (addition, multiplication, and subtraction). Now let's use these concepts to help us figure out some interesting probabilities.

3.10.1 *Some birthdays vs particular birthdays*

Suppose this is a leap year with 366 days. If we are in a room with 367 people, we would be 100% sure that at least two people in the room have the same birthday. How many people do we have to have in the room to be about 50% sure that at least two people will have the same birthday? It is not 183. The answer is just 23. About half the time when there are 23 people in the same room, two or more people will share the same birthday. You probably have 23 people in many of your classes. Chances are pretty good that at least two people will have the same birthday in your classes. Let's work this out.

Let's begin by just considering a room with 5 people. What is the number of ways to choose 5 birthdays? The first person could have any of the 366 birthdays, and so can the second, the third, the fourth, and the fifth. So, the total number of ways will be $366 \cdot 366 \cdot 366 \cdot 366 \cdot 366 = 366^5$.

What is the number of ways to choose 5 birthdays where no two repeat?

$$P_5^{366} = \frac{366!}{(366-5)!} = 366 \cdot 365 \cdot 364 \cdot 363 \cdot 362$$

So, the probability that no 2 people have the same birthday is

$$\frac{366 \cdot 365 \cdot 364 \cdot 363 \cdot 362}{366^5} = 0.9729$$

So, the probability that at least 2 people have the same birthday is

$$1 - 0.9729 = 0.02706 = 2.7\%$$

With only 5 people in the room, it is not very likely that two people will share the same birthday. But with 23 people in the room, we have

$$\frac{366 \cdot 365 \cdot 364 \cdots 344}{366^{23}} \approx 0.4936769$$

So, the probability that at least two people share the same birthday is $1 - 0.4936769 = 0.506323 \approx 50.6\%$. It is slightly more likely to happen than not.

Suppose we have about 30 people in the class. Then, the probability is significantly higher. The probability that no two people have the same birthday is

$$\frac{366 \cdot 365 \cdot 364 \cdots 337}{366^{30}} = \frac{2.3648 \times 10^{76}}{8.02476 \times 10^{76}} = 0.29469$$

So, the probability that at least two people share the same birthday is

$$1 - 0.29469 = 0.7053 = 70.53\%$$

So, the probability that at least two people share the same birthday in a 30-person class is very high. Most statistics professors would be more than willing to take a bet.

Now how about a **particular birthday**? What is the probability that someone has my birthday? Or what is the probability that today is someone's birthday? This is a very different question, and so is the answer.

The probability that today is **not** your birthday is

$$\frac{365}{366} = 0.997267$$

So, the probability that two people do **not** have a birthday today is

$$\left(\frac{365}{366}\right)^2 = 0.994542$$

And the probability that today is **not** 30 people's birthday is

$$\left(\frac{365}{366}\right)^{30} = 0.9211988$$

So, if there are 30 people in the room, there is only a $1 - 0.9211988 = 0.07880$ **or** 7.88% chance that today is someone's birthday. This is not very likely.

We actually need about 253 people in the room to be 50% sure that today is someone's birthday. Since

$$\left(\frac{365}{366}\right)^{253} = 0.50047$$

we will be $1 - 0.50047 = 0.499527 = 49.95\%$ sure today is someone's birthday with 253 people in the room. This is a lot of people, and a pretty big room just to be half sure.

Some unlikely event is very likely to occur, but it is very unlikely that a particular one will occur.

3.10.2 *Julius Caesar and you*

For this next example, you should sit back and take a very deep breath.

If Shakespeare is correct, Julius Caesar gasped "You too, Brutus" before breathing his last breath over 2,000 years ago. This was on March 15 in 44BC. Beware the "ides of March."

Assume that the air molecules Caesar exhaled long ago have spread fairly evenly around the world by now. What is the probability that we just inhaled at least one of these air molecules when we took our deep breath?

Let's parameterize the problem, and then substitute some reasonable numbers to get a plausible estimate. Assume that Caesar exhaled A molecules of air and that there are N molecules of air in the world. If I pick a molecule of air at random, the probability that it was exhaled by Caesar would be $\frac{A}{N}$. The probability that this random molecule of air was NOT exhaled by Caesar would be $1 - \frac{A}{N}$. If you take a very small breath and just inhale 3 molecules of air, the probability that all three of these molecules were NOT from Caesar would be $\left(1 - \frac{A}{N}\right) \cdot \left(1 - \frac{A}{N}\right) \cdot \left(1 - \frac{A}{N}\right) = \left(1 - \frac{A}{N}\right)^3$. This is the probability that the first molecule was not from Caesar AND the second was not from Caesar AND the third was not from Caesar.

If you were to take a larger breath and inhale B molecules of air, the probability that all B molecules were not from Caesar would be

$$\left(1 - \frac{A}{N}\right)^B$$

And the probability that you inhaled at least one molecule of air from Caesar would be

$$1 - \left(1 - \frac{A}{N}\right)^B$$

Now let us substitute for A, B, and N with some reasonable numbers. Let $A \approx 2.2 \times 10^{22}$ molecules, approximately 1/30 of a liter of air, let $B \approx A$, and let $N \approx 10^{44}$ molecules of air:

$$\begin{aligned} P\,(\text{inhale Caesar air}) &= 1 - \left(1 - \frac{2.2 \times 10^{22}}{10^{44}}\right)^{2.2\times 10^{22}} \\ &= 1 - \left(1 - 2.2 \times 10^{-22}\right)^{2.2\times 10^{22}} \approx 99\% \end{aligned}$$

There is more than a 99% chance that you just inhaled at least one air molecule from Caesar when you took that deep breath. Eventually, we are all part of one another.

3.11 Bayes Theorem

If we know $P[A\,|\,B]$, can we figure out $P[B\,|\,A]$?

Suppose we know the probability of breaking your leg if you go skiing. But now that you have broken your leg, we want to figure out the probability that you were actually skiing.

We know P[you break your leg | you are skiing] but want to know P[you are skiing | you break your leg]. How do we figure this out?

We know $P[A \cap B] = P[A] \cdot P[B\,|\,A]$ and $P[A \cap B] = P[B] \cdot P[A\,|\,B]$. Therefore, we know that $P[A] \cdot P[B\,|\,A] = P[B] \cdot P[A\,|\,B]$. If we rearrange this expression, we get one version of Bayes theorem:

$$P[B\,|\,A] = \frac{P[B] \cdot P[A\,|\,B]}{P[A]} \tag{3.13}$$

Also, recall the multiplication rule.

We have

$$P[A \cap B] = P[B] \cdot P[A\,|\,B]$$
$$P\left[A \cap \bar{B}\right] = P[\bar{B}] \cdot P[A\,|\,\bar{B}]$$

So,

$$P[A \cap B] + P\left[A \cap \bar{B}\right] = P[B] \cdot P[A\,|\,B] + P[\bar{B}] \cdot P[A\,|\,\bar{B}]$$

We note that $P[A] = P[A \cap B] + P[A \cap \bar{B}]$. The event A consists of the part of A that intersects B plus the part of A that does not intersect B.

So,

$$P[A] = P[B] \cdot P[A\,|\,B] + P[\bar{B}] \cdot P[A\,|\,\bar{B}]$$

If we move some of the terms around

$$P[A] = P[A\,|\,B] \cdot P[B] + P[A\,|\,\bar{B}] \cdot P[\bar{B}] \tag{3.14}$$

so Bayes theorem can be rewritten as follows:

$$P[B\,|\,A] = \frac{P[B] \cdot P[A\,|\,B]}{P[A]}$$

or

$$P[B \mid A] = \frac{P[A \mid B] \cdot P[B]}{P[A \mid B] \cdot P[B] + P[A \mid \bar{B}] \cdot P[\bar{B}]} \quad (3.15)$$

It is worth remembering that the expression in the numerator is the first part of the expression in the denominator.

3.11.1 *Lizzie Borden*

What is the probability that Lizzie Borden was guilty of murdering her father and stepmother in 1892 given that she was acquitted of the crimes? We have no idea. But what if we are willing to make some assumptions?

Suppose that 75% of all murder defendants are guilty, that 80% of guilty defendants are convicted, and that 85% of innocent defendants are acquitted. This means that 25% of murder defendants are innocent, that 20% of guilty defendants are acquitted, and that 15% of innocent defendants are convicted. The system is far from perfect (see Table 3.3). We want to know the probability of being guilty given that you have been acquitted. From Bayes theorem, we have

$$\begin{aligned}
P[\text{guilty} \mid \text{acquitted}] &= \frac{P[\text{guilty} \cap \text{acquitted}]}{P[\text{acquitted}]} \\
P[\text{guilty} \cap \text{acquitted}] &= P[\text{acquitted} \mid \text{guilty}] P[\text{guilty}] \\
&= (20\%)\,(75\%) = 15\% \\
P[\text{acquitted}] &= P[\text{acquitted} \mid \text{guilty}] P[\text{guilty}] \\
&\quad + P[\text{acquitted} \mid \text{innocent}] P[\text{innocent}] \\
&= (0.20)\,(0.75) + (0.85)\,(0.25) = 0.15 + 0.2125 \\
&= 0.3625 = 36.25\%
\end{aligned}$$

So,

$$P[\text{guilty} \mid \text{acquitted}] = \frac{0.15}{0.3625} = 0.41436 \approx 41.4\%$$

Note that $P[\text{guilty}] = 0.75$ before the trial. After the acquittal, the probability of being guilty has decreased to 41.4%.

An alternative approach to thinking about these kinds of problems is to create a table of all the possible states in the world. In this problem, individuals are either guilty or innocent. Individuals are also either convicted or acquitted. So, there are four possible scenarios. Individuals can be guilty and convicted, guilty and acquitted, innocent and convicted, or innocent and acquitted. We can create Table 3.3.

Table 3.3. Guilty and Convicted.

	Guilty	Innocent	
Convicted	$(0.8)(0.75) = 0.60$	$(0.15)(0.25) = 0.0375$	0.6375
Acquitted	$(0.2)(0.75) = 0.15$	$(0.85)(0.25) = 0.2125$	0.3625
	0.75	0.25	1.00

We can see that 63.75% of individuals are convicted, some guilty, and some innocent. And 36.25% of individuals are acquitted, some guilty, and some innocent. If you want to know the probability of being guilty given that you are acquitted, it would be $0.15/0.3625 = 0.41436$. This is the same as what we have above.

3.11.2 *HIV/AIDS?*

After a particularly wild weekend that you do not clearly remember, you decide to go down to the local clinic to be tested for HIV. The next day the doctor contacts you and tells you that the test came back positive. Should you worry? We observe that we don't really care if the test is positive or negative. What we really care about is whether or not you have HIV. You want to know the conditional probability of having HIV given that you just tested positive.

Assume that tests for HIV are 98% accurate. If you have HIV, the test is positive 98% of the time. If you don't have HIV, the test is negative 98% of the time. While it would be very unusual for both of these probabilities to be the same, you often hear the claim that a test is 98% accurate without clarification about what this really means. Assume also that 0.5% of the population has HIV. This means about 1 person in 200 has HIV. This is roughly correct for the United States.

Assume that 10,000 tests for HIV are administered (see Table 3.4). Of these, how many are going to be positive?

Table 3.4. HIV and Positive.

	HIV	Not HIV	
Positive Test	49	199	248
Negative Test	1	9,751	9,752
	50	9,950	10,000

Since 0.5% of the population has HIV, 50 of the 10,000 people actually have HIV. Of these, 98% will test positive, giving us 49 positive tests.

Of the 9,950 people without HIV, 2% will test positive. Since 2% of 9,950 is 199, we will see 199 positive tests from people who do not have HIV.

We will have a total of $49 + 199 = 248$ positive tests. But most (199) of these positive tests are false positives.

The probability that you actually have HIV is $P[HIV \mid \text{positive test}] = 49/248 = .1976 = 19.76\%$ when the $P[\text{positive test} \mid HIV] = 98\%$. Most tests are less accurate than 98%. Of course, a positive test result here is not good news. Before the test, $P[HIV] = 0.5\%$. After the test, the probability of HIV has gone up to 19.76%. Your doctor will probably run the test again.

We have just talked through the problem. Hopefully, you see what is going on. We are interested in finding $P[HIV \mid \text{positive test}]$. We can do this directly by using Bayes theorem. We should begin by defining the events here. You can have a positive test or a negative test. And you can have HIV or not have HIV. Let A be a positive test, and $\bar{A}$ be a negative test. Let B mean having HIV, and $\bar{B}$ mean not having HIV.

We are told that $P[B] = 0.5\%$, half a percent of the population has HIV. And the tests are 98% accurate. We take this to mean that $P[A \mid B] = 98\%$ and $P[\bar{A} \mid \bar{B}] = 98\%$. This also means that $P[\bar{B}] = 99.5\%$, $P[\bar{A} \mid B] = 2\%$, and $P[A \mid \bar{B}] = 2\%$.

We are interested in finding

$$P[B \mid A] = \frac{P[A \mid B]P[B]}{P[A]} = \frac{P[A \mid B]P[B]}{P[A \mid B]P[B] + P[A \mid \bar{B}]P[\bar{B}]}$$

First, we find

$$P[A] = P[A \mid B]P[B] + P[A \mid \bar{B}]P[\bar{B}] = \frac{98}{100}(0.005) + \frac{2}{100}(0.995)$$
$$= 0.0049 + 0.0199 = 0.0248 = 2.48\%$$

Therefore,

$$P[B \mid A] = \frac{P[A \mid B] \cdot P[B]}{P[A]} = \frac{\frac{98}{100} \cdot \frac{1}{200}}{0.0248} = 0.1976 = 19.76\%$$

We can also create a table with all the possible states of the world. You can have HIV or not have HIV. And the test can be positive or negative. With 10,000 people in the world, we can list the number of people we expect in every category. With these numbers, we can calculate any probabilities you might be interested in finding.

We can see that 248 individuals will have positive tests. Of these 248 individuals, only 49 actually have HIV. Thus, the probability of having HIV given a positive test is $49/248 = 0.1976 = 19.76\%$.

There is more than one way to think through these kinds of problems. But if you are thinking clearly, they will all lead you to the same answer. If you do a problem two different ways, and you get the same answer both ways, you probably have the right answer. If you do a problem two different ways, and you get different answers, then one or both of your answers are almost certainly wrong.

3.11.3 *Subjective probability of having a good date*

Suppose there are two types of people in this world, good people and bad people. The good people sleep a little better at night, and the bad people enjoy the waking hours a little more. Assume that in your experience there are more good people than bad people so that

$$P[\text{good date}] = 0.55$$
$$P[\text{bad date}] = 0.45$$

Suppose you also know that most good dates arrive on time, while most bad dates do not.

$$P[\text{on time} \mid \text{good date}] = 0.80$$
$$P[\text{on time} \mid \text{bad date}] = 0.30$$

What is the probability of having a good date given that your date arrives on time?

$$P[\text{good date} \mid \text{on time}] = \frac{P[\text{good date}]\, P[\text{on time} \mid \text{good date}]}{P[\text{on time}]}$$

where

$$\begin{aligned} P[\text{on time}] &= P[\text{on time} \mid \text{good date}]P[\text{good date}] \\ &\quad + P[\text{on time} \mid \text{bad date}]P[\text{bad date}] \\ P[\text{good date} \mid \text{on time}] &= \frac{(0.55)(0.80)}{(0.55)(0.80) + (0.30)(0.45)} = \frac{0.44}{0.575} \\ &= 0.7652 \end{aligned}$$

Bayesians make a distinction between our prior probability and our posterior probability. The prior probability is the probability an event will happen before you take any new evidence into account. The posterior probability is the probability an event will happen after the new evidence or background information is taken into account. When the date arrives on time, we have some new information. This new information increases the subjective probability of a good date from 55% to 76.5%. Our prior probability of a good date was 55%, but our posterior probability (after the date arrives on time) is 76.5%.

We could also create a table here of all the states of the world (see Table 3.5).

We see that 57.5 of the dates show up on time, but only 44 of these are actually good dates. So, the probability of a good date conditional on the date showing up on time is 44/57.5 = 76.5%.

Table 3.5. Good Date on Time.

	Good Date	Bad Date	
On Time	44	13.5	57.5
Not on Time	11	31.5	42.5
	55	45	100

3.11.4 *Miracle or a trick?*

Suppose your suitemate comes to you with a deck of cards and suggests playing some poker together. You are 99% sure that your suitemate is a trustworthy person. Thus, you have the following prior probabilities regarding your suitemate's deck of cards:

$$P[\text{standard deck}] = 99\%$$

$$P[\text{rigged deck}] = 1\%$$

On the very first hand, your suitemate deals himself a five-card hand with all four aces. Is your suitemate cheating or is she very lucky? There are 48 different ways to get a five-card hand with four aces. This is because the 5th card can be any of the remaining 48 cards. And there are $C_5^{52} = 2{,}598{,}960$ different five-card hands:

$$P[4 \text{ aces} \mid \text{standard deck}] = \frac{48}{2{,}598{,}960} = 0.0000184689$$

$$P[4 \text{ aces} \mid \text{rigged deck}] = 1.0$$

Before you started playing poker with your suitemate, you were 99% sure that your suitemate was trustworthy. This was your prior probability. But after this first-hand of poker, your posterior probability will be different. Now what is the probability that your suitemate is trustworthy and playing with a standard deck?

$$\begin{aligned} P[\text{standard deck} \mid 4 \text{ aces}] &= \frac{P[4 \text{ aces} \mid \text{standard deck}]P[\text{standard deck}]}{P[4 \text{ aces}]} \\ &= \frac{(0.0000184689)\,(0.99)}{(0.0000184689)\,(0.99) + (1.0)(0.01)} \\ &= \frac{0.0000182842}{0.01001828} = 0.001825 \approx 0.18\% \end{aligned}$$

This is your posterior probability that your suitemate is trustworthy.

So, $P[\text{rigged deck} \mid 4 \text{ aces}] = 1 - 0.001825 = 0.99817 \approx 99.8\%$.

You were 99% sure that your suitemate was trustworthy before playing cards with her. Now you are 99.8% sure that your suitemate is not trustworthy. You would be justified in throwing the cards in your suitemate's face.

You have a theory about the world. Over time you gather more and more evidence. If the evidence is consistent with the theory, then you become more confident that the theory is true. If the evidence is not consistent with the theory, you will consider abandoning the theory.

3.12 Exercises

(1) In a promotion for United Airlines, customers and potential customers were given vouchers. A 1/325 proportion of these vouchers were for a free round-trip ticket anywhere United flies. How many vouchers would an individual need to collect in order to have a 50% chance of winning at least one free trip? (225)

(2) The bad news is that you must have \$20 right away to pay off a loan shark. The good news is that you've already got \$10, and you're at a carnival with games of chance. Here are your choices:

  (a) For \$10, you can have the opportunity to flip a coin. You win \$20 if the coin lands heads giving you a 50% chance to win.

  (b) For \$10, you have the opportunity to roll a four-sided (pyramid-shaped) die twice. You win \$20 if the number 4 comes up, giving you two 25% chances to win.

Which one do you choose? Does it matter which one you choose? If so, why? (a)

(3) Baskin-Robbins ice-cream parlors advertise 31 different flavors of ice cream. They decide to offer a substantial prize to any customer who orders a triple scoop cone with the winning combination of flavors. What is the probability of winning if

(a) each flavor must be different and the order of the flavors does not matter?
(b) each flavor must be different and the order of the flavors does matter? (0.000222, 0.000037078)

(4) You need to borrow \$100,000 to attend college. There is a 90% probability that Wells Fargo will loan you \$100,000. There is an 80% probability that Bank of America will loan you \$60,000. There is a 70% probability that Washington Mutual will loan you \$40,000. Assume that all these loan decisions are independent. What is the probability that you will be able to borrow enough money? If Washington Mutual decides to give you the loan of \$40,000, what is the probability of being able to borrow enough money now? (0.9560, 0.9800)
(5) Two roommates, Elmer and Fudd, try to get dates for Friday night. Elmer has a 30% probability of getting a date. Fudd has a 40% probability of getting a date. Only one of them ends up getting a date. What is the probability that it was Elmer? (0.3913)
(6) Dan's Diner employs three dishwashers. Al washes 40% of the dishes and breaks only 1% of those he handles. Betty and Chuck each wash 30% of the dishes, and Betty breaks only 2% of hers, but Chuck breaks 3% of the dishes he washes. You go to Dan's for supper one night and hear a dish break at the sink. What is the probability that Chuck is on the job? (0.4736)
(7) Show that the probability of the union of the events A and B can be written $P(A \cup B) = P(A) + P(B)\,[1 - P(A \,|\, B)$.
(8) A hamburger chain found that 75% of all customers use mustard, 80% use ketchup, and 65% use both. What is the probability that a particular customer will use at least one of the two? What is the probability that a mustard user will use ketchup? (0.90, 0.8666)

(9) Let events A and B be independent. If $P(A) = 0.40$ and $P(B) = 0.50$, what is $P(A \text{ or } B)$, $P(A \text{ and } B)$, and $P(A \mid B)$? (0.70, 0.20, 0.40)

(10) Suppose the local electronics store has 60 Samsung Galaxy Note cell phones of which 8 have a defective battery. You and your friend just bought two of these Samsung cell phones. What is the probability that both of your phones have a defective battery? (0.01582)

Chapter 4

Probability Distributions

4.1 Introduction

Statistics show that 50% of marriages will end in divorce. If you think that is bad, the other 50% end in death.

There are often numbers associated with uncertain outcomes. What is the life expectancy of a 20-year-old woman in Los Angeles? What is the temperature in New York City? What is the unemployment rate in Chicago? What is the price of milk in Boise, Idaho? These are all random variables.

4.2 Random Variable

A random variable is a variable whose numerical value is determined by the outcome of an uncertain experiment. What is the number of heads you get when you toss two coins? The number of heads can be 0, 1, or 2. If X is the number of heads, we can have $X = 0$, $X = 1$, or $X = 2$ (see Table 4.1).

A random variable can be a discrete random variable such as the number of marriages in San Francisco tomorrow or the number of runs scored by the Boston Red Sox in their next game. A random variable can be a continuous random variable like your income in ten years or the life expectancy of your dog. If a and b are possible outcomes, all real values between a and b are also possible with a

Table 4.1. Toss two coins.

Outcome	# of Heads	Probability
Tail, Tail	0	1/4
Head, Tail or Tail, Head	1	1/2
Head, Head	2	1/4

continuous random variable. They are not possible with a discrete random variable.

In the previous chapter, we learned how to calculate the probabilities of these uncertain outcomes. Thus, we know how to assign probabilities to the possible outcomes of a random variable.

If we flip two coins, we can get the following number of heads with the following probabilities.

The listing of these probabilities with all the possible outcomes is called a probability distribution.

4.3 Probability Distribution

$P(x)$ is a function which gives the probability of each possible value x of a random variable X. We call $P(x)$ a probability distribution function:

$$P(x) = P(X = x)$$

If X is the number of heads you get when you toss two coins, $P(x)$ looks like Table 4.2.

Table 4.2. Toss two coins.

X	0	1	2	3
$P(X)$	1/4	1/2	1/4	0

We could graph this as shown in Figure 4.1.

If X is the number you get when you roll a fair six-sided die, $P(x)$ looks like Table 4.3. We could graph this as well (see Figure 4.2).

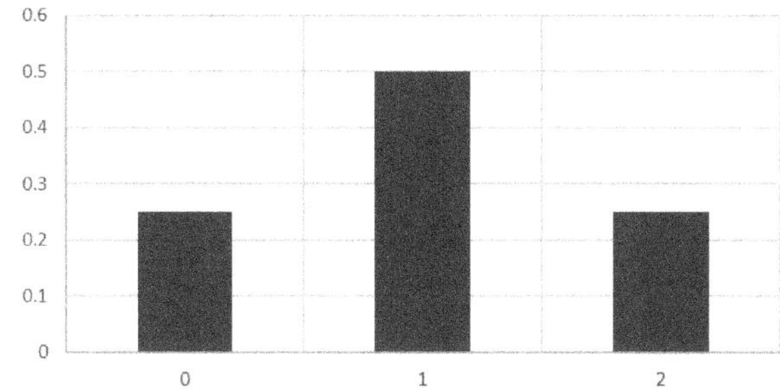

Fig. 4.1. Probability distributions.

Table 4.3. Roll die.

X	1	2	3	4	5	6
$P(X)$	1/6	1/6	1/6	1/6	1/6	1/6

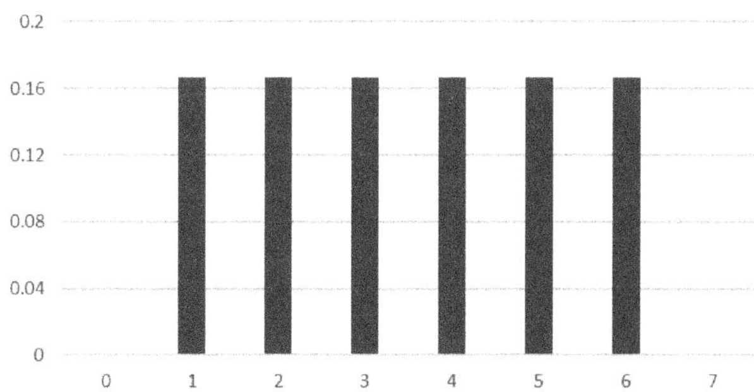

Fig. 4.2. Dice probability distribution.

We will note that $0 \leq P(x) \leq 1$ for all x. All probabilities must be between 0 and 1. Furthermore, for discrete random variables, the sum of all the individual probabilities must add up to 1. For continuous random variables, the integral[1] of the probability distribution

[1]If you have had some calculus, and this makes sense, then great. If not, please don't worry about it. But the discrete part should make sense.

function from negative infinity to positive infinity must be equal to 1. We are just saying that one of the possible outcomes must happen[2]:

$$\sum_x P(x) = 1 \quad \text{and} \quad \int_{-\infty}^{\infty} P(x)dx = 1 \tag{4.1}$$

When we see a probability distribution, we will want to be able to describe it. How might we characterize a probability distribution? We can start by describing the distribution by its center and its spread.

We can describe the center of a distribution with the expected value. The expected value, $E[X]$, of a random variable X is defined as

$$E[X] = \sum_x xP(x) = \mu_x \tag{4.2}$$

for discrete random variables where the notation indicates that summation extends over all possible values of x. If we have a continuous random variable, we will need to use some calculus:

$$E[X] = \int_{-\infty}^{\infty} xP(x)dx = \mu_x \tag{4.3}$$

The integral is over all possible values of x. If the calculus makes sense, then great. Otherwise, please don't worry about it. You can see that calculus is a way to deal with continuous variables the way we use summation signs to deal with discrete variables.

4.4 Laws of Expected Value

We will be using the notion of expected value over and over in this textbook. The following are some useful laws of expected value. If X and Y are random variables and c is any constant, then the following can be shown:

[2]There is a review of the summation operator Σ at the end of this chapter.

(1) $E[c] = c$
The expected value of a constant is the constant. This follows from the observation that $P[c] = 1$.

(2) The distributive property holds for the expectations operator so that

$$E[c + X + Y] = E[c] + E[X] + E[Y] = c + \mu_x + \mu_y$$

(3) The expected value of the multiple of a random variable is equal to the multiple of the expected value:

$$E[cX] = cE[X] = c\mu_x$$

(4) In general, if X is a random variable with probability distribution function $P(x)$, and $g(X)$ is some function of X, then the expected value of $g(X)$, $E[g(X)]$, is defined as

$$E[g(X)] = \sum_x g(x)P(x) = \int g(x)P(x)dx$$

for discrete variables and continuous variables, respectively.

(5) For example, the variance of a probability distribution is defined as the following expected value:

$$\sigma_x^2 = E[(X - \mu_x)^2] = \sum_x (x - \mu_x)^2 P(x) = \int (x - \mu_x)^2 P(x)dx$$

for discrete variables and continuous variables, respectively.

(6) With two random variables, the following holds from 2 above.

$$E[X - Y] = E[X] - E[Y] = \mu_x - \mu_y$$
$$E[X + Y] = E[X] + E[Y] = \mu_x + \mu_y$$

(7) And if X and Y are independent random variables, then

$$E[X \cdot Y] = E[X] \cdot E[Y]$$

(8) But be aware that, as a rule,

$$E\left(\frac{1}{X}\right) \neq \frac{1}{E[X]}$$

Suppose X is equal to 1 half the time and 3 half the time. Then, X is equal to 2 on average. But the inverse of X is equal to 1 half the time and 1/3 half the time. The average of the inverse of X is 2/3. And the inverse of 2 is not equal to 2/3.

4.5 Describing Probability Distributions

Now let's go back to describing probability distributions. We start with our measure of the center of a probability distribution. We call this the mean of the distribution.

4.5.1 *Mean μ of a probability distribution*

The mean of a probability distribution is the expected value of the random variable, a measure of central tendency, or the predicted long-run average:

$$\mu = E[X] = \sum_x xP(x) = \int xP(x)dx \tag{4.4}$$

for discrete and continuous random variables, respectively. The mean is the weighted average of all the possible outcomes where we use probabilities as weights. Please do not confuse the mean of a probability distribution with the mean of a sample which we discuss in earlier and later chapters.

4.5.1.1 *Toss two coins*

On average, how many heads do you get when you toss two coins?

$$\mu_x = \sum_x xP(x) = 0 \cdot P(X=0) + 1 \cdot P(X=1) + 2 \cdot P(X=2)$$
$$= 0 \cdot \frac{1}{4} + 1 \cdot \frac{1}{2} + 2 \cdot \frac{1}{4} = \frac{1}{2} + \frac{1}{2} = 1$$

If you flip a pair of coins a great many times, on average you will get one head.

4.5.1.2 *Sum of two dice*

When you roll 2 dice, the sum of the two numbers, X, has possible outcomes $X = 2, 3, \ldots, 12$. We find that the mean of X is $E[X] = 7$ (see Table 4.4).

4.5.1.3 *Chuck-A-Luck*

Chuck-A-Luck is a carnival game, sometimes called birdcage, played around the world. You pick a number between 1 and 6. The dealer

Table 4.4. Probability table.

X	$P(x)$	$xP(x)$
1	0	0
2	1/36	2/36
3	2/36	6/36
4	3/36	12/36
5	4/36	20/36
6	5/36	30/36
7	6/36	42/36
8	5/36	40/36
9	4/36	36/36
10	3/36	30/36
11	2/36	22/36
12	1/36	12/36
13	0	0
	$\sum xP(x)$	$\frac{252}{36} = 7$

will roll 3 dice. If your number comes up 3 times, you win \$3. If your number comes up 2 times, you win \$2. If your number comes up just once, you will win \$1. If your number does not come up at all, you lose \$1.

Let the random variable X be the amount of money you win when you play this game once. What is the $E[X]$?

$$P(\#\text{ comes up 3 times}) = \frac{1}{6} \cdot \frac{1}{6} \cdot \frac{1}{6} = \frac{1}{216}$$

$$P(\#\text{ comes up 2 times}) = C_2^3 \cdot \frac{5}{6} \cdot \frac{1}{6} \cdot \frac{1}{6} = \frac{15}{216}$$

$$P(\#\text{ comes up once}) = C_1^3 \cdot \frac{5}{6} \cdot \frac{5}{6} \cdot \frac{1}{6} = \frac{75}{216}$$

$$P(\#\text{ does not come up}) = 1 - \left(\frac{1}{216} + \frac{15}{216} + \frac{75}{216}\right) = \frac{125}{216}$$

$$= \left(\frac{5}{6}\right)\left(\frac{5}{6}\right)\left(\frac{5}{6}\right) = \frac{125}{216}$$

$$E[X] = \$3 \cdot \frac{1}{216} + \$2 \cdot \frac{15}{216} + \$1 \cdot \frac{75}{216} - \$1 \cdot \frac{125}{216}$$

$$= -\$0.08$$

So, on average, you lose 8¢ every time you play. You will lose less, on average, if you play roulette at a casino. You lose about 5.3¢ for every dollar you bet in the U.S., and only 2.7¢ for every dollar you bet in Europe. You will lose more, on average, if you play the state lotteries. You lose about 37¢ for every dollar you spend on state lotteries.

4.5.1.4 *St. Petersburg paradox*

The St. Petersburg paradox was first developed by Nicolas Bernoulli in the early 1700s. Consider the following experiment. Nicolas repeatedly tosses a coin until it comes up heads. You get \$2 if there is a head on the first toss, \$4 if the first head is on the second toss, \$8 if the first head is on the third toss, \$16 if the first head is on the fourth toss, etc. No matter what, you will win at least \$2. How much money can you expect to make playing this game?

$$\begin{aligned} E[X] &= \$2 \cdot \left(\frac{1}{2}\right) + \$4 \cdot \left(\frac{1}{4}\right) + \$8 \cdot \left(\frac{1}{8}\right) + \$16 \cdot \left(\frac{1}{16}\right) + \cdots \\ &= \$1 + \$1 + \$1 + \$1 + \cdots \\ &= \infty \end{aligned}$$

You can expect to make an infinite amount of money playing this game. Given that your expected payout is infinite, how much money are you willing to pay in order to play this game with Nicolas? Most people are only willing to pay a few dollars. This is the paradox. Why aren't people willing to pay more? If you could play this game as many times as you wanted, would you be willing to pay more? Why?

4.5.1.5 *Monte Carlo*

Here is an almost sure way to win \$1,000 in Monte Carlo. In French/European style roulette, there are 37 possible outcomes, the numbers 0 through 36. The number 0 is green, and all the other numbers are either red or black. The probability of landing on red is $18/37 = .486 \approx 0.50$. The probability of landing on black is also $18/37 = .486 \approx 0.50$. You begin by betting \$1,000 on red. If it comes up red, you will win \$1,000 and you can go home. If it comes up black, you should now bet \$2,000 on red. If it comes up red this time, you will win \$2,000. After accounting for the \$1,000 you lost in the first round, you will be up \$1,000 and you can go home. If it comes up black the second time, you should bet \$4,000 on the red in the following round, etc. As long as you leave the first time it comes up red, and double your bet every time, you are guaranteed to win \$1,000.

$$\begin{aligned}\text{Expected Winnings} &= \$1{,}000 \cdot \left(\frac{1}{2}\right) + \$1{,}000 \cdot \left(\frac{1}{4}\right) + \$1{,}000 \cdot \left(\frac{1}{8}\right) \\ &\quad + \$1{,}000 \cdot \left(\frac{1}{16}\right) + \$1{,}000 \cdot \left(\frac{1}{32}\right) \\ &\quad + \cdots = \$1{,}000\end{aligned}$$

The problem with this strategy is that you may not have enough money to double your bet every time, and there may be table limits which prevent you from betting as much as you want to bet. You will get a long series of black more frequently than you might think.

4.5.1.6 *Insurance*

In 2012, a one-year \$100,000 term life insurance policy for a 25-year-old woman cost about \$120. How much money can you expect to make if you buy this policy?

From 2017 Census Bureau estimates, of approximately 2.3 million 25-year-old women, about 1,175 will die before reaching their 26th birthday. So, the probability of death is

$$p = \frac{1{,}175}{2{,}308{,}000} = 0.000509$$

So, the expected payoff $= \$100{,}000 \cdot (0.000509) + \$0 \cdot (0.999491) =$ \$50.9.

A 50% benefit-to-premium ratio is typical of many insurance companies.

Here is an example of the structure of typical life insurance premiums (see Table 4.5).

Women pay less, and younger people pay less because they are less likely to pass away in any given year. Non-smokers also pay

Table 4.5. Insurance premiums.

Annual Premium, $100,000 Policy, Non-smokers		
Age	Male	Female
18–34	$144	$120
35–39	$156	$132
40–44	$216	$168
45–49	$324	$216
50–54	$540	$348
55–59	$840	$504
60–64	$1,260	$720
65–69	$1,992	$1,200
70–74	$3,000	$1,980
75–79	$4,992	$3,060

less. Insurance products marketed to individuals outside the workplace usually have different premiums for men and for women. But we typically see unisex rates on insurance products offered at the workplace. Life insurance, disability insurance, health insurance, annuities, or other ancillary products have premium rates which are typically unisex. Should life insurance companies move toward "unisex" rates where men and women pay equal premiums? Who would gain? Who would lose?

What if we are talking about defined pension benefits? A defined benefit pension plan is a type of pension plan in which an employer/sponsor promises a specified annual pension payment for as long as you live. Defined pension benefit programs can expect to pay out more to women because they live longer than men. So, should the annual premiums be higher as well?

4.5.1.7 *Medical clinic tests*

Assume there is a blood test for a sexually transmitted disease (STD) which affects 1/100 people. Every day about 50 people come to the clinic to be tested. You can either test everyone individually or initially pool all 50 blood samples and run one test. You might be able to clear everyone with just one test. What is the expected number of blood tests if we pool the blood? We only need one test if the pooled sample is negative. We need 51 tests if the pooled test is positive:

$P(\text{person is healthy}) = {}^{99}\!/_{100}$

$P(\text{50 people are healthy}) = \left({}^{99}\!/_{100}\right)^{50}$

So, the probability of one test is $\left({}^{99}\!/_{100}\right)^{50}$.

The probability of 51 tests is $\left[1 - \left({}^{99}\!/_{100}\right)^{50}\right]$:

$$E[\#\text{ of tests}] = \left[1 \cdot \left({}^{99}\!/_{100}\right)^{50}\right] + \left[51 \cdot \left[1 - \left({}^{99}\!/_{100}\right)^{50}\right]\right] \approx 21$$

Thus, we can decrease the average number of tests we run by initially pooling our sample. If these tests are expensive, we will want to minimize the number of tests.[3,4]

4.5.1.8 *Is life fair?*

Is there an advantage to being rich or poor in a fair game of chance? If the game is fair, both the rich person and the poor person must have an expected gain of zero. This means that the poor person is more likely to go home broke. Suppose the rich person is playing with \$90,000 and the poor person is playing with \$10,000, and they play poker until one of them is bankrupt. What is the probability that the rich person will win if they are both equally skilled and the game is fair? The rich person can win \$10,000 or lose \$90,000 and the expected gain is zero. This implies that the probability that the

[3]There is another way to do pooled testing. Suppose you have samples from 384 people and divide them into 48 pools so that each person's sample winds up in a unique set of six pools. You test each of the 48 pools. If one person is positive for the virus, then each of the six pools containing that sample should test positive — resulting in a unique combination of positive pools revealing the identity of the person (or people) carrying the virus. You have to optimize the design of the pools according to the expected prevalence of the virus, making it possible to pinpoint all of the positive individuals in a batch, as long as the total number of positives does not sharply exceed the expected number.

[4]In July 2020, the Food and Drug Administration (U.S.) authorized sample pooling in diagnostic testing for COVID-19.

rich person will win, p, is 90%:

$$\begin{aligned}(10{,}000)p + (-90{,}000)(1-p) &= 0\\ 100{,}000p &= 90{,}000\\ p &= 0.90\end{aligned}$$

With a 10% chance of winning, the poor person has zero expected gain:

$$(90{,}000)(0.10) + (-10{,}000)(0.90) = 0$$

The rich person is more likely to win but will lose more money if she doesn't win.

4.5.1.9 *Betting odds*

If you are betting on Brazil to win the next World Cup, and the odds are 7 to 1, you will win \$7 if Brazil wins the World Cup, and you will lose \$1 if Brazil loses the World Cup. Assuming that the betting markets are efficient, the expected winnings should be zero. So, if p is the subjective probability that Brazil will win the World Cup, the following should be true:

$$\begin{aligned}\$0 &= \$7 \cdot p - \$1 \cdot (1-p)\\ \$0 &= \$7p - \$1 + \$1p\\ \$0 &= \$8p - \$1\\ \$8p &= \$1\\ p &= \frac{1}{8} = 0.125 = 12.5\%\end{aligned}$$

The betting market's subjective probability that Brazil will win the next World Cup is 12.5%.

We have learned to describe the mean of a probability distribution. But people generally want to know much more about a probability distribution than just the mean. They also care about the spread of the distribution. At least since the work of Harry Markowitz and James Tobin in the 1950s, we have been aware that people make investment decisions based on both the mean and the variance of the return. This is known as mean–variance analysis, the process of weighing risk, expressed as variance, against the expected mean return.

Consider four examples of the return on a \$100 investment (see Table 4.6).

Table 4.6. Hypothetical investment returns.

Investment	Outcome	Expected Value	Variance	Std. Dev.
A	\$5 with certainty	\$5	0	\$0
B	\$10 with 50% \$0 with 50%	\$5	25	\$5
C	\$10 with 25% \$5 with 50% \$0 with 25%	\$5	12.5	\$3.54
D	\$105 with 25% \$5 with 50% −\$95 with 25%	\$5	5,000	\$70.71

The expected value of all the investments above is the same, but the variance is not. Would you be indifferent between all four investment opportunities? Most people are actually risk-averse. That is to say, if you want people to bear more risk, you have to reward them with a higher expected value. We care about more than just the expected value. We care about the risk or variance.

Here are the average annual total returns for holding stocks and bonds (see Table 4.7). You can see that stocks are much riskier than

Table 4.7. Investment returns.

Average Annual Total Returns (1926–2005) Nominal			
Asset	Mean	Std. Dev.	Variance
Treasury bills	3.8	3.1	9.6
Long-term treasury bonds	5.8	9.2	84.6
Long-term corp bonds	6.2	8.5	72.2
Large stocks	12.3	20.2	408.0
Small stocks	17.4	32.9	1,082.4
Inflation	3.1	4.3	18.5

bonds. This is one reason the mean rate of return is higher for stocks than for bonds.

4.5.2 *Variance* σ^2

The variance of a random variable X is defined as

$$\sigma^2 = E[(X-\mu)^2] = \sum_x (X-\mu)^2 P(x) = \int_{-\infty}^{\infty} (X-\mu)^2 P(x) dx \tag{4.5}$$

for discrete and continuous random variables, respectively. This measures how far we might expect X to be from its mean. We are talking about the variance of a probability distribution here. This is different from the variance of a sample which we discussed earlier. Please do not confuse these two concepts.

4.5.3 *Standard deviation* σ

The standard deviation σ is the square root of the variance σ^2:

$$\sigma = \sqrt{\sigma^2} = \sqrt{\sum\nolimits_x (X-\mu)^2 P(x)} \tag{4.6}$$

The units of σ will be the same as the units of X and easier to interpret than the variance. The standard deviation is the typical distance of X from its mean.

4.5.3.1 *Example* 1

Consider the number of heads you get when you flip two coins. We determined above that the expected value was equal to 1. Here we calculate the variance:

$$\begin{aligned}\sigma^2 &= \sum_x (X-\mu)^2 P(x) = (0-1)^2 \frac{1}{4} + (1-1)^2 \frac{1}{2} + (2-1)^2 \frac{1}{4} \\ &= \frac{1}{4} + 0 + \frac{1}{4} = \frac{1}{2} \\ \sigma &= \sqrt{\sigma^2} = \sqrt{\frac{1}{2}} = \frac{1}{\sqrt{2}}\end{aligned}$$

4.5.3.2 *Example 2*

Consider the number you get when you roll a single six-sided die. The mean is 3.5. The variance is as follows:

$$\begin{aligned}
\sigma^2 &= \sum_x (X-\mu)^2 P(x) \\
&= (1-3.5)^2\frac{1}{6} + (2-3.5)^2\frac{1}{6} + (3-3.5)^2\frac{1}{6} + (4-3.5)^2\frac{1}{6} \\
&\quad + (5-3.5)^2\frac{1}{6} + (6-3.5)^2\frac{1}{6} \\
&= (-2.5)^2\frac{1}{6} + (-1.5)^2\frac{1}{6} + (-0.5)^2\frac{1}{6} + (0.5)^2\frac{1}{6} \\
&\quad + (1.5)^2\frac{1}{6} + (2.5)^2\frac{1}{6} \\
&= \frac{6.25}{6} + \frac{2.25}{6} + \frac{0.25}{6} + \frac{0.25}{6} + \frac{2.25}{6} + \frac{6.25}{6} = \frac{35}{12} \\
&= 2.91666666
\end{aligned}$$

4.5.3.3 *Example 3*

When you play Chuck-A-Luck, on average, you will lose 8¢ every time you play. What is the variance?

$$\begin{aligned}
\sigma^2 &= \sum_x (X-\mu)^2 P(x) \\
&= (3-(-0.08))^2\frac{1}{216} + (2-(-0.08))^2\frac{15}{216} + (1-(-0.08))^2\frac{75}{216} \\
&\quad + (-1-(-008))^2\frac{125}{216} \\
&= 0.043 + 0.300 + 0.404 + 0.4911 = 1.239176 \\
\sigma &= \sqrt{1.239176} = 1.11318
\end{aligned}$$

We will frequently use the mean and the variance to describe the shape of a probability distribution. But we may want to know more about the shape of a distribution than the description provided by just these two numbers. Two distributions may have the same mean and variance but look very different. For example, you might want to ask if the distribution is symmetric or skewed. Or you may want to know if the distribution has one peak or multiple peaks.

4.5.4 *Skewness*

Consider two investment schemes, A and B (see Table 4.8 and Figure 4.3). For a \$100 investment, these are the returns along with their probabilities. These two investments "feel" very different. But these probability distributions have the same mean and the same variance. Check it out. The mean return is \$14 for both investments, and the standard deviation is \$29.04. But people may dislike investment B because they don't like the possibility of losing money. Thus, the mean and the variance may not be all the information you care about.

Table 4.8. Investment return.

Investment A	\$0 49%	\$5 2%	\$10 39%	\$100 10%
Investment B	−\$15.04 50%	\$43.04 50%		

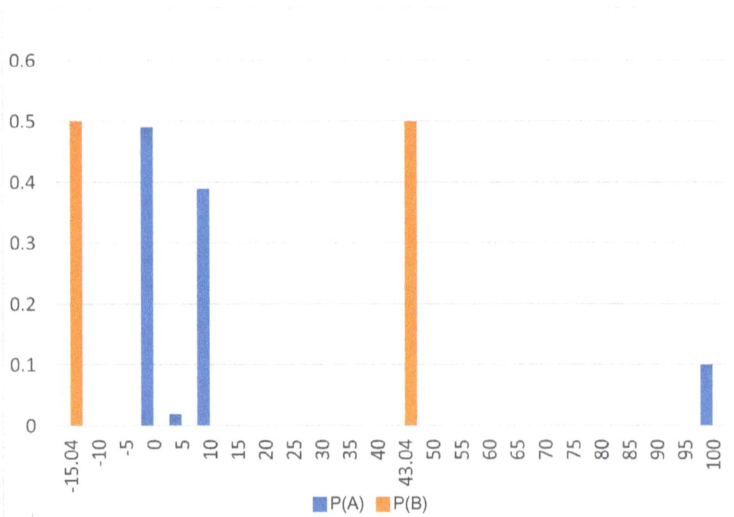

Fig. 4.3. Two distributions.

You might care if a probability distribution is skewed to the left or to the right. Investment A is skewed to the right. There is the possibility of doing much better than the mean. For a unimodal distribution, positive skew suggests that the tail is on the right side of the distribution, and negative skew suggests that the tail is on the left side of the distribution. A zero value for skew means that the tails on both sides of the mean balance out overall. One tail might be long and thin while the other is short and fat. A symmetric distribution will have a zero value for skew.

We also say that a distribution with a positive skew is "skewed right" and a distribution with a negative skew is "skewed left." Imagine someone taking the right tail of a distribution and pulling it right (skewed right), or someone taking the left tail of a distribution and pulling it left (skewed left) (see Figures 2.9 and 2.11).

One measure of skewness, developed by Karl Pearson (1857–1936), is the third standardized moment of a probability distribution defined as follows:

$$\tilde{\mu}_3 = E\left[\left(\frac{X-\mu}{\sigma}\right)^3\right] = \frac{E[(X-\mu)^3]}{(E[(X-\mu)^2])^{3/2}} \tag{4.7}$$

where μ is the mean and σ is the standard deviation. It is "standardized" because we subtract the mean μ from X and divide it by the standard deviation σ. For a sample of n observations, an estimate of skewness would be

$$\gamma = \frac{\frac{1}{n}\sum(X_i - \bar{X})^3}{\left[\frac{1}{n-1}\sum(X_i - \bar{X})^2\right]^{3/2}} \tag{4.8}$$

Any symmetric distribution will have a skewness of zero, $\gamma = 0$, if the third moment exists.

4.5.5 *Kurtosis*

When you look at probability distributions, you might also care about the frequency of extreme outliers. Kurtosis is a measure related to the tails of the distribution. Higher kurtosis is the result of extreme deviations or outliers. A few extreme outliers will tend to matter more than more frequent modestly sized deviations.

Table 4.9. Kurtosis.

Outcome	$P(X)$	$P(Y)$
−4	0.1	0.05
−2	0.2	0.4
0	0.4	0.1
2	0.2	0.4
4	0.1	0.05

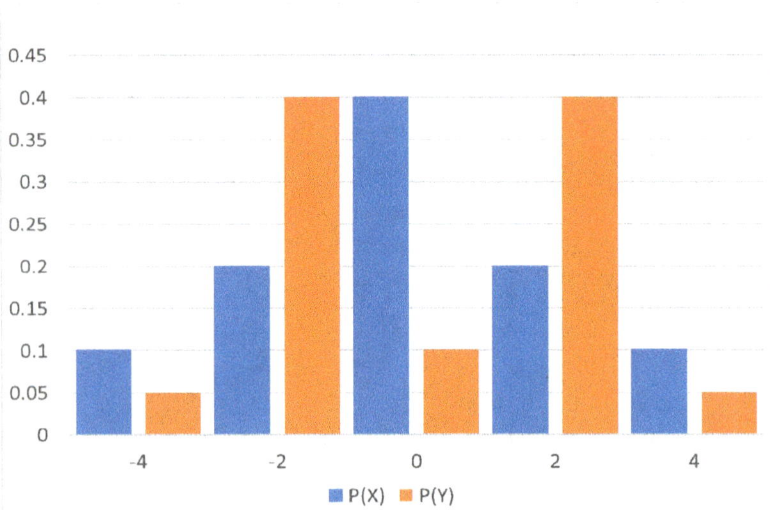

Fig. 4.4. Two distributions.

Consider two probability distributions, $P(X)$ and $P(Y)$, over the same range of outcomes (see Table 4.9 and Figure 4.4).

These two distributions have the same mean ($\mu = 0$), same variance ($\sigma^2 = 4.8$), and same skewness ($\tilde{\mu}_3 = 0$). But $P(X)$ has a higher degree of kurtosis. This is because of the higher tail probabilities.

Kurtosis is the fourth standardized moment of a probability distribution. It is defined as

$$\text{Kurt}[X] = E\left[\left(\frac{X-\mu}{\sigma}\right)^4\right] = \frac{E[(X-\mu)^4]}{(E[(X-\mu)^2])^2} \tag{4.9}$$

Since deviations from the mean are raised to the 4th power, higher tail probabilities will lead to a higher degree of kurtosis.

This brings us to a brief discussion of the "moments" of a distribution. The zeroth moment of a probability distribution is the total probability, i.e., one. The first moment of a probability distribution is the mean, the second moment is the variance, the third moment is the skewness, and the fourth moment is the kurtosis. The standardized moments μ_n of a probability distribution can be generally defined as

$$\mu_n = E\left[\left(\frac{X-\mu}{\sigma}\right)^n\right] = \sum_x \left(\frac{x-\mu}{\sigma}\right)^n P(x)$$
$$= \int_{-\infty}^{\infty} \left(\frac{x-\mu}{\sigma}\right)^n P(x)dx \tag{4.10}$$

for discrete and continuous variables respectively where μ is the mean, σ is the standard deviation, and μ_n is the nth moment of the distribution. The σ in the expression serves to "standardize" this measure by adjusting for the units of measure. All the moments together can perfectly describe the shape of a probability distribution. Unfortunately, some or all of these moments may be undefined for some probability distributions.

The probability distribution of a random variable can be characterized by its **moment-generating function**. The moment-generating function is a real function whose derivatives at zero are equal to the moments of the random variable. A probability distribution is uniquely determined by its moment-generating function, though not all random variables have a moment-generating function.

4.6 Linear Functions of Random Variables

We are often interested in the expected value or variance of a linear function of a random variable. For example, what is the mean and variance of playing Chuck-A-Luck if we bet \$50 rather than just \$1? What happens if we measure the height of basketball players in centimeters rather than inches? What if we measure Chicago temperatures in Celsius rather than Fahrenheit?

These are situations where we have a deterministic relationship between two random variables X and Y:

$$Y = a + bX$$

Since a and b are constants, when we know the value of X, we know the value of Y exactly.

For example, the temperature in Celsius is a linear function of the temperature in Fahrenheit. $C = \frac{5}{9}(F - 32) = -17.777 + \frac{5}{9}F$. When it is 32°F, we know it is 0°C. If we know the mean and variance of the temperature in Fahrenheit, can we figure out the mean and variance of the temperature in Celsius or Kelvin or Rankine?

Let X be a random variable with

$$\begin{aligned} \mu_x &= \text{mean of } x \\ \sigma_x^2 &= \text{variance of } x \end{aligned}$$

Let $Z = a + bX$ where a and b are fixed constants. Here, Z is a linear function of X.

What is the mean of Z?

$$\begin{aligned} E[Z] = \mu_Z &= \sum_z zP(z) = \sum_x (a + bx)P(x) \\ &= \sum aP(x) + \sum bxP(x) \\ &= a\sum P(x) + b\sum xP(x) = a + b\mu_x = \mu_z \end{aligned} \tag{4.11}$$

And what is the variance of Z?

$$\begin{aligned} V[Z] = \sigma_Z^2 &= E[(Z - \mu_Z)^2] = E[((a + bX) - (a + b\mu_x))^2] \\ &= E[(bX - b\mu_x)^2] = E[(b(X - \mu_x))^2] \\ &= E[b^2(X - \mu_x)^2] \\ &= b^2E[(X - \mu_x)^2] = b^2\sigma_x^2 \end{aligned} \tag{4.12}$$

Consequently, if $Z = a + X$,

$$\begin{aligned} E(Z) &= E(a + X) = a + \mu_x \\ V(Z) &= V(a + X) = \sigma_x^2 \end{aligned}$$

If you add a constant to a random variable, the mean will change, but the variance will stay the same.

If $Z = bX$,

$$E[Z] = E(bX) = b\mu_x$$
$$V(Z) = V(bX) = b^2\sigma_x^2$$

If you multiply a random variable by a number, the mean and the variance will change.

Let X be the number of heads you get when you toss two coins. We can describe the probability distribution of $X + 3$ and $2X$ if we know the mean of X, μ_x, and the variance of X, σ_x^2. What is the mean and the variance of these probability distributions? The mean of $X + 3$ is $\mu_x + 3$, and the variance of $X + 3$ is σ_x^2 The mean of $2X$ is $2\mu_x$, and the variance of $2X$ is $4\sigma_x^2$.

Suppose the average daily high temperature in Chicago is 58°F with a variance of 477. What is the mean, variance, and standard deviation of the high temperature in Celsius? We know that

$$C = \frac{5}{9}(F - 32) = -17.777 + \frac{5}{9}F$$
$$E(C) = \mu_C = \frac{5}{9}(\mu_F - 32) = \frac{5}{9}(58 - 32) = 14.44$$
$$V(C) = \sigma_C^2 = \left(\frac{5}{9}\right)^2 \sigma_F^2 = \left(\frac{5}{9}\right)^2 477 = 147.22$$
$$\text{SD}(C) = \sigma_C = \sqrt{147.22} = 12.13$$

4.7 Joint Probability Distributions

We now want to be able to describe the relationship between two random variables when there may or may not be a deterministic relationship. We turn our attention to joint probability distributions. We want to look at the probability of each possible outcome combination of the two variables being considered.

In the first example, we watch the LA Lakers (basketball) and the LA Kings (ice hockey) on a winter Friday night and see if they win or lose their games. Let X represent the outcome of the Kings game and Y represent the outcome of the Lakers game (see Table 4.10). We might represent the joint probability distribution as follows:

Table 4.10. Lakers and Kings.

Lakers and Kings		Y: LA Lakers		
		Lose: 0	Win: 1	
X: LA Kings	Lose: 0	0.22	0.33	0.55
	Win: 1	0.18	0.27	0.45
		0.40	0.60	1.00

$$\begin{aligned} P(x,y) &= P(X=x \quad \text{and} \quad Y=y) = P(X=x \cap Y=y) \\ P(0,1) &= P(X=0 \quad \text{and} \quad Y=1) = P(X=0 \cap Y=1) = 0.33 \\ P(1,0) &= P(X=1 \quad \text{and} \quad Y=0) = P(X=1 \cap Y=0) = 0.18 \end{aligned} \tag{4.13}$$

Here, the Kings win 45% of their games, and the Lakers win 60% of their games. The probability that both the Lakers and the Kings will win is 27%. The probability that they will both lose is 22%.

In the second example, we observe individuals who are being tried in a court of law. All the individuals are either guilty or innocent, and they are either acquitted or convicted of the charges. Let X represent whether the person is acquitted or convicted and Y represent whether the person is innocent or guilty. The joint probability distribution of all the possible outcomes appears in the following. Please note that these are hypothetical probabilities (see Table 4.11).

$$\begin{aligned} P(x,y) &= P(X=x \quad \text{and} \quad Y=y) = P(X=x \cap Y=y) \\ P(0,1) &= P(X=0 \quad \text{and} \quad Y=1) = P(X=0 \cap Y=1) = 0.15 \\ P(1,0) &= P(X=1 \quad \text{and} \quad Y=0) = P(X=1 \cap Y=0) = 0.0375 \end{aligned}$$

We note that all probabilities must be between 0 and 1:

$$0 \le P(xy) \le 1 \tag{4.14}$$

The sum of all the joint probabilities must be equal to 1:

$$\sum_x \sum_y P(x,y) = 1 \tag{4.15}$$

Table 4.11. Guilty and convicted.

Guilty and Convicted		Y		
		Innocent: 0	Guilty: 1	
$\boldsymbol{X}$	Acquitted: 0	0.2125	0.15	0.3625
	Convicted: 1	0.0375	0.60	0.6375
		0.25	0.75	1.00

Recall from our discussion of conditional probabilities that

$$P(A|B) = \frac{P(A \text{ and } B)}{P(B)} = \frac{P(A \cap B)}{P(B)}$$

But

$$P(x, y) = P(X = x \text{ and } Y = y) = P(X = x \cap Y = y)$$

So,

$$P(X = x|Y = y) = \frac{P(X = x \text{ and } Y = y)}{P(Y = y)} = \frac{P(x, y)}{P(y)} \tag{4.16}$$

In the Lakers and Kings case,

$$P(X = 1|Y = 1) = \frac{P(1, 1)}{P(Y = 1)} = \frac{0.27}{0.6} = 0.45 = 45\%$$

Note that $P(X = 1|Y = 1) = P(X = 1)$ here. If A and B are independent, then $P(A|B) = P(A)$ and $P(B|A) = P(B)$. The Lakers game has nothing to do with the Kings game.

In the Guilty and Convicted case,

$$P(X = 1|Y = 1) = \frac{P(X = 1 \text{ and } Y = 1)}{P(Y = 1)} = \frac{0.60}{0.75} = 0.80$$

We note that

$$P(X = 1|Y = 1) \neq P(X = 1)$$
$$0.80 \neq 0.6375$$

so X and Y are *not* independent here. If X and Y are independent, then $P(xy) = P(x) \cdot P(y)$ for all x and y. But being guilty is not independent of being convicted. Now let's further characterize the relationship between two variables.

4.7.1 *Covariance*

Covariance is a statistical measure of the linear mutual variability of two random variables. If the covariance is positive, both variables move together. When one variable increases, the other variable tends to increase as well. If the covariance is negative, then both variables move in opposite directions. When one variable increases, the other variable tends to decrease.

We expect to see a positive covariance between income and education, height and weight, and height and income. We tend to see a negative covariance between age and memory and between height and life expectancy.

We define the covariance between X and Y as

$$\begin{aligned}
\text{cov}(x, y) = \sigma_{xy} &= E[(X - \mu_x)(Y - \mu_y)] \\
&= \sum_x \sum_y (x - \mu_x)(y - \mu_y)P(x, y) \\
&= E[XY - \mu_x Y - \mu_y X + \mu_x\mu_y] \\
&= E[XY] - \mu_x E[Y] - \mu_y E[X] + \mu_x\mu_y \\
&= E[XY] - \mu_x\mu_y - \mu_x\mu_y + \mu_x\mu_y = E[XY] - \mu_x\mu_y \\
&= \sum_x \sum_y xyP(x, y) - \mu_x\mu_y \qquad (4.17)
\end{aligned}$$

Please note that this is the covariance of a joint probability distribution. This is different from the covariance of sample data discussed in an earlier chapter.

4.7.1.1 *Lakers and Kings*

Let us figure out the covariance between the winning performance of the Lakers and the Kings.

We first have to figure out the means of these variables:

$$\mu_x = E[X] = 1(0.45) + 0(0.55) = 0.45 \text{ Kings}$$

$$\mu_y = E[Y] = 1(0.60) + 0(0.40) = 0.60 \text{ Lakers}$$

$$\text{cov}(x, y) = \sigma_{xy} = \sum_x \sum_y xyP(x, y) - \mu_x\mu_y = 0.27 - (0.45)(0.6) = 0$$

Table 4.12. Calculating covariances.

x	y	xy	$P(x,y)$	$xyP(x,y)$
0	0	0	0.18	0
0	1	0	0.33	0
1	0	0	0.18	0
1	1	1	0.27	0.27
				$\sum_x \sum_y xyP(x,y) = 0.27$

The covariance between the Lakers winning and the Kings winning is zero (see Table 4.12). There is no relationship between the outcome of one game and the outcome of the other game.

4.7.1.2 *Guilty and convicted*

Now let us consider the joint probability case of being guilty and being convicted of a crime.

In order to figure out the covariance, we first have to figure out the means of the two variables:

$$\mu_x = E[X] = 0(0.3625) + 1(0.6375) = 0.6375$$

$$\mu_y = E[Y] = 0(0.25) + 1(0.75) = 0.75$$

$$\text{cov}(x,y) = \sigma_{xy} = \sum_x \sum_y xyP(x,y) - \mu_x\mu_y = 0.60 - (0.6375)(0.75)$$

$$= 0.121875$$

Here, we have a positive covariance between being guilty and being convicted (see Table 4.13). If you are guilty, you are more likely to be convicted with these hypothetical numbers. We certainly hope that these variables have a positive covariance.

If X and Y are independent, then $\text{cov}(x,y) = \sigma_{xy} = 0$. Please note that the inverse of this statement does not hold. Independence implies zero covariance, but zero covariance does not imply independence. This is because covariance measures the linear relationship between two variables. If there is a nonlinear relationship between the two variables, the covariance could be equal to zero even though the variables are not independent.

Table 4.13. Calculating covariances 2.

x	y	xy	$P(x,y)$	$xyP(x,y)$
0	0	0	0.2125	0
0	1	0	0.15	0
1	0	0	0.0375	0
1	1	1	0.60	0.60
				$\sum_x \sum_y xyP(x,y) = 0.60$

The sign of the covariance tells us if there is a positive or negative linear relationship between the two variables. But the magnitude of the covariance is difficult to interpret because it depends on the units being used to measure the two variables. The covariance will change if you change the units of measure. If you measure your variables in feet rather than inches, or pounds rather than tons, or millions rather than billions, or in yen rather than dollars, the covariance will change. The covariance measures the direction of the linear relationship but not its strength.

We can measure the strength of a linear relationship with the correlation coefficient.

4.7.2 *Correlation coefficient*

The correlation coefficient ρ (rho) is the covariance divided by the product of the variable standard deviations:

$$\rho = \frac{\sigma_{xy}}{\sigma_x \sigma_y} = \frac{\text{cov}(x, y)}{\text{SD}(x) \cdot \text{SD}(y)} \tag{4.18}$$

The correlation coefficient measures the direction *and* strength of the linear relationship between two variables. The correlation coefficient will always be between negative 1 and positive 1, $-1 \leq \rho \leq 1$. If X and Y are perfectly negatively correlated, perhaps $Y = -5X$, then $\rho = -1$. If X and Y are uncorrelated, then $\rho = 0$. And if X and Y are perfectly positively correlated, perhaps $Y = 2.54X$, then $\rho = 1$.

4.7.2.1 *Lakers and Kings*

In our Lakers and Kings example, the correlation coefficient will equal zero since the covariance was equal to zero. It does not matter what the standard deviations are.

4.7.2.2 *Guilty and convicted*

Let us consider the guilty and convicted example. What is the correlation coefficient between these variables? We calculated the covariance above, $\text{cov}_{xy} = 0.121875$. We now need to calculate the standard deviations of the two variables. We do this by calculating the variances first:

$$\begin{aligned} V(X) &= \sigma_x^2 = (0 - 0.6375)^2(0.3625) + (1 - 0.6375)^2(0.6375) \\ &= 0.147322 + 0.08377 = 0.2310934 \\ V(Y) &= \sigma_y^2 = (0 - 0.75)^2(0.25) + (1 - 0.75)^2(0.75) \\ &= 0.140625 + 0.046875 = 0.1875 \\ \rho &= \frac{\sigma_{xy}}{\sigma_x \sigma_y} = \frac{0.121875}{\sqrt{(0.23109)(0.1875)}} = 0.5854909 \end{aligned}$$

Here, we illustrate some possible cases with X, Y diagrams (see Figures 4.5–4.9):

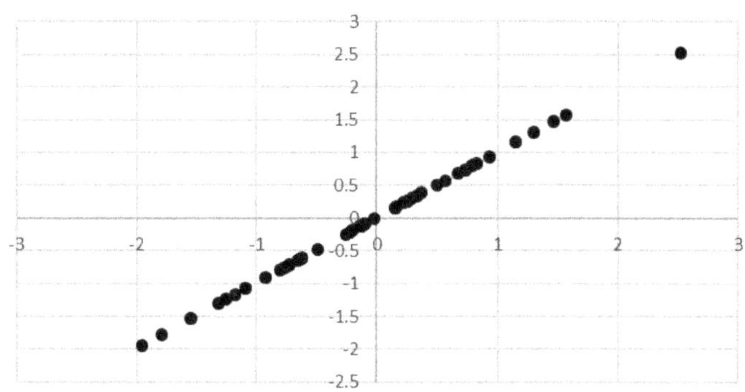

Fig. 4.5. $\rho = 1$.

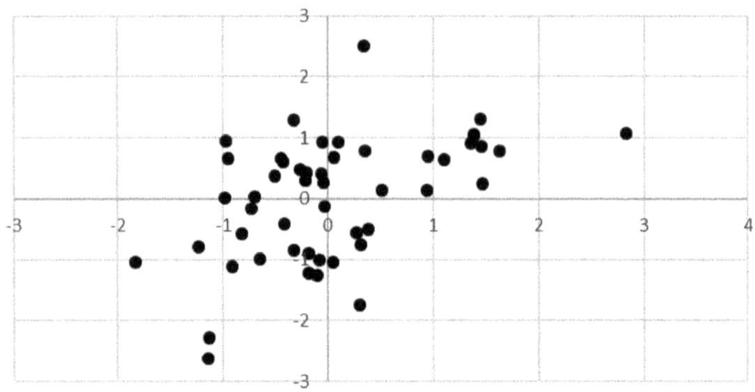

Fig. 4.6. $\rho = 0.5$.

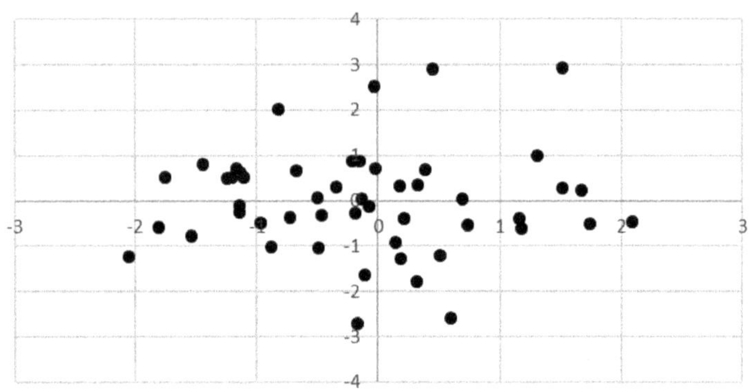

Fig. 4.7. $\rho = 0$.

If X and Y are independent, then $\rho = 0$. But $\rho = 0$ does not imply independence because correlation is merely a linear measure. Consider this example.

Let $Y = X^2$. Since Y is a function of X, they are clearly not independent. Now suppose X can take on three possible values with the following probabilities: $P_x(-1) = \frac{1}{4}, P_x(0) = \frac{1}{2}$ and $P_x(1) = \frac{1}{4}$. Since $Y = X^2$, Y can take on two possible values, 0 and 1. This gives us the following three possible outcome pairs (XY) with these probabilities: $P(-1,1) = \frac{1}{4}$, $P(0,0) = \frac{1}{2}$, and $P(1,1) = \frac{1}{4}$.

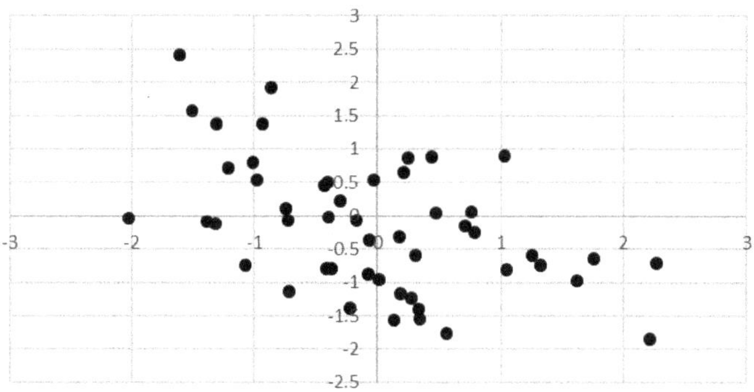

Fig. 4.8. $\rho = -0.5$.

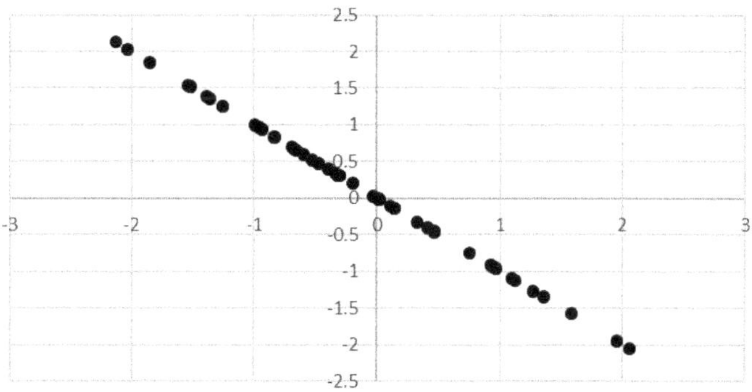

Fig. 4.9. $\rho = -1$.

The correlation coefficient $\sigma_{xy} = E[XY] - E[X]E[Y]$. We have $E[X] = 0$, $E[Y] = \frac{1}{2}$, and $E[XY] = 0$. Therefore, $\sigma_{xy} = 0$ and $\rho = 0$. Here the correlation coefficient is zero, but the two variables are not independent. The correlation coefficient only measures the strength of the linear relationship. But we have a nonlinear relationship between these two variables.

We should observe that correlation is *not* a transitive property. If A is correlated with B and B is correlated with C, A may or may not be correlated with C. Suppose $B = A + C$. We know that A is correlated with B and C is correlated with B, but we know nothing about the relationship between A and C.

Your total income is equal to your wage income and your interest income. When your wage income goes up, your total income will tend to go up. And when your interest income goes up, your total income will tend to go up. But there may be no relationship between your wage income and your interest income.

4.8 Linear Functions

We are often interested in the sum of two random variables. Your total income is the sum of your labor income and your capital income. Or you may be an orange grower with orange groves in California and Florida. Your annual earnings will depend on your earnings in California and your earnings in Florida.

Consider the sum of two random variables. If we know the mean and variance of the two random variables, can we say something about the mean and variance of the sum?

Let $Z = X + Y$

The mean of Z is

$$\mu_z = E[Z] = E[X + Y] = E[X] + E[Y] = \mu_x + \mu_y \tag{4.19}$$

The variance of Z is

$$\begin{aligned}
\sigma_z^2 &= E[(Z - \mu_z)^2] = E[((X + Y) - (\mu_x + \mu_y))^2] \\
&= E[((X - \mu_x) + (Y - \mu_y))^2] \\
&= E[(X - \mu_x)^2 + (Y - \mu_y)^2 + 2(X - \mu_x)(Y - \mu_y)] \\
&= E[(X - \mu_x)^2] + E[(Y - \mu_y)^2] + 2E[(X - \mu_x)(Y - \mu_y)] \\
&= \sigma_x^2 + \sigma_y^2 + 2\sigma_{xy}
\end{aligned} \tag{4.20}$$

4.8.1 *Restaurant example*

Suppose you are a tough restaurant critic. You enjoy 30% of your restaurant meals. You go to the same restaurant on Saturday and Sunday so that you can try a variety of things on the menu. How many good restaurant meals will you have over the weekend? What is the mean and the variance? Here we have a hypothetical joint

Table 4.14. Good Restaurants.

		Saturday: Y		
		Bad Meal: 0	Good Meal: 1	
Sunday: X	Bad Meal: 0	0.60	0.10	0.70
	Good Meal: 1	0.10	0.20	0.30
		0.70	0.30	1.00

probability distribution. Y is the quality of the Saturday meal and X is the quality of the Sunday meal (see Table 4.14).

First, we calculate the mean and the variance of X and Y:

$$E[X] = 0(0.7) + 1(0.3) = 0.30 = \mu_x$$
$$E[Y] = 0(0.7) + 1(0.3) = 0.30 = \mu_y$$
$$V[X] = (0 - 0.3)^2(0.7) + (1 - 0.3)^2(0.3) = 0.21 = \sigma_x^2$$
$$V[Y] = (0 - 0.3)^2(0.7) + (1 - 0.3)^2(0.3) = 0.21 = \sigma_y^2$$

Then we calculate the covariance and the correlation coefficient of X and Y:

$$\text{cov}(x, y) = \sigma_{xy} = \sum_x \sum_y xyP(x, y) - \mu_x\mu_y = 0.20 - (0.3)(0.3)$$
$$= 0.11$$
$$\rho = \frac{\text{cov}(x, y)}{\sqrt{\sigma_x^2\sigma_y^2}} = \frac{0.11}{\sqrt{(0.21)(0.21)}} = 0.523809$$

Now we can figure out the mean and variance of the sum:

$$Z = X + Y$$
$$E[Z] = \mu_z = \mu_x + \mu_y = 0.3 + 0.3 = 0.6$$
$$V[Z] = \sigma_z^2 = \sigma_x^2 + \sigma_y^2 + 2\sigma_{xy} = 0.21 + 0.21 + 2(0.11) = 0.64$$

The restaurant critic can expect to have 0.6 good meals over the weekend with a variance of 0.64. There is a positive correlation between the Saturday meal and the Sunday meal because you are eating at the same restaurant. But the correlation is not 1 because you are eating different items on the menu and the quality of service is different from day to day.

4.8.2 *Shiller example*

Suppose PF is the *ex post* rational stock market price[5] and P is the actual stock market price. We know that $PF = P + E$ where E should be a random error term which is uncorrelated with P and the expected value of P is equal to PF. Robert Shiller notes that since P and E are independent, then $V[PF] = \sigma_{pf}^2 = \sigma_p^2 + \sigma_e^2$ Consequently, it should be the case that $\sigma_{pf}^2 > \sigma_p^2$. The variance of the *ex post* rational stock market price should be larger than the variance of the actual stock market price. But he finds that *ex post* rational stock market prices are less volatile than actual stock market prices.[6] He finds excess volatility in the stock market and now has a Nobel Prize in Economics.

We can extend this idea as follows to any linear combination of X and Y. Let $Z = a + bX + cY$ where a, b, and c are constants. We assume we know the mean, variance, and covariance of X and Y. We want to figure out the mean and variance of Z.

The mean of Z is

$$\begin{aligned}\mu_z &= E[Z] = E[a + bX + cY] = E[a] + E[bX] + E[cY] \\ &= E[a] + bE[X] + cE[Y] = a + b\mu_x + c\mu_y \end{aligned} \tag{4.21}$$

The variance of Z is

$$\begin{aligned}\sigma_z^2 &= E[(Z - \mu_z)^2] = E[((a + bX + cY) - (a + b\mu_x + c\mu_y))^2] \\ &= E[((bX - b\mu_x) + (cY - c\mu_y))^2] \\ &= E[(bX - b\mu_x)^2 + (cY - c\mu_y)^2 + 2(bX - b\mu_x)(cY - c\mu_y)] \\ &= E[b^2(X - \mu_x)^2] + E[c^2(Y - \mu_y)^2] + 2bcE[(X - \mu_x)(Y - \mu_y)] \\ &= b^2\sigma_x^2 + c^2\sigma_y^2 + 2bc\sigma_{xy} \end{aligned} \tag{4.22}$$

[5]This is the appropriate stock price if the future was known with certainty.

[6]Shiller, "Do Stock Prices Move Too Much to be Justified by Subsequent Changes in Dividends?" *American Economic Review*, June 1981, pp. 421–436.

4.8.3 *Sample mean example*

Suppose X has a mean of 5 and a variance of 10. Suppose Y has a mean of 8 and a variance of 20. What are the mean and the variance of Z if Z is the average of X and Y? $Z = \frac{X+Y}{2} = \frac{1}{2}X + \frac{1}{2}Y$. Assume X and Y are independent so that the covariance is equal to zero.

The mean of Z is

$$\mu_z = E[Z] = E\left[\frac{1}{2}X + \frac{1}{2}Y\right] = \frac{1}{2}\mu_x + \frac{1}{2}\mu_y = \frac{1}{2}(5) + \frac{1}{2}(8) = 6.5$$

The mean of Z is the average of the mean of X and the mean of Y.

What is the variance of z?

$$\begin{aligned}\sigma_z^2 = E[(Z-\mu_z)^2] &= \left(\frac{1}{2}\right)^2 \sigma_x^2 + \left(\frac{1}{2}\right)^2 \sigma_y^2 + 2\left(\frac{1}{2}\right)\left(\frac{1}{2}\right)\sigma_{xy} \\ &= \frac{1}{4}(10) + \frac{1}{4}(20) + 0 = 7.5\end{aligned}$$

Note that the variance of the average, Z, is smaller than the variance of either X or Y. Since X and Y are not correlated, they will tend to offset each other. It will be unlikely for both X and Y to be unusually large at the same time, or unusually small at the same time. Thus, the average will not be as volatile as either X or Y.

4.8.4 *Hedge fund example*

In the old days, "hedge funds" were, in fact, hedge funds. They would buy a portfolio of assets as a hedge against the performance of the overall market, pairing both short and long positions. Suppose there are two firms in your portfolio, Umbrella.com (U) and Solar.com (S). Umbrella.com does well when it rains and poorly when it is sunny. And Solar.com does well when it is sunny and poorly when it rains. It is sunny half the time and rainy half the time. Your portfolio (P) consists of 50% Umbrella stock (U) and 50% Solar stock (S). $P = \frac{1}{2}U + \frac{1}{2}S$. Here are the rates of return (see Table 4.15).

Table 4.15. Hedge funds.

Rate of Return	Sunny (%)	Rainy (%)	Mean (%)	Std. Dev. (%)	Variance
Umbrella.Com	0	10	5	5	25
Solar.Com	10	0	5	5	25
Portfolio	5	5	5	0	0

The covariance between Umbrella.com and Solar.com is

$$\begin{aligned}\mathrm{cov}_{\mathrm{u,s}} = \sigma_{u,s} &= \sum\sum(U-\mu_u)(S-\mu_s)P(U,S)\\ &= (0-5)(10-5)\frac{1}{2} + (10-5)(0-5)\frac{1}{2} = -25\end{aligned}$$

So the variance of the portfolio P is

$$\begin{aligned}\sigma_P^2 &= \left(\frac{1}{2}\right)^2 \sigma_u^2 + \left(\frac{1}{2}\right)^2 \sigma_s^2 + 2\left(\frac{1}{2}\right)\left(\frac{1}{2}\right)\mathrm{cov}_{u,s}\\ &= \left(\frac{1}{2}\right)^2 25 + \left(\frac{1}{2}\right)^2 25 + 2\left(\frac{1}{2}\right)\left(\frac{1}{2}\right)(-25) = 0\end{aligned}$$

By buying stock in Solar.com, you are able to hedge your investment in Umbrella.com. There is a negative covariance between the two assets. You earn the same average rate of return, but you have zero risk. The variance on the rate of return on the portfolio is zero.

This is why people like to hold "negative beta" stocks, stocks which do well when the overall market does not. Think about mortuary companies and gold companies.

Finally, consider $Z = a + bX + cY + dW$ where a, b, c, d are all constants. Suppose we know the means, variances, and covariances of X, Y, and W. What is the mean and variance of Z?

The mean of Z is

$$\begin{aligned}\mu_z &= E[Z] = E[a + bX + cY + dW]\\ &= E[a] + E[bX] + E[cY] + E[dW]\\ &= E[a] + bE[X] + cE[Y] + dE[W] = a + b\mu_x + c\mu_y + d\mu_w\end{aligned} \tag{4.23}$$

The variance of Z is

$$\begin{aligned}
\sigma_z^2 &= E[(Z-\mu_z)^2] \\
&= E[((a+bX+cY+dW)-(a+b\mu_x+c\mu_y+d\mu_w))^2] \\
&= E[((bX-b\mu_x)+(cY-c\mu_y)+(dW-d\mu_w))^2] \\
&= E[(bX-b\mu_x)^2+(cY-c\mu_y)^2+(dW-d\mu_w)^2 \\
&\quad +2(bX-b\mu_x)(cY-c\mu_y)+2(bX-b\mu_x)(dW-d\mu_w) \\
&\quad +2(cY-c\mu_y)(dW-d\mu_w)] \\
&= E[b^2(X-\mu_x)^2]+E[c^2(Y-\mu_y)^2]+E[d^2(W-\mu_w)^2] \\
&\quad +2bcE[(X-\mu_x)(Y-\mu_y)]+2bdE[(X-\mu_x)(W-\mu_w)] \\
&\quad +2cdE[(Y-\mu_y)(W-\mu_w)] \\
&= b^2\sigma_x^2+c^2\sigma_y^2+d^2\sigma_w^2+2bc\sigma_{xy}+2bd\sigma_{xw}+2cd\sigma_{yw} \qquad (4.24)
\end{aligned}$$

Here we have the general solution above. In the simple case where $Z = X + Y + W$, we have the following.

The mean of Z is

$$\mu_z = \mu_x + \mu_y + \mu_w \qquad (4.25)$$

The variance of Z is

$$\sigma_z^2 = \sigma_x^2 + \sigma_y^2 + \sigma_w^2 + 2\sigma_{xy} + 2\sigma_{xw} + 2\sigma_{yw} \qquad (4.26)$$

And if we know that X, Y, and W are all independent, then the covariances are equal to zero, and we have

$$\sigma_z^2 = \sigma_x^2 + \sigma_y^2 + \sigma_w^2 \qquad (4.27)$$

In this special case, the variance of the sum is the sum of the variances. This only holds if X, Y, and W are independent.

If you have income from a number of independent businesses, the variance of your total income will be much higher than the variance of the income from any of your individual businesses.

4.9 Cumulative Distribution Functions

This entire chapter has been about probability distribution functions or pdf for short. A different representation of the same probability information appears with cumulative distribution functions or CDF for short. The cumulative distribution function of a real-valued random variable X, evaluated at x, gives us the probability that X will take a value less than or equal to x. Thus, as x moves from $-\infty$ to $+\infty$, the CDF will increase from 0 to 1. The probability that $X \leq \infty$ will be 1 for any random variable. Every probability distribution function has its own unique cumulative distribution function.

Let the probability distribution function, pdf, be represented by $f_x(x)$. We know that $f_x(x) \geq 0$ for all values of x and $P(a < X < b) = \sum_a^b f_x(x)$ or $\int_a^b f_x(x)dx$ for discrete and continuous random variables, respectively. And since $P(-\infty < X < \infty) = 1$, $\sum\limits_x f_x(x) = \int_{-\infty}^{\infty} f_x(x)dx = 1$.

The CDF $F_x(x)$ gives the probability that X does not exceed x as a function of x:

$$F_x(x) = P(X \leq x) = \sum_{X \leq x} f_x(x) \quad \text{or} \quad \int_{-\infty}^{x} f_x(x)dx \tag{4.28}$$

We observe that $F_x(-\infty) = 0$, $F_x(\infty) = 1$, and $P(a < X < b) = F_x(b) - F_x(a)$. For $a < b$.

Here are some examples of discrete cumulative distribution functions and some continuous cumulative distribution functions.

This is the probability distribution function and the cumulative distribution function for the outcome of rolling a fair six-sided die. This is a discrete random variable, so the CDF rises in steps (see Figures 4.10 and 4.11).

Here we have a continuous probability distribution function. We call this a uniform distribution. Imagine spinning the hands of a clock. The hands can land anywhere between 0 and 12. The pdf and the CDF look like this (see Figures 4.12 and 4.13).

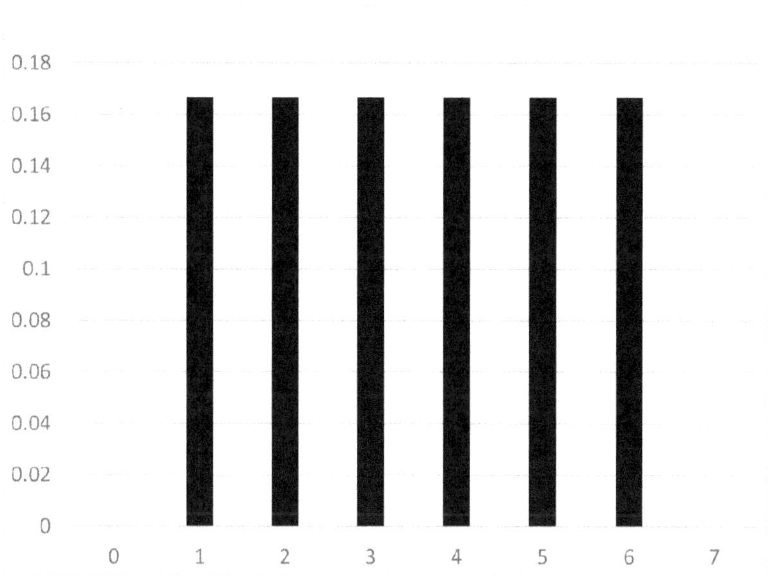

Fig. 4.10. Probability distribution function.

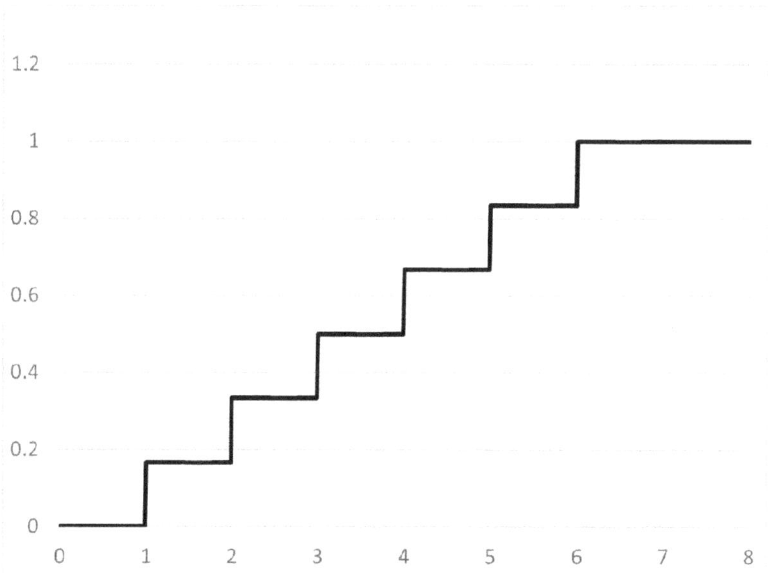

Fig. 4.11. Cumulative probability distribution.

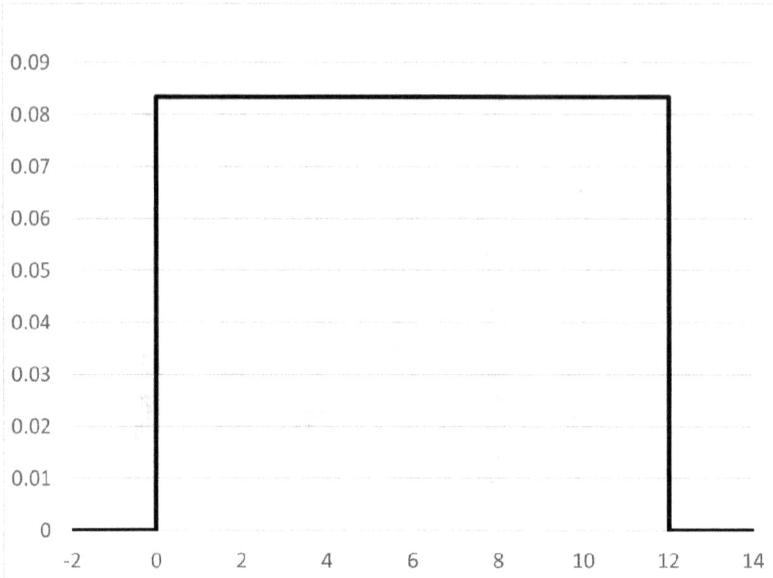

Fig. 4.12. Probability distribution function.

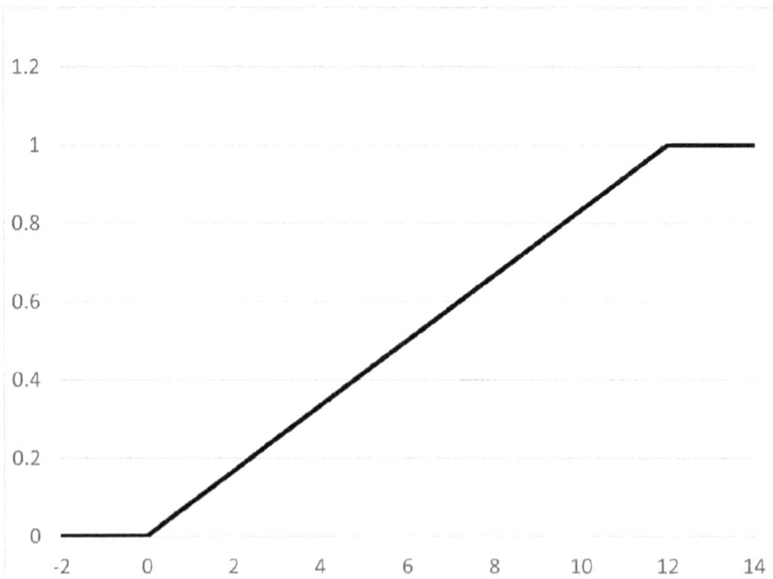

Fig. 4.13. Cumulative distribution function.

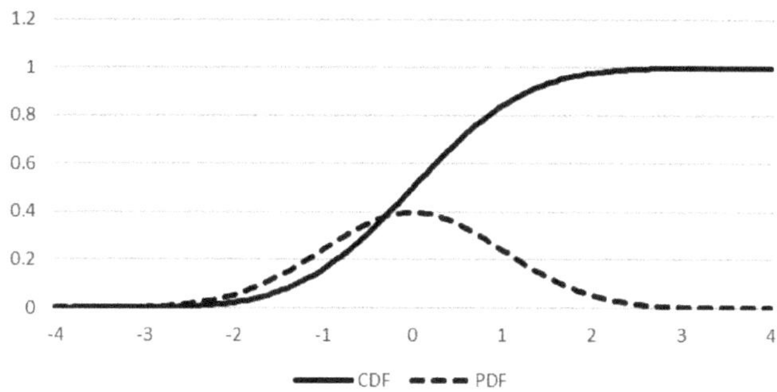

Fig. 4.14. Standard normal pdf and CDF.

Here we have another continuous random variable. The pdf is the dotted line, and the CDF is the solid line. Since the pdf is symmetric around zero, the CDF is equal to 0.5 when X is at zero (see Figure 4.14).

4.10 Summation Sign Notes

(1) The summation sign is defined as

$$\sum_{i=1}^{n} a_i = a_1 + a_2 + a_3 + \cdots + a_{n-1} + a_n$$

where i is the summation index and n is the boundary for the summation. For example, $\sum_{i=1}^{n} i = 1 + 2 + 3 + \cdots + (n-1) + n$.

(2) The summation of two variables with identical summation indices is the same as the sum of the two variables:

$$\begin{aligned}\sum_{i=1}^{n}(a_i + b_i) &= (a_1 + b_1) + (a_2 + b_2) + (a_3 + b_3) + \cdots + (a_n + b_n) \\ &= (a_1 + a_2 + \cdots + a_n) + (b_1 + b_2 + \cdots + b_n) \\ &= \sum_{i=1}^{n} a_i + \sum_{i=1}^{n} b_i\end{aligned}$$

(3) A multiplicative constant can be moved in front of the summation sign:

$$\sum_{i=1}^{n} ca_i = ca_1 + ca_2 + ca_3 + \cdots + ca_n$$
$$= c(a_1 + a_2 + a_3 + \cdots + a_n) = c\sum_{i=1}^{n} a_i$$

(4) An additive constant can be moved outside the summation sign:

$$\sum_{i=1}^{n}(a_i + c) = (a_1 + c) + (a_2 + c) + (a_3 + c) + \cdots + (a_n + c)$$
$$= (a_1 + a_2 + a_3 + \cdots + a_n) + nc = \sum_{i=1}^{n} a_i + nc$$

(5) The boundaries of the summation are often omitted when these are obvious:

$$\sum_{i=1}^{n} a_i = \sum_{i} a_i = \sum_{i}^{n} a_i = \sum a_i$$

(6) You can also have double summation signs as follows:

$$\sum_{i=1}^{n}\sum_{j=1}^{m} a_i b_j = a_1b_1 + a_1b_2 + a_1b_3 + \cdots + a_1b_m + a_2b_1 + a_2b_2$$
$$+ a_2b_3 + \cdots + a_2b_m + a_3b_1 + \cdots + a_3b_m$$
$$+ \cdots + a_nb_1 + a_nb_2 + a_nb_3 + \cdots a_nb_m$$

4.11 Exercises

(1) Suppose the heights of Americans, measured in inches, have a mean of 68 inches and a variance of 9. What would be the mean and variance of American heights if we measured them in centimeters? Remember that an inch is equal to 2.54 cm. (172.72, 58.064)

(2) The following table shows the joint distribution of two random variables X and Y.

		Y	
		0	5
X	0	.20	.10
	1	.10	.60

(a) What are the mean of X and mean of Y?
(b) What are the variance of X and variance of Y?
(c) What is the covariance of X and Y?
(d) What is the correlation coefficient?
$(0.7, 3.5, 0.21, 5.25, 0.55, 0.5238)$

(3) Suppose that in the land of Sigma income Y has a mean of 200 and a standard deviation of 50 and that taxes T has a mean of 100 and a standard deviation of 20. If the covariance of Y and T is 500, what is the standard deviation and variance of disposable income $Yd = Y - T$? (43.59, 1,900)

(4) Consider the following gambling game. You drop your pencil point into the middle of a table of random numbers and look at the digit on which it lands.

If it is a 7, you win \$5.
If it is a 1, you win \$2.
Otherwise, you win nothing.

Find the expected value of the amount you win in one play of this game. Is it your advantage to pay \$1 to play? (0.70, no)

(5) The correlation coefficient between two random variables X and Y is $\rho = 0.70$. It is given that $X = 1, 2$ or 3 with equal probability and $Y = -1, -2$ or -3 with equal probability. Calculate the covariance of X and Y. (0.466)

(6) Grove stock has a mean rate of return of 5% and a variance of 64. Motley stock has a mean rate of return of 15% and a variance of 200. The correlation coefficient of the returns on Grove stock and Motley stock is 0.40. Suppose we hold a portfolio which is 40% Grove stock and 60% Motley stock. What is the expected rate of return on the portfolio? What is the variance on the rate of return on the portfolio? (11%, 103.96)

(7) The weight of medium-sized tomatoes selected at random from a bin at the local supermarket is a random variable with a mean $\mu = 10$ ounces and a standard deviation $\sigma = 2$ ounces. Suppose we pick four tomatoes at random from the bin and put them in

a bag. The weight of the four tomatoes is a random variable. What are the mean and the standard deviation of the weight of the four tomatoes? (40, 4)

(8) For any two random variables X and Y, what is the relationship between the variance of $(X - Y)$ and the variance of $(Y - X)$? (same)

(9) An investment will be worth \$1,000, \$2,000, or \$5,000 at the end of the year. The probabilities of these values are 0.25, 0.60, and 0.15, respectively. Determine the mean and the variance of the value of this investment. (2,200, 156,0000)

(10) Let $F(x)$ be a cumulative probability distribution function. If $a > b$, can $F(a)$ be less than $F(b)$? Explain. (no)

Chapter 5

Special Probability Distributions

5.1 Introduction

> *Statistics show that Americans are living longer. The average American is now 12 months older than they were a year ago.*

In the previous chapter, we talked about probability distribution functions in general. In this chapter, we will discuss some special probability distribution functions which will be useful to us.

Since we have discrete random variables and continuous random variables, we have discrete probability distributions and continuous probability distributions. If a variable can take on any real value between two possible values, it is called a continuous variable. Otherwise, it is called a discrete variable. The number of heads you get could be any integer value between 0 and plus infinity depending on how many times you toss the coin. But it cannot take on any values between 1 and 2. So the number of heads will be discrete. Let's begin with some discrete probability distribution functions.

5.2 Discrete Probability Distributions

5.2.1 *Bernoulli trial probability distribution*

A Bernoulli trial (or binomial trial) is a random experiment with exactly two possible outcomes, arbitrarily called "success" and "failure," in which the probability of success is the same every time the experiment is conducted. The probability of "success" and "failure" need not be the same. Repeated trials are independent of each other.

The Bernoulli trial is named after Jacob Bernoulli (1655–1705), one of many famous mathematicians in the Bernoulli family.

A single coin flip could land heads or tails. You might roll a die when rolling a 6 is a success and rolling a 1, 2, 3, 4, or 5 is a failure. You might go to a movie and either like the movie or not like it. You might manufacture an airbag which is defective or not defective. Your date might be on time or might be late. Stock prices might rise or they might fall. It might rain and it might not.

Now let's consider the probability distribution of a Bernoulli trial. Let X represent the outcome of the Bernoulli trial. If the trial is a success, let $X = 1$, and if the trial is a failure, let $X = 0$. Furthermore, let $P(\text{success}) = \pi$ and $P(\text{failure}) = 1 - \pi$ where π is some constant such that $0 \leq \pi \leq 1$. Here $\pi \neq 3.141592$. Thus, we have the following discrete probability distribution function:

$$P(0) = 1 - \pi$$
$$P(1) = \pi$$

Here is a graph of this probability distribution with $\pi = 0.67$ (see Figure 5.1).

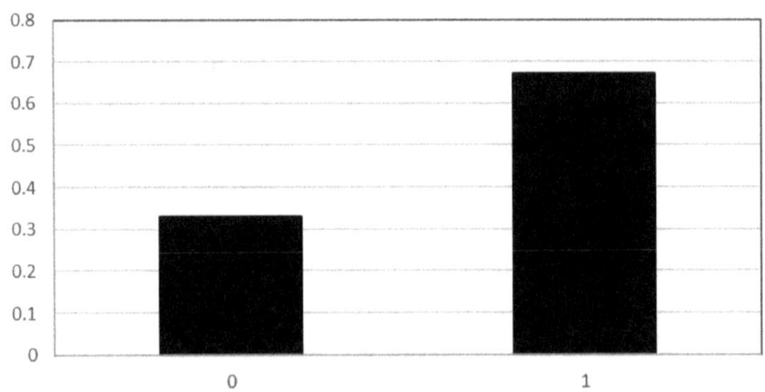

Fig. 5.1. Bernoulli trial probability distribution.

In order the characterize this distribution, we will look at the mean and the variance of the distribution. The mean of the distribution is

$$\mu_x = E[X] = \sum xP(x) = 0 \cdot (1-\pi) + 1 \cdot (\pi) = \pi \tag{5.1}$$

The variance of the probability distribution is

$$\begin{aligned}\sigma_x^2 &= E[(X-\mu_x)^2] = \sum (X-\mu_x)^2 P(x) \\ &= (0-\pi)^2(1-\pi) + (1-\pi)^2\pi \\ &= \pi^2(1-\pi) + (1-\pi)^2\pi \\ &= \pi(1-\pi)[\pi + (1-\pi)] = \pi(1-\pi) \end{aligned} \tag{5.2}$$

Thus, the mean of a Bernoulli trial is π and the variance is $\pi(1-\pi)$.

5.2.2 *Binomial probability distribution*

Suppose we are guessing on a multiple-choice exam. If there are 5 questions, what is the probability of getting 3 correct? Here we repeat a Bernoulli trial five times. Each time there is a probability of success equal to π and a probability of failure equal to $1-\pi$:

$$P(\text{success}) = P(S) = \pi$$
$$P(\text{failure}) = P(F) = 1-\pi$$

The probability of getting the first three questions correct and the last two questions wrong would be

$$P[\text{SSSFF}] = \pi\pi\pi(1-\pi)(1-\pi) = \pi^3(1-\pi)^2$$

The probability of getting the first one correct, the second wrong, the third correct, the fourth wrong, and the last one correct would be

$$P[\text{SFSFS}] = \pi(1-\pi)\pi(1-\pi)\pi = \pi^3(1-\pi)^2$$

We note that each possible sequence of 3 correct and 2 wrong answers has probability $\pi^3(1-\pi)^2$. How many such sequences are there? We know from our work on combinations that this answer is $C_3^5 = C_2^5$.

The number of ways to have 3 successes in 5 trials is the same as the number of ways to have 2 failures in 5 trials:

$$C_3^5 = C_2^5 = \frac{5!}{3!2!} = 10$$

So the probability of 3 successes in 5 trials would be $P[3\,\text{successes}] = 10\pi^3(1-\pi)^2$. If each of the questions is a multiple-choice question with five possible answers, and we know nothing about the subject of the exam, then $\pi = 20\%$. And the probability of 3 successes in 5 trials would be $10(.2)^3(1-.2)^2 = .0512 = 5.12\%$. You should probably study.

The binomial probability distribution is a series of Bernoulli trials. The outcome of each Bernoulli trial is independent of all the other outcomes. In n Bernoulli trials with probability π of success on each trial, the probability of exactly x successes is

$$\begin{aligned} P[x \text{ successes in } n \text{ trials}] &= C_x^n \pi^x (1-\pi)^{n-x} \\ &= \frac{n!}{x!(n-x)!}\pi^x(1-\pi)^{n-x} \qquad (5.3) \end{aligned}$$

This is the binomial probability distribution. Many statistics books have a table in the back listing the probabilities for various binomial probability distributions. The tables will present the probabilities for various combinations of n, x, and π.

5.2.2.1 *Shape of a binomial distribution*

Consider n independent Bernoulli trials, each with a probability of success π. We will denote $X_i = 1$ if the ith trial is a success and $X_i = 0$ if the ith trial is a failure. The total number of successes can be represented as

$$X = X_1 + X_2 + X_3 + \cdots + X_n$$

Recall that for each Bernoulli trial we have a mean or expected value $E[X_i] = \pi$, and we have a variance $V[X_i] = \pi(1-\pi)$. So for a binomial distribution, we have the following mean and variance:

$$\begin{aligned} E[X] &= E[X_1 + X_2 + X_3 + \cdots + X_n] \\ &= E[X_1] + E[X_2] + E[X_3] + \cdots + E[X_n] \\ &= \pi + \pi + \pi + \cdots + \pi = n\pi \end{aligned} \tag{5.4}$$

Since Bernoulli trials are independent from each other, all the covariances between the trials are zero. So we have the following variance:

$$\begin{aligned} V[X] &= V[X_1 + X_2 + X_3 + \cdots + X_n] \\ &= V[X_1] + V[X_2] + V[X_3] + \cdots + V[X_n] \\ &= \pi(1-\pi) + \pi(1-\pi) + \pi(1-\pi) + \cdots + \pi(1-\pi) \\ &= n\pi(1-\pi) \end{aligned} \tag{5.5}$$

We can summarize the mean and variance for a binomial distribution here:

$$\begin{aligned} \mu_x &= E[X] = n\pi \\ \sigma_x^2 &= V[X] = E[(X - \mu_x)^2] = n\pi(1-\pi) \end{aligned}$$

5.2.2.2 *Examples*

(1) Suppose you are guessing on a multiple-choice exam like the SAT. Before March 2016, there were five possible answers, A, B, C, D, and E, for each question so the uninformed guesser had a probability $\pi = 20\%$ of getting any answer correct by guessing. Each question is a Bernoulli trial.

If there are $n = 20$ questions, and X is the total number of successes (correct answers), how many questions can we expect to get correct?

$$E[X] = E[\#\text{ of successes}] = n\pi = 20(0.2) = 4$$

On a series of 20 question exams, we can expect to get 4 correct on average. But on any exam, a random guesser will probably get either more or less than 4 correct. What is the variance and the standard deviation here?

$$\begin{aligned} V[X] &= n\pi(1-\pi) = 20(0.2)(0.8) = 3.2 \\ \text{SD}[X] &= \sigma_x = \sqrt{\sigma_x^2} = \sqrt{3.2} = 1.7888 \end{aligned}$$

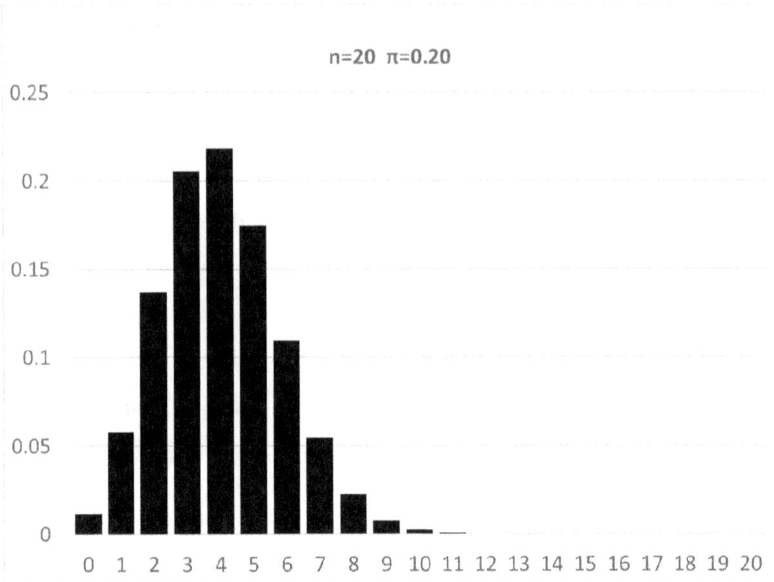

Fig. 5.2. Binomial distribution.

A random guesser will, on average, get 4 correct answers and 16 wrong answers. Suppose we give 1 point for correct answers, and $\frac{-1}{4}$ points for wrong answers. We penalize people for wrong answers. Then, the random guesser should expect to get a score of zero:

$$E[\text{score}] = 1(4) + \frac{-1}{4}(16) = 0$$

It will still make sense to guess if you can rule out some of the answers. But it will not help to guess if you know nothing (see Figure 5.2).

(2) Chances of a Run on a Bank. When you deposit money into your bank account, the bank wants to loan out those funds. The bank makes money by charging more on interest for their loans than they pay you on your deposits. While they would like to loan out as much as possible, they can't loan it all out because you may walk into the bank and ask for your money. So they need to keep enough reserves on hand to meet the withdrawal demands of their depositors. They do not want to be caught short when their depositors want to withdraw their money. How much do they need to keep in the vault?

Table 5.1. Bank withdrawals.

\$ Withdrawn	Probability
0	$C_0^2 0.1^0 0.9^2 = 0.81$
1	$C_1^2 0.1^1 0.9^1 = 0.18$
2	$C_2^2 0.1^2 0.9^0 = 0.01$

Let's assume each depositor deposits \$1, and there is a 10% chance of withdrawing the dollar on any given day. So if there is only \$1 on deposit at the bank, there is a 10% chance that it will be withdrawn today. If there is \$2 on deposit, then \$2, \$1, or \$0 may be withdrawn today. We can calculate the probabilities (see Table 5.1).

The bank can fairly safely loan out \$1 since the probability of \$2 being withdrawn is only 1%. It is unlikely that the bank will be caught short of cash if they loan out \$1.

Now suppose there is \$10 on deposit. Anywhere from \$0 to \$10 might be withdrawn on any given day. We can figure out the probabilities of all these different outcomes with the binomial distribution (see Table 5.2).

Table 5.2. Bank withdrawals 2.

\$ Withdrawn	Probability
0	$C_0^{10} 0.1^0 0.9^{10} = 0.3487$
1	$C_1^{10} 0.1^1 0.9^9 = 0.3874$
2	$C_2^{10} 0.1^2 0.9^8 = 0.1937$
3	$C_3^{10} 0.1^3 0.9^7 = 0.0574$
4	$C_4^{10} 0.1^4 0.9^6 = 0.0112$
5	$C_5^{10} 0.1^5 0.9^5 = 0.0015$
6	0.000137
7	0.000008748
8	0.000000364
9	0.000000009
10	0.0000000001

The probability of all deposits being withdrawn is $1/10^{10}$ = 1/10 billion. If you loan out half of the deposits, there is a 1/10,000 chance of being caught short. The most likely outcome is that \$1 will be withdrawn. And we only have \$10 on deposit here. As the amount of deposits increases, it becomes more and more certain that withdrawals will be extremely close to 10% of the deposits. With \$100 in deposit, there is only a 1/1,000 chance that more than 20% will be withdrawn. With \$1 million on deposit, almost 90% can be lent out safely. Bank of America has about \$1.3 trillion on deposit. So they can loan out quite a bit without getting into trouble.

One of the assumptions of the binomial distribution is that all the events are independent of each other. But if there is a financial crisis, everyone may want to withdraw their money at the same time. Then these events are no longer independent of each other. There could be a run on the bank, and the bank may not be able to meet the needs of its depositors. This can lead to a bank failure, even if you are the Bank of America.

5.2.3 *The Poisson distribution*

The Poisson distribution is a discrete probability distribution named after Siméon Denis Poisson (1781–1840). The Poisson distribution looks at the number of discrete occurrences over some time interval. This distribution might be used to describe the number of customer arrivals per minute at a bar, the number of text messages you receive per hour, the number of murders per day, the number of cyclists who ride by per minute, or the number of hazardous waste sites per county.

The Poisson distribution is a good approximation under the following assumptions:

(1) The expected number of occurrences in any time interval is constant over time.
(2) Each occurrence is independent of other occurrences.
(3) Two occurrences cannot occur at exactly the same moment in time.
(4) The number of occurrences is either 0 or a positive integer.

The Poisson probability distribution is expressed as follows:

$$P(X = x) = \frac{e^{-\lambda}\lambda^{x}}{x!} \tag{5.6}$$

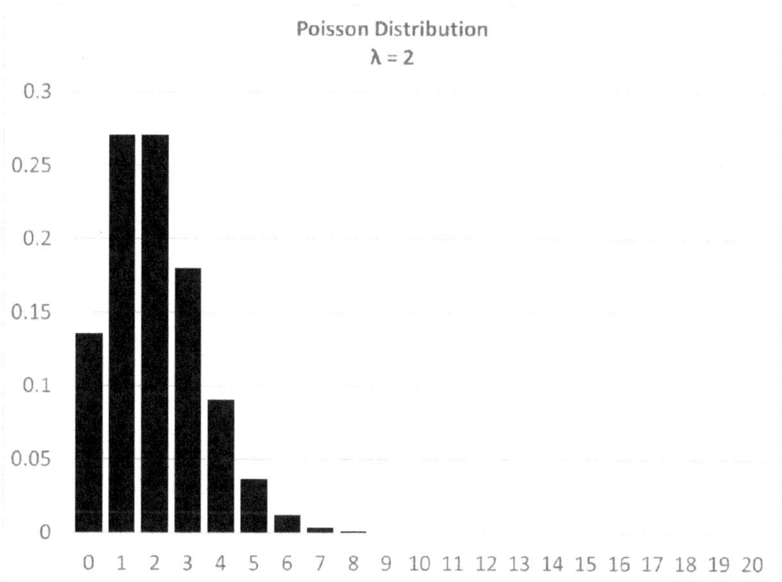

Fig. 5.3. Poisson distribution.

where x is a non-negative integer $(0, 1, 2, 3, \ldots), e = 2.71828$ (base of natural logarithms), and λ is the average number of occurrences in the relevant time period. The probability distribution is skewed to the right (see Figure 5.3).

As an exercise, you might go to the local bar during happy hour. Get a seat near the door, and order a non-alcoholic drink. Record the number of independent arrivals during every two-minute period from, say, 4pm to 6pm. If two people arrive as a couple, this is one arrival because they are not independent. The number of independent arrivals in every two-minute period should be well approximated by the Poisson distribution.

We will want to characterize the Poisson probability distribution. What does it look like? What is the mean and variance of the Poisson distribution?

If X has a Poisson probability distribution with parameter λ, then

$$E[X] = \lambda$$
$$V[X] = \lambda$$

Let's see why. This just requires a little algebra:

$$E[X] = \sum_{x=0}^{\infty} xP(x) = \sum_{x=0}^{\infty} x\frac{e^{-\lambda}\lambda^x}{x!} = \sum_{x=1}^{\infty} x\frac{e^{-\lambda}\lambda^x}{x!} = \sum_{x=1}^{\infty} \frac{e^{-\lambda}\lambda^x}{(x-1)!}$$
$$= \lambda\sum_{x=1}^{\infty} \frac{e^{-\lambda}\lambda^{x-1}}{(x-1)!}$$

Now let $z = x - 1$:

$$\sum_{x=1}^{\infty} \frac{e^{-\lambda}\lambda^{x-1}}{(x-1)!} = \sum_{z=0}^{\infty} \frac{e^{-\lambda}\lambda^{z}}{(z)!} = 1$$

This is the sum of all the probabilities of the Poisson distribution. The sum of the probabilities of any random variable must be equal to one since one of the outcomes must happen. So

$$E[X] = \lambda\sum_{z=0}^{\infty} \frac{e^{-\lambda}\lambda^{z}}{(z)!} = \lambda \cdot 1 = \lambda \tag{5.7}$$

We can also show that

$$V[X] = \lambda$$
$$V[X] = E[(X - \mu_x)^2] = E[(X-\lambda)^2] = E[X^2] - \lambda^2$$
$$E[X^2] = \sum_{x=0}^{\infty} x^2P(x) = \sum_{x=0}^{\infty} x^2\frac{e^{-\lambda}\lambda^x}{x!}$$

Let $x^2 = x(x-1) + x$

$$E[X^2] = \sum_{x=0}^{\infty} \{x(x-1) + x\}\frac{e^{-\lambda}\lambda^x}{x!}$$
$$= \sum_{x=0}^{\infty} x(x-1)\frac{e^{-\lambda}\lambda^x}{x!} + \sum_{x=0}^{\infty} x\frac{e^{-\lambda}\lambda^x}{x!}$$

So

$$E[X^2] = \sum_{x=0}^{\infty} x(x-1)\frac{e^{-\lambda}\lambda^x}{x!} + \lambda$$

The first term is zero for $x = 0$ and $x = 1$. So we can sum from $x = 2$, pull out a λ^2, and let $z = x - 2$:

$$E[X^2] = \lambda^2 \sum_{x=2}^{\infty} \frac{e^{-\lambda}\lambda^{x-2}}{(x-2)!} + \lambda = \lambda^2 \sum_{z=0}^{\infty} \frac{e^{-\lambda}\lambda^{z}}{z!} + \lambda = \lambda^2 + \lambda$$

So we have

$$V[X] = E[X^2] - \mu_x^2 = \lambda^2 + \lambda - \lambda^2 = \lambda \tag{5.8}$$

5.2.3.1 *Examples*

(1) Consider the number of arrivals at the Montclair Mall on a Saturday. Suppose there are 180 arrivals per hour "on average," so we have $180/60 = 3$ arrivals per minute. What is the probability that there will be 5 arrivals in the next minute?

Here $\lambda = 3$ so we have

$$P(X = 5) = \frac{e^{-3}3^5}{5!} = \frac{(0.049)(243)}{120} = 0.1008$$

(2) Suppose there are power outages in California as a result of faulty equipment and that these power outages occur randomly and independently. Let the average number of outages per 8-hour period be 4. Assume the distribution of power outages is stable.

What is the probability of zero outages in the next 8 hours?

$$P[\text{zero outages}] = \frac{e^{-\lambda}\lambda^x}{x!} = \frac{e^{-4}4^0}{0!} = 0.0183156$$

What is the probability of at most 2 outages in the first hour of the day? We have 4 outages per 8 hours or 1/2 outage per hour. We want to figure out

$$\begin{aligned} P[\text{at most } 2] &= P[0] + P[1] + P[2] \\ &= \frac{e^{-\frac{1}{2}}\frac{1}{2}^0}{0!} + \frac{e^{-\frac{1}{2}}\frac{1}{2}^1}{1!} + \frac{e^{-\frac{1}{2}}\frac{1}{2}^2}{2!} \\ &= 0.60653 + 0.30326 + 0.0758 \\ &= 0.9856 \end{aligned}$$

(3) Suppose you receive an average of 2.2 email messages per hour. What is the probability of receiving no email messages in a 30-minute

period? On average you get 1.1 email messages per 30 minutes, so $\lambda = 1.1$ here. Consequently,

$$P[0] = \frac{e^{-1.1}1.1^0}{0!} = 0.33287$$

What is the probability of getting 2 or more email messages in an hour?

$$\begin{aligned} P[2 \text{ or more}] &= 1 - P[0] - P[1] \\ &= 1 - \frac{e^{-2.2}2.2^0}{0!} - \frac{e^{-2.2}2.2^1}{1!} = 1 - 0.110803 - 0.243766 \\ &= 0.645431 \end{aligned}$$

5.3 Continuous Probability Distributions

Discrete random variables will have discrete probability distributions. Continuous random variables will have continuous probability distributions.

In music, a chromatic circle is a clock diagram which displays the relationship between 12 pitch classes (see Figure 5.4). Consider all the frequencies between middle C (261.63 Hz) and treble C (523.25 Hz). When you spin the arrow on the chromatic circle, the arrow can land on any of an infinite number of frequencies. Imagine an amateur

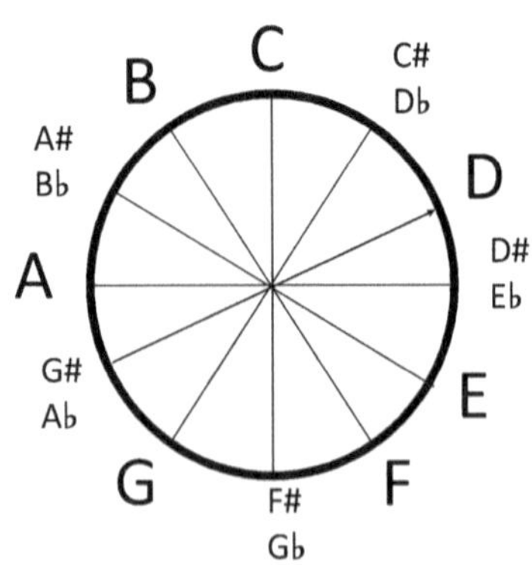

Fig. 5.4. Chromatic circle.

violinist. The point where the arrow lands is a continuous random variable. For our purposes here, let us think of the interval from C to C# or E to F as one note. Since there are 12 notes around the circle, the probability of landing in any one-note interval will be 1/12. If we were to divide each of these one-note intervals into 10 equal parts, the probability of landing in any 1/10 note interval would be 1/120 since there are now 120 such intervals around the circle. If we make these intervals smaller and smaller, the probability of landing in any interval becomes smaller and smaller. The probability of landing on any particular point or frequency is 0 because there are an infinite number of points around the chromatic circle:

$$P[\text{landing in any one note interval}] = 1/12$$

$$P[\text{landing in any } 1/10 \text{ note interval}] = 1/120$$

$$P[\text{landing in any } 1/100{,}000 \text{ note interval}] = 1/1{,}200{,}000$$

$$P[\text{landing on any particular frequency}] = 1/\infty = 0$$

Here we have a continuous random variable X. Variables like time, distance, temperature, height, weight, and age are all continuous random variables. All the possible outcomes are not countable, and each possible outcome has zero probability. An interval of possible outcomes has a non-zero probability. These continuous random variables are represented by a continuous probability density function.

With the chromatic circle, the probability of landing between E and F is calculated by looking at the area under the probability density function between E and F (see Figure 5.5). This is what we call a uniform probability distribution:

$$P[E \leq X \leq F] = (\text{base})(\text{height}) = (1)\left(\frac{1}{12}\right) = \frac{1}{12}$$

$$P[\text{middle } C \leq X \leq \text{treble } C] = (12)\left(\frac{1}{12}\right) = 1$$

5.3.1 *Uniform probability distribution*

We call the above probability distribution function a uniform probability distribution function.

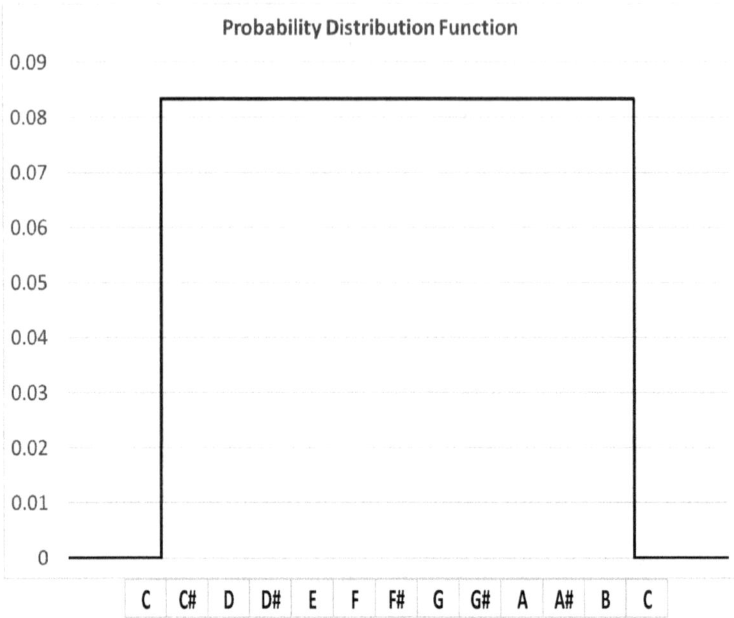

Fig. 5.5. Chromatic probability distribution.

(a) The probability that the outcome is any particular value is zero.
(b) The probability that the outcome is in any particular interval is the area under the probability distribution function between that interval:

$$P(x_1 < X < x_2) = base \cdot height$$
$$= (x_2 - x_1)\left(\frac{1}{b-a}\right) = \int_{x_1}^{x_2} \frac{1}{b-a} dx \quad (5.9)$$

(c) The total area under the probability distribution function is 1:

$$(b-a)\left(\frac{1}{b-a}\right) = 1$$

The uniform probability distribution function will look like this (Figure 5.6).

If we have a uniform probability distribution function between real numbers a and b, we have the following mean and variance.

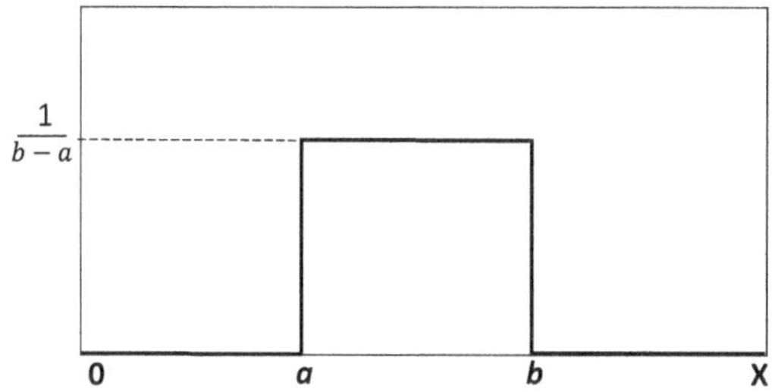

Fig. 5.6. Uniform probability distribution.

The expected value is

$$E[X] = \frac{a+b}{2} \tag{5.10}$$

The variance is

$$V[X] = \frac{(b-a)^2}{12} \tag{5.11}$$

With continuous probability distributions, we generally need some calculus to figure out expected values like the mean and the variance. If you are comfortable with calculus, the way to think about these is as follows:

$$E[X] = \int_a^b x\left(\frac{1}{b-a}\right)dx = \frac{a+b}{2} \tag{5.12}$$

$$V[X] = \int_a^b \left(x - \left(\frac{a+b}{2}\right)\right)^2 \left(\frac{1}{b-a}\right)dx = \frac{(b-a)^2}{12} \tag{5.13}$$

Suppose that you receive a podcast each day at a time that varies uniformly between 7am and 8am:

$$P[\text{delivery occurs between } 7:15 \text{ and } 7:30] = 1/4$$

5.3.2 *From binomial to the normal*

Now let's go back to our binomial probability distribution and consider the limit of a binomial probability distribution as $n \to \infty$. We are looking at the distribution of the number of successes when we do a Bernoulli trial over and over and over forever. This can be

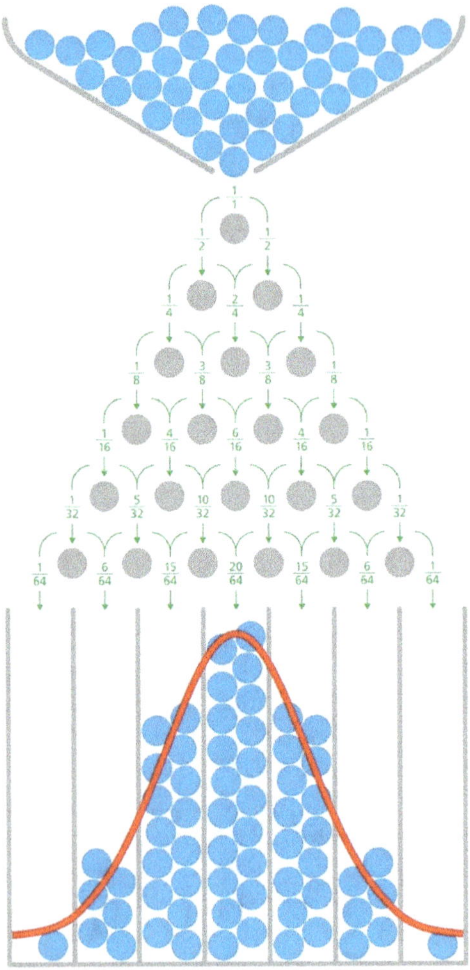

Fig. 5.7. Galton board.

illustrated on a Galton board, something designed by Francis Galton (1822–1911) (see Figure 5.7). The Boston Museum of Science has a Galton board the size of a room. The balls drop from the top of the board. They will hit a peg on the top row and must go right or left. This is the first Bernoulli trial. Then, the ball will hit a peg on the second row and again must go right or left. This is the second Bernoulli trial. There are rows and rows of pegs, and each row is another Bernoulli trial. Imagine having an infinite number of rows of pegs. We could define "success" as moving right and "failure" as moving left. A few balls will have a lot of successes and move far to the right. A few will move far to the left. But most balls will have some successes and some failures and pretty much end up in the middle. As the number of rows of pegs goes to infinity, the horizontal dispersion of the balls will approach the famous normal distribution.

DeMoivre (1733) showed that the binomial distribution with $\pi = 0.50$ approaches a normal distribution as the number of trials goes to infinity. Pierre-Simon Laplace (1749–1827) showed this was true for all binomial distributions with $0 < \pi < 1$.

You might think about the air molecules in the room. This is a three-dimensional version of a Galton board. Each molecule will be involved in about 60 million collisions in the next minute. Some will move a bit to the right. Some will move a bit to the left, or up, or down, or away. But most will pretty much end up about where they are now. Of course, there is some chance that all the air molecules will end up moving to a corner of the room. But luckily for us, this will happen very infrequently:

$$
\begin{aligned}
&P[\text{all air molecules suddenly move to a corner of the room}] \\
&\quad = 1/10^{3x10^{26}}\text{years}
\end{aligned}
$$

The physical movement of a particular air molecule over time is more generally described as Brownian motion. It is named after English botanist Robert Brown (1773–1858) who discovered it in 1827. The mathematical abstraction of the physical process is called a Weiner process, named after Norbert Weiner (1894–1964) of M.I.T.

5.3.3 *The normal distribution*

The normal probability distribution is the most popular probability distribution for reasons we will discuss later. It is bell-shaped and symmetrical. The probability distribution function is defined as

$$
\text{pdf}(x) = \frac{1}{\sqrt{2\pi\sigma^2}} e^{\frac{-(x-\mu)^2}{2\sigma^2}} \tag{5.14}
$$

where x is any real finite number $(-\infty < x < \infty)$, μ is any real finite number $(-\infty < \mu < \infty)$, σ^2 is a positive finite number $(0 < \sigma^2 < \infty), e = 2.71828$, and $\pi = 3.14159$. Note that here π represents the ratio of the circumference to the diameter of a circle. Do not worry. You will probably never need to use the normal equation above. But it is a special equation because it involves both e and π. It is almost as special as $e^{i\pi} = -1$.

Here x is a random variable with a normal probability distribution. There are a whole family of normal distributions depending on the values of μ and σ^2. The normal distribution is often called the Gaussian distribution after Carl Frederick Gauss (1777–1855) or sometimes the Laplace–Gauss distribution after Pierre-Simon Laplace. Karl Pearson started using the term "normal curve" in 1894.

As you might guess, the mean and variance of the normal distribution are defined by the parameters μ and σ^2:

$$\text{mean} = E[X] = \mu$$
$$\text{variance} = V[X] = E[(X - \mu)^2] = \sigma^2$$

Since the normal distribution is completely defined by these two parameters, we typically write $X \sim N(\mu, \sigma^2)$ meaning that the random variable X has a normal distribution (N) with mean μ and variance σ^2. If $X \sim N(24, 81)$, we have a random variable X which is normally distributed with a mean of 24, a variance of 81, and a standard deviation of 9. If the variance is σ^2, the standard deviation $\sigma = \sqrt{\sigma^2}$ (see Figures 5.8 and 5.9).

If X has a normal distribution, X will be within 2 standard deviations of the mean about 95% of the time. It is unlikely for X to be more than 3 standard deviations from the mean. An event is called a 3 sigma event (3σ) if we can expect it to happen only once in 370 trials (see Table 5.3).

If Z is a normal random variable with a mean of 0 and a variance of 1, then we write $Z \sim N(0, 1)$ and we say Z has a standard normal distribution.

To figure out probabilities for continuous random variables, we need to figure out the area under these probability density curves.

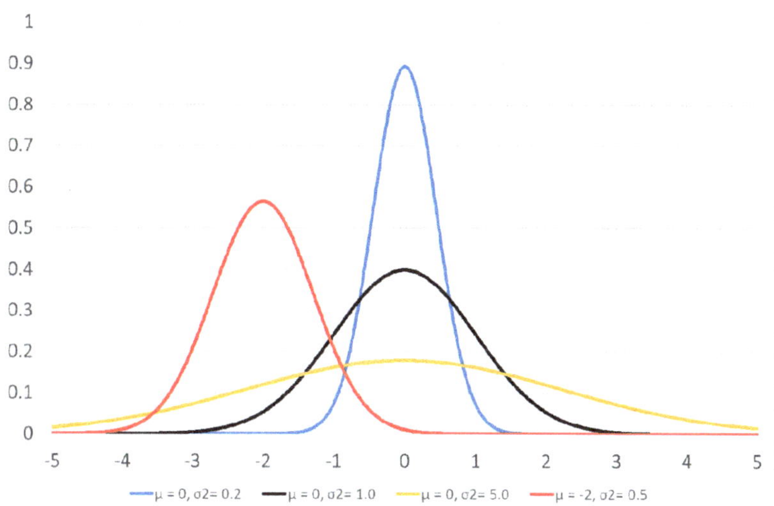

Fig. 5.8. Normal probability density function.

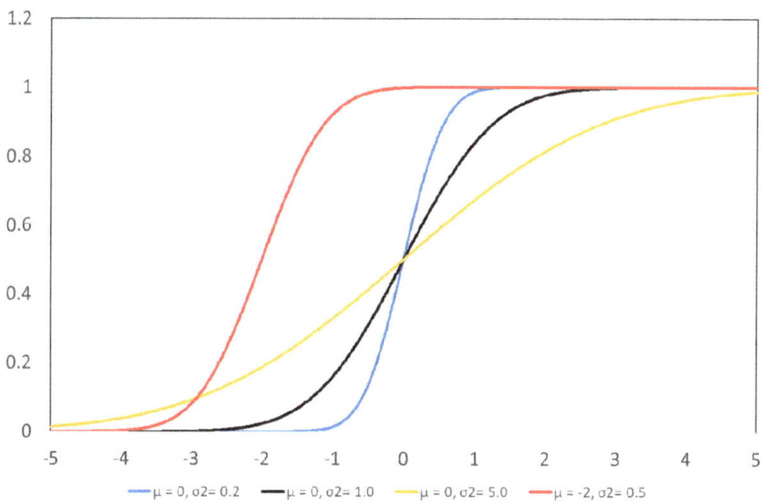

Fig. 5.9. Normal cumulative distribution function.

Table 5.3. Deviations relative to mean.

Range	Probability of Being in Range (%)	P(Outside of Range)1 in n
$+/-1\sigma$	68.80	3
$+/-2\sigma$	95.50	22
$+/-3\sigma$	99.70	370
$+/-4\sigma$	99.99	15,787
$+/-5\sigma$	100.00	1,744,278
$+/-6\sigma$	100.00	506,797,346

This technically involves some calculus and looks like this. The probability that a normal random variable X will fall between a and b is given by

$$P(a < X < b) = \int_a^b \frac{1}{\sqrt{2\pi\sigma^2}} e^{\frac{-(x-\mu)^2}{2\sigma^2}} dx \tag{5.15}$$

This integral is beyond the level of this textbook. And even if you have had calculus, you are probably not interested in calculating this integral every time you need to figure out some probability. Consequently, most people use the statistical tables in any statistics books or go online to figure out these probabilities.

Every statistics textbook has statistical tables at the back of the book. The tables may be arranged in slightly different ways. Let's look at the statistical tables in the Appendix. The table for the standard normal distribution, where $Z \sim N(0, 1)$, is Table A.1. These tables provide the probability that Z is less than some number z, $P(-\infty < Z < z)$. The table provides these probabilities for values of z from -3.09 to 3.09 in increments of 0.01. Values of z less than -3.09 or greater than 3.09 are not presented because the probability of Z being less than -3.09 or greater than 3.09 is essentially zero. To find the probability that Z is less than some number z, you look up z on the table. You need to find the first two digits of the number z along the left-hand column and the third digit of the number z along the top row. Since we only have these numbers in increments of 0.01, you can pick the number closest to the number of interest or you can interpolate the probabilities.

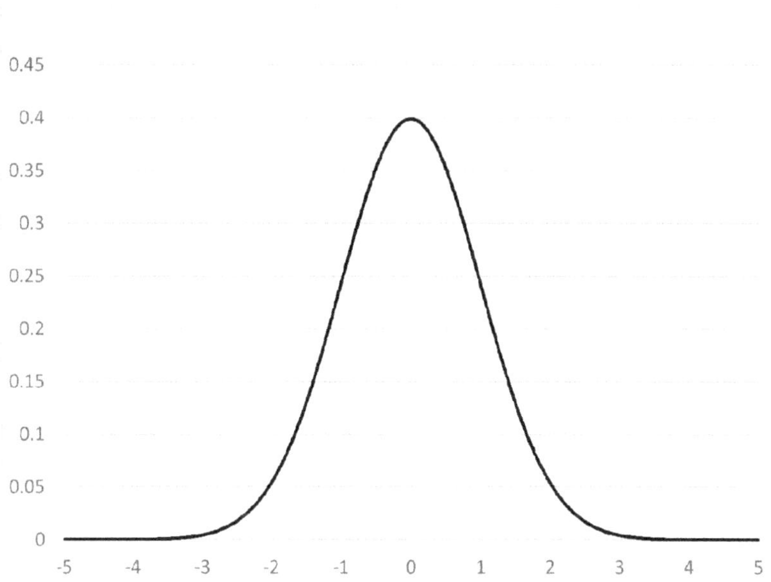

Fig. 5.10. Standard normal distribution.

Suppose $Z \sim N(0,1)$, and we want to find the probability $P(-\infty < Z < 0.75)$. First, we would look for the first two digits, 0.7, along the left-hand column. Then, we move along this row to the right until we are under the column headed by the third digit, 0.05. The table tells us that $P(-\infty < Z < 0.75) = 0.7734$.

There are some additional rules that will help you use statistical tables effectively. Here $Z \sim N(0,1)$ and c is a constant (see Figure 5.10).

1. The area under the normal distribution is equal to one:

$$P(-\infty < Z < \infty) = 1$$

   So $P(Z < c) = 1 - P(Z > c)$.

$$P(Z < 1.2) = 1 - P(Z > 1.2)$$

   And $P(Z > c) = 1 - P(Z < c)$.
   So $P(Z > 1.5) = 1 - P(Z < 1.5)$.
2. If Z has a continuous probability distribution, then $P(Z < c) = P(Z \leq c)$ because $P(Z = c) = 0$. Similarly, $P(Z > c) = P(Z \geq c)$.

3. The standard normal distribution is symmetric around zero:

$$P(Z > 0) = 0.50$$
$$P(Z < 0) = 0.50$$

4. Some standard normal tables report the probabilities for only positive values of c because for any $c > 0$,

$$P(0 < Z < \mathrm{c}) = P(-\mathrm{c} < Z < 0)$$

For example,

$$P(0 < Z < 1.2) = P(-1.2 < Z < 0)$$

This is because the standard normal distribution is symmetric around zero.

5. For any $c > 0$,

$$P(Z > \mathrm{c}) = 1 - P(Z < \mathrm{c}) = 1 - [P(Z < 0) + P(0 < Z < \mathrm{c})]$$

So $P(Z > 1.5) = 1 - [P(Z < 0) + P(0 < Z < 1.5)] = 1 - 0.5 - 0.4332 = 0.0668$.

6. The normal distribution is symmetric around 0. Since we know what the right half of the distribution looks like, we know what the left half of the distribution looks like:

$$\begin{aligned} P(-0.25 < Z < 0.50) &= P(-0.25 < Z < 0) + P(0 < Z < 0.50) \\ &= P(0 < Z < 0.25) + P(0 < Z < 0.50) \\ &= 0.0987 + 0.1915 = 0.2902 \end{aligned}$$

Now let's use a standard normal table to calculate some more probabilities. Make sure you understand how to calculate these kinds of probabilities.

Suppose you want to know the $P(-\infty < Z < 0.755)$. The table tells us that $P(-\infty < Z < 0.750) = 0.7734$. It also tells us that $P(-\infty < Z < 0.760) = 0.7764$. So if you want to estimate the probability $P(-\infty < Z < 0.755)$, we know the actual probability is between 0.7734 and 0.7764. We can estimate this probability by splitting the difference and going with $\frac{0.7734+0.7764}{2} = 0.7749$ as an approximation.

Given our understanding of the nature of the normal distribution, when the table tells us that $P(-\infty < Z < 0.75) = 0.7734$, it is actually telling us a lot more. For example, we also know that $P(Z > 0.75) = 1 - 0.7734 = 0.2266$ because all probabilities must add up to 1. We can also say that $P(Z < -0.75) = 0.2266$ because the normal distribution is symmetric around zero. And since $P(Z < 0) = 0.5$, we can also infer that $P(0 < Z < 0.75) = 0.7734 - 0.5 = 0.2734$. Similarly, $P(-0.75 < Z < 0) = 0.2734$ because the normal distribution is symmetric around zero. And finally, $P(-0.75 < Z < 0.75) = 0.2734 + 0.2734 = 0.5468$. It is often helpful to draw graphs to illustrate these probabilities. And always remember, if you ever get a probability greater than one or less than zero, you did something wrong.

Useful probabilities that we will use frequently include the following:

1. $P(-\infty < Z < 1.96) = 0.9750$. So we can infer that $P(-1.96 < Z < 1.96) = 0.95$ or 95%. You often hear that you will be within two standard deviations of the mean 95% of the time. We say this because 1.96 is pretty close to 2. For a standard normal distribution, $Z \sim N(0, 1)$, the variance and the standard deviation are equal to 1. Since $P(-\infty < Z < 2.00) = 0.9772$, we are actually within 2 standard deviations of the mean 95.44% of the time.
2. $P(-\infty < Z < 1.645) \approx 0.95$. We are interpolating between the probability values for 1.64 and 1.65. We can infer that $P(-1.645 < Z < 1.645) \approx 0.90$ or 90%.
3. $P(-\infty < Z < 1.28) = 0.8997 \approx 0.90$. So we know that $P(-1.28 < Z < 1.28) = 0.7994 \approx 0.80$ or 80%.
4. $P(-\infty < Z < 2.575) \approx 0.995$. We are interpolating between the probability values for 2.57 and 2.58. So we know that $P(-2.575 < Z < 2.575) \approx 0.99$ or 99%.

You should also be able to find z given a probability statement. For example, suppose you know that $Z \sim N(0, 1)$ and that $P(-\infty < Z < z) = 67\%$. Can you find z? On the normal table, you look for 0.6700 among the probabilities. Since the probabilities always increase with z, it is fairly easy to find 0.6700. You will find that it is associated with $z = 0.44$. So $P(-\infty < Z < 0.44) = 67\%$.

For an online table, you might try Stat Trek at https://stattrek.com/online-calculator/normal.aspx.

5.3.3.1 *Standardized normal random variable*

What if X is a normal random variable but not a standard normal? Suppose $X \sim N(24, 81)$. We have tables in the book for the standard normal, but we do not have tables for any other normal distribution. What do we do now? Here we have $X \sim N(\mu, \sigma^2)$ but not necessarily $X \sim N(0, 1)$.

Let's consider the transformed or standardized random variable:

$$Z = \frac{X - \mu}{\sigma}$$

Look at the mean and the variance of Z:

$$E[Z] = E\left[\frac{X - \mu}{\sigma}\right] = \frac{1}{\sigma}E[X - \mu] = \frac{1}{\sigma}[E[X] - \mu] = \frac{1}{\sigma}[\mu - \mu] = 0$$

$$V[Z] = V\left[\frac{X - \mu}{\sigma}\right] = \frac{1}{\sigma^2}V[X - \mu] = \frac{1}{\sigma^2}V[X] = \frac{\sigma^2}{\sigma^2} = 1$$

So the mean of Z is 0, and the variance of Z is 1. You will not be surprised to learn that

$$Z = \tfrac{X-\mu}{\sigma} \sim N(0, 1) \tag{5.16}$$

If X is a random variable with a normal distribution, a linear combination of X will also have a normal distribution. The proof involves using the moment generating function of the linear transformation of X. So we are asserting this without a proof here.

Now if $X \leq c$, where c is a constant, we know that

$$X - \mu \leq c - \mu$$

and

$$\frac{X - \mu}{\sigma} \leq \frac{c - \mu}{\sigma}$$

since $\sigma > 0$.

Consequently, $P(X \le c) = P(X-\mu \le c-\mu) = P\left(\frac{X-\mu}{\sigma} \le \frac{c-\mu}{\sigma}\right) = P\left(Z \le \frac{c-\mu}{\sigma}\right)$ where $Z = \frac{X-\mu}{\sigma} \sim N(0,1)$. We can figure out $P\left(Z \le \frac{c-\mu}{\sigma}\right)$ using the standard normal tables. Thus, we can figure out $P(X \le c)$ because they are equal.

Furthermore,

$$\begin{aligned} P(a \le X \le b) &= P(a-\mu \le X-\mu \le b-\mu) \\ &= P\left(\frac{a-\mu}{\sigma} \le \frac{X-\mu}{\sigma} \le \frac{b-\mu}{\sigma}\right) \\ &= P\left(\frac{a-\mu}{\sigma} \le Z \le \frac{b-\mu}{\sigma}\right) \end{aligned} \tag{5.17}$$

since $\sigma > 0$. Here $Z = \frac{X-\mu}{\sigma} \sim N(0,1)$, so we can calculate various probabilities by using the $N(0,1)$ tables from a textbook or online.

5.3.3.2 *Examples*

(1) Suppose that baby weights are normally distributed with $\mu = 7.25$ lbs and $\sigma = 1$ lb.

a. What is the probability that a randomly selected baby will weigh more than 8 lbs?

$$\begin{aligned} P(X > 8) = P(X-\mu > 8-\mu) &= P\left(\frac{X-\mu}{\sigma} > \frac{8-\mu}{\sigma}\right) \\ &= P\left(Z > \frac{8-7.25}{1}\right) = P(Z > 0.75) \\ &= 1 - 0.5 - 0.2734 = 0.2266 \end{aligned}$$

b. What is the probability that a randomly selected baby will weigh between 6.5 lbs and 8.5 lbs?

$$P(6.5 < X < 8.5) = ?$$

$$\begin{aligned} P(6.5 < X < 8.5) &= P(6.5-\mu < X-\mu < 8.5-\mu) \\ &= P\left(\frac{6.5-\mu}{\sigma} < \frac{X-\mu}{\sigma} < \frac{8.5-\mu}{\sigma}\right) \end{aligned}$$

$$= P\left(\frac{6.5 - 7.25}{1} < \frac{X - \mu}{\sigma} < \frac{8.5 - 7.25}{1}\right)$$
$$= P(-.75 < Z < 1.25) = 0.894 - .227 = 0.667$$

(2) SAT scores were originally designed to have a mean of 500 and a standard deviation of 100. What percent of students will get a score above 700 assuming a normal distribution?

$$P(X > 700) = P(X - \mu > 700 - \mu) = P\left(\frac{X - \mu}{\sigma} > \frac{700 - \mu}{\sigma}\right)$$
$$= P\left(Z > \frac{700 - 500}{100}\right) = P(Z > 2) = 0.023 = 2.3\%$$

What percent of students will get a score below 450?

$$P(X < 450) = P(X - \mu < 450 - \mu) = P\left(\frac{X - \mu}{\sigma} < \frac{450 - \mu}{\sigma}\right)$$
$$= P\left(Z < \frac{450 - 500}{100}\right) = P(Z < -0.5) = 0.309 = 30.9\%$$

(3) Suppose we want to give As to the top 30% of students on an exam. If the exam scores are normally distributed with a mean of 137 and a standard deviation of 35, what is the cutoff grade for an A? We want a cutoff grade c such that

$$P(X > c) = 30\%$$
$$P(X - \mu > c - \mu) = 30\%$$
$$P\left(\frac{X - \mu}{\sigma} > \frac{c - \mu}{\sigma}\right) = 30\%$$
$$P\left(Z > \frac{c - 137}{35}\right) = 30\%$$

We also know that $P(Z > 0.524) = 30\%$ from the tables. Therefore, $\frac{c-137}{35} = 0.524$ and $c = 155.34$.

(4) In the Boston Marathon, suppose that the average finishing time for registered runners is 195 minutes and 15% of the runners finish

in less than 150 minutes. If the finish times are normally distributed, what is the standard deviation of finish times?

$$P(X < 150) = P(X - \mu < 150 - \mu) = P\left(\frac{X-\mu}{\sigma} < \frac{150-\mu}{\sigma}\right)$$

$$= P\left(Z < \frac{150-195}{\sigma}\right) = P\left(Z < \frac{-45}{\sigma}\right) = 0.15 = 15\%$$

We know that $(Z < -1.036) = 0.15$ from the standard normal tables. So we have $-1.036 = \frac{-45}{\sigma}$ and $\sigma = 43.436$.

(5) The incomes of public school teachers have a fairly low standard deviation. Suppose the standard deviation of incomes is \$15,000 and 35% of teachers earn more than \$90,000 a year. What is the mean salary of public school teachers?

$$0.35 = P(X > 90{,}000) = P(X - \mu > 90{,}000 - \mu)$$
$$= P\left(\frac{X-\mu}{\sigma} > \frac{90{,}000-\mu}{\sigma}\right) = P\left(Z > \frac{90{,}000-\mu}{15{,}000}\right)$$

We know from our standard normal tables that $P(Z > 0.385) = 0.35$. Therefore, $0.385 = \frac{90{,}000-\mu}{15{,}000}$ and $\mu = 84{,}225$.

(6) Suppose that 20% of countries around the world have an inflation rate of less than 0% (deflation) and that 12% of countries have an inflation rate above 10%. If inflation rates are normally distributed, can we figure out the mean and variance of inflation rates?

$$0.20 = P(X < 0) = P(X - \mu < 0 - \mu) = P\left(\frac{X-\mu}{\sigma} < \frac{0-\mu}{\sigma}\right)$$
$$= P\left(Z < \frac{0-\mu}{\sigma}\right)$$

$$0.12 = P(X > 10) = P(X - \mu > 10 - \mu) = P\left(\frac{X-\mu}{\sigma} > \frac{10-\mu}{\sigma}\right)$$
$$= P\left(Z > \frac{10-\mu}{\sigma}\right)$$

We know from our standard normal tables that $0.20 = P(Z < -0.84)$ and $0.12 = P(Z > 1.175)$. Therefore, we know that $-0.84 = \frac{0-\mu}{\sigma}$ and

$1.175 = \frac{10-\mu}{\sigma}$. We have two equations with two unknowns, μ and σ. We can solve and find that $\mu = 4.16$ and $\sigma = 4.96$. The variance $\sigma^2 = 4.96^2 = 24.6$.

5.3.4 *The exponential distribution*

The exponential distribution is a continuous distribution which describes the time between random occurrences. How much time will it take before the next bus comes by? How many hours will this light bulb last? How much time will pass before I get another text message? Since we are interested in the amount of time it takes before something happens, the probability distribution will only take on positive values. The exponential distribution has a peak at zero, steadily decreases as time passes, and is skewed to the right (see Figures 5.11 and 5.12).

The exponential distribution is related to the Poisson distribution which describes the number of occurrences in a time interval. With the Poisson distribution, we are interested in the number of times something happens in a given time interval. For example, you might be interested in the probability that a certain number of car

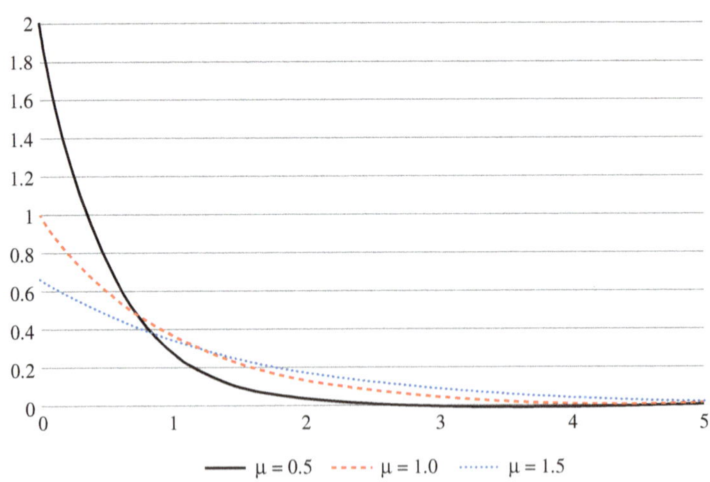

Fig. 5.11. Exponential probability distribution function.

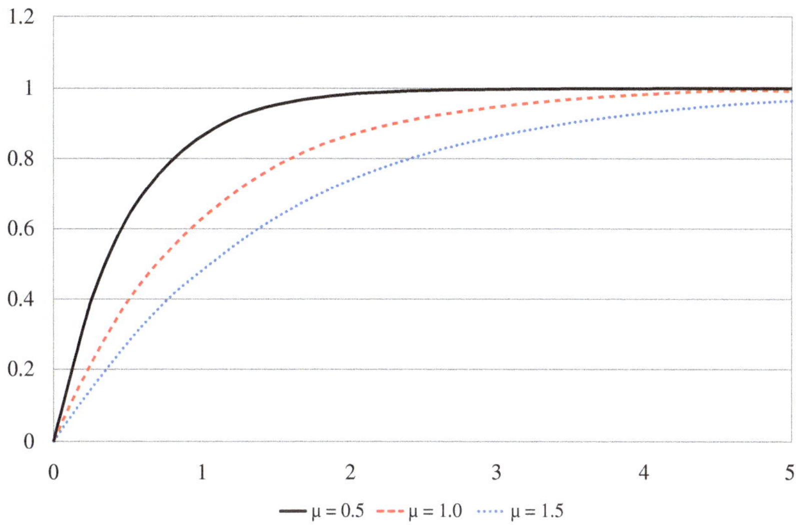

Fig. 5.12. Exponential cumulative distribution function.

accidents occur in a given hour on the highway. But with the exponential distribution, you are interested in the amount of time it takes before something happens. For example, you might be interested in the probability that a certain amount of time will elapse before the next car accident occurs on the highway.

The probability density function of the exponential distribution is given as

$$\text{pdf}(x) = \frac{1}{\mu} e^{\frac{-x}{\mu}} \tag{5.18}$$

where $e = 2.71828$ and μ is the mean or average time between events. The probability that something will happen within a certain amount of time x is given by

$$P(X \leq x) = \begin{cases} 0 & \text{for } x < 0 \\ 1 - e^{\frac{-x}{\mu}} & \text{for } x \geq 0 \end{cases} \tag{5.19}$$

The probability that something will take longer than a given amount of time x is given by

$$P(X \geq x) = \begin{cases} 1 & \text{for } x < 0 \\ e^{\frac{-x}{\mu}} & \text{for } x \geq 0 \end{cases} \tag{5.20}$$

If you know some calculus, you might be able to derive the cumulative distribution functions from the probability density function above.

We note here (without proof) that

$$E[X] = \mu$$
$$V[X] = \mu^2$$

With continuous probability distributions, you need to use calculus to figure out the expected value:

$$E[X] = \int_0^\infty xf(x)dx = \int_0^\infty x\frac{1}{\mu}e^{\frac{-x}{\mu}}dx = \mu$$

$$V[X] = E(x-\mu)^2 = \int_0^\infty (x-\mu)^2\frac{1}{\mu}e^{\frac{-x}{\mu}}dx = \mu^2$$

We leave this as an exercise for students who know some calculus. You will want to integrate this by parts. If you do not know calculus, you can start to see why calculus is valuable.

Memory: An important property of the exponential distribution is that it is memoryless. This means that if a random variable X is exponentially distributed, its conditional probability has the following property:

$$P(X > t + s | X > s) = P(X > t) \tag{5.21}$$

for all $s, t \geq 0$. The probability that X will not happen in the next t minutes does not depend on how much time s has already passed.

Suppose you have been waiting 20 minutes for the bus to arrive $(X > 20)$. With an exponential distribution, the probability that you will need to wait another 10 minutes for the bus to arrive $(X > 20 + 10)$ is the same as the initial probability that you would need to wait 10 minutes for the bus to arrive ($X > 10$) when you first got to the bus stop.

If the life of a lightbulb has an exponential distribution, it means the probability that the light bulb will last another t minutes is independent of how long (s minutes) the light bulb has already been on. The fact that something has not happened does not increase, or decrease, the probability of that event happening. This may or may not be a good assumption.

5.3.4.1 *Examples*

(1) Suppose you normally get 2.2 emails per hour. If emails are independent and follow an exponential distribution, find the probability that you will get an email within 30 minutes. Since you get 2.2 emails per hour, the mean time between emails is $60/2.2 = 27.3$ minutes. So the probability of getting an email within 30 minutes will be

$$P(X \leq x) = 1 - e^{\frac{-x}{\mu}}$$

$$P(X \leq 30) = 1 - e^{\frac{-30}{27.3}} = 1 - 0.33287 = 66.71\%$$

Note that we got the equivalent answer using the Poisson distribution when we were asked the probability of getting zero emails in the next 30 minutes. The probability of getting 0 emails in the next 30 minutes was 33.287%.

(2) Even hackers occasionally hit a hole-in-one on the golf course. Suppose the typical hacker hits one hole-in-one during every 5,000 rounds of golf, and these follow an exponential distribution. What is the probability of hitting a hole-in-one during a decade in which you play 1,000 rounds of golf?

$$P(X \leq x) = 1 - e^{\frac{-x}{\mu}}$$

$$P(X \leq 1{,}000) = 1 - e^{\frac{-1{,}000}{5{,}000}} = 1 - 0.8187 = 18.12\%$$

(3) Suppose there is an earthquake in Southern California (magnitude 4.0 or higher) every 21 days, and these follow an exponential distribution. What is the probability of going for a month (31 days)

without an earthquake?

$$P(X \geq x) = e^{\frac{-x}{\mu}}$$

$$P(X \geq 31) = e^{\frac{-31}{21}} = 0.2285 = 22.85\%$$

(4) Suppose the Minnesota Twins hit two home runs per game (9 innings) during the season. This is one home run every 4.5 innings. If these home runs are independent and follow an exponential distribution, what is the probability that the Twins will hit a home run in the next 3 innings (one-third of a game)?

$$P(X \leq x) = 1 - e^{\frac{-x}{\mu}}$$

$$P(X \leq 3) = 1 - e^{\frac{-3}{4.5}} = 0.4865 = 48.65\%$$

Use the Poisson distribution to figure out the same probability. Here $\lambda = 2/3$, the average number of home runs every 3 innings:

$$P(X \geq 1) = 1 - P(0) = 1 - \frac{e^{-\lambda}\lambda^x}{x!} = 1 - \frac{e^{-0.666}0.666^0}{0!} = 0.4865$$
$$= 48.65\%$$

(5) The number of days ahead travelers purchase their airline tickets can be modeled by an exponential distribution with the average amount of time equal to 15 days. Find the probability that a traveler will purchase a ticket fewer than 7 days in advance. How many days do half of all travelers wait?

$$P(X \leq 7) = 1 - e^{\frac{-x}{\mu}} = 1 - e^{\frac{-7}{15}} = 1 - 0.6271 = 0.3729$$

$$P(X \leq c) = 1 - e^{\frac{-x}{\mu}} = 1 - e^{\frac{-c}{15}} = 1 - 0.50 = 0.50$$

$$e^{\frac{-c}{15}} = 0.50$$

$$c = 10.397 \text{ days}$$

5.3.5 *Chi-Square distribution*

The chi-square distribution was developed by Friedrich Helmert (1843–1917) in 1876 and popularized by Karl Pearson (1857–1936) after 1900. This is often called the chi-squared distribution or the χ^2 distribution.[1]

If Z is a standard normal random variable ($Z \sim N(0,1)$), then Z^2 has a chi-square distribution with one degree of freedom. It is written as $Z^2 \sim \chi_1^2$. Since we are squaring the standard normal random variable, Z^2 can only take on positive values. The distribution will be skewed right with a range from 0 to infinity. Furthermore, the expected value of $Z^2 \sim \chi_1^2$ is equal to 1. This is because the standard deviation of Z is equal to 1. This means that Z is typically 1 unit away from its mean of 0. And $1^2 = (-1)^2 = 1$. So it should be reasonable that the expected value of Z^2 is unity and $E[\chi_1^2] = 1$.

If Z_1 and Z_2 are two independent standard normal random variables, then $Z_1^2 + Z_2^2$ has a chi-square distribution with 2 degrees of freedom and is written as χ_2^2. This distribution is still skewed to the right and now has an expected value of 2:

$$Z_1^2 + Z_2^2 \sim \chi_2^2$$

When we generalize, the sum of n independent standard normal random variables ($Z_i \sim N(0,1)$) which have all been squared, $\sum_1^n Z_i^2 = Z_1^2 + Z_2^2 + \cdots + Z_n^2$, has a chi-square distribution with n degrees of freedom and is written as χ_n^2:

$$Z_1^2 + Z_2^2 + \cdots + Z_n^2 \sim \chi_n^2 \tag{5.22}$$

There is an entire family of chi-square distributions, all depending on the number of degrees of freedom (see Figures 5.13 and 5.14). The expected value of a chi-square distribution with n degrees of freedom is n. This is because the expected value of χ_1^2 is one. If you add up n of these terms, the expected value will be n. The variance will be $2n$ and is just asserted here:

$$\text{Mean} = E(\chi_n^2) = n$$

$$\text{Variance} = V(\chi_n^2) = 2n$$

In order to quantify the probability distribution of a chi-square random variable, we will use the statistical tables in the Appendix.

[1] χ is the Greek letter chi.

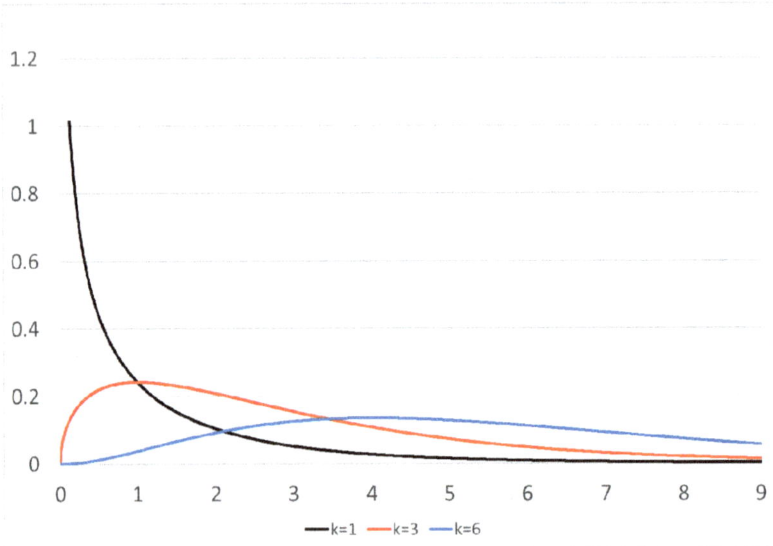

Fig. 5.13. Chi square probability distribution function.

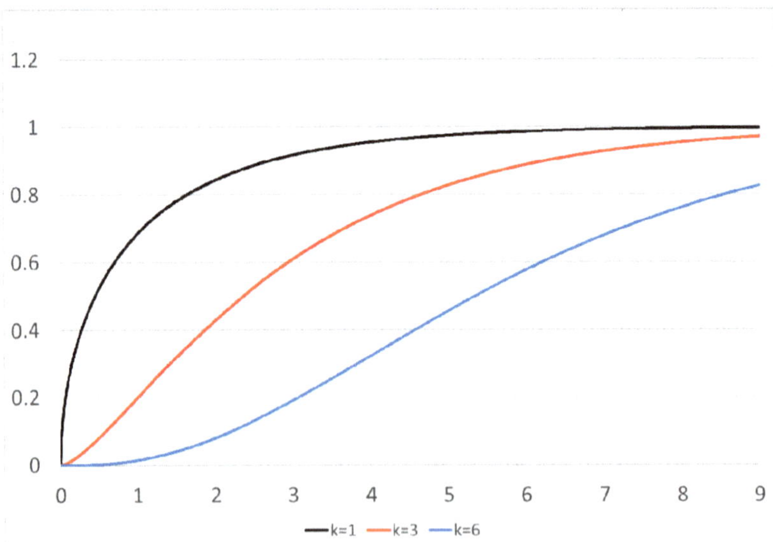

Fig. 5.14. Chi square cumulative distribution function.

These tables can be arranged in a number of different ways. If you are using a different chi-square table, please make sure you understand how it has been arranged.

Let's look at the statistical tables in the Appendix. The table for the chi-square distributions, χ_n^2, appears in Table A.2. The diagram in the upper right corner indicates that this table provides the probability that χ_n^2 is greater than various values c, $P(\chi_n^2 > c)$. This table provides much less information about the actual shape of the χ_n^2 distribution compared to the standard normal tables.

When you look at the chi-square tables, you must know the number of degrees of freedom for your chi-square variable. The degrees of freedom appear along the left-hand column of the table. This table includes degrees of freedom from 1 to 30, and then in increments of 10 up to 100. So if you are dealing with perhaps 55 degrees of freedom, you might interpolate between 50 and 60 or, better yet, go online.

For these various degrees of freedom, the next column on the table tells us the value c such that $P(\chi_n^2 > c) = 99.5\%$. The next column on the table tells us the value c such that $P(\chi_n^2 > c) = 99\%$. The next column on the table tells us the value c such that $P(\chi_n^2 > c) = 97.5\%$. The last column on the table tells us the value c such that $P(\chi_n^2 > c) = 0.5\%$. As you move from left to right, the probabilities get smaller, and the values of c get larger. The larger the value of c, the less likely a chi-square random variable will be larger than c.

You should be able to verify the following probability statements:

a. If $\Phi \sim \chi_5^2$, then $P(\Phi > 11.0705) = 5\%$.
b. If $\Phi \sim \chi_{10}^2$, then $P(\Phi > 23.2093) = 1\%$.
c. If $\Phi \sim \chi_{15}^2$, then $P(\Phi < 7.2609) = 5\%$.
d. If $\Phi \sim \chi_{18}^2$, then $P(\Phi > 10.8649) = 90\%$.
e. If $\Phi \sim \chi_{20}^2$, then $P(\Phi > 28.4120) = 10\%$.
f. If $\Phi \sim \chi_{30}^2$, then $P(20.5992 < \Phi < 40.2560) = 80\%$.

We should observe the following. When you add two independent chi-square random variables together, you get another chi-square random variable. Furthermore, the degrees of freedom of the resulting chi-square random variable will be the sum of the two original degrees of freedom:

$$\chi^2_m + \chi^2_n = \chi^2_{m+n}$$

It should also follow that

$$\chi^2_{m+n} - \chi^2_n = \chi^2_m$$

for $m, n \geq 1$. For example,

$$\chi^2_4 + \chi^2_5 = \chi^2_9$$
$$\chi^2_9 - \chi^2_3 = \chi^2_6$$

The chi-square distribution is used to study variances, to test independence, to test the homogeneity of two populations, and to test the goodness of fit. A classic example of a chi-square test is to test for fairness of a die where we test the hypothesis that all six possible outcomes are equally likely. We will return to the chi-square distribution later in the textbook. For now, we just want to understand what it is and how to use the chi-square tables in the Appendix.

5.3.6 *The Student's t-distribution*

The Student's t-distribution was developed by William Gosset (1876–1937) in 1908 while he was the Head Brewer for Guinness in Dublin. It is called Student's t-distribution because he published his work under the pseudonym "Student." He did not want Guinness to get credit for his work.

The Student's t-distribution is very similar to the standard normal distribution. It is symmetrical, is bell-shaped, and has a mean of zero. The Student's t-distribution has fatter tails than the $N(0, 1)$, so the variance is a little bigger than the variance of a $N(0, 1)$, in other words, a little bigger than 1. And while there is only one standard normal, there is a whole family of Student's t-distributions (as with the chi-square distribution) defined by the degrees of freedom.

If Z is a standard normal random variable, $Z \sim N(0, 1)$, and W is an independent chi-square random variable with n degrees of freedom ($W \sim \chi_n^2$), then $\frac{Z}{\sqrt{W/n}}$ has a Student's t-distribution with n degrees of freedom. We can write this using the following notation. If $Z \sim N(0,1)$ and $W \sim \chi_n^2$, then

$$\Psi_n = \frac{Z}{\sqrt{W/n}} \sim \text{Student's } t \text{ with } n \text{ degrees of freedom} \qquad (5.23)$$

Since $W \sim \chi_n^2$, we know that $E[W] = n$ (see Figures 5.15 and 5.16). So in the denominator of the Student's t random variable, we have a random variable W that we expect to be close to n divided by n. So the number in the denominator should be close to 1, and the square root of 1 is also 1. The Student's t random variable is merely the standard normal random variable divided by a random number close to 1. Thus, the Student's t random variable should look like a standard normal random variable except that it has a little more variability because of the noisy denominator close to 1. It should not be surprising that we have the following:

$$\text{Mean} = E(\Psi_n) = 0$$

$$\text{Variance} = V(\Psi_n) = \tfrac{n}{n-2} \quad \text{for } n > 2$$

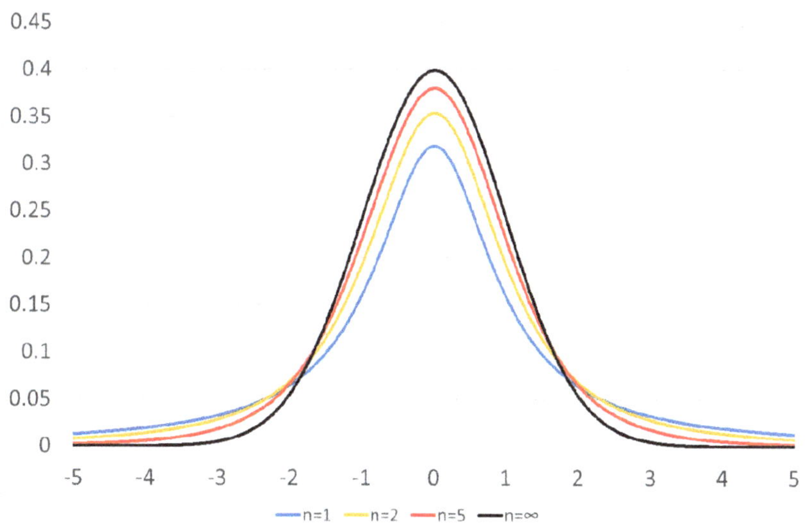

Fig. 5.15. Student's t probability distribution function.

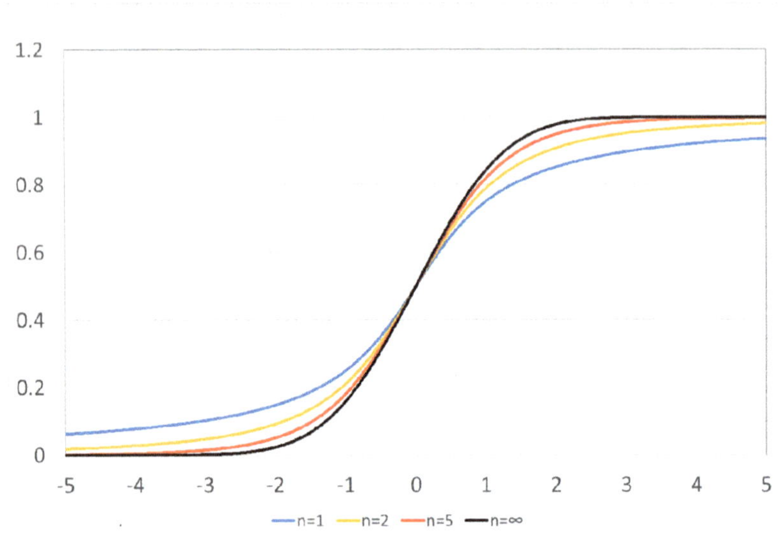

Fig. 5.16. Student's t cumulative distribution function.

Since Z has a standard normal distribution with a mean of 0, it makes sense that the Student's t-distribution also has a mean of zero. And the variance of the Student's t will be a little bit bigger than the variance of the standard normal. But as n approaches infinity, the Student's t-distribution approaches a $N(0, 1)$ distribution. This is because the denominator of the Student's t will approach 1. In the variance expression above, $\frac{n}{n-2} \to 1$ as $n \to \infty$.

The Student's t-distribution is useful in estimating the means of samples when the population variance is unknown, in estimating the differences between two means, and in analyzing regression results.

For now, we just want to learn the definition of the Student's t random variable and to use the Student's t tables in the Appendix or online.

Let's look at the statistical tables in the Appendix. The table for the Student's t-distributions appears in Table A.3. Let Ψ_n have a Student's t-distribution with n degrees of freedom.[2] The diagram in

[2]Ψ is the upper case Greek letter psi.

the upper right corner indicates that this table provides the probability that Ψ_n is greater than various values c, $P(\Psi_n > c)$. This table provides much less information about the actual shape of the Student's t-distribution compared to the standard normal tables.

When you look at the Student's t tables, you must know the number of degrees of freedom for your Student's t random variable. The degrees of freedom appear along the left-hand column of the table. This table includes degrees of freedom from 1 to 30, then in increments of 5 up to 100, and then increments of 10 up to 200 and then jumps to infinity. So if you are dealing with perhaps 300 degrees of freedom, you may want to look online. But the reality is that the Student's t-distribution does not look all that different whether you have 200 degrees of freedom or 300 degrees of freedom. So you could pick the closest degrees of freedom available on the table and be fairly close.

For these various degrees of freedom, the next column on the table tells us the value c such that $P(\Psi_n > c) = 10\%$. The next column on the table tells us the value c such that $P(\Psi_n > c) = 5\%$. The next column on the table tells us the value c such that $P(\Psi_n > c) = 2.5\%$. The last column on the table tells us the value c such that $P(\Psi_n > c) = 0.5\%$. As you move from left to right, the probabilities get smaller, and the values of c get larger. The larger the value of c, the less likely a Student's t random variable will be larger than c.

You should be able to confirm the following statements by looking at some Student's t tables:

(a) If $\Psi_5 \sim$ Student t with 5 degrees of freedom, then $P(\Psi_5 > 1.476) = 10\%$.
(b) If $\Psi_{10} \sim$ Student t with 10 degrees of freedom, then $P(\Psi_{10} > 1.812) = 5\%$.
(c) If $\Psi_{15} \sim$ Student t with 15 degrees of freedom, then $P(\Psi_{15} > 2.602) = 1\%$.
(d) If $\Psi_{30} \sim$ Student t with 30 degrees of freedom, then $P(0 < \Psi_{30} < 2.042) = 47.5\%$ since the Student's t-distribution is symmetric around zero.
(e) If $\Psi_\infty \sim$ Student t with ∞ degrees of freedom, then $P(-1.645 < \Psi_\infty < 1.645) = 90\%$. We note that this last probability is the

same as for a $N(0,1)$. This is because a Student's t-distribution with infinite degrees of freedom is the same as a $N(0,1)$.

5.3.7 *The F-distribution*

The F-distribution was developed by Sir Ronald A. Fisher (1890–1962) and George Snedecor (1881–1974). Snedecor named this distribution the "F"-distribution as a tribute to R. A. Fisher. This distribution is sometimes known as Snedecor's F-distribution or the Fisher–Snedecor distribution. This is a continuous probability distribution with a positive skew and range $(0, \infty)$ which depends on two parameters denoted m and n, the degrees of freedom in the numerator and the denominator.

The F-distribution is the ratio of two independent chi-square random variables which have been divided by their respective degrees of freedom.

If W is a chi-square random variable with m degrees of freedom ($W \sim \chi^2_m$) and Y is an independent chi-square random variable with n degrees of freedom ($Y \sim \chi^2_n$), then $\Omega = \frac{W/m}{Y/n} = \frac{\chi^2_m/m}{\chi^2_n/n}$ has an F-distribution with m degrees of freedom in the numerator and n degrees of freedom in the denominator. This is written as

$$\frac{W/m}{Y/n} \sim F(m,n) \tag{5.24}$$

For example, if $\Omega \sim F(2,4)$, then Ω has an F-distribution with 2 degrees of freedom in the numerator and 4 degrees of freedom in the denominator.

Since W is a chi-square random variable with m degrees of freedom, the expected value of W is m. And since Y is a chi-square random variable with n degrees of freedom, the expected value of Y is n. So we would expect W/m to be fairly close to 1. And we would expect Y/n to be fairly close to 1 as well. And so we would expect $\frac{W/m}{Y/n} \sim F(m,n)$ to be fairly close to 1. The expected value of $F(m,n)$ indeed approaches 1 as n gets larger and larger. Furthermore, we know that chi-square random variables can only take on positive values. Since the F-distribution is the ratio of two chi-square

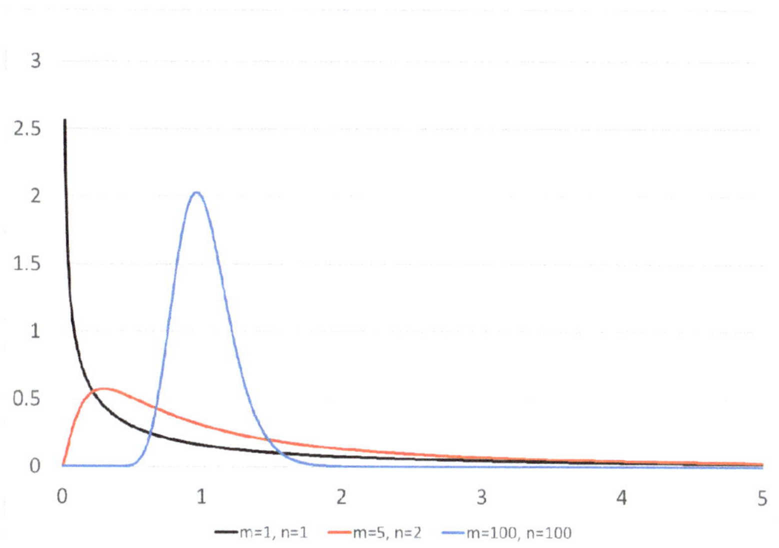

Fig. 5.17. Fisher–Snedecor probability distribution function.

random variables, the F-distribution can only take on positive values. Thus, the F-distribution will be centered near 1 and skewed to the right (see Figures 5.17 and 5.18).

If $\Omega \sim F(m, n)$, then $E(\Omega) = \frac{n}{n-2}$ for $n > 2$ and $V(\Omega) = \frac{2n^2(m+n-2)}{m(n-2)^2(n-4)}$ for $n > 4$. We are just asserting these here. The expected value should feel intuitively reasonable.

The F-distribution is useful when you are comparing the variances of two populations and when you are doing an analysis of variance (ANOVA).

You should learn to read the F-distribution tables. These statistical tables may be arranged differently in different textbooks and online. Let's look at the statistical tables in the Appendix. The tables for the F-distributions appear in Tables A.4(a)–(d). These tables provide the probability that Ω is greater than various values c, $P(\Omega > c)$, where $\Omega \sim F(m, n)$. This table provides much less information about the actual shape of the F distribution compared to the standard normal tables.

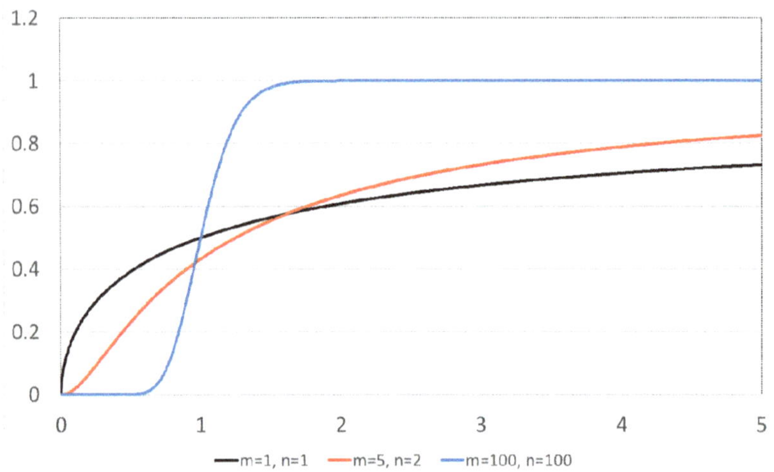

Fig. 5.18. Fisher–Snedecor cumulative distribution function.

When you look at the F-distribution tables, you must know the number of degrees of freedom for both the numerator and the denominator of your random F variable. The denominator degrees of freedom appear along the left-hand column of the table. These run from 1 to 20, then increments of 2 up to 30, then increments of 5 up to 50, then increments of 10 up to 100, and then increments of 20 up to 200 and then jump to infinity. The numerator degrees of freedom appear along the top of the table. These also run in increments from 1 all the way to infinity. There are actually four F tables here. Table A.4(a) is the 10% table, Table A.4(b) is the 5% table, Table A.4(c) is the 2.5% table, and Table A.4(d) is the 1% table. And each of these tables actually takes up three pages because of all the different possible numerator and denominator degrees of freedom combinations. Of course, all the possible numerator and denominator degrees of freedom combinations are not presented. Suppose you are dealing with $\Omega \sim F(32, 148)$. The table does not represent 32 degrees of freedom in the denominator or 148 degrees of freedom in the numerator. In this case, you might approximate the $F(32, 148)$ with an $F(30, 140)$

which does appear on the table. To be conservative, you should round down to the nearest appropriate degrees of freedom. The reality is that these distributions will be very close to each other. Alternatively, you can go online to get better numbers.

Now let's turn our attention to Table A.4(b), our 5% F-distribution table. If you have a random variable $\Omega \sim F(9, 16)$, we have 9 degrees of freedom in the numerator and 16 degrees of freedom in the denominator. If we look along the top row to "9" and along the left column to "16", we find the value 2.54 on the table. This tells us that if $\Omega \sim F(9, 16)$, then $P(\Omega > 2.54) = 5\%$.

Table A.4(c) is the 2.5% table. This table says "2.5%" at the top. If you have a random variable $\Omega \sim F(9, 16)$, we have 9 degrees of freedom in the numerator and 16 degrees of freedom in the denominator. If we look along the top row to "9" and along the left column to "16", we find the value 3.05 on the table. This tells us that if $\Omega \sim F(9, 16)$, then $P(\Omega > 3.05) = 2.5\%$. Using the information in these two tables, we can infer that $P(2.54 < \Omega < 3.05) = 2.5\%$ because $\Omega \sim F(9, 16)$ is bigger than 2.54 just 5% of the time and bigger than 3.05 just 2.5% of the time. So Ω must be between 2.54 and 3.05 exactly $5 - 2.5\% = 2.5\%$ of the time.

You should be able to confirm the following statements:

(a) If $\Omega \sim F(5, 10)$, then $P(\Omega > 3.33) = 5\%$.
(b) If $\Omega \sim F(10, 5)$, then $P(\Omega > 4.74) = 5\%$.
(c) If $\Omega \sim F(12, 8)$, then $P(\Omega > 0) = 100\%$.
(d) If $\Omega \sim F(5, 10)$, then $P(\Omega > 5.64) = 1\%$.
(e) If $\Omega \sim F(10, 5)$, then $P(\Omega > 10.05) = 1\%$.
(f) If $\Omega \sim F(5, 10)$, then $P(0 < \Omega < 3.33) = 95\%$.

Consider the following extension. If $\Psi_n \sim$ Student's t-distribution with n degrees of freedom, then $\Psi_n^2 \sim F(1, n)$. If you square a Student's t-distribution, you get an F-distribution. Recall that with a Student's t-distribution, $\Psi_n = \frac{Z}{\sqrt{W/n}}$ where $Z \sim N(0, 1)$ and $W \sim \chi_n^2$. So if we square Ψ_n, we get $\Psi_n^2 = \frac{Z^2}{W/n} = \frac{\chi_1^2/1}{\chi_n^2/n} \sim F(1, n)$. We are just saying that if you square a Student's t random variable, you will get a random variable with an F-distribution.

5.3.8 *Cauchy distribution*

The last special probability distribution we discuss will be the Cauchy distribution. You will probably never use the Cauchy distribution except to be pedantic. The Cauchy distribution is the exception to the rule that makes life difficult for statisticians. It violates all our standard assumptions and messes up all our results. It is useful to be aware of probability distributions like this one. If any of your variables have a Cauchy distribution, all bets will be off.

The Cauchy distribution is named after Augustin-Louis Cauchy (1789–1857). There may be more concepts and theorems named after Cauchy than any other mathematician.

We start with two independent normal random variables with a mean of zero. Let $X_a \sim N(0, \sigma_a^2)$ and $X_b \sim N(0, \sigma_b^2)$ where X_a and X_b are independent. Then, $\mathrm{K} = \frac{X_a}{X_b}$ has a standard Cauchy distribution. Since X_b has an expected value of 0, the value of K will often be very large or close to infinity. The tails of this distribution are very fat. Consequently, the expected value and the variance of the Cauchy distribution are undefined. The practical meaning of this is that collecting 1,000 data points gives you no more accurate estimate of the mean and standard deviation than a single point.

The standard Cauchy distribution has the following probability density function:

$$\mathrm{pdf}(x) = \frac{1}{\pi} \frac{\frac{\sigma_a}{\sigma_b}}{\left(\left(\frac{\sigma_a}{\sigma_b} \right)^2 + x^2 \right)} \tag{5.25}$$

Here $\pi \cong 3.1415926$. If you look at the pdf and the CDF of the Cauchy distribution, they look harmless enough (see Figures 5.19 and 5.20). Even though we have a perfectly well-defined probability density function, the Cauchy distribution does not have a moment-generating function. This simple probability density function can cause a lot of trouble.

You should have noted that all the probability distributions in this chapter are related to each other. You should keep those relationships in mind. There are many more probability density functions, both discrete and continuous. But the distributions covered in this chapter

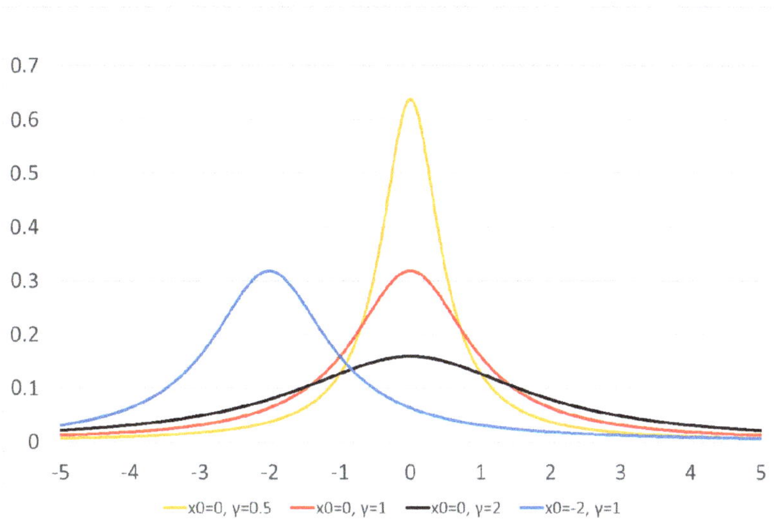

Fig. 5.19. Cauchy probability distribution function.

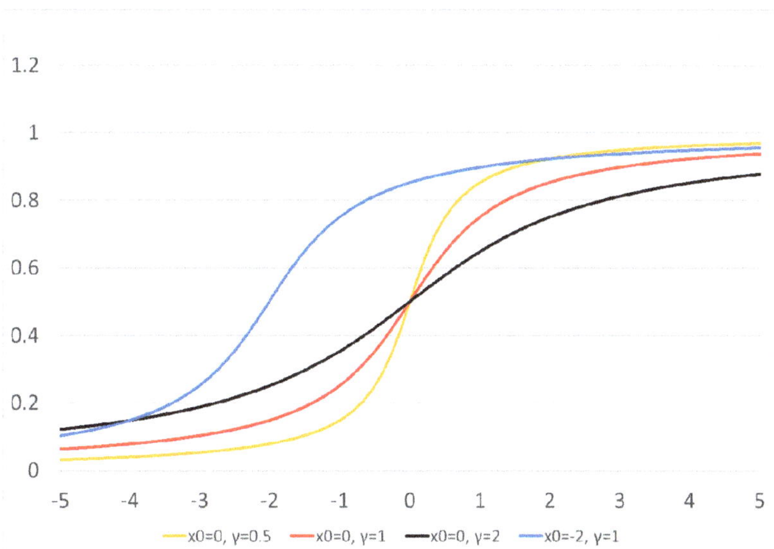

Fig. 5.20. Cauchy cumulative distribution function.

are all you will need to understand the essentials of statistics and econometrics.

5.4 Exercises

(1) Suppose Novak Djokovic makes a successful first serve about 65% of the time. If he serves six times, what is the probability that he gets

  (a) exactly 4 serves in?
  (b) no more than 4 serves in?
  (0.328, 0.6809)

(2) Small businesses are going bankrupt at a rate of 9.7 per month in Metropolis. Assuming a Poisson distribution, what is the probability of at least 3 going bankrupt next month of exactly 24 businesses going bankrupt? (0.9964, 0.00004755)

(3) The expected life of a computer component is an exponential random variable with a mean of 7 years. If the warranty period is 5 years, what proportion of the components can the manufacturer expect to replace under the warranty? What should the warranty period be if the manufacturer doesn't want to be bothered with having to replace more than 10% of the components? (0.510, 0.7375)

(4) Mensa is an organization whose members possess IQs in the top 2% of the population. To qualify, you must have an IQ greater than 133. If IQs are normally distributed with a mean of 100, what is the standard deviation and variance of IQs? (10.68, 114.05)

(5) Suppose 25% of the drivers who are members of the Teamsters Union earn over \$19.68 an hour, and about 10% of these drivers earn less than \$15.25 an hour. Assuming that these wages have a normal distribution, what are the mean, variance, and standard deviation of these wages? (18.15, 5.133, 2.266)

(6) The Beardstown Ladies wish to invest \$1,000 in common stock. They are considering two stocks, Holden stock and Sanborn stock. They both have a normal distribution of returns, as follows:

$$\text{Holden stock} \sim N(\$1{,}100,\ 1{,}600)$$

$$\text{Sanborn stock} \sim N(\$1{,}140,\ 2{,}500)$$

The Ladies only want to select one of the two stocks. Sanborn stock has a higher expected return, but it is also more risky in the sense that the variance of Sanborn's return is greater than that of Holden. The Beardstown Ladies want to choose the stock that has the smaller probability of returning less than \$1,000. Which stock should they choose? (Sanborn)

(7) The length of human pregnancies from conception to birth varies according to a distribution that is approximately normal with a mean of 266 days and a standard deviation of 16 days.

(a) What percent of pregnancies last less than 240 days (that's about 8 months)?
(b) What percent of pregnancies last between 240 and 270 days (roughly between 8 and 9 months)?
(c) How long do the longest 20% of pregnancies last?
(0.052, 0.5467, 279.46)

(8) Assume W is a random variable with a Student's t-distribution. Find the following probabilities:

(a) $P[0 \leq W \leq 6.31]$ when W has 1 degree of freedom.
(b) $P[-2.02 \leq W \leq 3.36]$ when W has 5 degree of freedom.
(c) $P[-1.30 \leq W \leq 1.30]$ when W has 40 degrees of freedom.
(d) $P[-1.96 \leq W \leq 1.96]$ when W has ∞ degrees of freedom.
(0.45, 0.94, .80, .95)

(9) A random variable has a χ^2 distribution with 9 degrees of freedom. What is the probability that the random variable will be between 16.919 and 21.666? Explain your work. (4%)

(10) Let Ω be distributed $F(5, 10)$ and let Ψ be distributed $F(10, 5)$. Which of the following probabilities is smaller, $P[\Omega \geq 3.3]$ or $P[\Psi \geq 3.3]$? Explain. ($P[\Omega \geq 3.3]$)

Chapter 6

Statistical Inference: Sampling and Sampling Distributions

6.1 Introduction

> *Statistics show that Hispanics are the fastest growing minority group. They are now almost 6 feet tall.*

We are ultimately interested in better understanding the world around us. In economics, we break up our questions about the world into two types: positive questions and normative questions. **Positive questions** seek to understand human behavior and the operation of the economic system without making judgments about whether the outcomes are good or bad. We seek to describe what is and how it works. **Normative questions** ask if the outcomes are good or bad and if we can make them better. They involve values, judgments, and prescriptions for preferred courses of action. A positive question is as follows: "Does Pepsi contain more sugar than Coke?" A normative question is as follows: "Does Pepsi taste better than Coke?" A positive question is as follows: "Would lowering the speed limit on highways decrease highway deaths?" A normative question is as follows: "Should we lower the speed limit on highways?" Both positive and normative questions are important. Statistics cannot answer the normative questions. But statistics can help us answer the positive questions about the world. And the answers to our positive questions are important to inform our normative decisions. Here are some positive questions:

What is the average income of an American household?
How much income inequality is there?
What percentage of teenagers are vaping?
How many hours of sleep do college students usually get?
Are Americans getting taller?

Since it is too expensive and too time-consuming to interview every single American about these kinds of questions, we will generally draw a random sample from the population and use statistical inference to learn what we can about the larger population. Statistical inference refers to the methods by which the characteristics of the population or phenomena are studied through the observation of sample data.

For example, suppose you have a hot tub in your backyard. It takes quite a while to heat up, so you are never quite sure when it is ready. When you think it might be ready, you don't just jump into the hot tub. You put a finger in the water to sample the temperature. You might move your finger around a bit to get a larger sample. You assume that the temperature around your finger will be a good estimate of the temperature of the water throughout the tub.

Thus from a larger population, we draw a smaller sample. The sample should be randomly or scientifically selected. Otherwise, it will be difficult or impossible to make inferences about the larger population.

6.2 Random Sample

A sample of size n out of a population of size N is said to be a random sample if every possible sample of n objects is equally likely to have been drawn.

It is important that every person or object in the population is equally likely to be selected to be in the sample. Otherwise, it may be difficult or impossible to make any statistical inferences.

In 1936, Alf Landon ran for president against F. D. Roosevelt. *Literary Digest*, a weekly magazine founded in 1890, polled 25% of all Americans.[1] This was an extremely large sample. They polled everyone listed in phone directories, everyone who had registered a car, and everyone who had subscribed to *Literary Digest*. They predicted that Alf Landon would win the election. They were wrong. They went out of business two years later.

Their mistake comes under the general heading of "**sample selection bias**." Their sample was not representative of the larger population. Back in 1936, rich people were more likely to own cars, rich people were more likely to have phones, rich people were more likely to subscribe to the *Literary Digest*, and rich people were more likely to vote Republican. Sample selection bias can happen for any number of reasons.

Caveman effect: We have data from caves about the lives of cavemen because it is more likely to survive the elements. But most prehistoric people may not have lived in caves or only lived in caves some of the time. Thus, the evidence may provide a misleading picture of the general lives of prehistoric people.

When we do a wage study, we only have wage data on people who are working. We do not have data on how much people who are not working would be earning if they were working. If people who are working are different from the people who are not working, it can be difficult to measure the effect of wages on the number of hours worked.

If you survey high school students on drug use, you are not going to capture students who have dropped out of high school or students who are out sick that day or students who are home-schooled. The rates of drug use may be very different for students in high school and high school dropouts.

Survivor bias: We can interview people who survive a plane crash, but we cannot interview those who did not. We can evaluate current

[1]They polled over 30 million people. By contrast, most Gallup polls today merely poll 1,000 or fewer people and get much more accurate results.

money managers and their performance, but it is harder to interview former money managers who lost their jobs due to poor performance. If the two groups are systematically different in important ways, we will have problems.

Healthy user bias: If you interview people on the street, you will be interviewing people who are fit enough to be walking around. Your sample is likely to be healthier than the general population which includes people in hospitals and people home in bed.

Self-selection bias: This bias occurs when the choice of being in or out of the sample is left to each person. This includes a "non-response bias" when potential respondents in a randomly selected sample refuse to be interviewed or refuse to answer certain questions. If people can choose to be in or out of the sample, we will have problems if those choosing to be in the sample are systematically different from those who choose not to be in the sample or if those who choose to answer your questions are systematically different from those who choose not to answer your questions.

Half a century ago (1975–1976) Ann Landers asked her readers the following question: "If you could do it all over again, would you have children?" Ten thousand people wrote into her column and 70% said "no." Are all individuals equally likely to respond to this prompt from this advice column? A year later 90% of the respondents to a national random sample poll said "yes," they would have children all over again. Who actually has the time to write to an advice column or call into a radio talk show?

Every time a faculty member is reviewed for promotion or tenure, we send out a survey to a randomly selected sample of their students. We feel very lucky if 30% of the students respond. Usually, only the students who have strong feelings about the professor respond. Thus, we will try to hound all the students in the sample to send in their evaluations. But we worry that students who are "hounded" may respond differently from students who are not "hounded."

There is a concern in the social sciences that most of our research is based on a "WEIRD" sample of people. WEIRD stands for western, educated, industrialized, rich, and democratic. People in WEIRD societies may represent 80% of study participants, but only 12% of the world population. For example, there is evidence that geometric illusions are perceived differently in WEIRD and non-WEIRD societies.[2]

It is important to have a sample which is representative of the larger population. Some researchers practice "snowball sampling" where research participants are asked to recruit other participants for a study. This is used when potential participants are hard to find. For example, suppose you want to interview immigrants from Sri Lanka. There may be very few immigrants from Sri Lanka in your neighborhood, and they may be difficult to find. But the immigrants from Sri Lanka probably know each other. So once you interview one person from Sri Lanka, you might ask this informant to recommend others. But if your informant from Sri Lanka is Tamil, this informant is likely to recommend others who are also Tamil while most people in Sri Lanka are Sinhalese. With snowball sampling, you can certainly learn something about your sample. But it is extremely difficult to make inferences about the larger population. You cannot determine the sampling error.

Another problem with survey data can be **response bias**. People are not always truthful, especially if they have an incentive to lie. This problem is not a sample selection problem. When you ask people about the number of sexual partners they have had, it appears that the average man has had more sexual partners than the average woman. If you are only surveying heterosexual people, this is impossible. Men tend to overstate the number, and women tend to understate the number.

There are a number of reasons why people provide misleading responses. Respondents may want to appear better than they are. Respondents may lie to build their self-worth by appearing cooler or richer or smarter. Yes, of course, I read seven books every week. Respondents may want to give socially desirable answers. Survey estimates of respondent voting are always higher than actual voter turnout. Since you are supposed to vote, people lie about having actually voted. Respondents are reluctant to answer questions about

---

[2]Segall, Campbell and Herskovit, "The influence of culture on visual perception", in *Social Perception*, Toch and Smith (eds.), 1968.

sensitive issues like sex, money, drugs, or illegal behavior. Respondents are more likely to lie or refuse to answer these kinds of questions. Respondents may want to give the answer they believe will "help" or "please" the researcher. Many people just want to help the researcher out. And so they make up responses based on their belief about what the researcher needs. The survey questions themselves may be leading, constructed in a way to encourage a particular kind of answer. And respondents might think they can influence the outcome of the research in their favor. If you absolutely love the product concept, you may say you will buy it more frequently than you actually think you will, in hopes of getting it introduced into the marketplace.

We lie to ourselves all the time. On Netflix, there is a big difference between the kinds of movies we place in our "My List" folder and the kinds of movies we actually watch. The "My List" folder is just for movies we "think" we should watch. So of course we will lie to survey takers.

6.3 Statistical Inference

Once we have gathered our sample data, we can try to learn something about the larger population. A statistic is a summary measure of the sample data used to infer something about the larger population. Prior to sampling, the statistic is called an estimator and is merely a formula. For example, the sample mean is this formula:

$$\bar{X} = \frac{1}{n} \sum_{n} X_i$$

Before we have any data, this is a random variable whose value is unknown. A specific value of an estimator is computed after collecting the sample data. After sampling, this statistic is called an estimate. For example, we might find that $\bar{X} = 68.23$ inches. This might be our estimate of the average height of an American.

The sample estimate will equal our population parameter of interest only by pure chance unless everyone in the population is exactly the same. Sometimes the sample estimate will be larger, sometimes it will be smaller, sometimes it will be close, and sometimes it will be way off. Thus, we are interested in the sampling distribution of the estimator and the probability distribution of this statistic. We need some sense of how this random variable behaves.

Suppose you are interested in some population mean μ. You might be interested in the average income, average hours of sleep, or the average number of children of all Americans or all human beings.

We draw a random sample from the population. We might collect the sample observations $X_1, X_2, X_3, \ldots, X_n$. Here the sample size is n. Once we have done this, what should we do with the data to come up with the best estimate of the population mean μ?

We could use the sample mean, the simple average of the data. We might use the sample mode, the most common value of the data. We might use the sample median, the middle value of the data. We might use the midpoint of the data, halfway between the largest and smallest value. We might use the lowest value of the data, or the day of the month, or my weight. How do we decide which estimator is the best one to use? Some might be better than others depending on the situation. And we will definitely need to think about what we mean by "best."

What estimators might we use if we are interested in the population variance σ^2? We could use the sample variance, the average squared deviation from the mean. We might use the sample standard deviation, the square root of the sample variance. We might use the range, the difference between the largest and the smallest value. We might use the sample average absolute deviation where we look at the absolute value of the deviation of each observation from the sample mean and average them. What is the best thing to do here?

And what estimator might we use if we are interested in the population proportion p, the percent of the population which shares a particular characteristic? Here $0 \leq p \leq 1$. We might use the sample proportion. Is there some other estimator which would be better? What should we do?

6.4 Properties of Estimators

We must choose an estimator in order to estimate some population parameter. Different estimators will have different properties.

There are a few properties we might like our estimator to have. This should inform our decision about the most appropriate estimator.

6.4.1 *Unbiasedness*

Everything else being the same, we would like our estimator to be unbiased. This means that, on average, our estimator will hit the population parameter on the nose. Suppose Θ is the population parameter we are estimating and θ is our estimator. If θ is an unbiased estimator of Θ, then $E(\theta) = \Theta$. We define the bias of an estimator as

$$\text{bias} = E(\theta) - \Theta \tag{6.1}$$

Hopefully, the bias is equal to 0.

6.4.2 *Consistency*

Consistency means that we can expect our estimator θ to be closer and closer to the true population parameter Θ as the sample size gets larger and larger. We write this as

$$\lim_{n \to \infty} P(|\theta - \Theta| \leq \varepsilon) = 1 \quad \text{for any } \varepsilon > 0 \tag{6.2}$$

If our sample size is large enough, we can be certain that our estimator θ will be arbitrarily close to the true population parameter Θ. The limit of the probability, as the sample size n goes to infinity, that the distance between θ and Θ will be less than ε is equal to 1. Equivalently, the probability that our estimate θ will be more than ε units away from the true population parameter Θ will become 0 as our sample size n increases. Thus, we can expect our parameter estimate to get closer and closer to the true population parameter as our sample size gets bigger and bigger.

6.4.3 *Efficiency*

If we have two unbiased estimators, we usually say one estimator is more efficient than the other estimator if the variance of the estimator is smaller for a given sample size. Suppose we have two unbiased estimators, θ_1 and θ_2, for some population parameter Θ. If the variance of θ_1 is smaller than the variance of θ_2, that is,

$$V(\theta_1) < V(\theta_2) \tag{6.3}$$

for the same sample size, then θ_1 is more efficient than θ_2. With a given sample size, θ_1 is more likely to give us an estimate closer to the true population parameter Θ than θ_2.

6.4.4 *Mean squared error*

Sometimes you may need to trade off one of these properties for another. For example, suppose you have a biased estimator and an unbiased estimator, but the biased estimator has a smaller variance than the unbiased estimator. Then which estimator would you choose? In these cases, you might look at the mean squared error (MSE) of the estimator. This measures the average of the squares of the errors, the average squared difference between the estimated values θ and the population parameter Θ. It can be shown that

$$\text{MSE}(\theta) = V(\theta) + \text{bias}(\theta, \Theta)^2 \tag{6.4}$$

The mean squared error is the variance of the estimator plus the squared bias. If you have two unbiased estimators, the estimator with the smallest variance will have the smallest mean squared error.

Let's focus on the sample mean, the sample variance, and the sample proportion. Before we gather any data, these are called estimators. These are random variables because their value depends on the particular sample we happen to draw. What does the sampling distribution of the sample mean look like? Since these are probability distributions, what is the mean and the variance of the distribution? We will start with the sample mean, and then move on to the other estimators.

6.5 The Sampling Distribution of the Sample Mean

Let us begin by assuming that X_i is a normally distributed random variable with a mean of μ and a variance of σ^2, $X_i \sim N(\mu, \sigma^2)$.

We will relax the normality assumption shortly. The sample mean is a statistic denoted by $\bar{X} = \frac{1}{n}\sum_1^n X_i$. Since the X_i are chosen randomly, the value of $\bar{X}$ is a random variable. All random variables have a probability distribution. We want to describe the probability distribution for the sample mean.

What is the mean of the probability distribution of $\bar{X}$? This may sound strange. We are looking for the mean of the mean. But remember that the sample mean is a random variable. And we are looking for the mean of this random variable:

$$\begin{aligned} E\left[\bar{X}\right] = E\left[\frac{1}{n}\sum_1^n X_i\right] &= \frac{1}{n}E\left[\sum_1^n X_i\right] = \frac{1}{n}E\left[X_1 + X_2 + \cdots + X_n\right] \\ &= \frac{1}{n}\left[E[X_1] + E\left[X_2\right] + \cdots + E[X_n]\right] \\ &= \frac{1}{n}[\mu + \mu + \cdots + \mu] = \frac{1}{n}[n\mu] = \mu \end{aligned} \tag{6.5}$$

Remember that $E[X_1] = E[X_2] = E[X_3] = E[X_n] = \mu$

So

$$E[\bar{X}] = \mu = \mu_{\bar{X}}$$

What is the variance of the probability distribution of $\bar{X}$?

$$\begin{aligned} V\left[\bar{X}\right] = V\left[\frac{1}{n}\sum_1^n X_i\right] &= \left(\frac{1}{n}\right)^2 V\left[\sum_1^n X_i\right] \\ &= \left(\frac{1}{n}\right)^2 V\left[X_1 + X_2 + \cdots + X_n\right] \\ &= \left(\frac{1}{n}\right)^2 \left[V\left[X_1\right] + V[X_2] + \cdots + V[X_n]\right] \\ &= \left(\frac{1}{n}\right)^2 \left[\sigma^2 + \sigma^2 + \cdots + \sigma^2\right] = \left(\frac{1}{n}\right)^2 \left[n\sigma^2\right] = \frac{\sigma^2}{n} \end{aligned}$$

$$V\left[\bar{X}\right] = \frac{\sigma^2}{n} \tag{6.6}$$

Recall that $V(cX) = c^2V(X)$ for any constant c and $V[X_1] = V[X_2] = V[X_3] = V[X_n] = \sigma^2$ since the variance of a sum is equal to the sum of the variances if all the variables are independent of each other as they are here. All the covariance terms are equal to zero because the X_i are independently distributed from each other.

Note that the variance of $\bar{X}$ approaches zero as n gets larger and larger. Since $V\left[\bar{X}\right] = \sigma_{\bar{X}}^2 = \frac{\sigma^2}{n}$, $\sigma_{\bar{X}}^2 \to 0$ as $n \to \infty$. The sampling distribution of $\bar{X}$ becomes more and more concentrated around the mean μ as the sample size n increases. $\bar{X}$ is a consistent estimate of the mean μ.

What is the standard deviation of the sampling distribution of $\bar{X}$? The standard deviation is the square root of the variance. So the standard deviation is

$$\mathrm{SD}\left[\bar{X}\right] = \sqrt{\frac{\sigma^2}{n}} = \frac{\sigma}{\sqrt{n}} \tag{6.7}$$

The larger the sample, the more likely that $\bar{X}$, the sample mean, is arbitrarily close of μ, the population mean. This is an example of the law of large numbers.

6.5.1 *Law of Large Numbers*

The **Law of Large Numbers** (LLN) is a theorem that describes the result of performing the same experiment a large number of times. The average of the results obtained from a large number of trials should be close to the expected value and will tend to become closer as more trials are performed.

For example, suppose Smallville is served by two hospitals. In the larger hospital, about 45 babies are born every day and in the smaller hospital, about 15 babies are born each day. As you know, about 50% of all babies are girls. However, the percentage varies from day to day. Sometimes it may be higher than 50%, sometimes lower. For a 1-year period, each hospital recorded the days when 60% or more of the babies were girls. Which hospital do you think recorded more such days?

The larger hospital? The smaller hospital? About the same number (i.e., within 5% of each other)?

From the Law of Large Numbers, we know that the answer is the smaller hospital. Since the larger hospital has more babies every day, the percent of babies who are girls is more likely to be closer to 50% every day. The smaller hospital is more likely to have some days when most of the babies are girls or most of the babies are boys.

The LLN is important because it guarantees stable long-term results for the averages of some random events. For example, while a casino may lose money in a single spin of the roulette wheel, its earnings will tend toward a predictable percentage over a large number of spins. Any winning streak by a player will eventually be overcome by the parameters of the game. It is important to remember that the law only applies (as the name indicates) when a large number of observations is considered. There is no principle that a small number of observations will coincide with the expected value or that a streak of one value will immediately be "balanced" by the others. If you have tossed a series of heads, it does not make a tail any more likely on the next coin toss.

6.5.2 *Sampling distribution of the sample mean $\bar{X}$ when X is normally distributed*

The linear combination of a bunch of normally distributed random variables will also be normally distributed. Since the X_i are normally distributed random variables, the sample mean will also be normally distributed. This is because $\bar{X}$ is a linear combination of a bunch of normally distributed random variables. We are asserting this here without a proof. The proof requires using moment-generating functions or other mathematical techniques.

Thus, we have $\bar{X} \sim N(\mu, \frac{\sigma^2}{n})$. We also know that if $X \sim N(\mu, \sigma^2)$, then $\frac{X-\mu}{\sigma} = Z \sim N(0,1)$. Similarly, since $\bar{X} \sim N(\mu, \frac{\sigma^2}{n})$, we can standardize $\bar{X}$ to get

$$Z = \frac{\bar{X} - \mu}{\sqrt{\sigma^2/n}} = \frac{\bar{X} - \mu}{\sigma/\sqrt{n}} \sim N(0,1) \tag{6.8}$$

This will allow us to solve many problems by taking advantage of the standard normal tables in the Appendix. Please note that we are assuming an infinite population here. If the population size N is smaller than infinite, this is not quite correct. As soon as $n = N$, $\bar{X} = \mu$ exactly. So you will need some finite sample corrections.

6.5.3 *Examples*

(1) Suppose that the starting salary of college graduates is normally distributed with a mean of \$54,400 and a standard deviation of \$11,000. If we randomly select 25 college graduates, what is the probability that the average salary of these graduates is between \$56,000 and \$58,000?

$$\begin{aligned}
P\left(56 < \bar{X} < 58\right) &= P\left(56 - \mu < \bar{X} - \mu < 58 - \mu\right) \\
&= P\left(\frac{56 - \mu}{\sqrt{\sigma^2/n}} < \frac{\bar{X} - \mu}{\sqrt{\sigma^2/n}} < \frac{58 - \mu}{\sqrt{\sigma^2/n}}\right) \\
&= P\left(\frac{56 - 54.4}{\sqrt{121/25}} < Z < \frac{58 - 54.4}{\sqrt{121/25}}\right) \\
&= P\left(0.727 < Z < 1.636\right) = 0.183
\end{aligned}$$

(2) Suppose that SAT scores are normally distributed with a mean of 500 and a standard deviation of 100. If we randomly select 10 Claremont high school students, what is the probability that their average SAT score is greater than 550?

$$\begin{aligned}
P\left(\bar{X} > 550\right) &= P\left(\bar{X} - \mu > 550 - \mu\right) = P\left(\frac{\bar{X} - \mu}{\sqrt{\sigma^2/n}} > \frac{550 - \mu}{\sqrt{\sigma^2/n}}\right) \\
&= P\left(Z > \frac{550 - 500}{\sqrt{10{,}000/10}}\right) = P\left(Z > 1.58\right) = 0.057 \\
&= 5.7\%
\end{aligned}$$

(3) Suppose that the annual return on the stock market is normally distributed with a mean of 12% and a standard deviation of 22%.

What is the probability that the average rate of return over an entire decade will be over 20% a year?

$$P\left(\bar{X} > 20\right) = P\left(\bar{X} - \mu > 20 - \mu\right) = P\left(\frac{\bar{X} - \mu}{\sqrt{\sigma^2/n}} > \frac{20 - \mu}{\sqrt{\sigma^2/n}}\right)$$

$$= P\left(Z > \frac{20 - 12}{\sqrt{484/10}}\right) = P\left(Z > 1.1499\right) = 0.125$$

$$= 12.5\%$$

(4) Suppose a life insurance company has written policies for 10,000 20-year-old men. Assume that the life expectancy for a 20-year-old man is 76.4 years with a standard deviation of 17 years. If the typical policyholder lives to be older than 76.4 years, the insurance company will do well. If the typical policyholder passes away much earlier than 76.4 years, the insurance company will lose money. The average age of death for the policyholder $\sim N(\mu, \frac{\sigma^2}{n}) = N(76.4, \frac{17^2}{10{,}000}) = N(76.4, 0.0289)$. We know from our standard normal tables that $P\left(Z < -2.33\right) = 1\%$. So we have $P\left(\frac{\bar{X}-76.4}{\sqrt{.0289}} < -2.33\right) = P\left(\bar{X} - 76.4 < -2.33\sqrt{.0289}\right) = P\left(\bar{X} < 76.4 - 0.3961\right) = P\left(\bar{X} < 76.00\right) = 1\%$. So there is only a 1% chance that the average policyholders will pass away more than 4.75 months (0.3961 years) early.

But what if X_i are *not* normally distributed? Strictly speaking, most random variables are not normally distributed. Are people's heights or weights normally distributed? Some people weigh hundreds of pounds above average, but no one weighs hundreds of pounds below average. Since heights and weights cannot be less than 0, they cannot range from $-\infty$ to $+\infty$. So strictly speaking, they are not normally distributed.

6.5.4 *Central limit theorem* (1930s)

Let X be a random variable having any distribution at all with a mean of μ and a variance of σ^2 with $-\infty < \mu < \infty$ and $0 < \sigma^2 < \infty$. We have a finite mean and a finite variance. Then the central limit theorem tells us that the probability distribution of $\bar{X}$ approaches that of a normal distribution as sample size n approaches infinity. As long as the underlying X has a finite mean and finite variance,[3] the sampling distribution of the sample mean will approach a normal distribution as the sample size gets larger and larger.

This theorem would not be very valuable if you needed an extremely large n before the probability distribution of $\bar{X}$ was remotely close to a normal distribution. But it turns out that $n = 25$ *or* 30 is usually all you need. This makes the central limit theorem very useful and celebrated. This is the most important theorem in statistics. This is also why the normal distribution is so popular.

The history of the central limit theorem dates to de Moivre (1733), Laplace (1812), and Lyapunov (1901). During the 1930s, progressively more general proofs of the central limit theorem were developed. Alan Turing (1934) proved the central limit theorem in his University of Cambridge dissertation only to find out later that the theorem had already been proved.

6.5.4.1 *Example*

Suppose your population has a unimodal (single peak) and symmetric distribution like a normal distribution with variance σ^2. Two unbiased estimators of the population mean are the sample mean and the sample median. The variance of the sample mean was shown to be $\frac{\sigma^2}{n}$. The variance of the sample median can be shown to be $\frac{\pi\sigma^2}{2n}$. We say the relative efficiency of two estimators, θ_1 and θ_2 is the ratio of their variances, $\frac{V(\theta_2)}{V(\theta_1)}$. The relative efficiency of the sample mean to the sample median is $\frac{\pi\sigma^2/2n}{\sigma^2/n} = \frac{\pi}{2} \approx 1.57$. Since the $\sqrt{\frac{\pi}{2}} \approx 1.25$, the standard deviation of the sample median will be about 25% larger than the standard deviation of the sample mean. Thus, the sample median is less efficient and more subject to sampling fluctuations. We prefer the sample mean. For non-normal distributions, the standard error of the median is difficult to compute.

---

[3]If the underlying Xs have a Cauchy distribution, all bets are off. Both the mean and the variance of a Cauchy distribution are undefined as we learned in the last chapter. But we generally do not face these unusual circumstances.

6.6 The Sampling Distribution of the Sample Variance

The population variance of a random variable X_i is

$$\sigma_x^2 = E[(X - \mu_x)^2] \tag{6.9}$$

Given a sample of n observations on X_i, how should we estimate the population variance σ_x^2?

The variance is the average squared deviation from the mean. We might think about using $\frac{1}{n}\sum (X_i - \mu_x)^2 = \frac{\sum(X_i-\mu_x)^2}{n}$. If we knew μ_x, this is exactly what we would do. But we generally do not know μ_x. Thus, we replace the population mean with the sample mean and define the sample variance as

$$s_x^2 = \frac{\sum (X_i - \bar{X})^2}{n-1} = \frac{1}{n-1}\sum (X_i - \bar{X})^2 \tag{6.10}$$

The reasons for this will become clear as we examine the nature of s_x^2. You should note that we divide by $n-1$ rather than by n. We divide by $n-1$ because we do not know the actual mean μ_x and use $\bar{X}$ as an estimate of the true population mean μ_x. By using $\bar{X}$, we are actually overfitting the data. So if we divided by n, we would underestimate the true variance. Since we had to estimate μ_x with the data, there is less independent information in the data for us to estimate the variance than would be indicated by the sample size n. We will see more on this in a moment.

We will use $s_x = \sqrt{s_x^2} = \sqrt{\frac{\sum(X_i-\bar{X})^2}{n-1}}$ as an estimate of the population standard deviation σ_x.

What is the sampling distribution of s_x^2? s_x^2 is a random variable with a probability distribution. We want to know something about the mean and variance of this distribution. We will begin by looking at the mean of s_x^2. We will find that $E\left[s_x^2\right] = \sigma_x^2$ and then go on to the variance of the distribution.

We have

$$s_x^2 = \frac{1}{n-1}\sum (X_i - \bar{X})^2$$

We begin with the summation term alone on the right. Let us add and subtract the population mean μ_x and manipulate:

$$\begin{aligned}
\sum(X_i - \bar{X})^2 &= \sum[(X_i - \mu_x) - (\bar{X} - \mu_x)]^2 \\
&= \sum\left[(X_i - \mu_x)^2 - 2(\bar{X} - \mu_x)(X_i - \mu_x) + (\bar{X} - \mu_x)^2\right] \\
&= \sum(X_i - \mu_x)^2 - 2(\bar{X} - \mu_x)\sum(X_i - \mu_x) + \sum(\bar{X} - \mu_x)^2 \\
&= \sum(X_i - \mu_x)^2 - 2(\bar{X} - \mu_x)(n\bar{X} - n\mu_x) + \sum(\bar{X} - \mu_x)^2 \\
&= \sum(X_i - \mu_x)^2 - 2n(\bar{X} - \mu_x)^2 + n(\bar{X} - \mu_x)^2 \\
&= \sum(X_i - \mu_x)^2 - n(\bar{X} - \mu_x)^2
\end{aligned}$$

So we have

$$\begin{aligned}
\sum(X_i - \bar{X})^2 &= \sum(X_i - \mu_x)^2 - n(\bar{X} - \mu_x)^2 \\
E\left[\sum(X_i - \bar{X})^2\right] &= E\left[\sum(X_i - \mu_x)^2\right] - nE\left[(\bar{X} - \mu_x)^2\right] \\
&= \sum[E[(X_i - \mu_x)^2]] - nE[(\bar{X} - \mu_x)^2] \\
&= \sum\sigma_x^2 - n\left(\frac{\sigma_x^2}{n}\right) = n\sigma_x^2 - \sigma_x^2 = (n-1)\sigma_x^2
\end{aligned} \tag{6.11}$$

So

$$E\left[\sum(X_i - \bar{X})^2\right] = (n-1)\sigma_x^2$$

Therefore, we have

$$\begin{aligned}
E\left[s_x^2\right] &= E\left[\frac{1}{n-1}\sum(X_i - \bar{X})^2\right] = \frac{1}{n-1}E\left[\sum(X_i - \bar{X})^2\right] \\
&= \frac{1}{n-1}(n-1)\sigma_x^2 = \sigma_x^2
\end{aligned} \tag{6.12}$$

and $s_x^2 = \frac{\sum(X_i - \bar{X})^2}{n-1}$ is an unbiased estimator of σ_x^2. This is why we divide by $(n-1)$.

What is the variance of s_x^2?

Recall that a chi-square random variable is the sum of the squares of n independent standard normal random variables. If $Z_i \sim N(0,1)$, then $\sum_n Z_i^2 \sim \chi_n^2$. Furthermore, the expected value of a chi-square random variable with n degrees of freedom is equal to n, and the variance is equal to $2n$. The mean of a χ_n^2 is $E[\chi_n^2] = n$ and the variance of a χ_n^2 is $V[\chi_n^2] = E[\chi_n^2 - n]^2 = 2n$.

If $X_i \sim N(\mu_x, \sigma_x^2)$, and $Z_i = \frac{X_i - \mu_x}{\sigma_x}$, we know that $\sum_n Z_i^2 = \sum(\frac{X_i-\mu_x}{\sigma_x})^2 \sim \chi_n^2$. Since $s_x^2 = \frac{\sum(X_i-\bar{X})^2}{n-1}$, we have $(n-1)s_x^2 = \sum(X_i - \bar{X})^2$. Dividing by σ_x^2, we get

$$\frac{(n-1)s_x^2}{\sigma_x^2} = \frac{\sum(X_i - \bar{X})^2}{\sigma_x^2} = \sum\left(\frac{X_i - \bar{X}}{\sigma_x}\right)^2$$

The random variable $\frac{(n-1)s_x^2}{\sigma_x^2} = \sum(\frac{X_i-\bar{X}}{\sigma_x})^2$ is very similar to $\sum(\frac{X_i-\mu_x}{\sigma_x})^2$. The only difference is that we have $\bar{X}$ in the expression instead of μ_x, and these two numbers should be pretty close to each other. Thus, we would expect their probability distributions to be very similar. While $\sum(\frac{X_i-\mu_x}{\sigma_x})^2 \sim \chi_n^2$, it turns out that $\frac{(n-1)s_x^2}{\sigma_x^2} = \sum(\frac{X_i-\bar{X}}{\sigma_x})^2 \sim \chi_{n-1}^2$. We lose a degree of freedom because of the uncertainty associated with our estimate of μ_x. Let us demonstrate that $\frac{(n-1)s_x^2}{\sigma_x^2} \sim \chi_{n-1}^2$.

Let us be more precise about the sampling distribution of s_x^2. We have $s_x^2 = \frac{1}{n-1}\sum(X_i - \bar{X})^2$. Let's look at the last summation term again. From equation 6.11, we have the following:

$$\sum(X_i - \bar{X})^2 = \sum(X_i - \mu_x)^2 - n(\bar{X} - \mu_x)^2$$

Divide everything by σ_x^2.

This gives us

$$\frac{\sum\left(X_i - \bar{X}\right)^2}{\sigma_x^2} = \frac{\sum(X_i - \mu_x)^2}{\sigma_x^2} - \frac{n\left(\bar{X} - \mu_x\right)^2}{\sigma_x^2}$$

$$\frac{\sum\left(X_i - \bar{X}\right)^2}{\sigma_x^2} = \frac{\sum(X_i - \mu_x)^2}{\sigma_x^2} - \frac{\left(\bar{X} - \mu_x\right)^2}{\sigma_x^2/n}$$

So $\frac{(n-1)s_x^2}{\sigma_x^2} = \frac{\sum(X_i-\bar{X})^2}{\sigma_x^2} = \frac{\sum(X_i-\mu_x)^2}{\sigma_x^2} - \frac{(\bar{X}-\mu_x)^2}{\sigma_x^2/n} = \sum(\frac{X_i-\mu_x}{\sigma_x})^2 - (\frac{\bar{X}-\mu_x}{\sigma_x/\sqrt{n}})^2$.

But $\sum(\frac{X_i-\mu_x}{\sigma_x})^2 \sim \chi_n^2$ and $(\frac{\bar{X}-\mu_x}{\sigma_x/\sqrt{n}})^2 \sim \chi_1^2$ since $\frac{\bar{X}-\mu_x}{\sigma_x/\sqrt{n}} \sim N(0,1)$.

So $\frac{(n-1)s_x^2}{\sigma_x^2} \sim \chi_n^2 - \chi_1^2 = \chi_{n-1}^2$

$$\frac{(n-1)\,s_x^2}{\sigma_x^2} \sim \chi_{n-1}^2 \tag{6.13}$$

Recall that $\chi_m^2 + \chi_n^2 = \chi_{m+n}^2$ or $\chi_m^2 = \chi_{m+n}^2 - \chi_n^2$. And please remember that we are assuming the population of X is normally distributed.

Since $\frac{(n-1)s_x^2}{\sigma_x^2} \sim \chi_{n-1}^2$, the variance of $\frac{(n-1)s_x^2}{\sigma_x^2} = 2(n-1)$. So we have $V(\chi_{n-1}^2) = V\left(\frac{(n-1)s_x^2}{\sigma_x^2}\right) = \frac{(n-1)^2}{\sigma_x^4}V(s_x^2) = 2(n-1)$, and so the variance of $s_x^2 = V(s_x^2) = \frac{2\sigma_x^4}{n-1}$. We also know that $E[\chi_{n-1}^2] = E\left[\frac{(n-1)s_x^2}{\sigma_x^2}\right] = n-1$ which implies that $E[s_x^2] = \sigma_x^2$ as we showed above. We have now derived the mean and the variance of s_x^2.

6.6.1 *Examples*

(1) We are concerned about income inequality. Assume family income in the U.S. is distributed normally with a mean of \$60K and a standard deviation of \$40K. Suppose we sample 20 families and measure the sample variance of their incomes, s_x^2. What is the probability that the sample variance will be bigger than 716?

$$\begin{aligned} P(s_x^2 > 716) &= P\left(\frac{(n-1)s_x^2}{\sigma_x^2} > \frac{(n-1)716}{\sigma_x^2}\right) \\ &= P\left(\chi_{20-1}^2 > \frac{(20-1)716}{1600}\right) = P(\chi_{19}^2 > 8.50) \\ &= 0.98 = 98\% \end{aligned}$$

(2) Suppose we are concerned about the variability of the number of raisins in a box of raisin bran. Assume that the number is distributed

normally. If a random sample of 16 boxes is taken, what is the probability that the sample variance will be more than twice the population variance?

$$P(s_x^2 > 2\sigma_x^2) = P\left(\frac{(n-1)s_x^2}{\sigma_x^2} > 2(n-1)\right) = P(\chi_{16-1}^2 > 2(16-1))$$
$$= P(\chi_{15}^2 > 30) = 1\%$$

6.7 The Sampling Distribution of the Population Proportion

In any election year, many, many polls are taken. Suppose you take a poll of 900 Americans and find that 279 identify as Democrats, 216 identify as Republicans, and 378 identify as Independents. How do we estimate the percent of Americans who identify as Independents? Our estimate, or sample proportion, would be $p = \frac{378}{900} = 0.42$ or 42%. What is the sampling distribution of the sample proportion? If we took this poll over and over, what would the distribution of p look like?

Let's start by thinking about this as a binomial distribution problem. Every time you interview someone, the person is either an independent or not an independent. Suppose that π represents the percent of all Americans who identify as an independent. You are trying to estimate π. (Please note that here π does NOT represent the ratio of the circumference to the diameter of a circle or 3.1415926.) We use π here to denote the percent of Americans who identify as an independent and is some number between 0 and 1.

In a survey of n Americans, let X be the number of Americans who identify as an independent. The count X has a binomial distribution with a probability of success equal to π. We know from the binomial distribution that

$$E[X] = \mu_x = n\pi$$
$$V[X] = \sigma_x^2 = n\pi(1-\pi)$$
$$\text{SD}(X) = \sigma_x = \sqrt{n\pi(1-\pi)}$$

Now the sample proportion $p = \frac{X}{n}$. We can figure out the mean and the variance of p:

$$E[p] = E\left[\frac{X}{n}\right] = \frac{1}{n}E[X] = \frac{1}{n}n\pi = \pi \tag{6.14}$$

$$V[p] = V\left[\frac{X}{n}\right] = \left(\frac{1}{n}\right)^2 V[X] = \left(\frac{1}{n}\right)^2 n\pi(1-\pi) = \frac{\pi(1-\pi)}{n} \tag{6.15}$$

$$\text{SD}[p] = \sqrt{\frac{\pi(1-\pi)}{n}} \tag{6.16}$$

We have the mean and the variance of the sampling distribution of p. But what kind of distribution do we have here? For a large enough sample, the distribution of p is normal. Ideally, the population should be more than 10 times larger than the sample to be sure our observations are independent. And we should have at least 10 successes and at least 10 failures in our sample, or $n\pi \geq 10$ and $n(1-\pi) \geq 10$ in expectation. Under these conditions, we can approximate the probability distribution of p with a normal distribution.

If $p = \frac{X}{n}$, then $p \approx N(\pi, \frac{\pi(1-\pi)}{n})$ for large enough n. It also follows that $Z = \frac{p-\pi}{\sqrt{\frac{\pi(1-\pi)}{n}}} \approx N(0,1)$ when we standardize the random variable p.

6.7.1 *Examples*

(1) Suppose that 38% of Americans believe in ghosts. If you randomly sample 180 Americans, what is the probability that more than 72 will believe in ghosts?

$$P\left(p > \frac{72}{180}\right) = P\left(p - \pi > \frac{72}{180} - \pi\right)$$
$$= P\left(\frac{p-\pi}{\sqrt{\frac{\pi(1-\pi)}{n}}} > \frac{\frac{72}{180} - \pi}{\sqrt{\frac{\pi(1-\pi)}{n}}}\right)$$

$$= P\left(Z > \frac{\frac{72}{180} - 0.38}{\sqrt{\frac{0.38(1-0.38)}{180}}}\right)$$

$$= P\,(Z > 0.553) = 0.29 = 29\%$$

(2) Suppose 60% of college students are female. If we randomly select 111 college students, what is the likelihood that majority will be male? Let p be the percent of our sample who is female:

$$P\,(p < .50) = P\,(p - \pi < 0.50 - \pi) = \left(\frac{p - \pi}{\sqrt{\frac{\pi(1-\pi)}{n}}} < \frac{0.5 - \pi}{\sqrt{\frac{\pi(1-\pi)}{n}}}\right)$$

$$= \left(Z < \frac{0.50 - 0.60}{\sqrt{\frac{0.60(1-0.60)}{111}}}\right)$$

$$= P\,(Z < -2.15) = 0.016 = 1.6\%$$

We have covered the probability distribution of the sample mean, the sample variance, and the sample proportion.

6.8 Exercises

(1) Suppose you sit near the entrance to the dining hall during the dinner hour and ask students to fill out a brief survey as they walk in. Some students fill out your survey and other students do not. Why might your sample be biased?

(2) Assume sumo wrestlers have an average weight of 328 lbs with a standard deviation of 52 lbs. If you randomly select six sumo wrestlers, what is the probability that they (all six together) will weigh over a ton? A short ton is 2,000 lbs. (0.4013)

(3) Suppose 66% of Americans support the legalization of marijuana. If we randomly survey 1,100 Americans, what is the probability that more than 750 people will say they support the legalization of marijuana? (.0633)

(4) Suppose newborn baby weights are normally distributed with a mean of 7.2 lbs and a standard deviation of 0.7 lbs. In a random sample of 20 newborn babies, what is the probability that the sample variance will be larger than 0.701? (0.10)

(5) Suppose that Faber College students exercise for 6.98 hours a week with a standard deviation of 6.35 hours. In a random survey of 10 students on their exercise habits, what is the probability that the sample mean $\bar{X}$ will exceed 8 hours? (0.306)

(6) Suppose the weights of bags of flour are normally distributed with a population standard deviation of $\sigma = 1.2$ ounces. Find the probability that a sample of 30 bags would have a sample standard deviation between 0.808 and 1.393 ounces. (0.85)

(7) In a sample of 23 basketball games, the Duncanville basketball team scores an average of 78.5 points with a sample variance of 176.3. What is the probability that the sample variance is less than 1/2 of the population variance? (0.025)

(8) Suppose that 63% of Americans say that guns make homes safer. In a random sample of 900 Americans, what is the probability that less than 550 will claim that having a gun makes them safer? (0.1324)

Chapter 7

Confidence Intervals

7.1 Introduction

Statistics means never having to say you are certain.

Suppose the average income of an American is some number μ, and we want to know what μ is. We might take a random sample of 25 Americans, ask them to report their income and calculate a sample mean $\bar{X} = \$50{,}752$. We now have an estimate of the population mean μ, but how sure are we of this estimate? Do we think the population mean is within a few dollars of \$50,752? Is it within a few hundred dollars or a few thousand dollars? How do we know? Can we say we are 95% sure that the population mean is within \$2,000 of our estimate or within \$5,000 of our estimate? Can we say we are 99% sure?

In this chapter, we will learn how to develop confidence intervals for four kinds of estimates. We will consider estimates of the population mean when we know the population variance and when we do not know the population variance. We will consider estimates of the population variance, and we will consider estimates of the population proportion.

7.2 Population Mean When We Know the Population Variance

We know that if $X_i \sim N(\mu, \sigma^2)$, then $\bar{X} \sim N\left(\mu, \frac{\sigma^2}{n}\right)$. Even if the X_i are not, strictly speaking, normally distributed, we know this is approximately true by the central limit theorem as long as the mean and variance are finite and the sample size n is reasonably large. And by reasonably large, we usually mean bigger than 30. By standardizing this random variable $\bar{X}$, we know that $\frac{\bar{X}-\mu}{\sqrt{\sigma^2/n}} = \frac{\bar{X}-\mu}{\sigma/\sqrt{n}} = Z \sim N(0,1)$.

Suppose you want a 90% confidence interval on your estimate of the population mean. From our standard normal tables, we know that

$$P(-1.645 < Z < 1.645) = 90\%$$

This means that

$$P\left(-1.645 < \frac{\bar{X}-\mu}{\sigma/\sqrt{n}} < 1.645\right) = 90\%$$

Multiply through by $\frac{\sigma}{\sqrt{n}}$

$$P\left(-1.645\frac{\sigma}{\sqrt{n}} < \bar{X} - \mu < 1.645\frac{\sigma}{\sqrt{n}}\right) = 90\%$$

Multiply by -1 noting that we need to invert the inequalities

$$P\left(1.645\frac{\sigma}{\sqrt{n}} > \mu - \bar{X} > -1.645\frac{\sigma}{\sqrt{n}}\right) = 90\%$$

Add $\bar{X}$ to all three terms in the parentheses

$$P\left(\bar{X} + 1.645\frac{\sigma}{\sqrt{n}} > \mu > \bar{X} - 1.645\frac{\sigma}{\sqrt{n}}\right) = 90\%$$

This can be rewritten as

$$P\left(\mu = \bar{X} \pm 1.645\frac{\sigma}{\sqrt{n}}\right) = 90\% \tag{7.1}$$

to give us a 90% confidence interval around our estimate $\bar{X}$.

7.2.1 *Examples*

(1) Suppose family incomes in the U.S. are normally distributed with a mean of μ and a population variance of 4 billion. You have a sample of 25 families and calculate a sample mean of \$90,021. What is the 90% confidence interval for the population mean?

$$P\left(\mu = \bar{X} \pm 1.645\frac{\sigma}{\sqrt{n}}\right) = 90\%$$

$$P\left(\mu = \$90{,}021 \pm 1.645\frac{63{,}245}{\sqrt{25}}\right) = 90\%$$

Since $\sigma = \sqrt{\sigma^2} = \sqrt{4 \text{ billion}} = 63{,}245$

$$P(\mu = \$90{,}021 \pm 20{,}808) = 90\%$$

$$P(\$69{,}213 < \mu < \$110{,}829) = 90\%$$

(2) What happens if the population variance is 8 billion? If there is a lot more income inequality in the general population, it is more likely for us to have drawn extreme observations in our sample. So we are less certain about our estimate:

$$P\left(\mu = \bar{X} \pm 1.645\frac{\sigma}{\sqrt{n}}\right) = 90\%$$

$$P\left(\mu = \$90{,}021 \pm 1.645\frac{89{,}443}{\sqrt{25}}\right) = 90\%$$

Since $\sigma = \sqrt{\sigma^2} = \sqrt{8 \text{ billion}} = 89{,}443$

$$P(\mu = \$90{,}021 \pm 29{,}427) = 90\%$$

$$P(\$60{,}594 < \mu < \$119{,}448) = 90\%$$

(3) What happens if the sample size is 50? Assume the population variance is 4 billion. If our sample size is larger, we have more data and should be more certain about our estimates:

$$P\left(\mu = \bar{X} \pm 1.645\frac{\sigma}{\sqrt{n}}\right) = 90\%$$

$$P\left(\mu = \$90{,}021 \pm 1.645\frac{63{,}245}{\sqrt{50}}\right) = 90\%$$

Since $\sigma = \sqrt{\sigma^2} = \sqrt{4 \text{ billion}} = 63{,}245$

$$P(\mu = \$90{,}021 \pm 14{,}713) = 90\%$$

$$P(\$75{,}308 < \mu < \$104{,}734) = 90\%$$

Instead of a 90% confidence interval, suppose you want a 95% confidence interval. We know from our standard normal tables that $P(-1.96 < Z < 1.96) = 95\%$

This means that

$$P\left(-1.96 < \frac{\bar{X} - \mu}{\sigma/\sqrt{n}} < 1.96\right) = 95\%$$

Multiply through by $\frac{\sigma}{\sqrt{n}}$

$$P\left(-1.96\frac{\sigma}{\sqrt{n}} < \bar{X} - \mu < 1.96\frac{\sigma}{\sqrt{n}}\right) = 95\%$$

Multiply by -1

$$P\left(1.96\frac{\sigma}{\sqrt{n}} > \mu - \bar{X} > -1.96\frac{\sigma}{\sqrt{n}}\right) = 95\%$$

Add $\bar{X}$ to all three terms

$$P\left(\bar{X} + 1.96\frac{\sigma}{\sqrt{n}} > \mu > \bar{X} - 1.96\frac{\sigma}{\sqrt{n}}\right) = 95\%$$

This can be rewritten as

$$P\left(\mu = \bar{X} \pm 1.96\frac{\sigma}{\sqrt{n}}\right) = 95\% \tag{7.2}$$

Suppose family incomes in the U.S. are normally distributed with a mean of μ and a population variance of 4 billion as above. You have a sample of 25 families and calculate a sample mean of \$90,021. What is the 95% confidence interval for the population mean?

$$P\left(\mu = \bar{X} \pm 1.96\frac{\sigma}{\sqrt{n}}\right) = 95\%$$

$$P\left(\mu = \$90{,}021 \pm 1.96\frac{63{,}245}{\sqrt{25}}\right) = 95\%$$

since $\sigma = \sqrt{\sigma^2} = \sqrt{4 \text{ billion}} = 63{,}245$.

$$P(\mu = \$90{,}021 \pm 24{,}792) = 95\%$$

$$P(\$65{,}229 < \mu < \$114{,}813) = 95\%$$

You will note that our confidence intervals will become larger for a number of reasons. If the population variance increases, we will be less certain of our estimates. There is more noise in the population, so it becomes harder to estimate anything. If the sample size decreases, we will be less certain of our estimates. We have less information, so we will be less certain. Or if we want a 95% confidence interval rather than a 90% confidence interval, the size of the confidence interval will increase.

If you want an 80% confidence interval, you would start with the fact that $P(-1.282 < Z < 1.282) = 80\%$. If you want a 99% confidence interval, you would start with $P(-2.576 < Z < 2.576) = 99\%$. Whatever the desired level of confidence, you can look up the appropriate critical values from the standard normal tables.

You should note that the higher the level of confidence you want, the wider the confidence interval will be. If you want to be 100% sure, then the confidence interval will be $(-\infty, +\infty)$ You can be certain that the population parameter will be within this interval.

7.3 Population Mean When We Do not Know the Population Variance (the Usual Case)

The above confidence intervals are all well and good except that in practice we will generally not know the true population variance. Why would we know the population variance but not know the mean? What do we do if we don't know the true population variance?

Now we have $X_i \sim N(\mu, \sigma^2)$, but both the mean μ and the variance σ^2 are unknown. This is the usual situation we will face in real life. First, we know that $\bar{X} \sim N\left(\mu, \frac{\sigma^2}{n}\right)$ so that by standardizing we have $\frac{\bar{X}-\mu}{\sqrt{\sigma^2/n}} = \frac{\bar{X}-\mu}{\sigma/\sqrt{n}} = Z \sim N(0,1)$ as before. We also know from the previous chapter that $\frac{(n-1)s_x^2}{\sigma^2}$ has a chi-square distribution with

$n-1$ degrees of freedom, $\frac{(n-1)s_x^2}{\sigma^2} \sim \chi^2_{n-1}$ where $s_x^2 = \frac{\sum(X_i-\bar{X})^2}{n-1}$. Now recall the definition of the Student's t-distribution. If $Z \sim N(0,1)$ and $W \sim \chi^2_n$, then $\frac{Z}{\sqrt{W/n}} = \Psi_n \sim$ Student's t with n degrees of freedom. Or if $Z \sim N(0,1)$ and $W \sim \chi^2_{n-1}$, then $\frac{Z}{\sqrt{W/(n-1)}} = \Psi_{n-1} \sim$ Student's t with $n-1$ degrees of freedom. We have our standard normal and we have our chi-square random variables above. We have $Z = \frac{\bar{X}-\mu}{\sigma/\sqrt{n}} \sim N(0,1)$ and $W = \frac{(n-1)s_x^2}{\sigma^2} \sim \chi^2_{n-1}$. So

$$\begin{aligned}\frac{Z}{\sqrt{W/(n-1)}} &= \frac{N(0,1)}{\sqrt{\chi^2_{n-1}/(n-1)}} = \frac{\frac{\bar{X}-\mu}{\sigma/\sqrt{n}}}{\sqrt{\frac{(n-1)s_x^2}{\sigma^2}\Big/(n-1)}} \\ &= \frac{\frac{\bar{X}-\mu}{\sigma/\sqrt{n}}}{\sqrt{\frac{s_x^2}{\sigma^2}}} = \frac{\bar{X}-\mu}{\sqrt{s_x^2/n}} \\ &= \frac{\bar{X}-\mu}{s_x/\sqrt{n}} \sim \text{Student's } t \text{ with } n-1 \text{ degrees of freedom}\end{aligned} \tag{7.3}$$

Since we don't know the population variance, the next best alternative is to estimate the population variance. We estimate the population variance with the sample variance, $s_x^2 = \frac{1}{n-1}\sum(X_i - \bar{X})^2$, and replace the population standard deviation with the sample standard deviation in our confidence interval equation. We have

$$\frac{\bar{X}-\mu}{\sigma/\sqrt{n}} \quad \text{vs} \quad \frac{\bar{X}-\mu}{s_x/\sqrt{n}} \tag{7.4}$$

But since we have some uncertainty regarding s_x, our estimate of the population standard deviation σ, this statistic on the right no longer has a standard normal distribution. The statistic has a Student's t-distribution. This is very similar to the normal, but the additional uncertainty is reflected in the fatter tails of the Student's t-distribution.

Now suppose we have a sample of size 30. We will be interested in the Student's t-distribution with $n-1$ degrees of freedom. In this case, we will have $30 - 1 = 29$ degrees of freedom. If we want a 90% confidence interval, we would look up the following from our Student's t tables. If Ψ_{29} has a Student's t-distribution with 29 degrees of freedom, we have

$$P(-1.699 < \Psi_{29} < 1.699) = 90\%$$

This means that

$$P\left(-1.699 < \frac{\bar{X} - \mu}{s/\sqrt{n}} < 1.699\right) = 90\%$$

Multiply through by $\frac{s}{\sqrt{n}}$

$$P\left(-1.699\frac{s}{\sqrt{n}} < \bar{X} - \mu < 1.699\frac{s}{\sqrt{n}}\right) = 90\%$$

Multiply by -1 noting that we need to invert the inequalities

$$P\left(1.699\frac{s}{\sqrt{n}} > \mu - \bar{X} > -1.699\frac{s}{\sqrt{n}}\right) = 90\%$$

Add $\bar{X}$ to all three terms

$$P\left(\bar{X} + 1.699\frac{s}{\sqrt{n}} > \mu > \bar{X} - 1.699\frac{s}{\sqrt{n}}\right) = 90\%$$

We can rewrite this as

$$P\left(\mu = \bar{X} \pm 1.699\frac{s}{\sqrt{n}}\right) = 90\% \tag{7.5}$$

when $n = 30$.

Suppose family incomes in the U.S. are normally distributed with a mean of μ and a variance σ^2, both unknown. We have a sample of 30 families and calculate a sample mean of \$90,021 and a sample variance of 5 billion. What is the 90% confidence interval for the population mean?

$$P\left(\mu = \bar{X} \pm 1.699\frac{s}{\sqrt{n}}\right) = 90\%$$

$$P\left(\mu = \$90{,}021 \pm 1.699\frac{70{,}711}{\sqrt{30}}\right) = 90\%$$

since $s = \sqrt{s^2} = \sqrt{5 \text{ billion}} = 70{,}711$.

$$P(\mu = \$90{,}021 \pm 21{,}934) = 90\%$$
$$P(\$68{,}087 < \mu < \$111{,}955) = 90\%$$

This is our 90% confidence interval. If we want a 95% confidence interval, and we have a sample of 30 observations, we go to your Student's t tables and look for $n - 1 = 30 - 1 = 29$ degrees of freedom:

$$P(-2.045 < \Psi_{29} < 2.045) = 95\%$$
$$P\left(-2.045 < \frac{\bar{X} - \mu}{s/\sqrt{n}} < 2.045\right) = 95\%$$

Move terms around to get

$$P\left(\mu = \bar{X} \pm 2.045\frac{s}{\sqrt{n}}\right) = 95\%$$
$$P\left(\mu = \$90{,}021 \pm 2.045\frac{70{,}711}{\sqrt{30}}\right) = 95\%$$

since $s = \sqrt{s^2} = \sqrt{5 \text{ billion}} = 70{,}711$.

$$P(\mu = \$90{,}021 \pm 26{,}400) = 95\%$$
$$P(\$63{,}620 < \mu < \$116{,}422) = 95\%$$

This is our 95% confidence interval. Note it is wider than our 90% confidence interval. When we don't know the population variance, we use the Student's t-distribution rather than the standard normal distribution.

7.4 Population Variance

Suppose family incomes in the U.S. are normally distributed with a mean of μ and a variance σ^2, both unknown. You have a sample of 25 families and calculate a sample mean of \$90,021 and a sample variance of 5 billion. What is the 90% confidence interval for the population variance, a measure of the amount of income inequality?

Our estimate is 5 billion. But the true population variance could be larger or smaller. How certain are we that it is 5 billion rather than 7 billion or 10 billion?

We learned in the last chapter that $\frac{(n-1)s_x^2}{\sigma_x^2} \sim \chi^2_{n-1}$ (chi-square distribution with $n-1$ degrees of freedom) where the sample variance $s_x^2 = \frac{\sum(X_i-\bar{X})^2}{n-1}$ and σ_x^2 is the true population variance. In our example above, we have a sample size of $n = 25$. So we know that $\frac{(n-1)s_x^2}{\sigma_x^2} \sim \chi^2_{25-1} = \chi^2_{24}$. If we look at our chi-square tables in our Appendix,[1] we can find the following about the distribution of χ^2_{24}:

$$P(12.4 < \chi^2_{24} < 39.4) = 95\%$$
$$P(0 < \chi^2_{24} < 36.4) = 95\%$$
$$P(13.9 < \chi^2_{24} < \infty) = 95\%$$

All three of these statements are true. If you think about it, you will realize that there are an infinite number of intervals with a 95% probability. We could put 2.5% of the probability on both tails, or 5% on one tail and 0% on the other tail, or 4% on one tail and 1% on the other tail. While the general practice is to put 2.5% on each tail, all of these are perfectly legitimate. So let's start with a more general statement. For some constants, a and b, the following will be true:

$$P(a < \chi^2_{24} < b) = 95\%$$
$$P\left(a < \frac{(n-1)s_x^2}{\sigma_x^2} < b\right) = 95\%$$

Let's invert all three elements and reverse the inequalities:

$$P\left(\frac{1}{a} > \frac{\sigma_x^2}{(n-1)s_x^2} > \frac{1}{b}\right) = 95\%$$

Multiply through by $(n-1)s_x^2$

$$P\left(\frac{(n-1)s_x^2}{a} > \sigma_x^2 > \frac{(n-1)s_x^2}{b}\right) = 95\%$$

[1]Not all chi-square tables will provide all this information, but online tables certainly will. Some tables will only give you the upper tail probabilities.

Or if you like the smaller quantities on the left,

$$P\left(\frac{(n-1)s_x^2}{b} < \sigma_x^2 < \frac{(n-1)s_x^2}{a}\right) = 95\% \tag{7.6}$$

We can plug in the appropriate values for a, b, and s_x^2, and we have our 95% confidence interval on the true population variance σ_x^2:

$$P(12.4 < \chi_{24}^2 < 39.4) = 95\%$$

$$P\left(12.4 < \frac{(n-1)s_x^2}{\sigma_x^2} < 39.4\right) = 95\%$$

$$P\left(\frac{1}{12.4} > \frac{\sigma_x^2}{(n-1)s_x^2} > \frac{1}{39.4}\right) = 95\%$$

$$P\left(\frac{(25-1)s_x^2}{39.4} < \sigma_x^2 < \frac{(25-1)s_x^2}{12.4}\right) = 95\%$$

$$P\left(\frac{(25-1)5}{39.4} < \sigma_x^2 < \frac{(25-1)5}{12.4}\right) = 95\%$$

$$P(3.046 < \sigma_x^2 < 9.68) = 95\%$$

We can also report the following 95% confidence intervals. Since

$$P(0 < \chi_{24}^2 < 36.4) = 95\%$$

$$P\left(0 < \frac{(n-1)s_x^2}{\sigma_x^2} < 36.4\right) = 95\%$$

we have

$$P(3.30 < \sigma_x^2 < \infty) = 95\%$$

And since we also have

$$P(13.9 < \chi_{24}^2 < \infty) = 95\%$$

$$P\left(13.9 < \frac{(n-1)s_x^2}{\sigma_x^2} < \infty\right) = 95\%$$

$$P(0 < \sigma_x^2 < 8.63) = 95\%$$

we have three 95% confidence intervals. These are all legitimate confidence intervals, though some of them might look a little strange.

There are an infinite number of 95% confidence intervals for any estimate depending on how you want to distribute the 5% probability across the two tails. Your statistics professor will probably accept any of these because they are all correct. But your boss at work will probably want you to put half the probability on each tail.

If we want a 90% confidence interval with a sample size of 25, we could start with the following statement about the chi-square distribution with $n-1=24$ degrees of freedom:

$$P(13.9 < \chi^2_{24} < 36.4) = 90\%$$

$$P\left(13.9 < \frac{(n-1)s_x^2}{\sigma_x^2} < 36.4\right) = 90\%$$

$$P\left(\frac{(25-1)s_x^2}{36.4} < \sigma_x^2 < \frac{(25-1)s_x^2}{13.9}\right) = 90\%$$

$$P(3.30 < \sigma_x^2 < 8.63) = 90\%$$

7.5 Population Proportion

Suppose you are interested in knowing what percent of adults in this world have bank accounts. You randomly select 1,000 adults around the world, and you ask them whether or not they have a bank account. Of your 1,000 respondents, 690 have bank accounts. So your estimate of the percent of adults who have bank accounts would be $\frac{690}{1{,}000} = 69\%$. Of course, 69% is just an estimate. How certain are you of this estimate? Could the true percentage be much higher or much lower?

In general, suppose X people out of your sample of size n have a particular characteristic. Your estimate of the percent of the population with this characteristic is $p = \frac{X}{n}$. In the last chapter, we learned that if $p = \frac{X}{n}$, then $p \approx N\left(\pi, \frac{\pi(1-\pi)}{n}\right)$ for large enough n. It follows that $\frac{p-\pi}{\sqrt{\frac{\pi(1-\pi)}{n}}} = Z \approx N(0,1)$.

We know from our standard normal tables that

$$P(-1.645 < Z < 1.645) = 90\%$$

This means that

$$P\left(-1.645 < \frac{p-\pi}{\sqrt{\frac{\pi(1-\pi)}{n}}} < 1.645\right) = 90\%$$

Multiply through by $\sqrt{\frac{\pi(1-\pi)}{n}}$

$$P\left(-1.645\sqrt{\frac{\pi(1-\pi)}{n}} < p-\pi < 1.645\sqrt{\frac{\pi(1-\pi)}{n}}\right) = 90\%$$

Multiply by -1 noting that we need to invert the inequalities

$$P\left(1.645\sqrt{\frac{\pi(1-\pi)}{n}} > \pi - p > -1.645\sqrt{\frac{\pi(1-\pi)}{n}}\right) = 90\%$$

Add p to all three terms

$$P\left(p + 1.645\sqrt{\frac{\pi(1-\pi)}{n}} > \pi > p - 1.645\sqrt{\frac{\pi(1-\pi)}{n}}\right) = 90\%$$

We can rewrite this as

$$P\left(\pi = p \pm 1.645\sqrt{\frac{\pi(1-\pi)}{n}}\right) = 90\% \tag{7.7}$$

So we have surveyed 1,000 adults and found that 690 respondents had bank accounts. Thus, our estimate of the proportion of adults with bank accounts was $\frac{690}{1{,}000} = .69 = 69\%$. What is our 90% confidence interval of this estimate?

$$P\left(\pi = p \pm 1.645\sqrt{\frac{\pi(1-\pi)}{n}}\right) = 90\%$$

$$P\left(\pi = .69 \pm 1.645\sqrt{\frac{.69(1-.69)}{1{,}000}}\right) = 90\%$$

$$P(\pi = .690 \pm .024) \cong 90\%$$

Please note that we do not know the true value of π and used our estimated value of p in the equation. Thus, this confidence interval is an approximation. If you try various estimates of p in the neighborhood of 0.69, you will see that the margin of error will not change very much. So for practical purposes, we are pretty comfortable with this approximation.

If we are interested in a 95% confidence interval, we would observe the following from our standard normal tables:

$$P(1.96 < Z < 1.96) = 95\%$$

This means that

$$P\left(-1.96 < \frac{p-\pi}{\sqrt{\frac{\pi(1-\pi)}{n}}} < 1.96\right) = 95\%$$

Multiply through by $\sqrt{\frac{\pi(1-\pi)}{n}}$ to get

$$P\left(-1.96\sqrt{\frac{\pi(1-\pi)}{n}} < p-\pi < 1.96\sqrt{\frac{\pi(1-\pi)}{n}}\right) = 95\%$$

Multiply by -1 noting that we need to invert the inequalities

$$P\left(1.96\sqrt{\frac{\pi(1-\pi)}{n}} > \pi - p > -1.96\sqrt{\frac{\pi(1-\pi)}{n}}\right) = 95\%$$

Add p to all three terms

$$P\left(p + 1.96\sqrt{\frac{\pi(1-\pi)}{n}} > \pi > p - 1.96\sqrt{\frac{\pi(1-\pi)}{n}}\right) = 95\%$$

This can be rewritten as

$$P\left(\pi = p \pm 1.96\sqrt{\frac{\pi(1-\pi)}{n}}\right) = 95\% \tag{7.8}$$

You will often see the results of polls on the evening news and in the newspaper. For example, a poll might report that 57% of Americans support a ban on the sale of semi-automatic weapons with a margin of error of 3.6%. Where does this 3.6% number come from?

Suppose you poll about 725 Americans on the sale of semi-automatic weapons. And suppose you find that 57% of your sample supports the ban, and 43% are on the other side. What is your 95% confidence interval on your estimate of the population proportion? We know the following:

$$P\left(\pi = p \pm 1.96\sqrt{\frac{\pi(1-\pi)}{n}}\right) = 95\%$$

$$P\left(\pi = .57 \pm 1.96\sqrt{\frac{.57(.43)}{725}}\right) = 95\%$$

$$P(\pi = .57 \pm .036) = 95\%$$

Suppose you poll 1,000 people on some issue. If the issue is controversial, about half of Americans will be on one side and half will be on the other side:

$$P\left(\pi = p \pm 1.96\sqrt{\frac{\pi(1-\pi)}{n}}\right) = 95\%$$

$$P\left(\pi = .50 \pm 1.96\sqrt{\frac{.5(.5)}{1000}}\right) = 95\%$$

$$P\left(\pi = .50 \pm .031\right) = 95\%$$

This is why poll results typically have a margin of error of 3% or 3.5%. Firms will poll anywhere from 600 to 1,000 people. And if public opinion is fairly split with π close to 50%, you will get a margin of error in this range. If public opinion is not split, no one is going to bother doing a poll. Why would anyone poll 1,000 people and ask them if they think puppies are cute?

How many people do we need to poll to get the margin of error down to 2% with 95% confidence? Assuming we are polling people on a controversial issue, we need the following to happen:

$$1.96\sqrt{\frac{.5(.5)}{n}} = 0.02$$

$$n = 2{,}401$$

And if we want a margin of error of just 1%,

$$1.96\sqrt{\frac{.5(.5)}{n}} = 0.01$$
$$n = 9{,}604$$

We "just" need to survey 1,000 people to get a margin of error of around 3%. But if we want a margin of error of 2%, we need to survey over 2,400 people. This will more than double our survey costs. And if we want a margin of error of 1%, we need to survey close to 10,000 people. That will really blow our budget. It also takes a lot of time to reach 10,000 people. Since public opinion changes over time, you cannot take a few months surveying people. The costs can rise very quickly.

7.6 Final Thoughts

To summarize this chapter, we can derive confidence intervals in the following four cases by observing the following relationships:

If we want a confidence interval on the population mean when the true variance is known, we use the fact that $\frac{\bar{X}-\mu}{\sigma/\sqrt{n}} \sim N(0,1)$.

If we want a confidence interval on the population mean when the true variance is unknown, we use the fact that $\frac{\bar{X}-\mu}{s_x/\sqrt{n}} \sim$ Student t with $n-1$ degrees of freedom.

If we want a confidence interval on the population variance, we use the fact that $\frac{(n-1)s_x^2}{\sigma_x^2} \sim \chi^2_{n-1}$.

And if we want a confidence interval on a population proportion, we use the fact that $p \sim N\left(\pi, \frac{p(1-p)}{n}\right)$.

The size of the confidence interval depends on several factors. If your sample size increases, the confidence interval will narrow. If the population variance is smaller, your confidence interval will narrow. If you only want 80% confidence rather than 90% confidence, the confidence interval will narrow.

Most people are more certain of their estimates than they should be. When you ask people to come up with 90% confidence intervals for various quantities, they will be wrong more than 10% of the time. For example, please write down 90% confidence intervals for the following from the top of your head:

(1) Martin Luther King's age at death,
(2) length of the Nile River (in miles),
(3) number of countries in OPEC,
(4) number of books in the Old Testament,
(5) diameter of the moon (in miles),
(6) weight of an empty Boeing 747 (in pounds),
(7) year in which Wolfgang Amadeus Mozart was born,
(8) gestation period for an Asian elephant (in days),
(9) air distance from London to Tokyo (in miles), and
(10) deepest known point in the ocean (in feet).

You can Google the correct answers and see how you did. You should have gotten nine out of the ten correct. If you got all 10 correct, then you were probably using 100% confidence intervals, not 90% confidence intervals. But most people find that their 90% confidence intervals are generally correct about 50% of the time and that their 98% confidence intervals are generally correct about 60% of the time. People are generally more confident of their estimates than they should be. Outcomes people indicate as being certain to occur happen about 80% of the time. And outcomes people deem as being impossible occur about 20% of the time.

In this chapter, we explained how to derive confidence intervals which look like the following:

$$P(3.30 < \sigma_x^2 < 8.63) = 90\%$$

Some people may be uncomfortable with this kind of probability statement. The population variance, σ_x^2, is some number. This number is either between 3.30 and 8.63 or it is not between these two numbers. It cannot be between these two numbers 90% of the time. It will be between those numbers 100% of the time or 0% of the time.

Confidence intervals need to be interpreted properly. If we gather the sample data again, calculate a new sample variance, work out a new confidence interval, and do this over and over and over, then 90% of the time, our confidence interval would contain the true population variance, and 10% of the time it would not. The confidence is not really about this particular interval. It is about all the intervals we would generate if we did the same experiment over and over and over.

7.7 Exercises

(1) The credit card debt of customers at Fidelity Fiduciary Bank has a population standard deviation of \$3,800. How big a sample is needed to estimate the mean debt with 95% confidence and a tolerable error of \$100? of \$200? (5548, 1387)

(2) Campus security is concerned about crime. A random sample of 15 campus thefts shows that the mean amount stolen was \$332 with a sample standard deviation of \$136. Construct a 90% confidence interval for the mean stolen amount for all such thefts. (270.16, 393.84)

(3) A pharmaceutical firm is bringing out a new sleeping pill. It is tested on a random sample of 18 people. The sample standard deviation of the time to sleep turns out to be 11 minutes. Construct an 80% confidence interval for the population variance of the time to sleep. (95.23, ∞)

(4) According to a Gallup poll, 76% of men and 65% of women claim to be "in love" with someone. The poll surveyed 502 men and 500 women by telephone.

    (a) Construct a 90% confidence interval for the proportion of men "in love."
    (b) Construct a 95% confidence interval for the proportion of women "in love." $(\pm 0.0313, \pm 0.0418)$

(5) In a random survey of 25 professional female tennis players, you find an average age of 25.6 years with a standard deviation of 3.8 years. Find the 95% confidence interval on the population variance. $(8.79, 27.95)$

(6) In a random survey of 850 people in Nigeria, 306 report having Internet access. What is the estimate of the percent of Nigerians who have Internet access? What is the 95% confidence interval on this estimate? (0.36 ± 0.0323)

(7) What happens to the width of the confidence interval as

   (a) the sample size increases
   (b) the variance of the population increases
   (c) the desired level of confidence increases (narrower, wider, wider)

(8) We know by the LLN that as the number of trials increases we get closer and closer to the mean. Suppose a coin is flipped 9,999 times with the coin landing on heads 4,998 times and tails 5,001 times. What is the probability that the next coin flip will land on heads? (0.50)

Chapter 8

Hypothesis Testing

8.1 Introduction

All knowledge is human belief, more accurately human opinion. What often happens in physical sciences is that there is a high degree of conformity of opinion. When this occurs, the opinion held by most is asserted to be an objective fact, and those who doubt it are labeled "nuts." But history is replete with examples of opinions losing majority status, with once objective "truths" shrinking into the dark corners of social intercourse.

—Ed Leamer, Economics, UCLA

On 4 July 2012, the ATLAS and CMS experiments at CERN's Large Hadron Collider in Switzerland announced they had each observed a new particle in the mass region around 126 GeV. This particle is consistent with the Higgs boson predicted by the Standard Model.

In the previous chapter, we learned about confidence intervals. We can make probability statements like $P(119.6 \text{ GeV} < \mu < 133.3 \text{ GeV}) = 90\%$. We might say that based on the available data, we are 90% sure that the mass μ is between 119.6 GeV and 133.3 GeV. We might say that based on the available data, we are 90% sure that this theory is true. A Bayesian would be comfortable with this. But a classical objectivist would not. A theory is either true or not true. It can't be true 90% of the time and false 10% of the time.

With hypothesis testing, we will take a different approach. Instead of asking "what is the probability that a theory is true given the observed data,"

$$P[\text{Theory is true} \mid \text{Observed data}] = ?$$

we will ask "what is the probability of seeing the observed data if the theory is true."

$$P[\text{Observed data} \mid \text{Theory is true}] = ?$$

Hypothesis tests are tests by statistical contradiction. If the theory is true, we can say that the sample data are likely to look like this and unlikely to look like that. If the sample data are of the likely kind, then the theory is supported. If the sample data are of the unlikely kind, then the theory is weakened. We can never be 100% sure of anything since unlikely things happen all the time.

8.2 Types of Errors

We begin by observing that there are two types of errors we can make. If we want to go out on Friday night, we might worry about two types of errors: We might ask someone out only to have them say "no." Or we might choose not to ask someone out who would have said "yes." Somehow we need to navigate between these two errors much like Odysseus had to navigate between Scylla and Charybdis. Perhaps we are guided by Alfred Tennyson's words "Tis better to have loved and lost, / Than never to have loved at all."

A **Type I error** is when a true hypothesis is rejected. A **Type II error** is when a false hypothesis is accepted. We would prefer not to make either of these kinds of errors.

When the government distributes welfare checks, we assume that most people are not needy. A stereotypical conservative is worried about a Type I error when the undeserving get welfare checks. A stereotypical liberal is worried about a Type II error when some needy folks do not get welfare checks.

When the government hands out criminal punishments, we assume people are innocent until proven guilty. A stereotypical liberal is worried about a Type I error when innocent people go to jail. And a stereotypical conservative is worried about a Type II error when guilty people are set free.

The FDA does not approve new drugs until the drugs are proven effective. The FDA assumes that new drugs are not effective. A Type I error would occur if the FDA approves a bad drug. A Type II error would occur if the FDA does not approve a good drug.

Blaise Pascal considered a wager on God's existence. A Type I error would be to accept God and act accordingly when God does not exist. And a Type II error would be to reject God and act accordingly when God does exist.

The probability of a Type I error is denoted by α, the significance level of the test. The probability of a Type II error is denoted by β. $(1-\beta)$ is called the power of the test. We would like to make α and β as small as possible. We can do this by gathering more information. But holding the amount of information constant, decreasing α means increasing β and visa versa (see Table 8.1).

Table 8.1. States of nature.

Decision	Null Hypothesis is True	Null Hypothesis is False
Accept Null	Correct Decision Probability $= 1 - \alpha$	Type II Error Probability $= \beta$
Reject Null	Type I Error Probability $= \alpha$ Significance Level of the Test	Correct Decision Probability $=$ $1 - \beta$ Power of Test

8.3 Hypothesis Testing

Let us begin with a nonstatistical example. Suppose a person is indicted for a crime and is being tried in a court of law. We are entertaining two hypotheses. The **null hypothesis** is a claim that is assumed to be true until it is declared false. In a court of law, the null hypothesis, denoted H_0, is that the person is innocent. The **alternative hypothesis**, denoted H_A, the claim we will adopt if the null hypothesis is rejected, is that the person is guilty.

Hypothesis testing procedures are conservative in nature. We assume the world is flat until we have enough evidence to suggest otherwise. We assume you are innocent until proven guilty. We use the old medicine until the new ones are proven to be better.[1] We do not accept new theories until we find evidence to support them. We will stick with the status quo until enough evidence suggests otherwise.

How much evidence do we need to reject the null hypothesis H_0? In a court of law, there are various standards. It could be "preponderance of the evidence," "clear and convincing evidence," or "beyond a reasonable doubt." If we do not ask for enough evidence before convicting someone, we will make a lot of Type I errors and send many innocent people to jail. If we ask for too much evidence before convicting someone, we will make a lot of Type II errors and set a lot of guilty people free. We need to find the right balance. In practice, we will choose the probability of a Type I error we are comfortable with, keeping in mind the implied probability of a Type II error.

8.3.1 *Hypothesis testing procedure*

There are five steps to formal hypothesis testing:

(1) We first state the null hypothesis and the alternative hypothesis. The null hypothesis, denoted H_0, is the statement being tested. It is usually a statement of "no effect" or "no difference" and reflects the status quo. We assume the null hypothesis is true until we have enough evidence to suggest otherwise. The alternative hypothesis, denoted H_A, is the hypothesis we accept if the given data do not conform with the null hypothesis.

(2) We choose the significance level of the test α. This is the probability of a Type I error. We usually set $\alpha = 5\%$. But we should report enough information so that a third party could choose their own level of α in order to make their own decisions.

---

[1] This is not quite correct. The FDA will approve a new drug if it is better than a placebo. You might only be interested in a new drug if it is better than the old drug. But all drugs have side effects and have different levels of efficacy on different people. So a drug that is better for you may not be better for someone else.

(3) Based on α, we need to determine the rejection region and acceptance region for our test statistic. This may be a $N(0,1)$, Student's t-statistic, an F statistic, or a chi-square statistic. We may have a one-tailed test or a two-tailed test. If our alternative hypothesis involves a "not equal" sign ($\neq$), then we will have a two-tailed test. If our alternative hypothesis involves a greater than sign ($>$ or $\geq$) or a less than sign ($<$ or $\leq$), we will have a one-tailed test. We will use a statistical table or go online to find the critical values.
(4) We calculate the test statistic using our sample data. The test statistic may have a $N(0,1)$, Student's t, F, or a chi-square distribution. We want to see if the test statistic falls in the rejection region or the acceptance region.
(5) We make a decision. If the test statistic falls in the rejection region, we will reject the null hypothesis in favor of the alternative hypothesis. We say the result is statistically significant at the α% level. If the test statistic falls in the acceptance region, we will not reject the null hypothesis.

Let's work through four different situations.

8.4 Testing Hypotheses About the Population Mean When the Population Variance Is Known

Suppose Key Review, an SAT prep course, claims to be able to improve your SAT score. In order to test their claim, we randomly select 25 high school students to take the Key Review course and have them take the SAT exam. After the course, their average score is 535. Is this enough evidence to conclude that the Key Review course is effective? We know that SAT scores are normally distributed with a mean of 500 and a variance of 10,000 by construction. $X_i \sim N(500, 10{,}000)$.

The null hypothesis here is that SAT scores measure scholastic aptitude and a cram course has no effect on your scores. $H_0 : \mu = 500$. The alternative hypothesis we will consider is that the cram course might help or hurt your performance on the SAT. The course might teach you useful facts and test strategies, or it might leave you exhausted and irritable. $H_A : \mu \neq 500$. We will consider a different alternative hypothesis later.

We will find evidence against the null hypothesis if our sample mean, $\bar{X}$, is either much larger than or much smaller than 500 given our alternative hypothesis. How much larger or smaller does it need to be? Unfortunately, we don't know the probability distribution of $\bar{X}$ *per se*. But we do know the following. If the $X_i \sim N(500, 10{,}000)$, then $\bar{X} \sim N(500, \frac{10{,}000}{n})$, and $\frac{\bar{X}-500}{\sqrt{10{,}000/n}} = Z \sim N(0,1)$. So the sample mean $\bar{X}$ will be too big or too small when $\frac{\bar{X}-500}{\sqrt{10{,}000/n}}$ is too big or too small. And we know the exact probability distribution of $\frac{\bar{X}-500}{\sqrt{10{,}000/n}} = Z$ under the null hypothesis.

We typically set $\alpha = 5\%$, and let's do so here. We are willing to risk making a Type I error 5% of the time. When the null hypothesis is true, we are willing to reject it 5% of the time. We also know from our statistical tables that $P(-1.96 < Z < 1.96) = 95\%$. So under the null hypothesis $P\left(-1.96 < \frac{\bar{X}-500}{\sqrt{10{,}000/n}} < 1.96\right) = 95\%$. If the null hypothesis is true, $\frac{\bar{X}-500}{\sqrt{10{,}000/n}} < -1.96$ or $1.96 < \frac{\bar{X}-500}{\sqrt{10{,}000/n}}$ only 5% of the time. Since this is somewhat unlikely, we will reject the null hypothesis in favor of the alternative hypothesis if this happens.

Now we can evaluate our test statistic. $\frac{\bar{X}-500}{\sqrt{10{,}000/n}} = \frac{535-500}{\sqrt{10{,}000/25}} = \frac{35}{20} = 1.75$. Since $-1.96 < 1.75 < 1.96$, we see nothing unusual here. Under the null hypothesis, this seems like a reasonably common outcome. Thus, the evidence does not suggest that Key Review is effective. We do not reject the null hypothesis. We summarize the hypothesis testing procedure in Table 8.2.

Let's consider this experiment again with a different alternative hypothesis. The null hypothesis will continue to be that SAT scores measure scholastic aptitude and a cram course has no effect on your scores. $H_0 : \mu = 500$. But let's consider a one-sided alternative hypothesis. We will only consider the possibility that the cram course will help your performance on the SAT. $H_A : \mu > 500$.

We will find evidence against the null hypothesis if our sample mean, $\bar{X}$, is much larger than 500. How much larger does it need to be? Unfortunately, we still don't know the probability distribution of $\bar{X}$ *per se*. But we do know the following. If the

Table 8.2. Hypothesis testing summary: $\mu = 500$, $\mu \neq 500$.

Hypothesis	$H_0 : \mu = 500 \; H_A : \mu \neq 500$
Significance Level	$\alpha = 5\%$
Acceptance Region	$-1.96 < \frac{\bar{X}-500}{\sqrt{10{,}000/n}} < 1.96$
Test Statistic	$\frac{\bar{X}-500}{\sqrt{10{,}000/n}} = \frac{535-500}{\sqrt{10{,}000/25}} = \frac{35}{20} = 1.75$
Decision	Since $-1.96 < 1.75 < 1.96$, do not reject H_0

$X_i \sim N(500, 10{,}000)$, then $\bar{X} \sim N\left(500, \frac{10{,}000}{n}\right)$, and $\frac{\bar{X}-500}{\sqrt{10{,}000/n}} = Z \sim N(0,1)$. So the sample mean $\bar{X}$ will be too big when $\frac{\bar{X}-500}{\sqrt{10{,}000/n}}$ is too big. And we know the exact probability distribution of $\frac{\bar{X}-500}{\sqrt{10{,}000/n}}$ under the null hypothesis.

We typically set $\alpha = 5\%$, and let's do so here. We are willing to risk making a Type I error 5% of the time. When the null hypothesis is true, we are willing to reject it 5% of the time. We also know from our statistical tables that $P(Z < 1.645) = 95\%$. So under the null hypothesis $P\left(\frac{\bar{X}-500}{\sqrt{10{,}000/n}} < 1.645\right) = 95\%$. Only 5% of the time, $1.645 < \frac{\bar{X}-500}{\sqrt{10{,}000/n}}$ if the null hypothesis is true. Since this is somewhat unlikely, we will reject the null hypothesis in favor of the alternative hypothesis if this happens.

Now we can evaluate our test statistic. $\frac{\bar{X}-500}{\sqrt{10{,}000/n}} = \frac{535-500}{\sqrt{10{,}000/25}} = \frac{35}{20} = 1.75$. Since $1.6456 < 1.75$, this is somewhat unusual. Under the null hypothesis, this is an unlikely outcome. Thus, the evidence suggests that we should reject the null hypothesis. There is enough evidence here that the Key Review cram course is effective (see Table 8.3).

Please note that $\frac{\bar{X}-\mu}{\sqrt{\sigma^2/n}} = \frac{\bar{X}-\mu}{\sigma/\sqrt{n}}$. You will see the test statistic expressed both ways.

Table 8.3. Hypothesis testing summary: $\mu = 500$, $\mu > 500$.

Hypothesis	$H_0 : \mu = 500$ $H_A : \mu > 500$
Significance Level	$\alpha = 5\%$
Acceptance Region	$\frac{\bar{X}-500}{\sqrt{10{,}000/n}} < 1.645$
Test Statistic	$\frac{\bar{X}-500}{\sqrt{10{,}000/n}} = \frac{535-500}{\sqrt{10{,}000/25}} = \frac{35}{20} = 1.75$
Decision	Since $1.75 > 1.645$, reject H_0

An important lesson here is that the alternative hypothesis matters. Depending on our specification of the alternative hypothesis, we reach a completely different conclusion regarding the effectiveness of this SAT cram course.

8.5 Testing Hypotheses About the Population Mean When the Population Variance Is Unknown

The SAT example is an unusual situation where we know the population variance. The exam is written to produce a variance of 10,000. Normally, we do not know the population variance. How do we test hypotheses about the mean when we don't know the population variance?

Suppose you are in charge of a school lunch program, and you want to make sure that your active students are consuming at least 2,400 calories per day. You monitor the calorie consumption of a random sample of 30 students and find a sample mean consumption of 2,387 calories with a sample variance of 1,512. Do you have enough evidence here to conclude that the average student is not consuming enough calories?

The null hypothesis here is your students are consuming at least 2,400 calories per day. $H_0 : \mu \geq 2{,}400$. The alternative hypothesis is that they are not consuming enough calories per day. $H_A : \mu < 2{,}400$.

We will find evidence against the null hypothesis if our sample mean, $\bar{X}$, is much smaller than 2,400. How much smaller does it need to be? Unfortunately, we don't know the probability distribution of $\bar{X}$ *per se*. But we do know the following: If the $X_i \sim N(2{,}400, \sigma^2)$, then $\bar{X} \sim N\left(2{,}400, \frac{\sigma^2}{n}\right)$, and $\frac{\bar{X}-2{,}400}{\sqrt{\sigma^2/n}} = Z \sim N(0,1)$. We also know that if s^2 is the sample variance, then $\frac{(n-1)s^2}{\sigma^2} \sim \chi^2_{n-1}$. And since $\frac{N(0,1)}{\sqrt{\chi^2_{n-1}/(n-1)}} \sim$ Student's t with $n-1$ degrees of freedom, we have $\frac{\bar{X}-2{,}400}{\sqrt{s^2/n}} \sim$ Student's t with $n-1$ degrees of freedom. So the sample mean $\bar{X}$ will be "too small" when $\frac{\bar{X}-2{,}400}{\sqrt{s^2/n}}$ is too small. And we know the exact probability distribution of $\frac{\bar{X}-2{,}400}{\sqrt{s^2/n}}$ under the null hypothesis.

We typically set $\alpha = 5\%$, and let's do so here. We are willing to risk making a Type I error 5% of the time. When the null hypothesis is true, we are willing to reject it 5% of the time. We also know from our Student's t tables that $P(\Psi_{29} > -1.699) = 95\%$. So under the null hypothesis $P\left(\frac{\bar{X}-2{,}400}{\sqrt{s^2/n}} > -1.699\right) = 95\%$. If the null hypothesis is true, $\frac{\bar{X}-2{,}400}{\sqrt{s^2/n}} < -1.699$ only 5% of the time. Since this is somewhat unlikely, we will reject the null hypothesis in favor of the alternative hypothesis if this happens.

Now we can evaluate our test statistic. $\frac{\bar{X}-2{,}400}{\sqrt{1{,}512/30}} = \frac{2{,}387-2{,}400}{\sqrt{1{,}512/30}} = \frac{-13}{7.099} = -1.83$. Since $-1.83 < -1.699$, this is somewhat unusual. Under the null hypothesis, this is an unlikely outcome. Thus, the evidence suggests that we should reject the null hypothesis. There is enough evidence here to conclude that these students are not consuming 2,400 calories per day (see Table 8.4).

Would our conclusion have been different if we were only willing to make a Type I error 3% of the time? Suppose we set our significance level $\alpha = 3\%$. Our hypothesis testing procedure would be exactly the same. The only difference would be that our critical value from the Student's t-distribution would be -1.957 instead of -1.699. Our test statistic would still be $\frac{\bar{X}-2{,}400}{\sqrt{1{,}512/30}} = \frac{2{,}387-2{,}400}{\sqrt{1{,}512/30}} = \frac{-13}{7.099} = -1.83$. But since $-1.83 > -1.957$, we would not reject the null hypothesis. We do not find sufficient evidence that your students are getting less

Table 8.4. Hypothesis testing summary: $\mu = 2400$, $\alpha = 5\%$.

Hypothesis	$H_0 : \mu \geq 2{,}400$ $H_A : \mu < 2{,}400$
Significance Level	$\alpha = 5\%$
Acceptance Region	$\dfrac{\bar{X} - 2{,}400}{\sqrt{s^2/n}} > -1.699$
Test Statistic	$\dfrac{\bar{X} - 2{,}400}{\sqrt{1,512/30}} = \dfrac{2{,}387 - 2{,}400}{\sqrt{1{,}512/30}} = \dfrac{-13}{7.099} = -1.83$
Decision	Since $-1.83 < -1.699$, reject H_0

than the recommended daily calories. Thus, the results can be very sensitive to your selection of the significance level α (see Table 8.5).

Table 8.5. Hypothesis testing summary: $\mu \geq 2400$, $\alpha = 3\%$.

Hypothesis	$H_0 : \mu \geq 2{,}400$ $H_A : \mu < 2{,}400$
Significance Level	$\alpha = 3\%$
Acceptance Region	$\dfrac{\bar{X} - 2{,}400}{\sqrt{s^2/n}} > -1.957$
Test Statistic	$\dfrac{\bar{X} - 2{,}400}{\sqrt{1{,}512/30}} = \dfrac{2{,}387 - 2{,}400}{\sqrt{1{,}512/30}} = \dfrac{-13}{7.099} = -1.83$
Decision	Since $-1.83 > -1.957$, do not reject H_0

8.6 Testing Hypotheses About the Population Variance

Suppose that you are a money manager, and your clients do not like bearing a lot of risk. You promise your clients that the population variance on the rate of return on your portfolio of stocks is less than 400. But one of your clients has looked at your rates of return over the past ten years ($n = 10$) and finds a sample variance of 660. Does your client have enough evidence to show that your portfolio has a population variance greater than 400?

The null hypothesis here is that there is limited risk in holding your portfolio. We are measuring risk here by the variance in the rate of return on the portfolio. $H_0 : \sigma^2 \leq 400$. The alternative hypothesis is that your portfolio is much riskier. $H_A : \sigma^2 > 400$.

We can estimate the population variance σ^2 with the sample variance s^2. If s^2 is much larger than 400, then we will reject the null hypothesis. But how much larger does s^2 need to be? We know s^2 is measured with error. We don't know the probability distribution of s^2, but we do know that $\frac{(n-1)s^2}{\sigma^2} \sim \chi^2_{n-1}$. And we know that s^2 is "too big" when $\frac{(n-1)s^2}{\sigma^2}$ is "too big" since $(n-1)$ and σ^2 are constants.

We typically set $\alpha = 5\%$, so let's change the pace by setting $\alpha = 10\%$ for no particular reason except to practice. We are willing to risk making a Type I error 10% of the time now. When the null hypothesis is true, we are willing to reject it 10% of the time. We also know from our chi-square tables that $P(0 < W_9 < 14.7) = 90\%$ for a χ^2_9 We look for a chi-square random variable with 9 degrees of freedom because we have $n - 1 = 10 - 1 = 9$ degrees of freedom. So under the null hypothesis $P\left(\frac{(n-1)s^2}{\sigma^2} < 14.7\right) = 90\%$. If the null hypothesis is true, $\frac{(n-1)s^2}{\sigma^2} > 14.7$ only 10% of the time. Since this is somewhat unlikely, we will reject the null hypothesis in favor of the alternative hypothesis if this happens. We can say s^2 is "too big" if this happens.

We can now evaluate our test statistic. $\frac{(n-1)s^2}{\sigma^2} = \frac{(10-1)660}{400} = 14.85$. Since $14.85 > 14.7$, we can reject the null hypothesis in favor of the alternative hypothesis. We can say s^2 is "too big." This portfolio appears to be riskier than it was claimed to be. We summarize the decision process in Table 8.6.

Table 8.6. Hypothesis testing summary: $\sigma^2 \leq 400$.

Hypothesis	$H_0 : \sigma^2 \leq 400$ $H_A : \sigma^2 > 400$
Significance Level	$\alpha = 10\%$
Acceptance Region	$\dfrac{(n-1)s^2}{\sigma^2} < 14.7$
Test Statistic	$\dfrac{(n-1)s^2}{\sigma^2} = \dfrac{(10-1)660}{400} = 14.85$
Decision	Since $14.85 > 14.7$, we reject H_0

8.7 Testing Hypotheses About the Population Proportion

Barak Obama, Oprah Winfrey, and Bill Gates are some famous left-handed people. About 10% of people are left-handed. Some people believe that left-handed tennis players have an advantage over right-handed tennis players. Think about Martina Navratilova or Rafael Nadal. Are the best tennis players more likely to be left-handed?

We might look at the 256 male and female tennis players who played in the main draw at Wimbledon over the summer. Suppose 32 of them are left-handed. Would this be convincing evidence that the best tennis players are more likely to be left-handed?

The null hypothesis here is that there is no difference between tennis players and everyone else. Ten percent of the best tennis players are left-handed. $H_0 : \pi = 0.10$. The alternative hypothesis we will consider is that the best tennis players are more likely to be left-handed. $H_A : \pi > 0.10$.

We can estimate π with $p = \frac{X}{n} = \frac{32}{256} = 0.125$. If p is much larger than 0.10, we will reject the null hypothesis. But p is just an estimate and estimated with error. So is p large enough for us to reject the null hypothesis? How large does p need to be?

Let's set our significance level $\alpha = 5\%$. We are willing to risk making a Type I error 5% of the time now. We are willing to reject a true null hypothesis 5% of the time.

From the previous chapters, we know that if the sample proportion $p = \frac{X}{n}$, then $p \approx N\left(\pi, \frac{\pi(1-\pi)}{n}\right)$ for large enough n. It follows that $\frac{p-\pi}{\sqrt{\frac{\pi(1-\pi)}{n}}} = Z \approx N(0,1)$. We also know from our standard normal tables that

$$P(Z < 1.645) = 95\%$$
$$P(Z > 1.645) = 5\%$$

Thus, we will evaluate our test statistic $\frac{p-\pi}{\sqrt{\frac{\pi(1-\pi)}{n}}}$. If it is larger than 1.645, we will reject our null hypothesis. Here $\frac{p-\pi}{\sqrt{\frac{\pi(1-\pi)}{n}}} = \frac{.125-.10}{\sqrt{\frac{.10(1-.10)}{256}}} =$

Table 8.7. Hypothesis testing summary: $\pi = 0.10$.

Hypothesis	$H_0 : \pi = 0.10$ $H_A : \pi > 0.10$
Significance Level	$\alpha = 5$
Acceptance Region	$\frac{p - \pi}{\sqrt{\frac{\pi(1-\pi)}{n}}} \cdot < 1.645$
Test Statistic	$\frac{p - \pi}{\sqrt{\frac{\pi(1-\pi)}{n}}} = \frac{.125 - .10}{\sqrt{\frac{.10(1-.10)}{256}}} = \frac{.025}{.01875} = 1.33$
Decision	Since $1.33 < 1.645$, we do not reject H_0

$\frac{.025}{.01875} = 1.33$. Since $1.33 < 1.645$, we will not reject our null hypothesis. We do not have enough evidence here to suggest that the best tennis players are any different from the rest of the population (see Table 8.7).

8.8 Observations

While the statements of the null hypothesis and the alternative hypothesis may seem *pro forma*, they are quite important. The specification of the alternative hypothesis will dictate the form of the rejection region (see Table 8.8). If the test statistic falls in the rejection region, we will reject the null hypothesis. So we must know the location of the rejection region. If you have a two-sided alternative hypothesis, you will use a two-tailed test. If you have a one-sided alternative hypothesis, you will use a one-tailed test. Which tail you will use depends on the one-sided alternative hypothesis.

Table 8.8. Alternative hypothesis and the rejection region.

Form of Null and Alternative Hypotheses	Rejection Region
$H_0 : \beta = 3.14$ and $H_A : \beta \neq 3.14$	Two-tailed test
$H_0 : \beta = 3.14$ and $H_A : \beta > 3.14$	One-tailed test, right tail rejection region
$H_0 : \beta = 3.14$ and $H_A : \beta < 3.14$	One-tailed test, left tail rejection region
$H_0 : \beta \leq 3.14$ and $H_A : \beta > 3.14$	One-tailed test, right tail rejection region
$H_0 : \beta \geq 3.14$ and $H_A : \beta < 3.14$	One-tailed test, left tail rejection region

The significance level of the test is the probability of a Type I error (rejecting the null hypothesis when it is true). We typically select the significance level α to be 5%. It reflects the amount of evidence against the null hypothesis we need in order to reject it. The significance level α must also be stated clearly. The level of α determines the size of the rejection region. Without knowing α, you cannot determine the acceptance and rejection regions.

You will often hear the term **p-value**. Assuming that the null hypothesis is true, the p-value is the probability that the test statistic would take a value as extreme or more extreme than that actually observed. The smaller the p-value, the stronger the evidence against the null hypothesis. If the p-value is less than α, we reject the null hypothesis.

In the earlier left-handed tennis player example, we found our test statistic to be $\frac{p-\pi}{\sqrt{\frac{\pi(1-\pi)}{n}}} = 1.33$ where $\frac{p-\pi}{\sqrt{\frac{\pi(1-\pi)}{n}}} = Z \sim N(0,1)$. From our standard normal tables, we know that $P(-1.33 < Z < 1.33) = 0.816$. So the probability of our test statistics being as large or larger (in absolute value) under the null hypothesis is $1 - 0.816 = 0.184 = 18.4\%$. The p-value here is 18.4%. Since 18.4% is larger than $\alpha = 5\%$, we do not reject the null hypothesis.

To summarize, when we do hypothesis testing, we will use the following test statistics in these specific cases:

If you are testing a hypothesis about the population mean when the true population variance is known, we will use the fact that $\frac{\bar{X}-\mu}{\sqrt{\sigma_x^2/n}} = \frac{\bar{X}-\mu}{\sigma_x/\sqrt{n}} \sim N(0,1)$.

If you are testing a hypothesis about the population mean when the true variance is unknown, we will use the fact that $\frac{\bar{X}-\mu}{\sqrt{s_x^2/n}} = \frac{\bar{X}-\mu}{s_x/\sqrt{n}} \sim$ Student's t with $n-1$ degrees of freedom.

If you are testing a hypothesis about the population variance, we will use the fact that $\frac{(n-1)s_x^2}{\sigma_x^2} \sim \chi^2_{n-1}$.

And if you are testing a hypothesis about a population proportion, you will use the fact that $p = \frac{X}{n} \sim N\left(\pi, \frac{\pi(1-\pi)}{n}\right)$.

Hypothesis testing does not tell you if the hypothesis is true or not true. It merely tells you if the evidence you have is likely under the null hypothesis or unlikely under the null hypothesis. Accepting the null hypothesis merely means that you do not have enough evidence to reject it. It does not mean the null hypothesis is true. And rejecting the null hypothesis means that your data would be unlikely if the null hypothesis was true. But you should be aware that unlikely things happen all the time.

8.9 Exercises

(1) Boys of a certain age are known to have a mean weight of $\mu = 85$ pounds with a standard deviation of $\sigma = 11.6$ pounds. Assume weights are normally distributed. A complaint is made that the boys living in a municipal children's home are underfed. As one bit of evidence, $n = 25$ boys (of the same age) are weighed and found to have a mean weight of $\bar{X} = 80.9$. Is the complaint justified? (yes, 5%, one-tailed)

(2) You are interested in studying the incomes of single women over 80 years of age in a certain large city. In a sample of 20 such women, you find an average income of \$17,500 with a standard deviation of \$6,200. Test the hypothesis that the true mean is \$20,000 at the 5% significance level. (accept)

(3) Bags of a certain brand of tortilla chips claim to have a net weight of 14 ounces. Net weights actually vary slightly from bag to bag and are normally distributed with mean μ. A representative of a consumer advocate group wishes to see if there is any evidence that the mean net weight is less than advertised. She selects 16 bags of this brand at random and determines the net weight of each. She finds the sample mean to be $\bar{X} = 13.82$ and the sample standard deviation to be $s = 0.24$. Test the hypothesis that the mean net weight is 14 ounces or more. (reject)

(4) We take a random sample of 15 female students and find that on average they are 64.5 inches tall with a standard deviation of 2.5 inches. Test the hypothesis that the true variance in heights is no larger than 5 at the 10% level. (accept)

(5) For many years, the Federal Aviation Administration has been giving a pilot's exam with a mean score of 85 and a variance

of 64. After a completely new exam is introduced, a sample of 15 persons take the exam, and the sample variance equals 36. Test the hypothesis that the variance of the exam scores for the new exam is the same as for the old at the 5% significance level. (accept)

(6) A noted psychic was tested for ESP. The psychic was presented with 200 cards face down and asked to determine if each card was one of five symbols: a star, cross, circle, square, or three wavy lines. The psychic was correct in 50 cases. Let π represent the probability that the psychic correctly identifies the symbol on the card in a random trial. Suppose you wished to see if there is evidence that the psychic is doing better than just guessing. Test the hypothesis that $H_0 : \pi = 0.20$ vs the alternative hypothesis $H_A : \pi > 0.20$. (reject, 5%)

(7) It is widely believed that autism (ASD) affects 2.3% of our children. A study of 384 children finds that 19 have autism. Is this strong evidence that the level of autism is higher? Test the hypothesis that the rate of autism is indeed 2.3%. (reject, 5%)

(8) Are Americans overweight? You select a random sample of 35 Americans and find an average weight of 161.94 lbs with a standard deviation of 35.88 lbs. Test the following hypotheses:

   (a) $H_0 : \mu = 152$ vs $H_A : \mu \neq 152$ at the 5% level.
   (b) $H_0 : \mu = 152$ vs $H_A : \mu < 152$ at the 5% level.
   (c) $H_0 : \mu = 152$ vs $H_A : \mu > 152$ at the 5% level.

   (accept, accept, reject).

Chapter 9

Hypothesis Testing with Two Samples

9.1 Introduction

There are two kinds of statistics, the kind you look up and the kind you make up.

—Archie Goodwin

In the previous chapter, we considered testing hypotheses about a population mean, population variance, or population proportion. In this chapter, we will consider testing hypotheses about differences in two population means, differences in two population variances, and differences in two population proportions. We will have two separate samples instead of one. Are grades higher in humanities classes than in social science classes? Is there more income inequality in South Africa than in the United States? Are Republicans more likely to be in love than Democrats?

9.2 Differences in Two Means

Suppose you have two random variables, X and Y, where $X_i \sim N(\mu_x, \sigma_x^2)$ and $Y_i \sim N(\mu_y, \sigma_y^2)$. You are curious if the means are the same, that is, if $\mu_x = \mu_y$. Are incomes higher in Ireland than in the United States? You survey a random sample of people in Ireland and a random sample of people in the United States. Assume we have n_x

observations on X_i and n_y observations on Y_i. How do we test this kind of hypothesis?

9.2.1 *Matched pairs*

We already know how to deal with this question in one particular situation. This is when we have "matched pairs" of data. Suppose you want to find out if the COVID-19 vaccine is effective. If we have a sample of 30 pairs of twins, we can do the following. With each pair of twins, one is given a placebo and the other is given the vaccine. We will have 30 placebo outcomes X_i and 30 vaccine outcomes Y_i. We can find out if there is a difference between the average placebo outcome, $\bar{X}$, and the average vaccine outcome, $\bar{Y}$. But in this case, we have more information because all the participants in the study have a twin. We can measure the difference in the outcomes for each pair of twins, $D_i = X_i - Y_i$, and see if the average D_i is equal to zero. We learned how to do this in the previous chapter.

For a numerical example, suppose you want to see if Joe Biden was more popular in the 2020 Presidential election than Hillary Clinton in the 2016 Presidential election. We can look at the percentage of the vote received by Biden and Clinton in all 50 states. In Virginia, Biden received 54.1% of the vote and Clinton received 49.7% of the vote for a difference of 4.4% points. If you look at the vote difference for all 50 states, you will find an average difference of 4.0% points with a standard deviation of 2.0% points.

We want to test the null hypothesis that Biden and Clinton were equally popular, $H_0 : \mu_d = 0$ where μ_d is the mean difference. We have 50 observations on the D_i and know that $\frac{\bar{D}-0}{s_d/\sqrt{50}}$ will have a Student's t-distribution under the null hypothesis with $50 - 1 = 49$ degrees of freedom. Here s_d is the sample standard deviation of the D_i. The Student's t critical values will be -2.008 and 2.008 for $\alpha = 5\%$. We have a test statistic $\frac{\bar{D}-0}{s_d/\sqrt{50}} = \frac{4.0-0}{2.0/\sqrt{50}} = 14.14$. Since $14.14 > 2.008$, we reject $H_0 : \mu_d = 0$. Biden was more popular than Clinton (see Table 9.1).

Table 9.1. Hypothesis testing summary: $\mu_d = 0$.

Hypothesis	$H_0 : \mu_d = 0 \quad H_A : \mu_d \neq 0$
Significance Level	$\alpha = 5\%$
Acceptance Region	$-2.008 < \frac{\bar{D} - 0}{s_d/\sqrt{n}} < 2.008$
Test Statistic	$\frac{\bar{D} - 0}{s_d/\sqrt{n}} = \frac{4.0 - 0}{2.0/\sqrt{50}} = 14.14$
Decision	Since $14.14 > 2.008$, reject H_0

9.2.2 *Population variances σ_x^2 and σ_y^2 are known*

We still have two random variables, X and Y, where $X_i \sim N(\mu_x, \sigma_x^2)$ and $Y_i \sim N(\mu_y, \sigma_y^2)$. We want to know if the means are the same, that is, if $\mu_x = \mu_y$. Let us assume we know σ_x^2 and σ_y^2. In general, we will not know the true population variances. But we will work through the logic here to lay down the groundwork for when we do not know the population variances. We have n_x observations on X_i and n_y observations on Y_i. We begin by estimating μ_x with $\bar{X} = \frac{1}{n_x}\sum X_i$ and μ_y with $\bar{Y} = \frac{1}{n_y}\sum Y_i$. Let $D = \bar{X} - \bar{Y}$. We know that

$$E[D] = \mu_D = E[\bar{X} - \bar{Y}] = E[\bar{X}] - E[\bar{Y}] = \mu_x - \mu_y \tag{9.1}$$

$$V(D) = \sigma_D^2 = V(\bar{X} - \bar{Y}) = V(\bar{X}) + V(\bar{Y}) = \frac{\sigma_x^2}{n_x} + \frac{\sigma_y^2}{n_y} \tag{9.2}$$

We are assuming here that the X_i and Y_i are all independent of each other. Thus, all the covariances are equal to zero. Since the X_i and Y_i are normally distributed, and D is a linear combination of the X_i and Y_i, then D must be normally distributed as well. Thus, we have $D = \bar{X} - \bar{Y} \sim N\left(\mu_x - \mu_y, \frac{\sigma_x^2}{n_x} + \frac{\sigma_y^2}{n_y}\right)$. And by normalizing, we have

$$\frac{(\bar{X} - \bar{Y}) - (\mu_x - \mu_y)}{\sqrt{\frac{\sigma_x^2}{n_x} + \frac{\sigma_y^2}{n_y}}} \sim N(0, 1) \tag{9.3}$$

9.2.2.1 *Example*

Since household incomes are about 20% higher in Connecticut than in Rhode Island, we want to see if SAT scores are higher in Connecticut than in Rhode Island. You randomly sample 25 high school students in Connecticut (X_i) and 30 high school students in Rhode Island (Y_i). Suppose that $\bar{X}$ is 523 and that $\bar{Y}$ is 497.5. Do we have enough evidence to conclude that the average scores are different in the two states? We assume that $X_i \sim N(\mu_x, 10{,}000)$ and $Y_i \sim N(\mu_y, 10{,}000)$.

Our null hypothesis here is that there is no difference in the two states. $H_0 : \mu_x = \mu_y \; or \; \mu_x - \mu_y = 0$. Since we have $\bar{X} > \bar{Y}$, let our alternative hypothesis be $H_A : \mu_x > \mu_y \; or \; \mu_x - \mu_y > 0$. With these data, we would never conclude that $\mu_x < \mu_y$. We will select a significance level $\alpha = 5\%$. We will want to reject H_0 if our estimate of $\mu_x - \mu_y$ is much bigger than 0. But how much bigger?

We will use the fact that $\frac{(\bar{X}-\bar{Y})-(\mu_x-\mu_y)}{\sqrt{\frac{\sigma_x^2}{n_x}+\frac{\sigma_y^2}{n_y}}} \sim N(0,1)$. From our normal tables, we know that $P(Z > 1.645) = 5\%$. So if our test statistic, $\frac{(\bar{X}-\bar{Y})-(\mu_x-\mu_y)}{\sqrt{\frac{\sigma_x^2}{n_x}+\frac{\sigma_y^2}{n_y}}}$, is bigger than 1.645, we will reject the null hypothesis.

Under the null hypothesis, our test statistic is $\frac{(\bar{X}-\bar{Y})-(\mu_x-\mu_y)}{\sqrt{\frac{\sigma_x^2}{n_x}+\frac{\sigma_y^2}{n_y}}} = \frac{(523-497.5)-(0)}{\sqrt{\frac{10{,}000}{25}+\frac{10{,}000}{30}}} = \frac{25.5}{27.08} = 0.942$. Since $0.942 < 1.645$, we do not reject H_0 at the 5% significance level. We do not have enough evidence to say that SAT scores are higher in Connecticut than in Rhode Island (see Table 9.2).

9.2.2.2 *Note on Group differences vs Individual differences*

What does the existence of group differences tell us about individual differences? The answer may not be a lot. On average, women do better on the reading and writing section of the SAT than men. Women have an average score of 534 on the reading and writing (ERW) section of the SAT while men have an average score of 529. If you randomly select a man and a woman who have just taken the

Table 9.2. Hypothesis testing summary: $\mu_x = \mu_y$, σ_x^2, σ_y^2 known.

Hypothesis	$H_0 : \mu_x = \mu_y \text{ or } \mu_x - \mu_y = 0$ $H_A : \mu_x > \mu_y \text{ or } \mu_x - \mu_y > 0$
Significance Level	$\alpha = 5\%$
Acceptance Region	$\dfrac{(\bar{X} - \bar{Y}) - (\mu_x - \mu_y)}{\sqrt{\frac{\sigma_x^2}{n_x} + \frac{\sigma_y^2}{n_y}}} < 1.645$
Test Statistic	$\dfrac{(\bar{X} - \bar{Y}) - (\mu_x - \mu_y)}{\sqrt{\frac{\sigma_x^2}{n_x} + \frac{\sigma_y^2}{n_y}}} = \dfrac{(523 - 497.5) - (0)}{\sqrt{\frac{10{,}000}{25} + \frac{10{,}000}{30}}}$ $= \dfrac{25.5}{27.08} = 0.942$
Decision	Since $0.942 < 1.645$, we do not reject H_0

SAT, what is the probability that the woman will have done better than the man in the reading and writing section?

Let the females scores $X \sim N(534,\ 10{,}000)$ and the male scores $Y \sim N(529,\ 10{,}000)$. If you randomly select a female student and a male student, what is the probability that the female student did better than the male student? We want to know $P(X > Y) = P(X - Y > 0)$.

We know that $X - Y \sim N(\mu_x - \mu_y, \sigma_x^2 + \sigma_y^2) = N(534 - 529,\ 20{,}000) = N(5,\ 20{,}000)$. So $P(X - Y > 0) = P((X - Y) - 5 > 0 - 5) = P\left(\frac{(X-Y)-5}{\sqrt{20{,}000}} > \frac{0-5}{\sqrt{20{,}000}}\right) = P(Z > -0.0353) = 0.514 = 51.4\%$. The female student may be more likely to have done better but not by much. It is still basically a toss up.

9.2.3 *Population variances σ_x^2 and σ_y^2 are unknown*

We still have two random variables, X and Y, where $X_i \sim N(\mu_x, \sigma_x^2)$ and $Y_i \sim N(\mu_y, \sigma_y^2)$. We want to know if the means are the same, that is, if $\mu_x = \mu_y$. We have n_x observations on X_i and n_y observations on Y_i. We do not know the true population variances, the usual situation. Here we need to think about several possible scenarios.

9.2.3.1 *Two population variances are the same $\sigma_x^2 = \sigma_y^2$*

Suppose the two population variances are the same. If we do not know the variances to be the same, we will normally want to test this assumption. We discuss how to do this shortly. But let's assume we know the variances to be the same or that we cannot reject the hypothesis that they are the same. Thus, $\sigma_x^2 = \sigma_y^2$.

If the variances are the same, we have $\sigma^2 = \sigma_x^2 = \sigma_y^2$.

Let $D = \bar{X} - \bar{Y}$. We know that

$$E[D] = \mu_D = E[\bar{X} - \bar{Y}] = E[\bar{X}] - E[\bar{Y}] = \mu_x - \mu_y \tag{9.4}$$

$$\begin{aligned} V(D) = \sigma_D^2 = V(\bar{X} - \bar{Y}) = V(\bar{X}) + V(\bar{Y}) &= \frac{\sigma_x^2}{n_x} + \frac{\sigma_y^2}{n_y} = \frac{\sigma^2}{n_x} + \frac{\sigma^2}{n_y} \\ &= \sigma^2\left(\frac{1}{n_x} + \frac{1}{n_y}\right) = \sigma^2\left(\frac{n_x + n_y}{n_x n_y}\right) \end{aligned} \tag{9.5}$$

Since D is a linear combination of some normally distributed random variables, we know that D is normally distributed as well. So we have

$$D = \bar{X} - \bar{Y} \sim N\left(\mu_x - \mu_y, \sigma^2\left(\frac{n_x + n_y}{n_x n_y}\right)\right) \tag{9.6}$$

And if we standardize this, we have

$$\frac{(\bar{X} - \bar{Y}) - (\mu_x - \mu_y)}{\sqrt{\sigma^2\left(\frac{n_x+n_y}{n_x n_y}\right)}} \sim N(0, 1) \tag{9.7}$$

We will come back to this.

Now recall that $\frac{(n_x-1)s_x^2}{\sigma_x^2} \sim \chi_{n_x-1}^2$ and $\frac{(n_y-1)s_y^2}{\sigma_y^2} \sim \chi_{n_y-1}^2$. We have two chi-square random variables. If we add them together, we get another chi-square random variable:

$$\begin{aligned} &\frac{(n_x - 1)s_x^2}{\sigma_x^2} + \frac{(n_y - 1)s_y^2}{\sigma_y^2} \\ &\quad \sim \chi_{n_x-1}^2 + \chi_{n_y-1}^2 = \chi_{n_x-1+n_y-1}^2 = \chi_{n_x+n_y-2}^2 \end{aligned}$$

Furthermore, since $\sigma^2 = \sigma_x^2 = \sigma_y^2$, we have

$$\frac{(n_x-1)s_x^2}{\sigma_x^2} + \frac{(n_y-1)s_y^2}{\sigma_y^2}$$

$$= \frac{(n_x-1)\,s_x^2}{\sigma^2} + \frac{(n_y-1)s_y^2}{\sigma^2} = \frac{(n_x-1)\,s_x^2 + (n_y-1)s_y^2}{\sigma^2}$$

So

$$\frac{(n_x-1)s_x^2 + (n_y-1)s_y^2}{\sigma^2} \sim \chi^2_{n_x+n_y-2} \tag{9.8}$$

Now we have a standard normal random variable (9.7) and a chi-square random variable (9.8). Let's divide the standard normal random variable by the square root of the chi-square random variable which has been divided by its degrees of freedom. This will give us a Student's t random variable:

$$\frac{\frac{(\bar{X}-\bar{Y})-(\mu_x-\mu_y)}{\sqrt{\sigma^2\left(\frac{n_x+n_y}{n_x n_y}\right)}}}{\sqrt{\frac{(n_x-1)s_x^2+(n_y-1)s_y^2}{\sigma^2}\Big/(n_x+n_y-2)}}$$

$$= \frac{(\bar{X}-\bar{Y})-(\mu_x-\mu_y)}{\sqrt{\frac{(n_x-1)s_x^2+(n_y-1)s_y^2}{n_x+n_y-2}\left(\frac{n_x+n_y}{n_x n_y}\right)}}$$

$$= \frac{(\bar{X}-\bar{Y})-(\mu_x-\mu_y)}{\sqrt{s^2\left(\frac{n_x+n_y}{n_x n_y}\right)}} \sim \text{Student's } t\text{-distribution} \tag{9.9}$$

with $n_x + n_y - 2$ degrees of freedom where $s^2 = \frac{(n_x-1)s_x^2+(n_y-1)s_y^2}{n_x+n_y-2}$.

You should note that s^2 is a weighted average of s_x^2 and s_y^2. Since $\sigma^2 = \sigma_x^2 = \sigma_y^2$, both s_x^2 and s_y^2 should be an estimate of σ^2. When you are doing your work, make sure that s^2 is between s_x^2 and s_y^2. If it is not, you made a mistake somewhere. Please also note that

$$s^2 = \frac{(n_x - 1)s_x^2 + (n_y - 1)s_y^2}{n_x + n_y - 2} = \frac{\sum (X_i - \bar{X})^2 + \sum (Y_i - \bar{Y})^2}{n_x + n_y - 2}$$

Depending on the situation, one may be easier to evaluate than the other. And to recap, we will use the fact that $\frac{(\bar{X}-\bar{Y})-(\mu_x-\mu_y)}{\sqrt{s^2\left(\frac{n_x+n_y}{n_x n_y}\right)}} \sim$ Student's t-distribution with $n_x + n_y - 2$ degrees of freedom.

9.2.3.2 *Example*

You want to see if college men are taller than college women. You have a random sample of 21 college men and a random sample of 24 college women. The men have an average height of $\bar{X} = 69.1$ inches with a sample variance of $s_x^2 = 9.6$. The women have an average height of $\bar{Y} = 63.7$ inches with a sample variance of $s_y^2 = 7.4$. We will assume that the population variances are the same for now. They are pretty close. We will test this assumption shortly.

Let's test the null hypothesis that, on average, male and female heights are the same. $H_0 : \mu_x - \mu_y = 0$. Our alternative hypothesis is that men are taller than women. $H_0 : \mu_x - \mu_y > 0$. We will use the 5% significance level. Our test statistic is $\frac{(\bar{X}-\bar{Y})-(\mu_x-\mu_y)}{\sqrt{s^2\left(\frac{n_x+n_y}{n_x n_y}\right)}} \sim$ Student's t with $n_x + n_y - 2$ degrees of freedom. We will reject the null hypothesis if our estimate of $\mu_x - \mu_y$ is much bigger than zero. How much bigger? We will look at the Student's t-distribution with $21 + 24 - 2 = 43$ degrees of freedom and put 5% on the right-hand tail. We have $P(\Psi_{43} > 1.681) = 5\%$ from the table.

We should begin by calculating $s^2 = \frac{(n_x-1)s_x^2+(n_y-1)s_y^2}{n_x+n_y-2} = \frac{(21-1)9.6+(24-1)7.4}{21+24-2} = \frac{362.2}{43} = 8.42$. Since 8.42 is between 9.6 and 7.4, we probably did the calculations correctly.

Then we will evaluate our test statistic. $\frac{(\bar{X}-\bar{Y})-(\mu_x-\mu_y)}{\sqrt{s^2\left(\frac{n_x+n_y}{n_x n_y}\right)}} = \frac{(69.1-63.7)-(0)}{\sqrt{8.42\left(\frac{21+24}{21\cdot 24}\right)}} = \frac{5.4}{0.867} = 6.227$.

Since $6.227 > 1.681$, we will reject our null hypothesis. Men appear to be taller than women even with fairly small sample sizes (see Table 9.3).

Table 9.3. Hypothesis testing summary: $\mu_x = \mu_y$, $\sigma_x^2 = \sigma_y^2$.

Hypothesis	$H_0 : \mu_x - \mu_y = 0 \quad H_0 : \mu_x - \mu_y > 0$
Significance Level	$\alpha = 5\%$
Acceptance Region	$\dfrac{(\bar{X} - \bar{Y}) - (\mu_x - \mu_y)}{\sqrt{s^2\left(\frac{n_x+n_y}{n_x n_y}\right)}} < 1.681$
Test Statistic	$\dfrac{(\bar{X} - \bar{Y}) - (\mu_x - \mu_y)}{\sqrt{s^2\left(\frac{n_x+n_y}{n_x n_y}\right)}} = \dfrac{(69.1 - 63.7) - (0)}{\sqrt{8.42\left(\frac{21+24}{21 \cdot 24}\right)}}$
	$= \dfrac{5.4}{0.867} = 6.227$
Decision	Since $6.227 > 1.681$, we reject H_0

9.2.3.3 *Two population variances are different, but sample sizes are really large*

If the two population variances are not the same, we are in a little bit of trouble. There is no procedure we can follow with well-defined probability distributions. We are forced to make some approximations. If our sample sizes are really, really big, we will assume that our estimates of the population variances are really, really good. We will assume that s_x^2 is really close to σ_x^2, and s_y^2 is really close to σ_y^2. Then it will be the case that

$$\frac{(\bar{X} - \bar{Y}) - (\mu_x - \mu_y)}{\sqrt{\frac{s_x^2}{n_x} + \frac{s_y^2}{n_y}}} \approx N(0,1) \tag{9.10}$$

9.2.3.4 *Example*

Suppose you want to see if, on average, men weigh more than women. You survey 1,352 men and find an average weight of $\bar{X} = 179.05$ lbs with a sample variance of 1,030.68. You also survey 2,221 women and find an average weight of $\bar{Y} = 151.42$ lbs with a sample variance of 1,157.31. Since our sample sizes are fairly large, we will assume we have very good estimates of the population variances. The population variances are close but not exactly the same.

The null hypothesis is that average weights are the same for men and women. $H_0 : \mu_x = \mu_y$ or $H_0 : \mu_x - \mu_y = 0$. Let the alternative hypothesis be $H_A : \mu_x \neq \mu_y$ or $H_A : \mu_x - \mu_y \neq 0$. You are comfortable with a significance level of $\alpha = 5\%$. We will reject the null hypothesis if our estimate of $\mu_x - \mu_y$ is very different from zero, either much bigger or much smaller than 0.

Assuming our estimates of the population variances are very, very good, our test statistic will have a $N(0,1)$ distribution:

$$\frac{(\bar{X} - \bar{Y}) - (\mu_x - \mu_y)}{\sqrt{\frac{s_x^2}{n_x} + \frac{s_y^2}{n_y}}} \approx N(0,1)$$

Since we have an alternative hypothesis $H_A : \mu_x - \mu_y \neq 0$, we will have a two-tailed rejection region. With $\alpha = 5\%$, we will put 2.5% of the rejection region on both tails. We know from our standard normal tables that

$$P(-1.96 < Z < 1.96) = 95\%$$

We evaluate our test statistic

$$\frac{(\bar{X} - \bar{Y}) - (\mu_x - \mu_y)}{\sqrt{\frac{s_x^2}{n_x} + \frac{s_y^2}{n_y}}} = \frac{(179.05 - 151.62) - (0)}{\sqrt{\frac{1{,}030.68}{1{,}352} + \frac{1{,}157.31}{2{,}221}}} = \frac{27.43}{1.1328} = 24.21$$

Since $24.21 > 1.96$, we can reject the null hypothesis at the 5% significance level. On average, men seem to weigh more than women (see Table 9.4).

9.2.3.5 *Two population variances are different, but sample sizes are small*

If the two population variances are different, but the sample sizes are small, then our estimates of the population variances, s_x^2 and s_y^2, may not be very close to σ_x^2 and σ_y^2. Thus, there will be more noise in our test statistic, $\frac{(\bar{X}-\bar{Y})-(\mu_x-\mu_y)}{\sqrt{\frac{s_x^2}{n_x}+\frac{s_y^2}{n_y}}}$, than would be the case if our sample sizes were really large. This noise will be reflected in fatter tails in the probability distribution. The Student's t-distribution is

Table 9.4. Hypothesis testing summary: $\mu_x = \mu_y$, n_x, n_y large.

Hypothesis	$H_0 : \mu_x = \mu_y$ or $H_0 : \mu_x - \mu_y = 0$
	$H_A : \mu_x \neq \mu_y$ or $H_A : \mu_x - \mu_y \neq 0$
Significance Level	$\alpha = 5\%$
Acceptance Region	$-1.96 < \frac{(\bar{X} - \bar{Y}) - (\mu_x - \mu_y)}{\sqrt{\frac{s_x^2}{n_x} + \frac{s_y^2}{n_y}}} < 1.96$
Test Statistic	$\frac{(\bar{X} - \bar{Y}) - (\mu_x - \mu_y)}{\sqrt{\frac{s_x^2}{n_x} + \frac{s_y^2}{n_y}}} = \frac{(179.05 - 151.62) - (0)}{\sqrt{\frac{1{,}030.68}{1{,}352} + \frac{1{,}157.31}{2{,}221}}}$
	$= \frac{27.43}{1.1328} = 24.21$
Decision	Since $24.21 > 1.96$, we reject H_0

very similar to a $N(0, 1)$ except that it has fatter tails. So we will approximate the probability distribution of $\frac{(\bar{X}-\bar{Y})-(\mu_x-\mu_y)}{\sqrt{\frac{s_x^2}{n_x}+\frac{s_y^2}{n_y}}}$ with a Student's t-distribution. The only remaining question is the appropriate degrees of freedom. While there are different algorithms for selecting the degrees of freedom, we will simply proceed with the smaller of $(n_x - 1)$ and $(n_y - 1)$ degrees of freedom to be conservative. It should be clear that this is just an approximation. This kind of approximation drives mathematicians crazy. But in the real world, decisions need to be made, and statisticians need a path forward whether or not it is paved.

9.2.3.6 *Example*

You are interested in comparing average incomes in Panama and Kazakhstan. Unfortunately, your samples' sizes are small because you do know very many people in these countries. You survey 21 people in Panama and find an average monthly wage $\bar{X} = \$1{,}423$ with a sample variance of $s_x^2 = 992{,}000$. You also survey 19 people in Kazakhstan and find an average monthly wage $\bar{Y} = \$1{,}536$ with a sample variance of $s_y^2 = 377{,}000$. You have converted local currencies into dollars using PPP exchange rates. There appears to be much more income inequality in Panama than in Kazakhstan.

The null hypothesis is that average monthly wages are the same in Panama and Kazakhstan. $H_0 : \mu_x = \mu_y$ or $H_0 : \mu_x - \mu_y = 0$. Let the alternative hypothesis be $H_A : \mu_x \neq \mu_y$ or $H_A : \mu_x - \mu_y \neq 0$. You are comfortable with a significance level of $\alpha = 5\%$. We will reject the null hypothesis if our estimate of $\mu_x - \mu_y$ is very different from zero, either much bigger or much smaller than 0.

Our test statistic, $\frac{(\bar{X}-\bar{Y})-(\mu_x-\mu_y)}{\sqrt{\frac{s_x^2}{n_x}+\frac{s_y^2}{n_y}}}$, has a Student's t-distribution with the smaller of $(n_x - 1)$ and $(n_y - 1)$ degrees. In this case, we have $19 - 1 = 18$ degrees of freedom. With a 2 tailed test, we want 2.5% of the probability on both tails. We go to our Student's t tables and find that

$$P(-2.101 < \Psi_{18} < 2.101) = 95\%$$

We evaluate our test statistic,

$$\frac{(\bar{X}-\bar{Y})-(\mu_x-\mu_y)}{\sqrt{\frac{s_x^2}{n_x}+\frac{s_y^2}{n_y}}} = \frac{(1{,}423 - 1{,}536) - (0)}{\sqrt{\frac{992{,}000}{21}+\frac{377{,}000}{19}}} = \frac{-113}{258.99} = -0.4363$$

Since $-2.101 < -0.4363 < 2.101$, we do not reject our null hypothesis. We do not have enough evidence here to conclude that average incomes are different in Panama and Kazakhstan (see Table 9.5).

Table 9.5. Hypothesis testing summary: $\mu_x = \mu_y$, n_x, n_y small.

Hypothesis	$H_0 : \mu_x = \mu_y$ or $H_0 : \mu_x - \mu_y = 0$ $H_A : \mu_x \neq \mu_y$ or $H_A : \mu_x - \mu_y \neq 0$
Significance Level	$\alpha = 5\%$
Acceptance Region	$-2.101 < \frac{(\bar{X}-\bar{Y})-(\mu_x-\mu_y)}{\sqrt{\frac{s_x^2}{n_x}+\frac{s_y^2}{n_y}}} < 2.101$
Test Statistic	$\frac{(\bar{X}-\bar{Y})-(\mu_x-\mu_y)}{\sqrt{\frac{s_x^2}{n_x}+\frac{s_y^2}{n_y}}} = \frac{(1{,}423 - 1{,}536) - (0)}{\sqrt{\frac{992{,}000}{21}+\frac{377{,}000}{19}}}$ $= \frac{-113}{258.99} = -0.4363$
Decision	Since $-2.101 < -0.4363 < 2.101$, we do not reject H_0

9.3 Differences in Two Variances

Suppose you want to test if the variance of X is different from the variance of Y. Is income inequality rising in the United States? Are stocks really riskier than bonds? Is climate change causing the weather to be more erratic? We have two random variables, X and Y, where $X_i \sim N(\mu_x, \sigma_x^2)$ and $Y_i \sim N(\mu_y, \sigma_y^2)$. We want to see if $\sigma_x^2 = \sigma_y^2$ or if $\sigma_x^2 \neq \sigma_y^2$. Assume we have n_x observations on X_i and n_y observations on Y_i.

We know that $\frac{(n_x-1)s_x^2}{\sigma_x^2} \sim \chi^2_{n_x-1}$ and $\frac{(n_y-1)s_y^2}{\sigma_y^2} \sim \chi^2_{n_y-1}$. We also recall the definition of the F-distribution. The F-distribution comes from the ratio of two chi-square random variables which have been divided by their degrees of freedom. We have two chi-square random variables here:

$$F = \frac{\chi^2_{n_x-1}/(n_x-1)}{\chi^2_{n_y-1}/(n_x-1)}$$

$$= \frac{\frac{(n_x-1)s_x^2}{\sigma_x^2} \Big/ (n_x-1)}{\frac{(n_y-1)s_y^2}{\sigma_y^2} \Big/ (n_y-1)} = \frac{s_x^2/\sigma_x^2}{s_y^2/\sigma_y^2} \sim F(n_x-1, n_y-1)$$

If you want to test the null hypothesis that $\sigma_x^2 = \sigma_y^2$, then under the null hypothesis, the above simplifies to

$$\frac{s_x^2/\sigma_x^2}{s_y^2/\sigma_y^2} = \frac{s_x^2}{s_y^2} \sim F(n_x-1, n_y-1) \tag{9.11}$$

Please note that we also have due to symmetry

$$\frac{s_y^2/\sigma_y^2}{s_x^2/\sigma_x^2} = \frac{s_y^2}{s_x^2} \sim F(n_y-1, n_x-1) \tag{9.12}$$

Let's test the assumption we made earlier that the variance in male heights is equal to the variance in female heights.

We have a random sample of 21 college men and a random sample of 24 college women. The men have an average height of $\bar{X} = 69.1$ inches with a sample variance of $s_x^2 = 9.6$. The women have an average height of $\bar{Y} = 63.7$ inches with a sample variance of $s_y^2 = 7.4$. Are the population variances the same?

The null hypothesis is that the population variances are the same. $H_0 : \sigma_x^2 = \sigma_y^2$. Since $s_x^2 > s_y^2$, the alternative hypothesis will be that $H_A : \sigma_x^2 > \sigma_y^2$. There is no way we are going to conclude that $\sigma_x^2 < \sigma_y^2$ when $s_x^2 > s_y^2$. And we will set our significance level $\alpha = 5\%$. Our test statistic will be

$$\frac{s_x^2}{s_y^2} \sim F(n_x - 1, n_y - 1) = F(21 - 1, 24 - 1) = F(20, 23)$$

We will reject the null in favor of the alternative if s_x^2 is much bigger than s_y^2 or if $\frac{s_x^2}{s_y^2}$ is really big. We want to have the 5% rejection region on the right tail of the $F(20, 23)$ distribution. We look at our statistical tables to find that $P(F_{20,23} > 2.05) = 5\%$.

Our test statistic is $\frac{s_x^2}{s_y^2} = \frac{9.6}{7.4} = 1.297$. Since $1.297 < 2.05$, we do not reject our null hypothesis. It is acceptable to assume that the two variances are the same here, as we did above (see Table 9.6).

Please note that most statistical tables only provide the critical values on the right-hand tail of the F-distribution. This will only allow for one-tailed tests. You will not be able to do a two-tailed test. You would need to look online to find the critical values on

Table 9.6. Hypothesis testing summary: $\sigma_x^2 = \sigma_y^2$.

Hypothesis	$H_0 : \sigma_x^2 = \sigma_y^2 \quad H_A : \sigma_x^2 > \sigma_y^2$
Significance Level	$\alpha = 5\%$
Acceptance Region	$\frac{s_x^2}{s_y^2} < 2.05$
Test Statistic	$\frac{s_x^2}{s_y^2} = \frac{9.6}{7.4} = 1.297$
Decision	Since $1.297 < 2.05$, we do not reject H_0

the left-hand tail. If you are constrained by your access to an online table, perhaps during an in-class exam, you will need to do a one-tailed test. In this case, you must put the larger of s_x^2 and s_y^2 on the top of the test statistic. This will allow you to do a one-tailed test with a right-hand side rejection region (see Table 9.7).

Table 9.7. Two variances.

Sample Variance Estimates	$s_x^2 > s_y^2$	$s_x^2 < s_y^2$
H_0	$\sigma_x^2 = \sigma_y^2$	$\sigma_x^2 = \sigma_y^2$
H_A	$\sigma_x^2 > \sigma_y^2$	$\sigma_x^2 < \sigma_y^2$
Test Statistic	s_x^2/s_y^2	s_y^2/s_x^2
Rejection Region	Right tail	Right tail

9.4 Differences in Two Population Proportions

If X is the number of "successes" in n trials, we learned earlier that the proportion of successes, $p = \frac{X}{n}$, will be distributed $N\left(\pi, \frac{\pi(1-\pi)}{n}\right)$ for large enough n where π is the population proportion.

Suppose you want to know if Republicans are more likely to be in love than Democrats. Let π_1 be the proportion of Republicans who are in love, and let π_2 be the proportion of Democrats who are in love. You might survey n_1 Republicans and find that X_1 of them are in love. And you might survey n_2 Democrats and find that X_2 of them are in love. Let $p_1 = \frac{X_1}{n_1}$ be our sample proportion of Republicans who are in love, and $p_2 = \frac{X_2}{n_2}$ be our sample proportion of Democrats who are in love. We know that $p_1 \sim N\left(\pi_1, \frac{\pi_1(1-\pi_1)}{n_1}\right)$ and $p_2 \sim N\left(\pi_2, \frac{\pi_2(1-\pi_2)}{n_2}\right)$. Since p_1 and p_2 are independent, we know that $p_1 - p_2 \sim N\left(\pi_1 - \pi_2, \frac{\pi_1(1-\pi_1)}{n_1} + \frac{\pi_2(1-\pi_2)}{n_2}\right)$. The expected value of a difference is the difference in the expected values. And the variance of a difference is the sum of the variances as long as the variables are independent.

Let our null hypothesis be that $\pi_1 = \pi_2$ or that $\pi_1 - \pi_2 = 0$. $H_0 : \pi_1 - \pi_2 = 0$. And our alternative hypothesis is $H_A : \pi_1 - \pi_2 \neq 0$. And let our significance level $\alpha = 5\%$.

If the null hypothesis is true, we have $\pi = \pi_1 = \pi_2$.

The variance of $p_1 - p_2$ is

$$\begin{aligned}
&\frac{\pi_1(1-\pi_1)}{n_1} + \frac{\pi_2(1-\pi_2)}{n_2} \\
&\quad = \frac{\pi(1-\pi)}{n_1} + \frac{\pi(1-\pi)}{n_2} = \pi(1-\pi)\left(\frac{1}{n_1} + \frac{1}{n_2}\right) \\
&\quad = \pi(1-\pi)\left(\frac{n_1+n_2}{n_1 \cdot n_2}\right)
\end{aligned}$$

Unfortunately, we do not know π. But both p_1 and p_2 are estimates of π under the null hypothesis. We will use a weighted average of p_1 and p_2 as our estimate of π. We will use

$$\hat{p} = \frac{X_1 + X_2}{n_1 + n_2}$$

When you calculate $\hat{p}$ you should get a number between of p_1 and p_2, and they should all be numbers between 0 and 1. We approximate the variance of the difference in proportions $p_1 - p_2$ with

$$\hat{p}(1-\hat{p})\left(\frac{n_1+n_2}{n_1 \cdot n_2}\right)$$

So under the null hypothesis

$$p_1 - p_2 \approx N\left(\pi_1 - \pi_2, \hat{p}(1-\hat{p})\left(\frac{n_1+n_2}{n_1 \cdot n_2}\right)\right) \tag{9.13}$$

So if we standardize this random variable

$$\frac{(p_1 - p_2) - (\pi_1 - \pi_2)}{\sqrt{\hat{p}(1-\hat{p})\left(\frac{n_1+n_2}{n_1 \cdot n_2}\right)}} \approx N(0,1) \tag{9.14}$$

Under the null hypothesis, we have $\pi_1 - \pi_2 = 0$:

$$\frac{(p_1 - p_2) - (0)}{\sqrt{\hat{p}(1-\hat{p})\left(\frac{n_1+n_2}{n_1 \cdot n_2}\right)}} \approx N(0,1) \tag{9.15}$$

where $\hat{p} = \frac{X_1+X_2}{n_1+n_2}$.

Since we set $\alpha = 5\%$ and $H_A : \pi_1 - \pi_2 \neq 0$, we will need a two-tailed rejection region with 2.5% probability on each of the tails. From our $N(0,1)$ tables, we know that

$$P(-1.96 < Z < 1.96) = 95\%$$

So if our test statistic is outside these bounds, we would reject the null hypothesis.

9.4.1 *Example*

Now let's plug in some numbers. Suppose you survey 363 Republicans and find that 280 of them are in love. And you survey 309 Democrats and find that 188 of them are in love. So your estimates are that $p_1 = \frac{280}{363} = 0.77 = 77\%$ of Republicans are in love and that $p_2 = \frac{188}{309} = 0.61 = 61\%$ of Democrats are in love. Are these two proportions statistically different from each other?

Our null hypothesis is that $\pi_1 = \pi_2$ or that $\pi_1 - \pi_2 = 0$. $H_0 : \pi_1 - \pi_2 = 0$. And our alternative hypothesis is $H_A : \pi_1 - \pi_2 \neq 0$. And our significance level $\alpha = 5\%$. We will use the fact that, under the null hypothesis,

$$\frac{(p_1 - p_2) - (0)}{\sqrt{\hat{p}(1-\hat{p})\left(\frac{n_1+n_2}{n_1 \cdot n_2}\right)}} \approx N(0,1)$$

And

$$P\left(-1.96 < \frac{(p_1 - p_2) - (0)}{\sqrt{\hat{p}(1-\hat{p})\left(\frac{n_1+n_2}{n_1 \cdot n_2}\right)}} < 1.96\right) = 0.95$$

Here $\hat{p} = \frac{X_1+X_2}{n_1+n_2} = \frac{280+188}{363+309} = \frac{468}{672} = 0.696 = 69.6\%$. Plugging in the rest of the numbers we have

$$\frac{(p_1 - p_2) - (0)}{\sqrt{\hat{p}(1-\hat{p})\left(\frac{n_1+n_2}{n_1 \cdot n_2}\right)}}$$

$$= \frac{(0.77 - 0.61) - (0)}{\sqrt{0.696(1-0.696)\left(\frac{363+309}{363 \cdot 309}\right)}} = \frac{0.16}{0.0356} = 4.49$$

Since $4.49 > 1.96$, we would reject the null hypothesis that $\pi_1 = \pi_2$. Republicans are more likely to be in love than Democrats (see Table 9.8).

Table 9.8. Hypothesis testing summary: $\pi_1 - \pi_2 = 0$.

Hypothesis	$H_0 : \pi_1 - \pi_2 = 0$ $H_A : \pi_1 - \pi_2 \neq 0$
Significance Level	$\alpha = 5\%$
Acceptance Region	$-1.96 < \frac{(p_1 - p_2) - (0)}{\sqrt{\hat{p}(1-\hat{p})\left(\frac{n_1+n_2}{n_1 \cdot n_2}\right)}} < 1.96$
Test Statistic	$\frac{(p_1 - p_2) - (0)}{\sqrt{\hat{p}(1-\hat{p})\left(\frac{n_1+n_2}{n_1 \cdot n_2}\right)}} = \frac{(0.77 - 0.61) - (0)}{\sqrt{0.696(1-0.696)\left(\frac{363+309}{363 \cdot 309}\right)}}$ $= \frac{0.16}{0.0356} = 4.49$
Decision	Since $4.49 > 1.96$, we reject H_0

9.5 Exercises

(1) Suppose you want to see if women have a higher body mass index (BMI) than men. You have a sample of 15 women with an average BMI of 29.6 with a standard deviation of 5.9. You have a sample of 18 men with an average BMI of 29.1 with a standard deviation of 4.6. Test the hypothesis that, on average, women and men have the same BMI at the 5% level. (accept)

(2) It is claimed that the variance of the weekly income of economics majors is higher than the variance of the income of computer and information system majors. Two random samples revealed the following weekly incomes (in \$1000):

Economics majors: 1.0, 2.0, 3.0, 6.0 ($\bar{X} = 3$, $s_x = 2.1602$)
CIS majors: 1.0, 2.0, 3.0 ($\bar{Y} = 2$, $s_y = 1$)

Assuming normality, use a 1% significance level to test the hypothesis $H_0 : \sigma_x^2 = \sigma_y^2$ against the alternative $H_A : \sigma_x^2 > \sigma_y^2$ where σ_x^2 and σ_y^2 are, respectively, the variances of economics major incomes and CIS major incomes. (accept)

(3) In a sample of 16 American Airlines flights, the planes arrived 10.437 *minutes late* on average with a standard deviation of 8.647 minutes. In a sample of 19 Delta Airlines flights, the planes arrived 1.474 *minutes early* on average with a standard deviation of 5.680 minutes. Test the hypothesis that American Airlines and Delta Airlines are equally good at prompt arrivals. (reject)

(4) A simple random sample (SRS) of 298 male faculty members at a large public university found that 119 felt that the university was supportive of female and minority faculty. An independent SRS of 151 female faculty found that 38 felt that the university was supportive of female and minority faculty. Let π_1 and π_2 represent the proportion of all male and female faculty, respectively, at the university who felt that the university was supportive of female and minority faculty at the time of the survey. Test the hypothesis that $\pi_1 = \pi_2$ at the 5% level. (reject)

(5) Suppose an examination of the credit card balances of people in Alaska and Connecticut yields the following figures:

Alaska: $n_x = 26$, $\bar{X} = \$7{,}089$, $s_x = \$4{,}700$
Connecticut: $n_y = 36$, $\bar{Y} = \$6{,}237$, $s_y = \$5{,}100$

where s_x and s_y are the sample estimates of the standard deviation in Alaska and Connecticut, respectively.

(a) Test the hypothesis that the variances are the same at the 5% level. (accept)
(b) Test the hypothesis that the difference between the two means is zero at the 5% level. (accept)

(6) Suppose you record the daily high Fahrenheit temperature in New York City and Paris for 365 days and find the following:

New York City: $\bar{X} = 62.5$, $s_x = 16.0$
Paris: $\bar{Y} = 59.8$, $s_y = 12.0$

(a) Test the hypothesis that the variance in NYC temperatures is the same as the variance in Paris temperatures at the 5% level. (reject)
(b) Test the hypothesis that the average temperature in NYC is the same as the average temperature in Paris at the 5% level. (reject)

Chapter 10

Simple Regression

10.1 Introduction

> *Statistics show that 60% of murder victims knew their assailants. Evidently they did not know them well enough.*

With simple linear regression, we are interested in relationships between different variables. We might be interested in the relationship between smoking and lung cancer, or interest rates and stock prices, or hours spent studying and grades, or education and income.

We want to study how one variable tends to change as other variables change. We want to determine if a relationship exists or not. And if a relationship exists, we would like to know the direction of the relationship, the strength of the relationship, and the magnitude of the relationship.

We have several statistical tools to explore the relationship between two variables. First, we can start with a graph or a scatterplot. A picture is worth a thousand words (see Figure 10.1).

Second, we can move on to some summary statistical measures like the sample covariance or the sample correlation coefficient as estimates of the population covariance or population correlation coefficient.

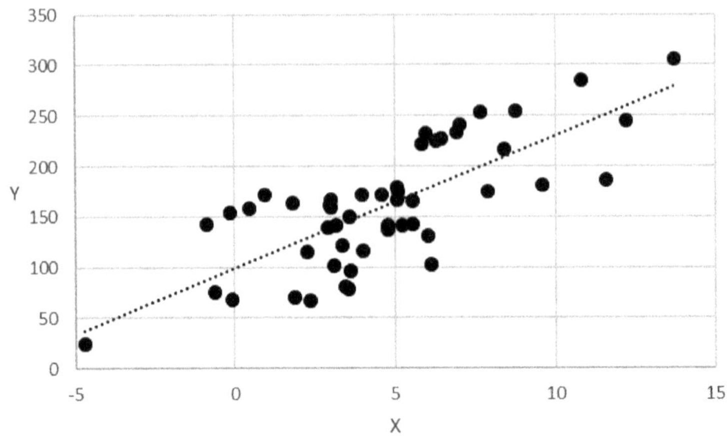

Fig. 10.1. Scatterplot.

Sample correlation coefficient

$$r = \frac{1}{n-1}\left\{\sum_{i=1}^{n}\left(\frac{X_i - \bar{X}}{s_x}\right)\left(\frac{Y_i - \bar{Y}}{s_y}\right)\right\}$$

Population correlation coefficient

$$\rho = \frac{\sigma_{xy}}{\sigma_x \sigma_y} = \frac{\text{cov}_{xy}}{\text{SD}_x \text{SD}_y}$$

And third, we can build a mathematical model of the relationship. This is called regression analysis and is the topic of this chapter. We might estimate relationships between variables with an equation like this. Here the value of the dependent variable Y depends on two independent variables X_2 and X_3 along with a stochastic error term u_i:

$$Y_i = \beta_1 + \beta_2 X_2 + \beta_3 X_3 + u_i$$

Before we get ahead of ourselves, we should clarify the difference between deterministic relationships and stochastic relationships.

In **deterministic relationships**, the dependent Y variable is fully determined by the parameter values and the explanatory X variables. There is an exact relationship between the variables. Consider the temperature measured in Celsius and the temperature measured in Fahrenheit. If you know one, you can figure out the exact value of the other. If you know the distance in miles, you know the distance in kilometers. If you know the height in inches, you know the height in meters. If you know the weight in pounds, you know the weight in kilograms.

A deterministic relationship might look like

$$Y_i = \beta_1 + \beta_2 X_i \tag{10.1}$$

where β_1 is the intercept and β_2 is the slope. These are both fixed parameters. The value of the ith observation on variable Y_i can be perfectly predicted given the value of X_i. If you know the Fahrenheit temperature, you can figure out the Celsius temperature with certainty:

$$C_i = \frac{5}{9}(F_i - 32)$$

Stochastic relationships possess some inherent randomness. The same set of parameter values and explanatory variables will lead to a range of different outcomes. Think about the relationship between consumption and income, or interest rates and stock prices, or height and weight. Knowing someone's income gives you some sense of their consumption but not an exact value. There is a stochastic element in the level of consumption even if you know the income.

A stochastic relationship might look like

$$Y_i = \beta_1 + \beta_2 X_i + u_i \tag{10.2}$$

where u_i is a random variable, a random disturbance term, and a random error term. On average, the error term is assumed to be zero. The dependent variable Y is determined in part by the independent variable X and in part by the disturbance term u_i. Holding X constant, we can observe different values for Y across different observations:

$$E(Y_i|X_i = x_i) = \beta_1 + \beta_2 x_i \tag{10.3}$$

The error term u_i can represent measurement error on the Y_i and/or the multitude of other factors which might influence Y_i.

10.2 Regression Analysis

Suppose we have a stochastic relationship represented by

$$Y_i = \beta_1 + \beta_2 X_i + u_i$$

We want to estimate β_1 and β_2 by looking at data on pairs (X_i, Y_i). Regression analysis is a way of estimating the true parameters β_1 and β_2 from some sample data.

10.2.1 *Example 1: Random numbers*

Let's consider some hypothetical data on variables X and Y (see Table 10.1).

Table 10.1. Sample data.

X	Y
2	3
4	2
5	6
8	5
9	8

Here is a scatterplot of the sample data with these five data points (see Figure 10.2).

We first observe that no straight line will go through all five data points. But what if we try to imagine a line which fits the five data points better than any other line? What would that line look like?

Just by eyeballing the data, suppose we consider a line like $Y = 1 + 0.7X$. This line will do pretty well even if it is not necessarily the very "best" line, whatever that might mean. Let's think about how well this line does.

The purpose of a stochastic model is to predict Y given X or a bunch of Xs. Once we have estimated the coefficients in the equation, how well can we predict Y for any particular value of X or set of Xs?

Let's look at the very first point (2,3). When $X = 2$, our equation $Y = 1 + 0.7X$ gives us a predicted $Y = Yhat = \hat{Y} =$

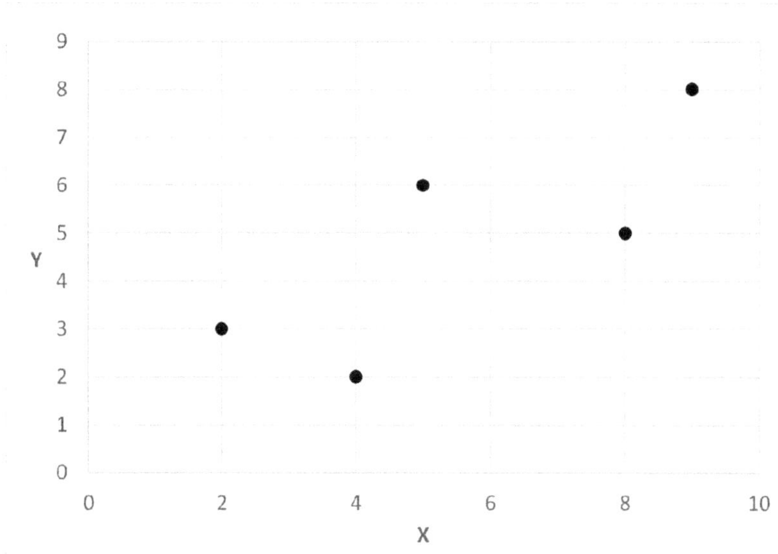

Fig. 10.2. Sample data.

$1 + 0.7(2) = 2.4$. But the actual $Y = 3$ when $X = 2$. The prediction error is the difference between the actual Y and the predicted Y or $Y - \hat{Y} = 3 - 2.4 = 0.6$. We would like to pick a line with very small prediction errors. Here are the prediction errors for this line $Y = 1 + 0.7X$ (see Table 10.2).

Table 10.2. Sample fit.

X	Y	$\hat{Y} = 1 + 0.7X$	Error	Error^2	|Error|
2	3	2.4	0.6	0.36	0.6
4	2	3.8	−1.8	3.24	1.8
5	6	4.5	1.5	2.25	1.5
8	5	6.6	−1.6	2.56	1.6
9	8	7.3	0.7	0.49	0.7
		$\sum$	−0.6	8.9	6.2

We would like the errors to be as small as possible. We probably want to make the sum of the errors as close to 0 as possible. But we note the following problem. If we merely sum all the errors, large positive errors merely cancel out the large negative errors. There will be an infinite number of lines where the sum of the errors will equal zero. Thus, it is good to have the sum of the errors equal zero but that will not be enough.

One way to avoid the problem of large positive errors canceling out large negative errors is to look at the absolute value of the errors. We may want to minimize the sum of the absolute values of all the errors. We could choose the line which minimizes $\sum |Y - \hat{Y}|$. Under some circumstances, this will turn out to be a very good strategy.

But another way to avoid the problem of large positive errors canceling out large negative errors is to square all the errors. We could minimize the sum of all the errors squared. We could choose the line which minimizes $\sum (Y - \hat{Y})^2$. This is what we will normally want to do.

What we should do depends on the nature of the error terms u_i. Under most circumstances, it will be better to minimize the sum of the squared errors. But if your errors have infinite variance, as with a Cauchy distribution, it is better to minimize the absolute values of the errors. But normally we will assume our errors have finite variance. We will discuss the proof a bit later.

If you minimize the sum of the squared errors here, you will get the following line:

$$Y = 1.156627 + 0.65X$$

With this line, the sum of the squared errors is equal to 8.74. With our eyeball line, $Y = 1 + 0.7X$, the sum of the squared errors was equal to 8.9. We were pretty close.

10.2.2 *Example 2: Hanford Site*

The Hanford Site is a decommissioned nuclear production complex in Washington state. It was the first full-scale plutonium production reactor in the world. From 1944 to 1971, it released radioactive waste into the Columbia River which flows along the Washington/Oregon border out to the Pacific Ocean (see

Fig. 10.3. Columbia river.

Figure 10.3). People who consumed fish from the Columbia River were exposed to this radiation. Scientists looked at the data to see if exposure to the radiation affected cancer rates in various communities. Here are some data from 9 Oregon counties (see Table 10.3).

Table 10.3. Hanford data.

Oregon County	Exposure Index	Cancer Mortality Rate
Portland	11.64	207.5
Clatsop	8.34	210.3
Columbia	6.41	177.9
Hood River	3.83	162.3
Gilliam	3.41	129.9
Morrow	2.57	130.1
Umatilla	2.49	147.1
Wasco	1.62	137.5
Sherman	1.25	113.5

Suppose we try to estimate the following relationship:

$$\text{CancerMortality}_i = \beta_1 + \beta_2 \ \text{RadiationExposure}_i + u_i$$

We are interested in seeing if there is any relationship between radiation exposure and cancer mortality rates. Is $\beta_2 = 0$? If there is a relationship, it is a positive one? Is $\beta_2 > 0$? Or is there a negative relationship? Is $\beta_2 < 0$. And if $\beta_2 \neq 0$, how big is β_2? Does radiation have a big effect on cancer mortality rates?

If we choose the line which minimizes the sum of the squared errors, we will get

$$\widehat{\text{CancerMortality}} = 114.7 + 9.23 \ \text{RadiationExposure}$$

Since the coefficient on *RadiationExposure* is positive, it means that when *RadiationExposure* increases, *CancerMortality* increases. This suggests that increasing radiation exposure leads to higher cancer mortality rates. But these coefficient estimates are just estimates. They are estimated with error (see Table 10.4). We only have 9 data points. How certain are we of our estimates? We need to understand where these estimates come from and what they really mean.

The technique of choosing the line which minimizes the sum of the squared errors is called "ordinary least squares" or OLS. The coefficient estimates are called the OLS estimates. Sometimes this technique is also called direct least squares. We will first discuss

Table 10.4. Hanford data fit.

Cancer Y	Exposure X	$\hat{Y}$	Error	Error^2
207.5	11.64	219.76	−12.26	150.3076
210.3	8.34	190.06	20.24	409.6576
177.9	6.41	172.69	5.21	27.1441
162.3	3.83	149.47	12.83	164.6089
129.9	3.41	145.69	−15.79	249.3241
130.1	2.57	138.13	−8.03	64.4809
147.1	2.49	137.41	9.69	93.8961
137.5	1.62	129.58	7.92	62.7264
113.5	1.25	126.25	−12.75	162.5625

how we arrive at the OLS estimates. Then we will discuss the sampling distribution of the OLS estimates. We will consider why this might be what we want to do. And then we will finish with some hypothesis testing. Do we have enough evidence here to conclude that radiation exposure leads to higher cancer mortality rates?

10.3 Point Estimation

We start with a regression model like

$$Y_i = \beta_1 + \beta_2 X_i + u_i$$

and gather some data on Y and X. How do we determine the coefficient estimates for β_1 and β_2 which minimize the sum of the squared errors? Anytime you want to minimize or maximize something, you probably want to use some calculus, and this time is no exception. We will need to use a wee bit of calculus, and a bit more of algebra to figure out how to estimate the coefficients here. If you are unfamiliar with calculus, you are welcome to skip any discussion involving calculus without losing the logic of the methodology. But first we need to define some notation.

10.3.1 *Notation*

We will assume that the true relationship between the dependent variable and the independent variable is represented by

$$Y_i = \beta_1 + \beta_2 X_i + u_i$$

We assume that the $u_i \sim N(0, \sigma_u^2)$. Y_i is a stochastic variable because it depends on the value of u_i The X_i is a nonstochastic variable because it does not depend on u_i or any other stochastic variable. And we assume we will never know the true values of β_1, β_2, or u_i.

Our estimated relationship will be

$$Y_i = b_1 + b_2 X_i + e_i \tag{10.4}$$

where b_1 is our estimate of β_1, b_2 is our estimate of β_2, and e_i is our estimate of u_i. Note that there is only one b_1 and one b_2 but N values of e_i where N is the sample size.

Our predicted value of Y, predicted Y, or $Yhat$ is

$$\hat{Y}_i = b_1 + b_2 X_i \tag{10.5}$$

The fitted error

$$e_i = Y_i - \hat{Y}_i = Y_i - b_1 - b_2 X_i \tag{10.6}$$

With ordinary least squares (OLS), we choose the values of b_1 and b_2 to minimize the sum of the squared errors:

$$\min_{b_1, b_2} \sum_{i=1}^{n} e_i^2 = \sum (Y_i - b_1 - b_2 X_i)^2 \tag{10.7}$$

Under OLS, the following will be true. $\sum e_i = 0$ and $\sum e_i X_i = 0$. The average error is equal to zero, and the errors are orthogonal to (uncorrelated with) X. If the errors were correlated with X, then you could choose a slightly different estimate for b_2 to get slightly smaller errors.

The regression line is chosen so that the sum of the squared deviations of the actual sample data from the regression line is minimized. We need to use a little calculus here to minimize the sum. Feel free to cut to the chase.

We want to

$$\min_{b_1,b_2} D = \sum_{i=1}^{N}[Y_i - b_1 - b_2 X_i]^2 = \sum e_i^2$$

To minimize the sum of the squared errors, we just take derivatives with respect to the parameters and set them equal to zero. These are the first-order conditions

$$(1)\ \frac{\partial D}{\partial b_1} = \sum_{i=1}^{N} 2[Y_i - b_1 - b_2 X_i][-1] = 0 \tag{10.8}$$

$$(2)\ \frac{\partial D}{\partial b_2} = \sum_{i=1}^{N} 2[Y_i - b_1 - b_2 X_i][-X_i] = 0 \tag{10.9}$$

Simplifying we get

$$\begin{aligned}&(1)\ \textstyle\sum Y_i - Nb_1 - b_2 \sum X_i = 0\\&(2)\ \textstyle\sum X_i Y_i - b_1 \sum X_i - b_2 \sum X_i^2 = 0\end{aligned}$$

From 1 above, solve for b_1 and we get

$$b_1 = \frac{1}{N}[\Sigma Y_i - b_2 \Sigma X_i]$$

$$b_1 = \bar{Y} - b_2 \bar{X} \tag{10.10}$$

This is the estimate of the intercept β_1. Note that the OLS line goes through the average value of Y and the average value of X.

Substitute for b_1 into (2) above and solve for b_2

$$\Sigma X_i Y_i - \frac{1}{N}[\Sigma Y_i - b_2 \Sigma X_i]\Sigma X_i - b_2 \Sigma X_i^2 = 0$$

$$\Sigma X_i Y_i - \frac{1}{N}(\Sigma Y_i)(\Sigma X_i) + b_2 \frac{1}{N}(\Sigma X_i)^2 - b_2 \Sigma X_i^2 = 0$$

$$\Sigma X_i Y_i - \frac{1}{N}(\Sigma Y_i)(\Sigma X_i) = b_2 \left[\Sigma X_i^2 - \frac{1}{N}(\Sigma X_i)^2\right]$$

Multiply both sides by N and move the b_2 term to the left

$$b_2[N\Sigma X_i^2 - (\Sigma X_i)^2] = N\Sigma X_i Y_i - (\Sigma Y_i)(\Sigma X_i)$$

$$b_2 = \frac{N\Sigma X_i Y_i - (\Sigma Y_i)(\Sigma X_i)}{\mathrm{N}\Sigma X_i^2 - (\Sigma X_i)^2}$$

Divide everything by N

$$b_2 = \frac{\Sigma X_i Y_i - \Sigma \bar{X}\bar{Y}}{\Sigma X_i^2 - (\mathrm{N}\bar{X})^2} = \frac{\Sigma X_i Y_i - \Sigma \bar{X}\bar{Y}}{\Sigma X_i^2 - (\Sigma \bar{X})^2}$$

$$b_2 = \frac{\Sigma X_i Y_i - \Sigma \bar{X}\bar{Y}}{\Sigma X_i^2 - 2\bar{X}\Sigma X_i + (\Sigma \bar{X})^2} = \frac{\Sigma X_i Y_i - \Sigma X_i \bar{Y} - \Sigma \bar{X} Y_i + \Sigma \bar{X}\bar{Y}}{\Sigma X_i^2 - 2\bar{X}\Sigma X_i + (\Sigma \bar{X})^2}$$

$$b_2 = \frac{\Sigma(X_i - \bar{X})(Y_i - \bar{Y})}{\Sigma(X_i - \bar{X})^2} \tag{10.11}$$

Now let $x_i = X_i - \bar{X}$ and $y_i = Y_i - \bar{Y}$ where we measure the variables as deviations from their mean. Then we can write this as follows:

$$b_2 = \frac{\sum x_i y_i}{\sum x_i^2} \tag{10.12}$$

This is the estimate of the slope β_2. We now have the point estimates for both the slope and the intercept. When we estimate simple regression lines, the computer does not "try" a whole bunch of lines to see which one has the smallest sum of squared errors.[1] We merely plug the data into these formulas to obtain our OLS coefficient estimates:

$$b_1 = \bar{Y} - b_2\bar{X}_2 \quad \text{and} \quad b_2 = \frac{\sum x_i y_i}{\sum x_i^2} \tag{10.13}$$

Of course, our estimates are just estimates. The true parameter values are likely to be larger or smaller than our estimates. How close are we to the true parameters' values? We need to know something about the sampling distribution of these estimates.

[1]There are some procedures in regression analysis where we do "try" various parameters to see which one works the best. If the underlying function is not well defined or well behaved, we may have to use numerical methods to find the best fit.

10.4 Sampling Distribution

We will begin with the mean and the variance of these OLS estimators. We will consider the estimator of the slope and then move on to the estimator for the intercept. Are our estimates unbiased estimates? On average, will they hit our targets on the mark? And how close will our estimate be to the true population parameters? What is the sampling variance of our estimates?

10.4.1 *Slope estimates*

We have this true relationship

$$Y_i = \beta_1 + \beta_2 X_i + u_i$$

with $u_i \sim N(0, \sigma_u^2)$. Our estimate of the slope β_2 is written as follows:

$$b_2 = \frac{\sum x_i y_i}{\sum x_i^2} = \frac{\sum x_i(Y_i - \bar{Y})}{\sum x_i^2} = \frac{\sum x_i Y_i}{\sum x_i^2}$$

Let

$$k_i = \frac{x_i}{\sum x_i^2}$$

$$b_2 = \sum k_i Y_i$$

Note that

(1) the k_i are nonstochastic since the x_i are nonstochastic
(2) $\sum k_i = 0$ since $\sum x_i = 0$
(3) $\sum k_i^2 = \frac{1}{\sum x_i^2}$
(4) $\sum k_i x_i = \sum k_i X_i = 1$

Since

$$
\begin{aligned}
Y_i &= \beta_1 + \beta_2 X_i + u_i \\
b_2 &= \sum k_i Y_i = \sum k_i(\beta_1 + \beta_2 X_i + u_i) \\
&= \beta_1 \sum k_i + \beta_2 \sum k_i X_i + \sum k_i u_i = \beta_2 + \sum k_i u_i \\
E[b_2] &= \beta_2 + E\left[\sum k_i u_i\right] = \beta_2 + \sum k_i E[u_i] = \beta_2 \qquad (10.14)
\end{aligned}
$$

Therefore, the ordinary least squares estimator of the slope is an unbiased estimator of the slope. Now let us look at the variance of the estimator. What is the variance of the OLS estimator b_2?

$$V(b_2) = E(b_2 - E[b_2])^2 = E(b_2 - \beta_2)^2 \text{ since } E[b_2] = \beta_2.$$

We also have from above that $b_2 = \beta_2 + \sum k_i u_i$ thus $b_2 - \beta_2 = \sum k_i u_i$.

So

$$
\begin{aligned}
V(b_2) &= E(b_2 - \beta_2)^2 = E\left(\sum k_i u_i\right)^2 \\
&= E(k_1^2 u_1^2 + k_2^2 u_2^2 + \cdots + \text{ cross terms}) \\
&= \sum k_i^2 \sigma_i^2 = \sigma_u^2 \sum k_i^2 = \frac{\sigma_u^2}{\sum x_i^2} \qquad (10.15)
\end{aligned}
$$

Since the errors are independent of each other, $E(u_i \cdot u_j) = 0$ for $i \neq j$, all the cross terms are zero. We also have $E(u_i^2) = \sigma_u^2$.

Note that the $V(b_2) = \frac{\sigma_u^2}{\sum x_i^2} \to 0 \; as \; N \to \infty$. As the sample size increases, the term in the denominator can only increase, causing the variance to get smaller and smaller. Thus, the precision of our estimate only improves with more data. This is a consistent estimator.

For a given sample size, the precision of our estimate will be higher if the variance of the errors is smaller. The more accurate our data, the better our estimate of the slope. We will also have a better estimate of the slope if $\sum x_i^2 = \sum(X_i - \bar{X})^2$ is larger. This term will be larger if the X data are very spread out. You want to have very small u_i and a very large dispersion for your Xs to get a good estimate of the slope coefficient.

Our OLS slope estimate, $b_2 = \frac{\sum x_i y_i}{\sum x_i^2}$, is both unbiased and consistent with variance $V(b_2) = \frac{\sigma_u^2}{\sum x_i^2}$.

10.4.2 *Intercept estimate*

Now let's look at our estimator for the intercept. We will begin by showing that we have an unbiased estimator, $E[b_1] = \beta_1$. We have

$$b_1 = \bar{Y} - b_2\bar{X} = \beta_1 + \beta_2\bar{X} + \bar{u} - b_2\bar{X}$$

$$E[b_1] = E[\beta_1 + \beta_2\bar{X} + \bar{u} - b_2\bar{X}] = \beta_1 + E[\beta_2\bar{X}] + E[\bar{u}] - E[b_2\bar{X}]$$

$$= \beta_1 + \beta_2\bar{X} + E[\bar{u}] - \bar{X}E[b_2] = \beta_1 \tag{10.16}$$

Since $E[b_2] = \beta_2$ and $E[u] = 0$. So $E[b_1] = \beta_1$. Our intercept estimate will be unbiased. On average, we will hit the target on the mark.

What is the variance of $b_1 = V(b_1)$?

$$b_1 = \bar{Y} - b_2\bar{X} = \frac{1}{N}\sum Y_i - \sum k_i Y_i \bar{X}$$

Since $k_i = \frac{X_i - \bar{X}}{\sum(X_i - \bar{X})^2} = \frac{x_i}{\sum x_i^2}$ and $b_2 = \sum k_i Y_i$:

$$b_1 = \frac{1}{N}\sum Y_i - \bar{X}\sum k_i Y_i = \sum\left(\frac{1}{N} - \bar{X}k_i\right)Y_i$$

Each Y_i is independent with variance σ_u^2

$$V(b_1) = \sum\left(\frac{1}{N} - \bar{X}k_i\right)^2\sigma_u^2 = \sum\left(\frac{1}{N^2} - \frac{2}{N}\bar{X}k_i + \bar{X}^2k_i^2\right)\sigma_u^2$$

$$= \left(\frac{1}{N} - \frac{2}{N}\bar{X}\sum k_i + \bar{X}^2\sum k_i^2\right)\sigma_u^2$$

But we have $\sum k_i = 0$ and $\sum k_i^2 = \frac{1}{\sum(X_i - \bar{X})^2}$, so

$$V(b_1) = \left(\frac{1}{N} + \frac{\bar{X}^2}{\sum(X_i - \bar{X})^2}\right)\sigma_u^2 = \left(\frac{\sum(X_i - \bar{X})^2 + N\bar{X}^2}{N\sum(X_i - \bar{X})^2}\right)\sigma_u^2$$

$$= \left(\frac{\sum X_i^2}{N\sum(X_i - \bar{X})^2}\right)\sigma_u^2 = \frac{\sigma_u^2\sum X_i^2}{N\sum(X_i - \bar{X})^2} \tag{10.17}$$

Note that the $V(b_1) = \frac{\sigma_u^2\sum X_i^2}{N\sum(X_i - \bar{X})^2} \to 0$ as $N \to \infty$. As the sample size increases, the terms in the denominator will increase more quickly than the numerator, causing the variance to get smaller and smaller. Thus, the precision of our estimate only improves with more data. This is a consistent estimator.

For a given sample size, the precision of our estimate will be larger if the variance of the errors is smaller. The more accurate our data, the better our estimate of the intercept. We will also have a better estimate of the intercept if $\sum x_i^2 = \sum(X_i - \bar{X})^2$ is larger. This term will be larger if the X data are very spread out. You want to have very small and very large Xs. And the more data you have, the larger your N, the smaller the variance of b_1 will be. You also want to have a lot of Xs near zero to keep the numerator smaller. You are trying to estimate the intercept here, the value of Y when $X = 0$. So the more data you have near $X = 0$, the better off you will be.

Thus, we have shown that the OLS estimate of the intercept is unbiased and consistent.

10.4.3 *Sampling distribution*

We would like to know a little more about the sampling distribution than just the mean and the variance. With our OLS estimators

$$b_1 = \bar{Y} - b_2\bar{X}$$

and

$$b_2 = \frac{\Sigma(X_i - \bar{X})(Y_i - \bar{Y})}{\Sigma(X_i - \bar{X})^2} = \frac{\sum x_i y_i}{\sum x_i^2}$$

We have unbiased estimators:

$$E[b_1] = \beta_1$$
$$E[b_2] = \beta_2$$

And we have the variance of our estimators as follows:

$$V(b_1) = \frac{\sigma^2 \sum X_i^2}{N\sum(X_i - \bar{X})^2}$$

$$V(b_2) = \frac{\sigma^2}{\sum(X_i - \bar{X})^2} = \frac{\sigma^2}{\sum x_i^2}$$

Since the u_i are distributed normally, the Y_i are distributed normally, and since b_1 and b_2 are weighted averages of Y_i, b_1 and b_2 will also be distributed normally. So we have

$$b_1 \sim N\left(\beta_1, \frac{\sigma^2 \sum X_i^2}{N\sum(X_i - \bar{X})^2}\right)$$

$$b_2 \sim N\left(\beta_2, \frac{\sigma^2}{\sum(X_i - \bar{X})^2}\right)$$

Since $b_1 \sim N\left(\beta_1, \frac{\sigma^2 \sum X_i^2}{N\sum(X_i-\bar{X})^2}\right)$, then we can standardize this normal random variable as

$$\frac{b_1 - \beta_1}{\sqrt{\frac{\sigma^2 \sum X_i^2}{N\sum(X_i-\bar{X})^2}}} \sim N(0,1) \tag{10.18}$$

And since $b_2 \sim N\left(\beta_2, \frac{\sigma^2}{\sum(X_i-\bar{X})^2}\right)$, we can standardize this normal random variable as

$$\frac{b_2 - \beta_2}{\sqrt{\frac{\sigma^2}{\sum(X_i-\bar{X})^2}}} \sim N(0,1) \tag{10.19}$$

This is the sampling distribution of our OLS estimators. We have learned that OLS is unbiased and consistent. But is it efficient?

10.5 Efficiency

Why do we use OLS? Is this the "best" we can do? Is OLS more efficient than any other estimator? Is the variance of the OLS estimator smaller than the variance of any other linear unbiased estimator? Let's find out.

10.5.1 *Efficiency of slope estimates*

We begin with our estimator for the slope:

$$b_2 = \frac{\sum x_i y_i}{\sum x_i^2} = \frac{\sum x_i Y_i}{\sum x_i^2}$$

Let

$$k_i = \frac{x_i}{\sum x_i^2}$$

so

$$b_2 = \sum k_i Y_i$$

Now consider any other linear unbiased estimator of β_2. Call it b twiddle or b squiggly:

$$\tilde{b}_2 = \sum w_i Y_i$$

where w_i are weights not necessarily equal to k_i. Now

$$\begin{aligned} E[\tilde{b}_2] &= \sum w_i E[Y_i] = \sum w_i(\beta_1 + \beta_2 X_i + u_i) \\ &= \beta_1 \sum w_i + \beta_2 \sum w_i X_i + \sum w_i u_i \end{aligned}$$

For $\tilde{b}_2$ to be unbiased, we need $\sum w_i = 0$ and $\sum w_i X_i = 1$. We also know that $E[u_i] = 0$.

The variance of

$$\begin{aligned} \tilde{b}_2 = V(\tilde{b}_2) &= V\left(\sum w_i Y_i\right) = \sum w_i^2 V(Y_i) \\ &= \sum w_i^2 V(u_i) = \sigma_u^2 \sum w_i^2 = \sigma_u^2 \sum \left(w_i - \frac{x_i}{\sum x_i^2} + \frac{x_i}{\sum x_i^2}\right)^2 \\ &= \sigma_u^2 \sum \left(w_i - \frac{x_i}{\sum x_i^2}\right)^2 + \sigma_u^2 \sum \left(\frac{x_i}{\sum x_i^2}\right)^2 \\ &\quad + 2\sigma_u^2 \sum \left(w_i - \frac{x_i}{\sum x_i^2}\right)\left(\frac{x_i}{\sum x_i^2}\right) \\ &= \sigma_u^2 \sum \left(w_i - \frac{x_i}{\sum x_i^2}\right)^2 + \sigma_u^2 \sum \left(\frac{x_i}{\sum x_i^2}\right)^2 \\ &= \sigma_u^2 \sum \left(w_i - \frac{x_i}{\sum x_i^2}\right)^2 + \text{constant} \end{aligned}$$

because the third term in the cross product

$$\sum\left(w_i - \frac{x_i}{\sum x_i^2}\right)\left(\frac{x_i}{\sum x_i^2}\right) = \sum\frac{w_i x_i}{\sum x_i^2} - \frac{\sum x_i^2}{\left(\sum x_i^2\right)^2}$$
$$= \sum\frac{w_i x_i}{\sum x_i^2} - \frac{1}{\sum x_i^2}$$
$$= \sum\frac{w_i X_i}{\sum x_i^2} - \frac{1}{\sum x_i^2} = 0$$

since

$$\sum w_i X_i = 1 \quad \text{and} \quad \sum w_i \bar{X} = 0 \quad \text{with} \quad \sum w_i = 0$$

We minimize $V(\tilde{b}_2)$ by setting $w_i = \frac{x_i}{\sum x_i^2}$ so the first term goes to zero. Then $V(\tilde{b}_2) = \frac{\sigma_u^2}{\sum x_i^2} = V(b_2)$. Thus, OLS is the minimum variance estimator. OLS is indeed the best linear unbiased estimator of the slope.

10.5.2 *Efficiency of intercept estimates*

Let's now look at the efficiency of the OLS estimator for the intercept:

$$b_1 = \bar{Y} - b_2\bar{X} = \frac{1}{N}\sum Y_i - \bar{X}\sum k_i Y_i = \sum\left(\frac{1}{N} - \bar{X}k_i\right)Y_i$$

from before, and $\sum k_i = 0$ and $\sum k_i^2 = \frac{1}{\sum(X_i - \bar{X})^2} = \frac{1}{\sum x_i^2}$.

We know that

$$V(b_1) = \frac{\sigma_u^2 \sum X_i^2}{N\sum(X_i - \bar{X})^2}$$

Let $\tilde{b}_1$ (b twiddle or b squiggly) be any other linear unbiased estimator

$$\tilde{b}_1 = \sum w_i Y_i = \sum w_i(\beta_1 + \beta_2 X_i + u_i)$$
$$= \sum w_i\beta_1 + \sum w_i\beta_2 X_i + \sum w_i u_i$$

For unbiasedness, we must have $\sum w_i = 1$ and $\sum w_i X_i = 0$:

$$
\begin{aligned}
V(\tilde{b}_1) &= V\left(\sum w_i Y_i\right) = \sum w_i^2 V(Y_i) = \sum w_i^2 \sigma_u^2 \\
&= \sigma_u^2 \sum \left(\left[w_i - \frac{1}{N} + \bar{X}k_i\right] + \left[\frac{1}{N} - \bar{X}k_i\right]\right)^2 \\
&= \sigma_u^2 \sum \left(w_i - \frac{1}{N} + \bar{X}k_i\right)^2 + \sigma_u^2 \sum \left(\frac{1}{N} - \bar{X}k_i\right)^2 \\
&\quad + 2\sigma_u^2 \sum \left(w_i - \frac{1}{N} + \bar{X}k_i\right)\left(\frac{1}{N} - \bar{X}k_i\right)
\end{aligned}
$$

But

$$
\begin{aligned}
&\sum \left(w_i - \frac{1}{N} + \bar{X}k_i\right)\left(\frac{1}{N} - \bar{X}k_i\right) \\
&= \sum w_i \left(\frac{1}{N} - \bar{X}k_i\right) - \sum \left(\frac{1}{N} - \bar{X}k_i\right)^2 \\
&= \frac{1}{N}\sum w_i - \bar{X}\sum w_i k_i - \sum \left(\frac{1}{N^2} - \frac{2}{N}\bar{X}k_i + \bar{X}^2 k_i^2\right) \\
&= \frac{1}{N}\sum w_i - \frac{\bar{X}\sum w_i (X_i - \bar{X})}{\sum (X_i - \bar{X})^2} - \frac{N}{N^2} + \frac{2\bar{X}}{N}\sum k_i + \bar{X}^2 \sum k_i^2 \\
&= \frac{1}{N} - \frac{\bar{X}^2}{\sum (X_i - \bar{X})^2} - \frac{1}{N} + 0 + \frac{\bar{X}^2}{\sum (X_i - \bar{X})^2} = 0
\end{aligned}
$$

So

$$
\begin{aligned}
V(\tilde{b}_1) = V\left(\sum w_i Y_i\right) &= \sigma_u^2 \sum \left(w_i - \frac{1}{N} + \bar{X}k_i\right)^2 \\
&\quad + \sigma_u^2 \sum \left(\frac{1}{N} - \bar{X}k_i\right)^2
\end{aligned}
$$

This is minimized by setting $w_i = \frac{1}{N} - \bar{X}k_i$ so that the first term drops out. This means that

$$\begin{aligned}
\tilde{b}_1 &= \sum w_i Y_i = \sum \left(\frac{1}{N} - \bar{X}k_i\right) Y_i = \frac{1}{N}\sum Y_i - \bar{X}\sum k_i Y_i \\
&= \bar{Y} - \bar{X}\frac{\sum(X_i - \bar{X})Y_i}{\sum(X_i - \bar{X})^2} = \bar{Y} - \bar{X}\frac{\sum(X_i - \bar{X})(Y_i - \bar{Y})}{\sum(X_i - \bar{X})^2} \\
&= \bar{Y} - \bar{X}\frac{\sum x_i y_i}{\sum x_i^2} = \bar{Y} - b_2\bar{X} = b_1
\end{aligned}$$

Thus, OLS gives us a linear unbiased estimator of the intercept with the smallest possible variance. OLS is an efficient estimator.

The OLS estimates of the slope and the intercept are unbiased, consistent, and efficient. We call these estimators BLUE for "best linear unbiased estimators." Among the class of unbiased estimators, OLS has the smallest variance. OLS is the most efficient. We have just proven the Gauss–Markov theorem for simple linear regressions. The Gauss–Markov theorem, named after Carl Friedrich Gauss and Andrey Markov, is the most important theorem in regression analysis. It explains why we use OLS all the time. We will discuss this theorem more thoroughly in the following chapter.

10.6 Hypothesis Testing

We showed above that the sampling distributions for b_1 and b_2 are as follows:

Since $b_1 \sim N\left(\beta_1, \frac{\sigma_u^2 \sum X_i^2}{N\sum(X_i - \bar{X})^2}\right)$, we have the standardized normal random variable

$$\frac{b_1 - \beta_1}{\sqrt{\frac{\sigma_u^2 \sum X_i^2}{N\sum(X_i - \bar{X})^2}}} \sim N(0,1)$$

And since $b_2 \sim N\left(\beta_2, \frac{\sigma_u^2}{\sum(X_i-\bar{X})^2}\right)$, we have the standardized normal random variable

$$\frac{b_2 - \beta_2}{\sqrt{\frac{\sigma_u^2}{\sum(X_i-\bar{X})^2}}} \sim N(0,1)$$

We would like to use these distributions in order to do hypothesis testing. However, we don't know σ^2. We will need to estimate it. We have

$$\begin{aligned}
Y_i &= \beta_1 + \beta_2 X_i + u_i \text{ (true relationship)}\\
Y_i &= b_1 + b_2 X_i + e_i \text{ (estimated relationship)}\\
\hat{Y}_i &= b_1 + b_2 X_i \text{ (fitted values of } Y_i\text{)}\\
e_i &= Y_i - \hat{Y}_i \text{ (fitted errors)}\\
\sigma_u^2 &= V(u_i) = E(u_i^2)
\end{aligned}$$

We will estimate σ_u^2 with $s_u^2 = \frac{\sum e_i^2}{N-2} = \frac{\sum(Y_i-b_1-b_2X_i)^2}{N-2} = \frac{\sum(Y_i-\hat{Y}_i)^2}{N-2}$. The residual variance s_u^2 is an unbiased and consistent estimator for σ_u^2. We divide by $N-2$ because we have N data points, but we had to estimate b_1 and b_2. So we lose two degrees of freedom in the process. We will demonstrate all this momentarily. We call $s_u = \sqrt{s_u^2}$ the **standard error of the regression** or the **root MSE** (square root of the mean squared error).

Let us show that s_u^2 is an unbiased estimate of σ_u^2. We have

$$\begin{aligned}
Y_i &= \beta_1 + \beta_2 X_i + u_i\\
\bar{Y} &= \beta_1 + \beta_2 \bar{X} + \bar{u}
\end{aligned}$$

Subtract the second equation from the first equation

$$Y_i - \bar{Y} = \beta_2(X_i - \bar{X}) + u_i - \bar{u}$$

Measure the variables as deviations from their mean with

$$\begin{aligned}
y_i &= Y_i - \bar{Y}\\
x_i &= X_i - \bar{X}
\end{aligned}$$

So

$$y_i = \beta_2 x_i + (u_i - \bar{u}) \tag{10.20}$$

We also have the following:

$$\begin{aligned} Y_i &= b_1 + b_2 X_i + e_i \\ \bar{Y} &= b_1 + b_2 \bar{X} \end{aligned}$$

with $\sum e_i = 0$ and $\bar{e} = 0$.

If we subtract the second from the first and use the notation for deviations from the mean,

$$y_i = b_2 x_i + e_i$$

so

$$e_i = y_i - b_2 x_i \tag{10.21}$$

So from 10.20 and 10.21 we have

$$\begin{aligned} e_i &= \beta_2 x_i + (u_i - \bar{u}) - b_2 x_i = (\beta_2 - b_2) x_i + (u_i - \bar{u}) \\ \sum e_i^2 &= (\beta_2 - b_2)^2 \sum x_i^2 + \sum (u_i - \bar{u})^2 \\ &\quad + 2(\beta_2 - b_2) \sum x_i (u_i - \bar{u}) \\ E\left[\sum e_i^2\right] &= \sum x_i^2 E[(\beta_2 - b_2)^2] + E\left[\sum (u_i - \bar{u})^2\right] \\ &\quad + 2E\left[(\beta_2 - b_2) \sum x_i (u_i - \bar{u})\right] \\ E\left[\sum e_i^2\right] &= \sum x_i^2 E[(\beta_2 - b_2)^2] + E\left[\sum (u_i - \bar{u})^2\right] \\ &\quad - 2E\left[(b_2 - \beta_2) \sum x_i (u_i - \bar{u})\right] \end{aligned}$$

There are three terms on the right-hand side here. The third term here needs a little more consideration.

Let's start with the following:

$$b_2 = \frac{\sum x_i y_i}{\sum x_i^2} = \frac{\sum x_i(\beta_2 x_i + (u_i - \bar{u}))}{\sum x_i^2}$$
$$= \beta_2 + \frac{\sum x_i u_i}{\sum x_i^2} + \frac{\sum x_i \bar{u}}{\sum x_i^2} = \beta_2 + \frac{\sum x_i u_i}{\sum x_i^2} + \frac{\bar{u}\sum x_i}{\sum x_i^2}$$
$$b_2 - \beta_2 = \frac{\sum x_i u_i}{\sum x_i^2} = \sum k_i u_i$$

where $k_i = \frac{x_i}{\sum x_i^2}$ and $\sum x_i = 0$. We can now write the third term above as

$$(b_2 - \beta_2)\sum x_i(u_i - \bar{u}) = \sum k_i u_i \sum x_i(u_i - \bar{u})$$
$$= \sum k_i u_i \left(\sum x_i u_i - \sum x_i \bar{u}\right)$$
$$= \sum k_i u_i \sum x_i u_i - \bar{u}\sum k_i u_i \sum x_i$$

Since $\sum x_i = 0$

$$(b_2 - \beta_2)\sum x_i(u_i - \bar{u}) = \sum k_i u_i \sum x_i u_i$$
$$= (k_1 u_1 + k_2 u_2 + \cdots)(x_1 u_1 + x_2 u_2 + \cdots)$$
$$= k_1 x_1 u_1^2 + k_2 x_2 u_2^2 + \cdots + \text{cross terms}$$

But $E[u_i^2] = \sigma_u^2$ and $E[u_i u_j] = 0$ for $i \neq j$ since the errors are independent. So

$$E\left[(b_2 - \beta_2)\sum x_i(u_i - \bar{u})\right] = E[k_1 x_1 u_1^2 + k_2 x_2 u_2^2 + \cdots]$$
$$= \sum k_i x_i \sigma_u^2 = \frac{\sum x_i^2}{\sum x_i^2}\sigma_u^2 = \sigma_u^2$$

Now we return to the expression we had earlier

$$E\left[\sum e_i^2\right] = \sum x_i^2 E[(\beta_2 - b_2)^2] + E\left[\sum (u_i - \bar{u})^2\right]$$
$$- 2E\left[(b_2 - \beta_2)\sum x_i(u_i - \bar{u})\right]$$

The first term is $\sum x_i^2$ times the variance of b_2. The second term would be the variance of u_i if we divided it by $(n-1)$ And the third term simplifies to two times σ_u^2:

$$E\left[\sum e_i^2\right] = \sum x_i^2 \frac{\sigma_u^2}{\sum x_i^2} + (n-1)\sigma_u^2 - 2\sigma_u^2 = (n-2)\sigma_u^2$$

So $E\left[\frac{\sum e_i^2}{n-2}\right] = \sigma_u^2$ where $s_u^2 = \frac{\sum e_i^2}{n-2} = \frac{\sum(Y_i - b_1 - b_2 X_i)^2}{n-2} = \frac{\sum(Y_i - \hat{Y}_i)^2}{n-2}$. We have an unbiased estimator for σ_u^2.

What is the probability distribution of $\sum e_i^2$? It turns out that $\frac{(n-2)s_u^2}{\sigma_u^2} = \frac{\sum e_i^2}{\sigma_u^2} \sim \chi_{n-2}^2$. Proving this is a bit beyond the level of this course, but we can get about halfway there and take a leap. We have $s_u^2 = \frac{\sum e_i^2}{n-2} = \frac{\sum(Y_i - b_1 - b_2 X_i)^2}{n-2} = \frac{\sum(Y_i - \hat{Y}_i)^2}{n-2}$.

From above we have

$$\begin{aligned}
\sum e_i^2 &= (\beta_2 - b_2)^2 \sum x_i^2 + \sum (u_i - \bar{u})^2 + 2(\beta_2 - b_2) \sum x_i(u_i - \bar{u}) \\
&= (\beta_2 - b_2)^2 \sum x_i^2 + \sum (u_i - \bar{u})^2 - 2(b_2 - \beta_2) \sum x_i(u_i - \bar{u}) \\
&= (\beta_2 - b_2)^2 \sum x_i^2 + \sum (u_i - \bar{u})^2 - 2 \sum k_i u_i \sum x_i u_i \\
\frac{\sum e_i^2}{\sigma_u^2} = \frac{(n-2)s_u^2}{\sigma_u^2} &= \frac{(\beta_2 - b_2)^2}{\sigma_u^2 / \sum x_i^2} + \frac{\sum (u_i - \bar{u})^2}{\sigma_u^2} - 2\frac{\sum k_i u_i \sum x_i u_i}{\sigma_u^2} \\
&= \left(\frac{\beta_2 - b_2}{\sigma_u \Big/ \sqrt{\sum x_i^2}} \right)^2 + \sum \left(\frac{u_i - \bar{u}}{\sigma_u} \right)^2 \\
&\quad - 2 \left(\sum k_i x_i \left(\frac{u_i}{\sigma_u} \right)^2 + \text{ cross terms} \right)
\end{aligned}$$

The first term here is just the square of a $N(0,1)$ and thus has a χ_1^2 distribution. Remember that $b_2 \sim N\left(\beta_2, \frac{\sigma_u^2}{\sum x_i^2}\right)$. The second term has a χ_{n-1}^2 distribution because we have $\bar{u}$ in the expression rather than the population mean 0. And the third term is unfortunately more appropriate for an advanced course. But because $\left(\frac{u_i}{\sigma_u}\right)^2 \sim \chi_1^2$, $\sum k_i x_i = 1$, and the cross terms equal zero in expectation, it may not surprise you that this has a χ_2^2 distribution. Thus, we have $\frac{\sum e_i^2}{\sigma_u^2} \sim \chi_1^2 + \chi_{n-1}^2 - \chi_2^2 = \chi_{n-2}^2$.

Now let's recap.

Since $b_1 \sim N\left(\beta_1, \frac{\sigma^2 \sum X_i^2}{N\sum(X_i-\bar{X})^2}\right)$, we have

$$\frac{b_1 - \beta_1}{\sqrt{\frac{\sigma^2 \sum X_i^2}{N\sum(X_i-\bar{X})^2}}} \sim N(0,1)$$

and $b_2 \sim N\left(\beta_2, \frac{\sigma^2}{\sum(X_i-\bar{X})^2}\right)$ so

$$\frac{b_2 - \beta_2}{\sqrt{\frac{\sigma^2}{\sum(X_i-\bar{X})^2}}} \sim N(0,1)$$

While we don't know σ^2, we have the following:

$$\frac{(n-2)s_u^2}{\sigma_u^2} = \frac{\sum e_i^2}{\sigma_u^2} \sim \chi_{n-2}^2 \tag{10.22}$$

Recall that if $Z \sim N(0,1)$ and $W \sim \chi_k^2$, and Z and W are independently distributed, then

$$\begin{aligned} t &= \frac{N(0,1)}{\sqrt{\chi_k^2/k}} = \frac{Z}{\sqrt{W/k}} \\ &= \frac{Z\sqrt{k}}{\sqrt{W}} \sim \text{Student's } t \text{ with } k \text{ degrees of freedom} \end{aligned} \tag{10.23}$$

So for our intercept estimate, we have $\frac{N(0,1)}{\sqrt{\chi_{n-2}^2/n-2}} = \frac{\frac{b_1-\beta_1}{\sqrt{\frac{\sigma^2\sum X_i^2}{n\sum(X_i-\bar{X})^2}}}}{\sqrt{\frac{(n-2)s_u^2}{\sigma_u^2}/n-2}} = \frac{b_1-\beta_1}{\sqrt{\frac{s_u^2\sum X_i^2}{n\sum(X_i-\bar{X})^2}}} = \frac{b_1-\beta_1}{SE_{b1}} \sim$ Student's t with $n-2$ degrees of freedom.

The term on the bottom is called the **standard error of** b_1, $SE_{b_1} = \sqrt{\frac{s_u^2\sum X_i^2}{n\sum(X_i-\bar{X})^2}}$.

And for our slope estimate, we have

$$\frac{N(0,1)}{\sqrt{\chi^2_{n-2}/n-2}} = \frac{\frac{b_2-\beta_2}{\sqrt{\frac{\sigma^2}{\sum(X_i-\bar{X})^2}}}}{\sqrt{\frac{(n-2)s_u^2}{\sigma_u^2}\Big/n-2}} = \frac{b_2-\beta_2}{\sqrt{\frac{s_u^2}{\sum(X_i-\bar{X})^2}}} = \frac{b_2-\beta_2}{SE_{b_2}} \sim \text{Student's } t$$

with $n-2$ degrees of freedom. The term on the bottom is called the **standard error of b_2**, $SE_{b_2} = \sqrt{\frac{s_u^2}{\sum(X_i-\bar{X})^2}}$.

We can now test simple hypotheses like $H_0 : \beta = 0$ by using the fact that $\frac{b-\beta}{SE_b} \sim$ Student's t-distribution with $n-2$ degrees of freedom.

10.7 Example: Hanford Site II

We started the chapter with some data on radiation exposure and cancer mortality rates along the Columbia River in nine Oregon counties. We estimated the following linear relationship:

$$\text{CancerMortality}_i = \beta_1 + \beta_2 \text{ RadiationExposure}_i + u_i$$

using ordinary least squares. Our OLS estimates were

$$\widehat{\text{CancerMortality}} = 114.715 + 9.231 \text{ RadiationExposure}$$

We can also report that the standard error of b_1 is 8.045 and the standard error of b_2 is 1.419. The standard error of the regression is 14.009.

We are interested in seeing if there is any relationship between radiation exposure and cancer mortality rates. Is $\beta_2 = 0$? And if there is a relationship, is it a positive one? Is $\beta_2 > 0$? Let's test the null hypothesis $H_0 : \beta_2 = 0$ against the alternative hypothesis $H_A : \beta_2 > 0$. We will set our significance level $\alpha = 5\%$.

Our test statistic $\frac{b_2-\beta_2}{SE_{b_2}} \sim$ Student's t with $N-2$ degrees of freedom. In this case, we have $N = 9$, so $N - 2 = 7$. Since we have a one-sided alternative hypothesis, we will use a one-tailed test. Since we have a greater than sign in the alternative hypothesis, we will put our 5% rejection region on the right-hand tail. If we look at the

Student's t tables with 7 degrees of freedom, we find the following:

$$P(\Psi_7 < 1.895) = 95\% \quad \text{or} \quad P(\Psi_7 > 1.895) = 5\%$$

Under the null hypothesis, our test statistic is

$$\frac{b_2 - \beta_2}{SE_{b_2}} = \frac{9.231 - 0}{1.419} = 6.506$$

Since $6.506 > 1.895$, we will reject the null hypothesis in favor of the alternative hypothesis. We find statistically significant evidence that radiation exposure increases cancer mortality rates. The radioactive waste from the Hanford site increased cancer mortality rates along the Columbia River (see Table 10.5).

Table 10.5. Hypothesis testing summary: Columbia River.

Hypothesis	$H_0 : \beta_2 = 0 \; H_A : \beta_2 > 0$
Significance Level	$\alpha = 5\%$
Acceptance Region	$\frac{b_2 - \beta_2}{SE_{b_2}} < 1.895$
Test Statistic	$\frac{b_2 - \beta_2}{SE_{b_2}} = \frac{9.231 - 0}{1.419} = 6.506$
Decision	Since $6.506 > 1.895$, reject H_0

10.8 Direction of Causality

When we measure the correlation coefficient between Y_i and X_i, we treat both variables symmetrically. The correlation coefficient is equal to $\frac{\text{cov}(Y_i,X_i)}{\sigma_{y_i}\sigma_{x_i}} = \frac{\text{cov}(X_i,Y_i)}{\sigma_{x_i}\sigma_{y_i}}$ and the order of the variables does not matter. The correlation of Y_i with X_i is the same as the correlation of X_i with Y_i.

When we run a regression, we *assume* that the X variable causes the Y variable. We assume the existence of and the direction of causality. We test to see if we can confirm these *a priori* assumptions. Of course, we cannot prove there is any causality. We can only find correlation. And correlation is not the same as causality. In a

19th-century study of medicine in Africa, the number of doctors in a region was strongly correlated with the prevalence of disease in the same region. The doctors went to the regions with the prevalence of disease. The doctors did not cause the disease.

The independent variable X and the dependent variable Y are not treated symmetrically in a linear regression. The dependent variable Y is assumed to be stochastic because its value depends, in part, on the value of the error term u_i. The independent variable, X, is assumed to be fixed or nonstochastic.

If we estimate the relationship $Y_i = \beta_1 + \beta_2 X_{2i} + u_i$, we will get a slope estimate $b_2 = \frac{\sum x_i y_i}{\sum x_i^2}$. But what if we rewrite $Y_i = \beta_1 + \beta_2 X_{2i}$ $+ u_i$ as follows:

$$\begin{aligned}\beta_2 X_i &= Y_i - \beta_1 - u_i \\ X_i &= \frac{1}{\beta_2} Y_i - \frac{\beta_1}{\beta_2} - \frac{u_i}{\beta_2} = -\frac{\beta_1}{\beta_2} + \frac{1}{\beta_2} Y_i - \frac{u_i}{\beta_2}\end{aligned}$$

So suppose we estimate the relationship $X_i = \alpha_1 + \alpha_2 Y_i + \varepsilon_i$ Here $\alpha_1 = \frac{-\beta_1}{\beta_2}$ and $\alpha_2 = \frac{1}{\beta_2}$. We get the estimates $\hat{X}_i = a_1 + a_2 Y_i$. We will get an estimate of $\alpha_2 = a_2 = \frac{\sum x_i y_i}{\sum y_i^2}$. Will $b_2 = \frac{1}{a_2}$? Generally, the answer will be no. If $b_2 = 1$ and all the data points fall directly on the regression line, then the answer is yes. But for all practical purposes, the answer is no. $b_2 = \frac{\sum x_i y_i}{\sum x_i^2}$ and $a_2 = \frac{\sum x_i y_i}{\sum y_i^2}$. They are not likely to be reciprocals of each other. Thus, it matters which variable is put on the right-hand side of the equation. We are assuming that X causes Y, and not the other way around.

10.9 Covariance Between the Slope and the Intercept

A final note on the covariance between the estimates of the slope and the intercept should be made. Our OLS slope and intercept estimates are not independent of each other. They will be correlated with each other. If we overestimate one, we will tend to underestimate the other if the Xs are positive:

$$\operatorname{cov}(b_1, b_2) = E[(b_1 - E[b_1])(b_2 - E[b_2])] = E[(b_1 - \beta_1)(b_2 - \beta_2)]$$

But

$$b_1 = \bar{Y} - b_2\bar{X}$$

and

$$E[b_1] = E[\bar{Y} - b_2\bar{X}] = \bar{Y} - \beta_2\bar{X}$$

So

$$\begin{aligned} b_1 - E[b_1] &= (\bar{Y} - b_2\bar{X}) - (\bar{Y} - \beta_2\bar{X}) = -\bar{X}(b_2 - \beta_2) \\ \operatorname{cov}(b_1, b_2) &= E[-\bar{X}(b_2 - \beta_2)(b_2 - \beta_2)] = -\bar{X}E(b_2 - \beta_2)^2 \\ &= -\bar{X}V(b_2) = -\bar{X}\frac{\sigma_u^2}{\sum x_i^2} \end{aligned} \quad (10.24)$$

When $\bar{X} > 0$, there is a negative covariance between the slope and the intercept estimates. If we overestimate the slope, we will tend to underestimate the intercept, and vice versa.

10.10 Exercises

(1) Suppose we estimate the following regression equation in order to understand the relationship between height and weight in a sample of 99 Americans. We estimated the following linear relationship:

$$Y_i = \beta_1 + \beta_2 X_i + u_i$$

using ordinary least squares where Y_i is weight in pounds and X_i is height in inches. Our estimated equation is

$$\begin{aligned} \hat{Y} = {} & -211.388 + 5.71774X \\ & (64.52) \qquad (0.97) \end{aligned}$$

The standard errors are reported in the parentheses. The standard error of the regression is 35.54.
We are interested in seeing if there is any relationship between height and weight. Test the null hypothesis $H_0 : \beta_2 = 0$ against the alternative hypothesis $H_A : \beta_2 > 0$. Set the significance level $\alpha = 5\%$. (reject)

(2) Suppose we estimate the following regression equation in order to understand the relationship between happiness and per capita GDP in a sample of 141 countries. We estimated the following linear relationship:

$$\text{Happiness}_i = \beta_1 + \beta_2 \text{GDPpc}_i + u_i$$

using ordinary least squares where Happiness_i is self-reported happiness on a scale from 0 to 10 and GDPpc_i is GDP per capita in thousands of dollars in 2020. Our estimated equation is

$$\begin{aligned}\widehat{\text{Happiness}} &= 4.734 + 0.039\text{GDPpc} \\ &\quad\ (0.089) \quad (0.003)\end{aligned}$$

The standard errors are reported in the parentheses. The standard error of the regression is 0.740.

We are interested in seeing if there is any relationship between GDPpc and happiness. Test the null hypothesis $H_0 : \beta_2 = 0$ against the alternative hypothesis $H_A : \beta_2 > 0$. Set the significance level $\alpha = 5\%$. (reject)

(3) With global warming, you might expect ski resorts to get less snow. We have 53 years of annual snowfall data from Mammoth Mountain in California. We used ordinary least squares to estimate the relationship between annual inches of snowfall and calendar year. Our estimated equation is

$$\begin{aligned}\widehat{\text{Snowfall}} &= -2{,}618.17 + 1.486 \text{ Year} \\ &\quad\ (2302.85) \qquad (1.1537)\end{aligned}$$

The standard errors are reported in the parentheses. The standard error of the regression is 128.48.

We are interested in seeing if there is any relationship between inches of snowfall and year. Test the null hypothesis $H_0 : \beta_2 = 0$ against the alternative hypothesis $H_A : \beta_2 > 0$. Set the significance level $\alpha = 5\%$. (accept)

(4) Larger houses typically cost more than smaller houses. Using data on 40 houses for sale in Claremont, CA, we estimated the

following regression equation:

$$\widehat{\text{Price}} = 221{,}943 + 387.8\text{SQFT}$$
$$(66629.9) \qquad (22.6)$$

The standard errors are reported in the parentheses. The standard error of the regression is 19,9696. $N = 40$.

We are interested in understanding the relationship between the price of a house and the size (square feet) of the house. Test the null hypothesis $H_0 : \beta_2 = 400$ that the price of a house increases by \$400 with every additional square foot. Set the significance level $\alpha = 5\%$. (accept)

(5) Estimate the regression equation $Y_i = \beta_1 + \beta_2 X_i + u_i$ using the following sample data:

X	Y
-1	0
0	2
1	4
2	5

(intercept 1.9, slope 1.7).

Chapter 11

Multiple Regression

11.1 Introduction

A statistician is a person whose lifetime ambition is to be wrong 5% of the time.

In this chapter, we will extend the analysis in Chapter 10 to multiple regression. In our simple linear regressions, we only had one independent variable on the right-hand side of the equation. In the real world, there are probably multiple independent X variables which help determine the value of the dependent variable Y. For example, your salary may depend on your level of education, your years of experience, your occupation, your industry, and where you live.

11.2 Notation

The true relationship between the variables is

$$Y_i = \beta_1 + \beta_2 X_{2i} + \beta_3 X_{3i} + \cdots + \beta_k X_{ki} + u_i$$

with $u_i \sim N(0, \sigma_u^2)$. We have $(k-1)$ explanatory variables here.

Using ordinary least squares (OLS), our estimated relationship is

$$Y_i = b_1 + b_2 X_{2i} + b_3 X_{3i} + \cdots + b_k X_{ki} + e_i$$

The fitted value of Y, predicted Y, or Y-hat is

$$\hat{Y}_i = b_1 + b_2 X_{2i} + b_3 X_{3i} + \cdots + b_k X_{ki}$$

Our fitted errors are

$$\begin{aligned} e_i &= Y_i - \hat{Y}_i = Y_i - (b_1 + b_2X_{2i} + b_3X_{3i} + \cdots + b_kX_{ki}) \\ &= Y_i - b_1 - b_2X_{2i} - b_3X_{3i} - \cdots - b_kX_{ki} \end{aligned}$$

Ordinary least squares (OLS) selects the estimates b_i which minimize the sum of the squared errors:

$$\min \sum_{i=1}^{n} e_i^2 = \sum (Y_i - b_1 - b_2X_{2i} - b_3X_{3i} - \cdots - b_kX_{ki})^2$$

Under OLS, it will be the case that $\sum e_i = 0$ and $\sum e_iX_i = 0$.

11.3 Gauss–Markov

Why do we use ordinary least squares? The Gauss–Markov theorem tells us that under the appropriate circumstances, ordinary least squares will give us the "best" estimates of the equation parameters. What are these circumstances? We will discuss the maintained assumptions here.

11.3.1 *Gauss–Markov assumptions*

(1) The model we are estimating is correctly specified. It is the true relationship between the variables. All the Xs which belong in the equation are in the equation. The model is linear in terms of the parameters as specified, though not necessarily linear in terms of the variables.
(2) The Y variable is stochastic, but the Xs are nonstochastic. The causality runs from the Xs to the Y. The Y variable may be measured with error, but the Xs can not be measured with error.
(3) $E(u_i) = 0$ or $E(Y_i - \beta_1 - \beta_2X_2 \cdots - \beta_kX_k) = 0$. On average, the errors are expected to equal zero. This means that the data points will be centered on the regression line. This assumption is unverifiable.
(4) $E(u_i \mid X) = 0$ or $\text{cov}(u_i, X) = 0$. The error terms are independent of the Xs. The error terms are uncorrelated with the Xs. There

is no relationship between any of the Xs and the value of the error terms.

(5) $V(u_i) = \sigma_u^2$ for all i with $0 \leq \sigma_u^2 < \infty$. The variance of the error is constant across observations and the variance is finite. The degree of spread of the Ys around the regression line does not change. For example, the spread of the Ys does not change with the values of X.

(6) $E(u_i \cdot u_j) = 0$ for all $i \neq j$. The error terms are independent of each other. The error terms are uncorrelated with each other. The value of one error term has no influence on the value of another error term. The amount that a particular Y_i is above or below the regression line does not influence the specific location of any other Y_j.

(7) $u_i \sim i.i.d.\ N(0, \sigma_u^2)$. This means that the error terms are independently and identically distributed (*i.i.d.*) with a normal distribution. The distribution of the values of Y is unimodal and symmetric. We are repeating the idea that the mean of the errors is zero and the variance is constant.

Ideal regression errors are often described as Gaussian "white noise." White light is light that is made up of all of the different colors (frequencies) of light combined together. White noise is noise that is produced by combining sounds of all different frequencies together. Regression errors should be "white noise" because there should be no dominant frequencies in the errors, and there should be no patterns in the errors. They should be completely random.

For computational reasons, we will need to make three more assumptions:

(1) We assume that the Xs vary. We assume that X is not constant. Otherwise, it will be impossible to estimate the effect of a change in X on Y.

(2) We assume that there is no exact linear relationship between the Xs. If X_2 and X_3 are the same, it will be impossible to distinguish the effect of X_2 from the effect of X_3.

(3) We assume that we have enough data such that $N > k$, the number of observations exceeds the number of parameters being estimated.

11.3.2 *Gauss–Markov theorem*

Under the assumptions we have stated, the ordinary least squares (OLS) estimators of the βs are the **b**est **l**inear **u**nbiased **e**stimators (BLUE) of the regression coefficients. By unbiased estimators, we mean that, on average, these estimators hit the true parameter values on the mark. The OLS estimators are consistent estimators. The variance of the estimate goes toward zero as the sample size increases. And by "best," we mean that these estimators have the minimum variance of all linear unbiased estimators. OLS estimators are efficient estimators. In short, OLS is BLUE.

We will not prove the Gauss–Markov theorem here. We proved the Gauss–Markov theorem in the case of a simple linear regression in the previous chapter. It required a lot of summation signs. In the case of multiple regression with many explanatory variables, we would need to use linear algebra to make the notation manageable. The usefulness of linear algebra is demonstrated in the Appendix to this chapter.

All the assumptions behind the Gauss–Markov theorem are not equally important. We have three assumptions here just to make ordinary least squares computationally feasible. Assumptions 1, 2, 3, and 4 are necessary for the unbiasedness of the coefficient estimates and for meaningful standard errors. Assumptions 5 and 6 are necessary for the efficiency of the estimates and for good estimates of the standard errors. But they are not necessary for the unbiasedness of OLS. The normality assumption in assumption 7 is not all that critical because we can rely on the central limit theorem with sample sizes $(N - k)$ larger than 30.

11.4 Goodness of Fit

You can always stick a regression line through some data. But sometimes the regression line fits the data fairly well, and other times there is very little relationship between the line and the data.

We want a measure of the extent to which the regression line fits the sample data points. A good regression equation explains or accounts for a large proportion of the variation in Y. And we would like to use a measure of the goodness of fit that is unit-free.

We can break up the deviation of any observation Y_i from the mean of Y, $\bar{Y}$, into two parts, by adding and subtracting $\hat{Y}_i$:

$$Y_i - \bar{Y} = (Y_i - \hat{Y}_i) + (\hat{Y}_i - \bar{Y})$$

where $(Y_i - \hat{Y}_i) = e_i$ is the unexplained part and $(\hat{Y}_i - \bar{Y})$ is the explained part of the deviation. Remember that $\hat{Y}_i$ is the fitted value of Y, the expected value of Y given the explanatory variables.

Suppose we look at the total variation in Y around its mean:

$$\text{Variation}(Y) = \sum (Y_i - \bar{Y})^2$$

Note that this is not the variance of Y because we are not dividing it by $(N - 1)$. It turns out that

$$\sum (Y_i - \bar{Y})^2 = \sum (Y_i - \hat{Y}_i)^2 + \sum (\hat{Y}_i - \bar{Y})^2$$

This is because the e_i are orthogonal to the Xs. And the explained part of the deviation is just a linear combination of the Xs and lies in the space of the Xs. This is really nothing more than the Pythagorean theorem, $a^2 + b^2 = c^2$, with three sides of a right triangle. We can show this as follows:

$$\begin{aligned}\sum (Y_i - \bar{Y})^2 &= \sum ((Y_i - \hat{Y}_i) + (\hat{Y}_i - \bar{Y}))^2 \\ &= \sum (Y_i - \hat{Y}_i)^2 + \sum (\hat{Y}_i - \bar{Y})^2 \\ &\quad + 2 \sum (Y_i - \hat{Y}_i)(\hat{Y}_i - \bar{Y})\end{aligned}$$

But the last term here equals zero:

$$\sum (Y_i - \hat{Y}_i)(\hat{Y}_i - \bar{Y}) = 0$$

$$\sum (Y_i - \hat{Y}_i)(\hat{Y}_i - \bar{Y}) = \sum e_i(\hat{Y}_i - \bar{Y}) = \sum e_i(b_1 + b_2 X_i - \bar{Y}) = 0$$

since $\sum e_i = 0$ and $\sum e_i X_i = 0$. The errors e_i lie in a space orthogonal to the Xs.

Note that

$$\sum (Y_i - \hat{Y}_i)^2 = \sum e_i^2$$

So

$$\sum (Y_i - \bar{Y})^2 = \sum e_i^2 + \sum (\hat{Y}_i - \bar{Y})^2$$

We have the Total Variation of Y = Residual Sum of Squares + Explained Sum of Squares or the Total Sum of Squares (TSS) = Residual Sum of Squares (RSS) + Explained Sum of Squares (ESS):

$$\text{TSS} = \text{RSS} + \text{ESS}$$

One measure of the goodness of fit is the R-squared, R^2, the percent of the total variation in Y which is explained by the Xs:

$$R^2 = \frac{\text{ESS}}{\text{TSS}} = 1 - \frac{\text{RSS}}{\text{TSS}} = 1 - \frac{\sum e_i^2}{\sum (Y_i - \bar{Y})^2}$$

$$0 \leq R^2 \leq 1$$

Unfortunately, there is one problem with the R^2 as a measure of goodness of fit. The R^2 can only increase as you add more Xs to the regression equation. The R^2 pertains to the explained and unexplained variation in Y but does not account for the number of Xs in the regression equation. When the number of parameters in the regression, k, is equal to the sample size N, the $R^2 = 1$. We may not necessarily want a goodness of fit measure which is just measuring the number of explanatory variables we have thrown into the equation.

Thus, consider a measure of the goodness of fit which adjusts for the number of Xs in the regression. Consider the adjusted R-squared, or the R bar squared, written as $\bar{R}^2$, where

$$\bar{R}^2 = 1 - \frac{\sum e_i^2/(N-k)}{\sum (Y_i - \bar{Y})^2/(N-1)} = 1 - \frac{s_u^2}{s_y^2} = 1 - \frac{V(u)}{V(Y)}$$

When additional X variables are added to the regression equation, the R^2 will go up, but the $\bar{R}^2$ could go down. You will be penalized for adding too many Xs to your regression equation with the adjusted $\bar{R}^2$.

A little algebra will illustrate the relationship between R^2 and $\bar{R}^2$:

$$1 - (1 - R^2)\left(\frac{N-1}{N-k}\right) = \bar{R}^2$$

If you know the R^2, N, and k, you can figure out the $\bar{R}^2$. Let us make a few observations here:

1. If $k = 1$, $\bar{R}^2 = R^2$
2. If $k > 1$, $\bar{R}^2 \leq R^2$
3. If $N = k$, $R^2 = 1$
4. $\bar{R}^2$ can be negative
5. $0 \leq R^2 \leq 1$

If you ever find $R^2 = 1$, you know you have messed up. You either have too many Xs in your equation or not enough data points N. In either case, your results are meaningless.

Everything else being the same, a higher $\bar{R}^2$ is better than a lower $\bar{R}^2$. But everything else is rarely the same, and you should not be overly concerned about the $\bar{R}^2$. With cross-section data, an $\bar{R}^2$ near 0.50 would seem typical. With time series data, an $\bar{R}^2$ near 0.90 would seem normal.

11.4.1 *Why is the R^2 called the R^2?*

In a simple regression, the R^2 will be the square of the sample correlation coefficient between the Y and X variables. We usually denote the sample correlation coefficient between two variables with the letter $r_{xy} = \frac{\text{cov}_{xy}}{s_x \cdot s_y}$. Since $-1 \leq r_{xy} \leq 1$, we will have $0 \leq R^2 \leq 1$:

$$r_{xy} = \frac{\sum x_i y_i/(N-1)}{\sqrt{\sum x_i^2/(N-1)}\sqrt{\sum y_i^2/(N-1)}} = \frac{\sum x_i y_i}{\sqrt{\sum x_i^2}\sqrt{\sum y_i^2}}$$

So $r_{xy}^2 = \frac{(\sum x_i y_i)^2}{\sum x_i^2 \sum y_i^2}$

But $R^2 = \frac{\text{ESS}}{\text{TSS}} = \frac{\sum(\hat{Y}_i - \bar{Y})^2}{\sum(Y_i - \bar{Y})^2} = \frac{\sum((b_1+b_2X_2)-(b_1+b_2\bar{X}))^2}{\sum(Y_i-\bar{Y})^2} = \frac{b_2^2 \sum x_i^2}{\sum y_i^2} = \frac{\left(\frac{\sum x_i y_i}{\sum x_i^2}\right)^2 \sum x_i^2}{\sum y_i^2} = \frac{(\sum x_i y_i)^2}{\sum x_i^2 \sum y_i^2}$. QED.

11.5 Hypothesis Testing

We assume we have the true relationship

$$Y_i = \beta_1 + \beta_2 X_{2i} + \beta_3 X_{3i} + \cdots + \beta_k X_{ki} + u_i$$

with $u_i \sim N(0, \sigma_u^2)$.

We have estimated the relationship

$$Y_i = b_1 + b_2 X_{2i} + b_3 X_{3i} + \cdots + b_k X_{ki} + e_i$$

Suppose we want to test the hypothesis $H_0 : \beta_2 = 0$. Here we will extend the analysis from the previous chapter on simple regressions where we only had one X variable on the right-hand side. Now we have $(k-1)$ X variables on the right-hand side.

We know that $\frac{b_i - \beta_i}{SD_{b_i}} \sim N(0,1)$ where SD_{b_i} is the standard deviation of b_i. But now we estimate σ_u^2 with $s_u^2 = \frac{\sum e_i^2}{N-k} = \frac{\sum(Y_i - b_1 - b_2 X_{2i} - b_3 X_{3i} - \cdots - b_k X_{ki})^2}{N-k}$. We divide by $N-k$ rather than $N-2$ because we had to estimate k parameters. Thus, we now have $\frac{(N-k)s_u^2}{\sigma_u^2} = \frac{\sum e_i^2}{\sigma_u^2} = \frac{\sum(Y_i - b_1 - b_2 X_{2i} - b_3 X_{3i} - \cdots - b_k X_{ki})^2}{\sigma_u^2} \sim \chi^2_{N-k}$. We do not prove this here. But the intuition should follow from all the work we have done. We know the following:

$$\frac{\sum(Y_i - \mu_y)^2}{\sigma^2} \sim \chi^2_N$$

$$\frac{\sum(Y_i - \bar{Y})^2}{\sigma^2} \sim \chi^2_{N-1}$$

$$\frac{\sum(Y_i - b_1 - b_2X_2)^2}{\sigma^2} \sim \chi^2_{N-2}$$

$$\frac{\sum(Y_i - b_1 - b_2X_{2i} - b_3X_{3i} - \cdots - b_kX_{ki})^2}{\sigma^2} \sim \chi^2_{N-k}$$

We lose a degree of freedom with every parameter we estimate from the data. Since $\frac{b_i-\beta_i}{SD_{b_i}} \sim N(0,1)$, and $\frac{(N-k)s_u^2}{\sigma_u^2} \sim \chi^2_{N-k}$, we can form the following test statistic with a Student's t-distribution.

$$\frac{N(0,1)}{\sqrt{\chi^2_{N-k}/(N-k)}} = \frac{\frac{b_i-\beta_i}{SD_{b_i}}}{\sqrt{\frac{(N-k)s_u^2}{\sigma_u^2}/(N-k)}} = \frac{b_i-\beta_i}{SD_{b_i}\sqrt{\frac{s_u^2}{\sigma_u^2}}} = \frac{b_i-\beta_i}{SE_{b_i}} \sim \text{Student's}$$

t-distribution with $N-k$ degrees of freedom where SE_{b_i} is the standard error of b_i. If the null hypothesis is that $\beta_i = 0$, then $\frac{b_i}{SE_{b_i}}$ will have a Student's t-distribution with $N-k$ degrees of freedom.

11.6 Example

The Current Population Survey (CPS), sponsored jointly by the U.S. Census Bureau and the U.S. Bureau of Labor Statistics (BLS), is the primary source of labor force statistics for the population of the United States. We take a random sample of 774 observations from the March 2014 CPS survey and run the following regression. We have the natural log of weekly earnings, years of education, years of experience, and years of experience squared:

$$\ln\text{Wage}_i = \beta_1 + \beta_2\text{EDU}_i + \beta_3\text{EXP}_i + \beta_4\text{EXP}_i^2 + u_i$$

The estimated regression equation is

$$\begin{aligned}\ln\text{Wage}_i = \quad & 9.265 \quad + 0.0946\text{EDU}_i + 0.0453\text{EXP}_i - 0.0007\text{EXP}_i^2 \\ & (0.19202) \qquad (0.0082) \qquad\quad (0.0111) \qquad\quad (0.0002)\end{aligned}$$

Here the standard errors appear in parentheses. $\bar{R}^2 = 0.174$, and the regression $F = 55.169$.

Suppose we want to see if the level of education affects earnings. Our null hypothesis is $H_0 : \beta_2 = 0$ and our alternative hypothesis is

$H_A : \beta_2 \neq 0$. Let's set our significance level $\alpha = 5\%$. We know that $\frac{b_2-\beta_2}{SE_{b_2}}$ has a Student's t-distribution with $N-k$ degrees of freedom. In this case, we have $N-k = 774-4 = 770$ degrees of freedom. From our Student's t tables, we know that $P\left(-1.963 < \frac{b_2-\beta_2}{SE_{b_2}} < 1.963\right) = 95\%$. Under the null hypothesis, $\frac{b_2-\beta_2}{SE_{b_2}} = \frac{0.0946-0}{0.0082} = 11.505$. Since $11.505 > 1.963$, we reject $H_0 : \beta_2 = 0$ at the 5% significance level. The evidence suggests that education improves your earnings (see Table 11.1).

Table 11.1. Hypothesis testing summary: education and earings.

Hypothesis	$H_0 : \beta_2 = 0 \quad H_A : \beta_2 \neq 0$
Significance Level	$\alpha = 5\%$
Acceptance Region	$-1.963 < \dfrac{b_2 - \beta_2}{SE_{b_2}} < 1.963$
Test Statistic	$\dfrac{b_2 - \beta_2}{SE_{b_2}} = \dfrac{0.0946 - 0}{0.0082} = 11.505$
Decision	Since $11.505 > 1.963$, reject H_0

11.7 Regression *F*-Statistic

Suppose you run a regression

$$Y_i = \beta_1 + \beta_2 X_{2i} + \beta_3 X_{3i} + \cdots + \beta_k X_{ki} + u_i$$

and want to test the hypothesis that none of the Xs matter. You want to see if you are just wasting your time. Your null hypothesis is $H_0 : \beta_2 = \beta_3 = \cdots = \beta_k = 0$.

We know that $s_u^2 = \frac{1}{N-k}\sum(Y_i - b_1 - b_2X_{2i} - b_3X_{3i} - \cdots - b_kX_{ki})^2 = \frac{\sum e_i^2}{N-k} = \frac{\text{RSS}}{N-k}$ and $\frac{(N-k)s_u^2}{\sigma_u^2} = \frac{\text{RSS}}{\sigma_u^2} \sim \chi^2_{N-k}$.

We also know that $s_y^2 = \frac{1}{N-1}\sum(Y_i - \bar{Y})^2 = \frac{\text{TSS}}{N-1}$ and $\frac{(N-1)s_y^2}{\sigma_y^2} = \frac{\text{TSS}}{\sigma_y^2} \sim \chi^2_{N-1}$.

We have $\frac{\text{TSS}}{\sigma_y^2} \sim \chi^2_{N-1}$ and $\frac{\text{RSS}}{\sigma_u^2} \sim \chi^2_{N-k}$, two chi-square random variables. If we subtract one chi-square random variable from another chi-square, we get another chi-square random variable as long as the degrees of freedom of the first exceeds the degrees of freedom of the second:

$$\frac{\text{TSS}}{\sigma_y^2} - \frac{\text{RSS}}{\sigma_u^2} \sim \chi^2_{N-1} - \chi^2_{N-k} = \chi^2_{(N-1)-(N-k)} = \chi^2_{k-1}$$

If we take the ratio of two chi-square random variables which have been divided by their degrees of freedom, we will get a random variable with an F-distribution:

$$\frac{\left(\frac{\text{TSS}}{\sigma_y^2} - \frac{\text{RSS}}{\sigma_u^2}\right)/(k-1)}{\left(\frac{\text{RSS}}{\sigma_u^2}\right)/(N-k)} \sim F(k-1, N-k)$$

Our regression equation is

$$Y_i = \beta_1 + \beta_2 X_{2i} + \beta_3 X_{3i} + \cdots + \beta_k X_{ki} + u_i$$

Under the null hypothesis, we have $\beta_2 = \beta_3 = \cdots = \beta_k = 0$, so $Y_i = \beta_1 + u_i$. This would mean that the $V(Y_i) = V(u_i)$ and that $\sigma_y^2 = \sigma_u^2 = \sigma^2$ since β_1 is a constant. So if the null hypothesis is correct, we have the following:

$$\begin{aligned}&\frac{\left(\frac{\text{TSS}}{\sigma^2} - \frac{\text{RSS}}{\sigma^2}\right)/(k-1)}{\left(\frac{\text{RSS}}{\sigma^2}\right)/(N-k)}\\ &\quad = \frac{(\text{TSS} - \text{RSS})/(k-1)}{(\text{RSS})/(N-k)} = \frac{\text{ESS}/(k-1)}{\text{RSS}/(N-k)} \sim F(k-1, N-k)\end{aligned}$$

We will reject H_0 if TSS is much bigger than RSS or if this F-statistics is much bigger than 0. Remember that k is the number of parameters being estimated in the regression which is one larger than the number of Xs because of the constant term.

11.8 F-statistic and the R^2

There is a relationship between the regression F-statistic and the R^2:

$$F = \frac{\text{ESS}/(k-1)}{\text{RSS}/(N-k)}$$

$$= \frac{\frac{\text{ESS}}{\text{TSS}}/(k-1)}{\frac{\text{RSS}}{\text{TSS}}/(N-k)} = \frac{R^2/(k-1)}{(1-R^2)/(N-k)} \sim F(k-1, N-k)$$

The higher the R^2, the higher the F-statistic.

11.8.1 *Example*

Let's go back to the regression we just ran with CPS data. We have a random sample of 774 observations from the March 2014 CPS survey and ran the following regression. We have the natural log of weekly earnings, years of education, years of experience, and years of experience squared:

$$\ln\text{Wage}_i = \beta_1 + \beta_2\text{EDU}_i + \beta_3\text{EXP}_i + \beta_4\text{EXP}_i^2 + u_i$$

The estimated regression equation is

$$\begin{array}{rcccc} \ln\text{Wage}_i = & 9.265 & +\,0.0946\text{EDU}_i & +\,0.0453\text{EXP}_i & -\,0.0007\text{EXP}_i^2 \\ & (0.19202) & (0.0082) & (0.0111) & (0.0002) \end{array}$$

Here the standard errors appear in parentheses. $\bar{R}^2 = 0.174$, and the regression reports that TSS $= 421.156$, RSS $= 346.647$, and ESS $= 74.509$. We want to test the hypothesis that none of the Xs matter and that $H_0 : \beta_2 = \beta_3 = \beta_4 = 0$. Our alternative hypothesis is that $H_A : \beta_2 \neq \beta_3 \neq \beta_4 \neq 0$. Let's set our significance level $\alpha = 5\%$. Under the null hypothesis, $\frac{\text{ESS}/(k-1)}{\text{RSS}/(N-k)} \sim F(k-1,\ N-k)$. In our regression, $k = 4$ and $N = 774$. So our test statistic will have an $F(4-1{,}774-4) = F(3{,}770)$ distribution. From our F tables, we know that $P(F(3{,}770) < 2.62) = 95\%$. We calculate our test statistic $\frac{\text{ESS}/(k-1)}{\text{RSS}/(N-k)} = \frac{74.509/3}{346.647/770} = 55.168$. Most regression software will automatically report this F-statistic. Since $55.168 > 2.62$, we reject H_0 (see Table 11.2).

Table 11.2. Hypothesis testing summary: $\beta_2 = \beta_3 = \beta_4 = 0$.

Hypothesis	$H_0 : \beta_2 = \beta_3 = \beta_4 = 0$
	$H_A : \beta_2 \neq \beta_3 \neq \beta_4 \neq 0$
Significance Level	$\alpha = 5\%$
Acceptance Region	$\dfrac{\text{ESS}/(k-1)}{\text{RSS}/(N-k)} < 2.62$
Test Statistic	$\dfrac{\text{ESS}/(k-1)}{\text{RSS}/(N-k)} = \dfrac{74.509/3}{346.647/770} = 55.168$
Decision	Since $55.168 > 2.62$, we reject H_0

11.9 Generalized *F*-Tests

Let's generalize this F-test to test other hypotheses. We start with the following regression equation:

$$Y_i = \beta_1 + \beta_2 X_{2i} + \beta_3 X_{3i} + \cdots + \beta_k X_{ki} + u_i$$

Suppose we want to test the hypothesis that a subset of these coefficients is equal to zero.

We begin by rewriting the equation above as follows:

$$\begin{aligned} Y = {} & \beta_1 + \beta_2 X_2 + \cdots + \beta_{k-q} X_{k-q} + \beta_{k-q+1} X_{k-q+1} \\ & + \cdots + \beta_k X_k + u \end{aligned}$$

where we have dropped the subscript i. We want to test the null hypothesis that the last q coefficients are jointly equal to zero:

$$H_o\colon \beta_{k-q+1} = \cdots = \beta_k = 0$$

(1) We begin by estimating the "unrestricted model" above:

$$Y = \beta_1 + \beta_2 X_2 + \beta_3 X_3 + \cdots + \beta_k X_k + u$$

We call this the "unrestricted model" because all the coefficients are allowed to be whatever they want to be. We note the following:

$$\frac{(N-k)s^2}{\sigma_U^2} = \frac{\text{RSS}_U}{\sigma_U^2} \sim \chi^2_{N-k}$$

where RSS_U is the "residual sum of squares" from the unrestricted model, σ_U^2 is the variance of the error u in the unrestricted model, and

$$s^2 = \frac{1}{N-k}\sum e_i^2$$

where e_i are the fitted errors.

(2) We then impose our hypothesis H_o: $\beta_{k-q+1} = \cdots = \beta_k = 0$ on the regression equation by estimating the following "restricted model":

$$Y = \beta_1 + \beta_2 X_2 + \cdots + \beta_{k-q} X_{k-q} + u$$

By dropping the last q Xs from the regression, we force their coefficients to equal zero. We note the following:

$$\frac{(N-(k-q))s^2}{\sigma_R^2} = \frac{\text{RSS}_R}{\sigma_R^2} \sim \chi^2_{N-(k-q)}$$

where RSS_R is the "residual sum of squares" from the restricted model, σ_R^2 is the variance of the error u in the restricted model, and

$$s^2 = \frac{1}{N-(k-q)}\sum e_i^2$$

(3) If the null hypothesis is true, observe that $\sigma_U^2 = \sigma_R^2 = \sigma^2$.

(4) When we take the difference between two chi-square random variables, we get another chi-square random variable. We have

$$\frac{\text{RSS}_R}{\sigma^2} - \frac{\text{RSS}_U}{\sigma^2} = \frac{\text{RSS}_R - \text{RSS}_U}{\sigma^2} \sim \chi^2_{N-(k-q)-(N-k)} = \chi^2_q$$

Note that q will be equal to the number of restrictions in the null hypothesis. This is also the number of equal signs in the null hypothesis.

(5) The ratio of two chi-square random variables which have been divided by their degrees of freedom follows an F distribution.

Consequently,

$$\frac{\frac{\text{RSS}_R - \text{RSS}_U}{\sigma^2}/q}{\frac{\text{RSS}_U}{\sigma^2}/(N-k)} = \frac{(\text{RSS}_R - \text{RSS}_U)/q}{\text{RSS}_U/(N-k)} \sim F(q, N-k)$$

If the null hypothesis is false (i.e., the restrictions are false), then $\text{RSS}_R \gg \text{RSS}_U$. The restricted regression just won't fit the data quite as well. The F-statistics will be very large, and we will reject the null hypothesis. Note that $\text{RSS}_R \geq \text{RSS}_U$ always. If you ever find that $\text{RSS}_R < \text{RSS}_U$, giving you a negative F-statistics, you have messed up!

11.10 Example

Let's test another hypothesis with the CPS regression. We have a random sample of 774 observations from the March 2014 CPS survey and ran the following regression. We have the natural log of weekly earnings, years of education, years of experience, and years of experience squared:

$$\ln\text{Wage}_i = \beta_1 + \beta_2\text{EDU}_i + \beta_3\text{EXP}_i + \beta_4\text{EXP}_i^2 + u_i$$

The estimated regression equation is

$$\begin{array}{rcccc} \ln\text{Wage}_i = & 9.265 & + 0.0946\text{EDU}_i & + 0.0453\text{EXP}_i & - 0.0007\text{EXP}_i^2 \\ & (0.19202) & (0.0082) & (0.0111) & (0.0002) \end{array}$$

Here the standard errors appear in parentheses. $\bar{R}^2 = 0.174$, and the regression reports that TSS $= 421.156$, RSS $= 346.647$, and ESS $= 74.509$. $N - k = 774 - 4 = 770$.

Suppose we want to test the hypothesis that experience and experience squared do not matter. $H_0 : \beta_3 = \beta_4 = 0$ vs the alternative hypothesis $H_A : \beta_3 \neq \beta_4 \neq 0$. Note that $q = 2$ here. We will use the significance level $\alpha = 5\%$. We have already run the "unrestricted" regression. We now need to run the "restricted" regression where we impose our null hypothesis on the regression equation. We run the regression

$$\ln\text{Wage}_i = \beta_1 + \beta_2\text{EDU}_i + v_i$$

and get the follow regression estimates:

$$\begin{array}{rcc} \ln\text{Wage}_i = & 9.9079 & + 0.0953\text{EDU}_i \\ & (0.1111) & (0.0079) \end{array}$$

Here the standard errors appear in parentheses. $\bar{R}^2 = 0.157$, and the regression reports that TSS = 421.156, RSS = 354.570, and ESS = 66.586.

Our test statistic, $\frac{(\text{RSS}_R - \text{RSS}_U)/q}{\text{RSS}_U/(N-k)}$, has an $F(2{,}770)$ distribution. We know from our F tables that $P(F(2{,}770) < 3.01) = 95\%$. We calculate our test statistic. $\frac{(\text{RSS}_R - \text{RSS}_U)/q}{\text{RSS}_U/(N-k)} = \frac{(354.570-346.647)/2}{346.647/(774-4)} = \frac{181.246}{0.45} = 402.59$. Since $402.59 > 3.01$, we reject our null hypothesis (see Table 11.3).

Table 11.3. Hypothesis testing summary: $\beta_3 = \beta_4 = 0$.

Hypothesis	$H_0 : \beta_3 = \beta_4 = 0$
	$H_A : \beta_3 \neq \beta_4 \neq 0$
Significance Level	$\alpha = 5\%$
Acceptance Region	$P(F(2{,}770) < 3.01) = 95\%$
Test Statistic	$\frac{(\text{RSS}_R - \text{RSS}_U)/q}{\text{RSS}_U/(N-k)} = \frac{(354.570 - 346.647)/2}{346.647/(774-4)}$
	$= \frac{181.246}{0.45} = 402.59$
Decision	Since $402.59 > 3.01$, we reject H_0

11.11 Testing Linear Equality Constraints

We will consider four different kinds of equality constraints.

11.11.1 *Single linear equality constraint*

Suppose we have a Cobb–Douglas production function where output Q is a function of capital K and labor L:

$$Q = F(K, L) = AK^{\alpha}L^{\beta}$$

where A, the level of technology, along with α and β are constants. We might want to test for constant returns to scale, $H_0 : \alpha + \beta = 1$. If we have constant returns to scale, our output will double if we double our capital and double our labor. We can estimate our production function by taking logs:

$$\ln Q = \ln A + \alpha \ln K + \beta \ln L$$

This gives us the regression equation

$$\ln Q = \gamma + \alpha \ln K + \beta \ln L + u$$

We could run this regression and test to see if $\alpha + \beta = 1$. Let's generalize the regression specification a bit to

$$Y = \beta_1 + \beta_2 X_2 + \beta_3 X_3 + \cdots + \beta_k X_k + u$$

We will call this our "unrestricted" regression for reasons we will see shortly. We can run this regression and generate the "unrestricted" sum of squared residuals from this regression $\text{RSS}_U = \sum e_i^2$. We know that $\frac{\text{RSS}_U}{\sigma_u^2} = \frac{(N-k)s_u^2}{\sigma_u^2} \sim \chi^2_{N-k}$.

Suppose our null hypothesis is $H_0 : \beta_2 + \beta_3 = 1$. We could also write that as $H_0 : \beta_2 = 1 - \beta_3$. Let's impose this restriction on the regression equation. We would then have

$$\begin{aligned}
Y &= \beta_1 + (1 - \beta_3)\, X_2 + \beta_3 X_3 + \cdots + \beta_k X_k + u \\
Y &= \beta_1 + X_2 + \beta_3 (X_3 - X_2) + \cdots + \beta_k X_k + u \\
Y - X_2 &= \beta_1 + \beta_3 (X_3 - X_2) + \cdots + \beta_k X_k + u \\
Z = Y - X_2 &= \beta_1 + \beta_3 (X_3 - X_2) + \cdots + \beta_k X_k + u
\end{aligned}$$

Let's call this our "restricted" regression because we have imposed our null hypothesis on this equation. We would create the variables $Y - X_2$ and $X_3 - X_2$. We can then run this regression and generate the "restricted" sum of the squared residuals, $\text{RSS}_R = \sum e_i^2$. We know that $\frac{\text{RSS}_R}{\sigma_u^2} \sim \chi^2_{N-(k-1)}$. This is because we are estimating $k - 1$ parameters on the right-hand side of the equation. If the null hypothesis is true, the variance of the errors in the two regressions will be the same. So under the null hypothesis, $\frac{\text{RSS}_R}{\sigma^2} - \frac{\text{RSS}_U}{\sigma^2} \sim \chi^2_{N-(k-1)-(N-k)} = \chi^2_1$.

Thus, we have two chi-square random variables and can form the following F-statistic. Under the null hypothesis, all the σ^2 drop out, and we have

$$\frac{(\text{RSS}_R - \text{RSS}_U)/1}{\text{RSS}_U/(N-k)} \sim F(1, N-k)$$

If the null hypothesis is false, the restricted regression will not fit the data nearly as well as the unrestricted regression. We would reject the null hypothesis if $\text{RSS}_R \gg \text{RSS}_U$, if the F-statistic is really big. If the null hypothesis is true, we expect $\text{RSS}_R \approx \text{RSS}_U$, and the F-statistics will be very small. If $\text{RSS}_R < \text{RSS}_U$, then you have messed up. All F-statistics must be positive.

11.11.2 *Multiple linear equality constraints*

This framework will allow us to test multiple linear equality constraints at the same time. We have the general regression specification:

$$Y = \beta_1 + \beta_2 X_2 + \beta_3 X_3 + \cdots + \beta_k X_k + u$$

We can run this regression and generate the "unrestricted" sum of the squared residuals, $\text{RSS}_U = \sum e_i^2$. We know that $\frac{\text{RSS}_U}{\sigma_U^2} = \frac{(N-k)s_u^2}{\sigma_U^2} \sim \chi^2_{N-k}$.

Suppose you want to test the following null hypothesis: $H_0 : \beta_2 = \beta_3$ and $\beta_4 = 2\beta_5$. We have two linear equality constraints here. We can form the "restricted" regression by imposing the null hypotheses on the coefficients:

$$Y = \beta_1 + \beta_2 X_2 + \beta_2 X_3 + 2\beta_5 X_4 + \beta_5 X_5 \cdots + \beta_k X_k + u$$
$$Y = \beta_1 + \beta_2 (X_2 + X_3) + \beta_5 (2X_4 + X_5) \cdots + \beta_k X_k + u$$

We call this our "restricted" regression because we have imposed our null hypotheses on this equation. We can create the variables $X_2 + X_3$ and $2X_4 + X_5$. We can then run this regression and generate the "restricted" sum of the squared residuals, $\text{RSS}_R = \sum e_i^2$. We know that $\frac{\text{RSS}_R}{\sigma_R^2} \sim \chi^2_{N-(k-2)}$. If the null hypothesis is true, the variance of the error in the two regressions will be the same. So under the null hypothesis, $\frac{\text{RSS}_R}{\sigma^2} - \frac{\text{RSS}_U}{\sigma^2} \sim \chi^2_{N-(k-2)-(N-k)} = \chi^2_2$.

With these two chi-square random variables, we can form our F-statistic. Under the null hypothesis,

$$\frac{(\text{RSS}_R - \text{RSS}_U)/2}{\text{RSS}_U/(N-k)} \sim F(2, N-k)$$

The degrees of freedom in the numerator represent the number of constraints in the null hypothesis. This will be the same as the number of equal (=) signs in the null hypothesis.

In general, we have

$$\frac{(\text{RSS}_R - \text{RSS}_U)/m}{\text{RSS}_U/(N-k)} \sim F(m, N-k)$$

where m is the number of restrictions in the null hypothesis. We will reject the null hypothesis if F is too big.

11.11.3 *Equality of coefficients across regressions*

Sometimes we want to test for the equality of regression coefficients across regressions. Do men face the same labor market as women? Is the consumption function the same during periods of war and periods of peace? Is the demand for money in Japan and the United States the same? We can test these kinds of hypotheses with an F-test.

If men and women face the same labor market, standard wage equations for men should look similar to wage equations for women. Suppose we have labor market data with N_m observations on men and N_w observations on women. We can estimate this regression on the sample of N_m men:

$$Y_i = \beta_1 + \beta_2 X_{2i} + \beta_3 X_{3i} + \cdots + \beta_k X_{ki} + u_i$$

We run this regression and generate the residual sum of squares which we call RSS_m. And we can run the following regression on the sample of N_w women:

$$Y_j = \alpha_1 + \alpha_2 X_{2j} + \alpha_3 X_{3j} + \cdots + \alpha_k X_{kj} + u_j$$

We run this regression and generate the residual sum of squares which we call RSS_w. We know that $\frac{\text{RSS}_m}{\sigma_i^2} \sim \chi^2_{N_m-k}$ and $\frac{\text{RSS}_w}{\sigma_j^2} \sim \chi^2_{N_w-k}$. We will assume that $u_i \sim N(0,\sigma^2)$ and $u_j \sim N(0,\sigma^2)$ with σ^2 same. We will also assume that u_i and u_j are independently distributed. Then we can add the two chi-square random variables to get

$$\begin{aligned}\frac{\text{RSS}_U}{\sigma^2} &= \frac{\text{RSS}_m}{\sigma^2} + \frac{\text{RSS}_w}{\sigma^2} \sim \chi^2_{N_m-k} + \chi^2_{N_w-k} \\ &= \chi^2_{(N_m-k)+(N_m-k)} = \chi^2_{N_m+N_w-2k}\end{aligned}$$

Our null hypothesis is that all the coefficients are the same across the two regressions. $H_0 : \alpha_1 = \beta_1, \alpha_2 = \beta_2, \ldots \alpha_k = \beta_k$ or $H_0 : \alpha_i = \beta_i$ for all i. To test this, we then combine all the data on men and women to run the following regression:

$$Y_i = \gamma_1 + \gamma_2 X_{2i} + \gamma_3 X_{3i} + \cdots + \gamma_k X_{ki} + u_i$$

with $N = N_m + N_w$ observations. By combining all the data, we force the coefficients in the "restricted" regression to be the same for men and women. The residual sum of squares from this "restricted" regression is RSS_R where

$$\frac{\text{RSS}_R}{\sigma^2} \sim \chi^2_{N-k}$$

We now have two chi-square random variables and can form our F-statistic. If the null hypothesis is true, the variance of the errors will be the same for RSS_U and RSS_R:

$$\frac{(\text{RSS}_R - \text{RSS}_U)/k}{\text{RSS}_U/(N-2k)} \sim F(k, N-2k)$$

where $N = N_m + N_w$. If the null hypothesis is true, we expect F to be close to zero. If the null hypothesis is false, the fit of our restricted regression will be significantly worse than the fit of our two separate regressions. We will have $\text{RSS}_R \gg \text{RSS}_U$, giving us a very big F-statistic. We will then reject the null hypothesis. If the F-statistic is ever negative, you have messed up.

11.11.4 *Example*

Using our CPS data, we run the following regression on the entire sample of men and women:

$$\ln\text{Wage}_i = \gamma_1 + \gamma_2\text{EDU}_i + \gamma_3\text{EXP}_i + \gamma_4\text{EXP}_i^2 + \varepsilon_i$$

With a sample size of 774, we get the following regression results:

$$\begin{aligned}\ln\text{Wage}_i = {} & 9.265 + 0.0946\text{EDU}_i + 0.0453\text{EXP}_i - 0.0007\text{EXP}_i^2 \\ & (0.19202) \quad (0.0082) \qquad (0.0111) \qquad (0.0002)\end{aligned}$$

Here the standard errors appear in parentheses. $\bar{R}^2 = 0.174$, and the regression reports that TSS = 421.156, RSS = 346.647, and ESS = 74.509.

Then we run the following regression over our sample of 405 men:

$$\ln\text{Wage}_i = \beta_1 + \beta_2\text{EDU}_i + \beta_3\text{EXP}_i + \beta_4\text{EXP}_i^2 + u_i$$

We get the following regression results:

$$\begin{aligned}\ln\text{Wage}_i = {} & 9.1019 + 0.1005\text{EDU}_i + 0.0590\text{EXP}_i - 0.0009\text{EXP}_i^2 \\ & (0.2583) \qquad (0.0106) \qquad (0.0152) \qquad (0.0002)\end{aligned}$$

Here the standard errors appear in parentheses. $\bar{R}^2 = 0.209$, and the regression reports that TSS = 215.402, RSS = 168.932, and ESS = 46.469.

Then we run the regression on the sample of 369 women:

$$\ln\text{Wage}_i = \alpha_1 + \alpha_2\text{EDU}_i + \alpha_3\text{EXP}_i + \alpha_4\text{EXP}_i^2 + v_i$$

We get the following regression results:

$$\begin{aligned}\ln\text{Wage}_i = {} & 9.3083 + 0.0929\text{EDU}_i + 0.0343\text{EXP}_i - 0.0005\text{EXP}_i^2 \\ & (0.2786) \qquad (0.0125) \qquad (0.0156) \qquad (0.0002)\end{aligned}$$

Here the standard errors appear in parentheses. $\bar{R}^2 = 0.155$, and the regression reports that TSS = 194.987, RSS = 163.351, and ESS = 31.636.

We want to test the null hypothesis $H_0 : \alpha_1 = \beta_1$, $\alpha_2 = \beta_2$, $\alpha_3 = \beta_3$, $\alpha_4 = \beta_4$ with an alternative hypothesis $H_A : \alpha_1 \neq \beta_1$,

$\alpha_2 \neq \beta_2$, $\alpha_3 \neq \beta_3$, $\alpha_4 \neq \beta_4$. Let us set our significance level $\alpha =$ 5%. Under the null hypothesis, we know our test statistic has the following probability distribution:

$$\frac{(\text{RSS}_R - \text{RSS}_U)/k}{\text{RSS}_U/(N-2k)} \sim F(k, N-2k) = F(4{,}766)$$

From our statistical tables, we know that $P(F(4{,}766) < 2.38) = 95\%$. We calculate our test statistic. We know that $\text{RSS}_R = 346.647$, and $\text{RSS}_U = \text{RSS}_m + \text{RSS}_w = 168.932 + 163.351 = 332.283$. Remember that $\text{RSS}_U < \text{RSS}_R$ always. Our test statistic is

$$\frac{(\text{RSS}_R - \text{RSS}_U)/k}{\text{RSS}_U/(N-2k)} = \frac{(346.647 - 332.283)/4}{332.283/(774 - 2(4))} = \frac{3.591}{0.4337} = 8.278$$

Since $8.278 > 2.38$, we will reject our null hypothesis H_0. The labor market experience of men appears to be different from that of women (see Table 11.4).

Table 11.4. Hypothesis testing summary: $\alpha_1 = \beta_1$, $\alpha_2 = \beta_2$, $\alpha_3 = \beta_3$, $\alpha_4 = \beta_4$.

Hypothesis	$H_0 : \alpha_1 = \beta_1,\ \alpha_2 = \beta_2,\ \alpha_3 = \beta_3,\ \alpha_4 = \beta_4$
	$H_A : \alpha_1 \neq \beta_1,\ \alpha_2 \neq \beta_2,\ \alpha_3 \neq \beta_3,\ \alpha_4 \neq \beta_4$
Significance Level	$\alpha = 5\%$
Acceptance Region	$P(0 < F(4{,}766) < 2.38) = 95\%$
Test Statistic	$\frac{(\text{RSS}_R - \text{RSS}_U)/k}{\text{RSS}_U/(N-2k)} = \frac{(346.647 - 332.283)/4}{332.283/(774 - 2(4))}$
	$= \frac{3.591}{0.4337} = 8.278$
Decision	Since $8.278 > 2.38$, we reject H_0

11.11.5 *Structural difference with small samples*

With time series data, we may be interested in a change in some relationship over time. With cross-section data, we may be interested in the differences across ethnic groups. But we may not always have enough data to run two regressions over two sample periods or two ethnic groups. For example, with time series data, you might be working with annual data from 1947 to 2020 but think the world is different since Trump became President in 2017. You only have four data points from 2017 to 2020. You may not be able to run a regression on just the Trump years. Or if you have cross-section data, you might have labor market data on 100 White Americans but only 5 Native Americans. You may not be able to run a regression on the Native Americans alone. In these cases, we will use a modified version of these F-tests. We follow this procedure in cases where the additional sample is too small.

Suppose we have the general regression equation

$$Y_i = \beta_1 + \beta_2 X_{2i} + \beta_3 X_{3i} + \cdots + \beta_k X_{ki} + u_i$$

We have $N_1 + N_2 = N$ observations where $N_1 > k$ and $N_2 < k$. We cannot run the regression over the last N_2 observations. So we do the following.

We first run the regression over the N_1 observations. We will call the sum of squared residuals from this regression RSS_1. We know that $\frac{\text{RSS}_1}{\sigma^2} \sim \chi^2_{N_1-k}$:

$$Y_i = \beta_1 + \beta_2 X_{2i} + \beta_3 X_{3i} + \cdots + \beta_k X_{ki} + u_i$$

Then we run the regression over the entire dataset with N observations. We will call the sum of squared residuals from this regression RSS_0. We know that $\frac{\text{RSS}_0}{\sigma^2} \sim \chi^2_{N-k}$:

$$Y_j = \alpha_1 + \alpha_2 X_{2j} + \alpha_3 X_{3j} + \cdots + \alpha_k X_{kj} + u_j$$

Our null hypothesis is that there is no structural difference over the last N_2 observations, $H_0 : \alpha_1 = \beta_1, \alpha_2 = \beta_2, \ldots \alpha_k = \beta_k$ or $H_0 : \alpha_i = \beta_i$ for all i. If there is no difference, both equations should fit the data equally well. If there is a structural change, this second regression of all N observations will not fit the data very well. We will get an unusually large RSS_0.

We know that $\frac{\text{RSS}_0}{\sigma^2} - \frac{\text{RSS}_1}{\sigma^2} \sim \chi^2_{N-k} - \chi^2_{N_1-k} = \chi^2_{N-k-(N_1-k)} = \chi^2_{N-N_1} = \chi^2_{N_2}$. If we take the ratio of these two chi-square random variables divided by their degrees of freedom, under the null hypothesis we have

$$\frac{\left(\frac{\text{RSS}_0}{\sigma^2} - \frac{\text{RSS}_1}{\sigma^2}\right) / N_2}{\frac{\text{RSS}_1}{\sigma^2} / (N_1 - k)} = \frac{(\text{RSS}_0 - \text{RSS}_1)/N_2}{\text{RSS}_1(N_1 - k)} \sim F(N_2, N_1 - k)$$

We will reject H_0 if F is very big.

11.12 *t*-test vs *F*-test

Anytime you have a simple hypothesis like $H_0: \beta_2 = \beta_3$ where there is only one equal sign in the hypothesis, you will always be able to test the hypothesis with a t-test or an F-test. If there are two ways to test the same hypothesis, one would hope that the results of the two tests would be the same. It would be awkward if the t-test rejected the null hypothesis while the F-test accepted the null hypothesis. You would not be able to sleep at night. Luckily for us, this will never happen.

Remember the definition of a Student's t-distribution. $\frac{N(0,1)}{\sqrt{\chi_k^2/k}} \sim$ Student's t with k degrees of freedom. If we square a Student's t random variable, we get $\frac{[N(0,1)]^2}{\chi_k^2/k} = \frac{\chi_1^2/1}{\chi_k^2/k} \sim F(1,k)$. The square of the t-statistic will be equal to the F-statistic for the same hypothesis. If you examine your statistical tables, you will also find that the critical values for the $F(1,k)$ distribution are the square of the critical values for the Student's t-distribution with k degrees of freedom. So the test results will always be the same.

11.12.1 *Example*

Suppose we have a simple regression $Y_i = \beta_1 + \beta_2 X_2 + u_i$. We want to test the null hypothesis that $\beta_2 = 0$. We know that $\frac{b_2-\beta_2}{SD_{b_2}} = \frac{b_2-\beta_2}{\sqrt{\sigma^2/\sum x_i^2}} \sim N(0,1)$ and $\frac{(N-2)s^2}{\sigma^2} \sim \chi_{N-2}^2$. So we have $\frac{N(0,1)}{\sqrt{\chi_{N-2}^2/(N-2)}} = \frac{\frac{b_2-\beta_2}{\sqrt{\sigma^2/\sum x_i^2}}}{\sqrt{\frac{(N-2)s^2}{\sigma^2}/(N-2)}} = \frac{b_2-\beta_2}{\sqrt{s^2/\sum x_i^2}} = \frac{b_2-\beta_2}{SE_{b_2}} \sim$ Student's t with $N-2$ degrees of freedom.

Under the null hypothesis that $\beta_2 = 0$, we can do a t-test with $\frac{b_2}{\sqrt{s^2 \sum x_i^2}} \sim$ Student's t with $N-2$ degrees of freedom. But if we square a Student's t random variable with $N-2$ degrees of freedom, we get a random variable with an $F(1, N-2)$ degrees of freedom:

$$t^2 = \left[\frac{b_2}{\sqrt{s^2/\sum x_i^2}}\right]^2 = \frac{b_2^2 \sum x_i^2}{s^2} = \frac{\text{ESS}/1}{\text{RSS}/(N-2)} \sim F(1, N-2)$$

since

$$\begin{aligned}\text{ESS} &= \sum(\hat{Y} - \bar{Y})^2 = \sum((b_1 + b_2X_2) - (b_1 + b_2\bar{X}))^2 \\ &= \sum(b_2(X_i - \bar{X}))^2 = b_2^2 \sum x_i^2\end{aligned}$$

11.13 Linear Algebra

You may note that the notation in the last two chapters has become a little painful. Econometrics is a lot easier to explain if we know a little linear algebra. If you have taken linear algebra, you might appreciate the following. When we run regressions, we assume the true relationship is

$$\boldsymbol{y} = X\boldsymbol{\beta} + \boldsymbol{u}$$

where

$$\begin{bmatrix} y_1 \\ \vdots \\ y_n \end{bmatrix} = \begin{bmatrix} X_{11} & \cdots & X_{k1} \\ \vdots & \ddots & \vdots \\ X_{1n} & \cdots & X_{kn} \end{bmatrix} \begin{bmatrix} \beta_1 \\ \vdots \\ \beta_k \end{bmatrix} + \begin{bmatrix} u_1 \\ \vdots \\ u_n \end{bmatrix}$$

We allow for a constant term by letting X_{11} through X_{1n} be identically equal to 1.

Our estimated equation will look like the following:

$$\boldsymbol{y} = X\boldsymbol{b} + \boldsymbol{e}$$

$$\begin{bmatrix} y_1 \\ \vdots \\ y_n \end{bmatrix} = \begin{bmatrix} X_{11} & \cdots & X_{k1} \\ \vdots & \ddots & \vdots \\ X_{1n} & \cdots & X_{kn} \end{bmatrix} \begin{bmatrix} b_1 \\ \vdots \\ b_k \end{bmatrix} + \begin{bmatrix} e_1 \\ \vdots \\ e_n \end{bmatrix}$$

We choose our OLS estimates $\boldsymbol{b}$ by minimizing the sum of squared residuals $\boldsymbol{e}'\boldsymbol{e}$:

$$\begin{aligned}\boldsymbol{e}'\boldsymbol{e} &= (\boldsymbol{y} - X\boldsymbol{b})'(\boldsymbol{y} - X\boldsymbol{b}) \\ &= \boldsymbol{y}'\boldsymbol{y} - \boldsymbol{b}'X'\boldsymbol{y} - \boldsymbol{y}'X\boldsymbol{b} + \boldsymbol{b}'X'X\boldsymbol{b} \\ &= \boldsymbol{y}'\boldsymbol{y} - 2\boldsymbol{b}'X'\boldsymbol{y} + \boldsymbol{b}'X'X\boldsymbol{b}\end{aligned}$$

To minimize this, we take the derivative with respect to $\boldsymbol{b}$ and set it equal to zero:

$$\frac{\partial \boldsymbol{e}'\boldsymbol{e}}{\partial \boldsymbol{b}} = -2X'\boldsymbol{y} + 2X'X\boldsymbol{b} = 0$$

So our ordinary least squares estimate will be

$$\boldsymbol{b} = (X'X)^{-1}(X'\boldsymbol{y})$$

Isn't this a lot easier than using all those subscripts and summation signs?

11.14 Exercises

(1) Using U.S. state-level data, we want to understand the relationship between the COVID death rate and vaccination rates, obesity rates, and population density. We estimate the following relationship:

$$\begin{aligned}\text{CovidDR} = \ & \underset{(110.25)}{133.24} - \underset{(1.10)}{3.00}\text{Vax} + \underset{(2.23)}{5.17}\text{Obesity} + \underset{(0.03)}{0.18}\text{PopDensity}\end{aligned}$$

Standard errors appear in parentheses. The standard error of the regression is 46.95. $N = 50$. And $R^2 = 0.49$. Test the hypothesis, $H_0 : \beta_2 = 0$, to see if higher vaccination rates decrease the COVID death rate at the 5% level. (reject)

(2) Consider a regression of the log of output Q on the log of capital stock K, the log of employment L, and a time trend:

$$\ln Q_t = \beta_1 + \beta_2 \text{time} + \beta_3 \ln L_t + \beta_4 \ln K_t + u_t$$

Test the hypothesis of constant returns to scale, $H_0 : \beta_3 + \beta_4 = 1$, given the following regression output with annual U.S. data from 1950–2019:

$$\ln Q = \underset{(0.742)}{-7.292} + \underset{(0.001)}{0.005}\text{time} + \underset{(0.089)}{0.194}\ln L + \underset{(0.073)}{0.799}\ln K$$

$$\text{RSS} = 0.038160 \quad N = 70$$

$$\ln Q - \ln L = -7.371 + 0.005\text{time} + 0.800(\ln K - \ln L)$$
$$(0.382) \quad (0.0009) \quad (0.072)$$
$$\text{RSS} = 0.38169 \quad N = 70$$

(accept)

(3) We want to see what determines a student's test score at different schools. The dependent variable, testscr, is the average test score of a school, str is the student-teacher ratio of the school (number of students per teacher), and avginc is the average income of families (in thousands) in the school district. The student–teacher ratio captures how the class size can affect students' learning, while average income indirectly captures the intensity of human capital investment from the family. Here we estimate

$$\text{testscr}_i = \beta_1 + \beta_2\text{str}_i + \beta_3\text{avginc}_i + \beta_4\text{avginc}_i^2 + \beta_5\text{avginc}_i^3 + u_i$$

where the square and cube of average income are also included. Test the hypothesis $H_0 : \beta_3 = \beta_4 = \beta_5 = 0$ at the 5% level given the regression output presented here:

$$\text{testscr}_i = 617.897 - 0.927\text{str}_i + 5.125\text{avginc}_i - 0.101\text{avginc}_i^2 + 0.0007\text{avginc}_i^3$$
$$N = 420 \quad \text{RSS} = 65{,}964.6 \quad R^2 = 0.57$$
$$\text{testscr}_i = 698.933 - 2.2798\text{str}_i$$
$$N = 420 \quad \text{RSS} = 144{,}315.5 \quad R^2 = 0.05$$

(reject)

(4) We estimate the consumption function using monthly U.S. data from 1959 to 2022. Here CON is personal consumption expenditures and DPI is disposable personal income. Standard errors are in parentheses:

$$\text{CON} = 27.867 + 0.886\,\text{DPI}$$
$$(17.70) \quad (0.002241)$$
$$R^2 = 0.99 \quad N = 761 \quad F = 156{,}320.03$$

(a) Explain the meaning of the F-statistic.
(b) What is the t-statistic for DPI? (395.373)
(c) What is the relationship between this t-statistic and the regression F-statistic?

(5) Using quarterly U.S. data from 1947 to 2021, we run a regression on imports (IMP) with income (GDP), consumer price index (CPI), and the exchange rate (EXCH) as independent variables. All variables are logged. Standard errors are in parentheses:

$$\text{IMP} = -5.192 + 1.207\text{GDP} + 0.272\text{CPI} - 0.033\text{EXCH}$$
$$(0.2835) \quad (0.0416) \quad (0.0699) \quad (0.0575)$$
$$R^2 = 0.997 \quad N = 300 \quad \text{RSS} = 3.06245$$

(a) Using a t-test, test the hypothesis that EXCH has no influence on IMP. (accept)

$$\text{IMP} = -5.353 + 1.207\text{GDP} + 0.273\text{CPI}$$
$$(0.0409) \quad (0.0416) \quad (0.0697)$$
$$R^2 = 0.997 \quad N = 300 \quad \text{RSS} = 3.06585$$

(b) Using an F-test, test the hypothesis that EXCH has no influence on IMP. (accept)
(c) How are these two tests related?

Chapter 12

Interpreting Regression Results

12.1 Introduction

Old statisticians never die. They just become insignificant.

When we run regressions, it is important to properly interpret the regression results. In this chapter, we will address some important issues and common mistakes.

12.2 Regression to the Mean

Why is OLS called a "regression"?

In the late 1800s, Sir Francis Galton looked at some data on the heights of fathers and their sons. He estimated the following OLS regression equation (without a computer):

$$\text{Son's Height} = 33.78 + 0.516 \text{ Father's Height}$$

He found that unusually short fathers tend to have taller sons. If the father is 59 inches tall, his son is expected to be 64.5 inches tall.

He also found that unusually tall fathers tend to have shorter sons. If the father is 75 inches tall, his son is expected to be 72 inches tall.

Francis Galton published a paper titled "Regression towards mediocrity in hereditary stature," and the term "regression toward the mean" was born. This is the observation that variables which are extreme on their first measurement tend to be closer to their average on their second measurement. And if a variable is extreme on their second measurement, they will tend to have been closer to average on the first measurement.

Why is this the case? First, very tall men are likely to marry women who are perhaps above average in height but not as exceptionally tall. And very short men are likely to marry women who are perhaps below average in height but not as exceptionally short. And second, protein consumption, exercise, sleep, and the environment are also likely to affect your height. You may have an unusually tall father. But it is unlikely that all the other variables which affect your height will be equally exceptional. Your height is influenced by a number of chance events. They are not all likely to fall the same way. So the offspring of unusually tall fathers are not likely to be as unusually tall as their fathers.

Does this mean that we will all soon be the same height? No. If we flip the axes around, we will see that very tall people had shorter parents. Very short people had taller parents. But our heights are not diverging either.

We see the phenomenon of "regression toward the mean" in many different places. People who do poorly on the PSAT do relatively better on the SAT. People who do well on the PSAT do relatively less well on the SAT. People with unusually high (low) incomes this year are likely to earn less (more) next year. Basketball players who make an unusually high (low) number of baskets in today's game are likely to make fewer (more) baskets in tomorrow's game.

When I played high school soccer, I had a coach who would yell at us when we played poorly but did not praise us when we played well. The coach was convinced that when he yelled at us after a poor performance, we would play better in the following game. However, if he praised us after a strong performance, he found that we would play worse in the following game. Do you think his yelling really improved our play? Or was he just experiencing "regression toward the mean"?

12.3 Functional Forms

One of the assumptions of the Gauss–Markov theorem is that we have the correct functional form for the regression equation. If we have the wrong function form, the results are not strictly valid. Since most of the relationships in this world are probably nonlinear, you might worry about running linear regressions. But linear regression just means that the models are linear in terms of the parameters but not necessarily in terms of the variables. Here are some models or transformations of models which are linear in the parameters but not in terms of the variables. We actually have a lot of flexibility in how we specify our models.

(1) Normal Linear

$$Y_i = \beta_1 + \beta_2 X_2 + \beta_3 X_3 + u_i$$

(2) Log-Linear Model

$$ln\, Y_i = \beta_1 + \beta_2 X_2 + \beta_3 X_3 + u_i$$

(3) Linear-Log Model

$$Y_i = \beta_1 + \beta_2\, ln\, X_2 + \beta_3\, ln\, X_3 + u_i$$

(4) Interactive Model

$$Y_i = \beta_1 + \beta_2 X_2 + \beta_3 X_3 + \beta_4 (X_2 \cdot X_3) + u_i$$

(5) Multiplicative Model (log-log)

$$Y_i = \alpha_1 X_2^{\beta_2} X_3^{\beta_3} \varepsilon_i$$
$$\ln Y_i = \ln \alpha_1 + \beta_2 \ln X_2 + \beta_3 \ln X_3 + \ln \varepsilon_i$$
$$\ln Y_i = \beta_1 + \beta_2 \ln X_2 + \beta_3 \ln X_3 + u_i$$

(6) Exponential Model

$$Y_i = e^{\beta_1 + \beta_2 X_2 + \beta_3 X_3 + u_i}$$
$$ln\, Y_i = \beta_1 + \beta_2 X_2 + \beta_3 X_3 + u_i$$

(7) Reciprocal Models

$$\frac{1}{Y_i} = \beta_1 + \beta_2 X_2 + \beta_3 X_3 + u_i$$

or

$$Y_i = \beta_1 + \beta_2 \left(\frac{1}{X_2}\right) + \beta_3 \left(\frac{1}{X_3}\right) + u_i$$

or

$$\frac{1}{Y_i} = \beta_1 + \beta_2 \left(\frac{1}{X_2}\right) + \beta_3 X_3 + u_i$$

(8) Polynomial Model

$$Y_i = \beta_1 + \beta_2 X_i + \beta_3 X_i^2 + \beta_4 X_i^3 + u_i$$

(9) Combination of the above

$$Y_i = \beta_1 + \beta_2 X_2 + \beta_3 X_2^2 + \beta_4 \ln X_3 + \beta_5 \frac{1}{X_4} + \beta_6 X_2 X_3 + u_i$$

The relationship between Y and the Xs may indeed be quite complicated over the entire range of Xs. But we are usually just interested in understanding these relationships over a narrow range of Xs. For example, we might be interested in the effects of marginal changes in public policy. What happens if we change the sales tax from 8% to 10%? We are not trying to figure out what happens if the sales tax goes from 8% to 500%. And for these small changes, the functional forms above may be more than adequate.

12.4 Growth Rates

We often work with the growth rates of variables like population, GDP, money supply, employment, and productivity. We can consider continuous growth rates and discrete growth rates.

12.4.1 *Continuous growth rates*

12.4.1.1 *Constant continuous growth rates*

If we assume a constant continuous growth rate, we have

$$Y_t = Y_o e^{rt}$$

where e is the base of the natural log (2.71828), r is the continuous growth rate, t is a measure of time, and Y_o is the value of Y in year 0. If we take logs, we get

$$\ln Y_t = \ln Y_o + rt$$

so our regression model is

$$\ln Y_t = \beta_1 + \beta_2 t + u_t$$

where t is a time trend and b_2 (our OLS estimate of β_2) is our estimate of the instantaneous growth rate r:

$$b_2 = \frac{\text{relative change in } Y}{\text{absolute change in } t}$$

12.4.1.2 *Changing continuous growth rates*

If we want to let the continuous growth rate change over time, we have

$$Y_t = Y_o e^{r_1 t + r_2 t^2}$$
$$\ln Y_t = \ln Y_o + r_1 t + r_2 t^2$$

so our regression model is

$$\ln Y_t = \beta_1 + \beta_2 t + \beta_3 t^2 + u_t$$

and the instantaneous growth rate is estimated to be

$$\frac{d \ln Y}{dt} = b_2 + 2b_3 t$$

12.4.2 *Discrete growth rates*

If we have discrete growth rates like annual, quarterly, or monthly growth rates, we would express the growth like the following:

$$Y_t = Y_o(1+r)^t$$

where Y_0 is the value of Y in period 0. Taking logs, we have

$$\ln Y_t = \ln Y_o + t\ln(1+r)$$

so our regression model is

$$\ln Y_t = \beta_1 + \beta_2 t + u_t$$

and our OLS estimate of β_2 is

$$b_2 = \ln(1+r)$$

so the compound growth rate r is estimated to be $\hat{r} = e^{b_2} - 1$. Note that $\ln(1+r) \approx r$ for r near 0. Also, note that all these can be rates of growth or rates of decay.

12.5 Elasticity

The price elasticity of demand is a measure used in economics to show the responsiveness of the quantity demanded of a good to a change in its price. More precisely, it gives the percentage change in quantity demanded Q in response to a 1% change in price P (holding constant all the other determinants of demand, such as income). It was devised by Alfred Marshall in 1890. Elasticity ε can be defined using a number of numerical expressions:

$$\varepsilon = \frac{\%\Delta Q}{\%\Delta P} = \frac{\Delta Q/Q}{\Delta P/P} = \frac{\Delta Q}{\Delta P}\cdot\frac{P}{Q} = \frac{dQ}{dP}\cdot\frac{P}{Q} = \frac{d(\log Q)}{d(\log P)} \tag{12.1}$$

So if we estimate a demand function

$$Q = \beta_1 + \beta_2 P + u$$

our OLS estimate of β_2 is

$$b_2 = \frac{dQ}{dP} = \frac{\Delta Q}{\Delta P}$$

and we can estimate the elasticity ε as

$$\varepsilon \approx b_2 \cdot \frac{\bar{P}}{\bar{Q}}$$

This is the elasticity at the point of the means $(\bar{P}, \bar{Q})$, or an average elasticity, on the demand curve. In general, elasticities are not constant but change when measured at different points along the demand curve or regression line. If you have a straight line demand curve like $Q = \beta_1 + \beta_2 P + u$, the elasticity will be different at every single point on the curve.

But what if we consider the following demand curve?

$Q = AP^{-\alpha}$ with constants A and α. Taking logs, this can be written as

$$\ln Q = \ln A - \alpha \ln P$$

giving us the regression equation

$$\ln Q = \beta_1 + \beta_2 \ln P + u$$

Then using a little calculus, our slope estimate b_2 is

$$b_2 = \frac{d(\ln Q)}{d(\ln P)} = \frac{\frac{1}{Q}dQ}{\frac{1}{P}dP} = \frac{dQ}{dP} \cdot \frac{P}{Q} = \varepsilon$$

In this case, the OLS coefficient b_2 is the elasticity estimate. When the variables are measured in logs as we do here, we are assuming we have a demand curve with a constant elasticity of demand. So this log-log model assumes the elasticity does not change. This makes the elasticity much easier to estimate.

12.6 Statistical Significance

If you run a regression and find that a variable X is statistically significant at the 5% level, what does that mean? It could mean that variable X actually matters in the determination of Y. But you should be aware that at the 5% significance level, this will happen in 1 out of 20 regressions just by chance when the true value of β is zero and X does not matter. Or you might have a specification error problem. If X is correlated with some other variable Z which is not in the regression, X may be picking up the effect of Z on Y when X itself does not matter. For example, if you run a regression of SAT scores on the number of televisions in the home, the number of televisions will probably be statistically significant. But the number of televisions probably does not matter and is merely correlated with family income. I would not go out and buy more televisions to improve your SAT scores.

What does it mean if a variable is statistically insignificant? If you run a regression and find that the variable X is statistically insignificant, it may mean that X does not matter in the determination of Y. But other things may be going on. It may be the case that X does matter but that you do not have enough data to measure the effect of X on Y. Or it may be the case that X does matter, but X is too highly correlated with another variable in the regression equation for you to see the effect. If you run a regression of consumption on income and wealth, it can be very difficult to tease out the independent effects of income and wealth because they are so highly correlated. It may also be the case that X does matter, but you have misspecified the functional form of the regression.

12.7 Scaling and Units of Measure

We have the following linear regression model:

$$Y_i = \beta_1 + \beta_2 X_2 + \beta_3 X_3 + u_i$$

and get the following OLS estimates:

$$Y_i = b_1 + b_2 X_2 + b_3 X_3 + e_i$$

We know that b_1, the estimate of the intercept, depends on the units of the dependent variable Y_i. If you change the units of Y_i, then the magnitude of b_1 will change. If Y_i is measured in pounds, then b_1 will be measured in pounds. The e_i will also be measured in pounds along with the standard error of the regression.

The coefficient estimate b_2 measures a rate of change and depends on the units of Y_i and the units of X_2:

$$b_2 = \frac{\Delta Y}{\Delta X_2} = \frac{\text{units of } Y}{\text{units of } X_2}$$

Thus, the magnitude of b_2 will change when you change the units of measure for Y and/or X_2. We can make the magnitude of b_2 as large or as small as we want by changing the units of measure of these variables. Thus, you must pay close attention to the units of measure in order to properly interpret the meaning of your coefficient estimates.

The following four regressions were run with the same data on consumption and income. Consumption and income were measured in either millions of dollars or billions of dollars. You should note that R^2 is unaffected by changes in the units of measure. But the intercept and the slope do change from regression to regression. Can you determine the units of consumption (CON) and income (INC) in each of the following regressions?

(1) CON $= -92.149084 + 0.0009534247$ INC $\quad R^2 = 0.971773$

(a) CON in billions, INC in billions
(b) CON in millions, INC in billions
(c) CON in billions, INC in millions
(d) CON in millions, INC in millions

(2) CON $= -92.149084 + 0.9534247$ INC $\quad R^2 = 0.971773$

(a) CON in billions, INC in billions
(b) CON in millions, INC in billions
(c) CON in billions, INC in millions
(d) CON in millions, INC in millions

(3) CON $= -92149.084 + 0.9534247$ INC $\quad R^2 = 0.971773$

(a) CON in billions, INC in billions
(b) CON in millions, INC in billions
(c) CON in billions, INC in millions
(d) CON in millions, INC in millions

(4) $\text{CON} = -92149.084 + 953.4247\ \text{INC} \quad R^2 = 0.971773$

(a) CON in billions, INC in billions
(b) CON in millions, INC in billions
(c) CON in billions, INC in millions
(d) CON in millions, INC in millions

The intercept indicates the units of the dependent variable. Since −92,149.084 million = −92.149084 billion, the dependent variable is measured in billions in *1* and *2* but millions in 3 and 4. And the slope is measured in units of Y over units of X. If income increases by a dollar, we expect consumption to increase by around 95¢. So in *2* and *3*, both income and consumption must be measured in the same units.

The moral of this illustration is that you can make the actual coefficients as large or as small as you want by changing the units of measure. *Thus, the actual size of the coefficient is meaningless.* You must pay attention to the units of measure in order to properly interpret the coefficients.

12.8 Beta Star Coefficients

There is a difference between statistical significance and economic significance. An X variable may be statistically significant but economically insignificant. Statistical significance tells us whether or not there is a relationship between the dependent and independent variables. Economic significance tells us about the magnitude of that relationship. An X variable may be statistically significant, but the magnitude of the effect may be very, very small. If we have two statistically significant variables, X_2 and X_3, how do we determine which one is more economically significant? We just learned that we cannot look at the size of the coefficient. We can make the coefficients as large as we want by using different units of measure. Thus, we need to adjust the coefficients for the units of measure. The "beta star coefficient" is used to make statements about the relative importance of independent variables in a multiple regression.

We have the following linear regression model:

$$Y_i = \beta_1 + \beta_2 X_2 + \beta_3 X_3 + u_i$$

and get the following OLS estimates:

$$Y_i = b_1 + b_2 X_2 + b_3 X_3 + e_i$$

If both X_2 and X_3 are statistically significant, we determine which variable is more economically significant by evaluating the "beta star coefficients" for X_2 and X_3 as follows:

$$\beta_2^* = \left| b_2 \cdot \frac{s_{x2}}{s_y} \right|$$

where b_2 is the OLS coefficient, s_{x_2} is the standard deviation of X_2 (independent variable), and s_y is the standard deviation of Y (dependent variable):

$$\beta_3^* = \left| b_3 \cdot \frac{s_{x3}}{s_y} \right|$$

where b_3 is the OLS coefficient, s_{x_3} is the standard deviation of X_3 (independent variable), and s_y is the standard deviation of Y (dependent variable).

If $\beta_2^* = 0.7$, it means a 1 standard deviation change in the independent variable (X_2) will lead to a 0.7 standard deviation change in the dependent variable. We pay attention to the absolute value of the beta star coefficient. The larger the absolute value, the larger the economic significance of the independent variable. So if $\beta_3^* = 0.9$, then X_3 is economically more significant than X_2.

The magnitude of the OLS coefficients in a regression will depend on the units of measure being used for both the independent variable X and the dependent variable Y. But the "beta star coefficient" will be unit-free. We are adjusting the coefficients for the units of measure.

12.8.1 *Example*

We ran the following regression using Current Population Survey data from 2014:

$$\ln\text{WAGE} = \beta_1 + \beta_2\,\text{EDUCATION} + \beta_2\,\text{EXPERIENCE} + u_i$$

The regression results with 11,412 observations show that both Education and Experience are statistically significant in explaining lnWages (see Table 12.1).

Table 12.1. Regression results.

lnWage	Coefficient	Std. Error
EDUCATION	0.1128994	0.0024321
EXPERIENCE	0.0063399	0.0005762
Constant	9.445748	0.0424301

While both Education and Experience are statistically significant, we want to know which variable is more economically significant. What matters more? The summary statistics are provided on Table 12.2.

Table 12.2. Summary statistics.

Variable	OBS	Mean	Std. Dev.
lnWage	11,412	11.21929	0.7528082
EDUCATION	11,412	14.03207	2.747498
EXPERIENCE	11,412	29.86269	11.59761

We can calculate the beta star coefficients for both Education and Experience as follows:

$$\beta^*_{\text{EDUCATION}} = \left|0.1128994 \cdot \frac{2.747498}{0.7528082}\right| = 0.4120$$

$$\beta^*_{\text{EXPERIENCE}} = \left|0.0063399 \cdot \frac{11.58761}{0.7528082}\right| = 0.0976$$

A one standard deviation increase in the amount of education leads to a 0.412 standard deviation increase in your ln(wage), but a one standard deviation increase in the amount of experience only leads to a 0.0976 standard deviation increase in your ln(wage). Thus, education is more economically significant than experience.

12.9 Stepwise Linear Regression

Stepwise regression is a practice by some researchers in which the right-hand side variables are selected in a step-by-step manner. The procedure adds or removes independent variables one at a time using the variable's purported statistical significance. You will either add the most significant variable or remove the least significant variable. This is an automatic procedure based on some prespecified criterion usually taking the form of a sequence of F-tests or t-tests.

The basic problem is that stepwise regression involves running numerous regressions which are misspecified. Since these regressions are misspecified, the regression results are invalid, and the resulting F-tests and t-tests are meaningless. The decision to either include or not include a variable is based on these meaningless test statistics.

This procedure is an extreme form of data mining. The final regression results from stepwise regression are not adjusted for this model-building procedure. If you follow this procedure, you must properly adjust for the model uncertainty. Otherwise, the practice should be stopped altogether.

12.10 Common Regression Mistakes

12.10.1 *Garbage in, garbage out*

Today, we have enormous amounts of data available to us and the computing power to look at it carefully. Thus, the tools of statistics become more important and more valuable every day.

It is important to work with adequate amounts of good data. You must have enough data which is accurately measuring what you want to measure. If you have very little data, you cannot expect to learn much about the world. If you have very bad data, you cannot expect to learn much about the world.

A census was taken in the Soviet Union in 1937 during the Great Purge. Stalin thought the population figures were too low and arrested the statistics officials responsible. He ordered a new census in 1939. When the new numbers were still considered too low, Stalin just announced that the population was 170.5 million. Every now and then people will basically make up numbers. You have to be careful what you do with these numbers.

12.10.2 *Functional form of the regression equation must be correct*

Make sure all the important variables appear on the right-hand side. Otherwise, you have a specification error problem, and your results are invalid. Make sure your variables measure what you want to measure. Do not use income to measure wealth or wealth to measure GDP or GDP to measure money supply. Make sure to use the correct functional form. Do not use a linear specification to describe a nonlinear relationship. Weight typically rises with age but only to a point. After the age of 54, weight seems to fall with age. You want to take these nonlinearities into account.

12.10.3 *Multicollinearity*

If your X variables are highly correlated with each other, you will have trouble estimating the individual effects of your variables. Suppose you want to know if it is more important to have an educated father or an educated mother for success in school. The problem is that educated fathers tend to marry educated mothers. So it will be difficult to tease out the effect of one without the other. These variables may appear to be statistically insignificant even when they matter.

12.10.4 *Omitted variable bias*

Suppose someone runs some regressions and concludes that "golfers are more prone to heart disease, cancer, and arthritis." This researcher probably forgot to include age in their regression. Since older people are more likely to play golf, the golf variable was inadvertently picking up the effect of age on heart disease.

You might find a positive relationship between school spending and test scores. Does this mean we should spend more on schools? Maybe. But if you do not have family income in your regression equation, it may be the case that family income drives both test scores and school spending and that school spending has no effect on test scores. You have to make sure that all the important variables are in the regression.

12.10.5 *Data mining*

If you stick 20 meaningless variables on the right-hand side of a regression equation, you should expect one to be statistically significant at the 5% level just by chance.

If you run 20 regressions with a meaningless variable X, you should expect this variable to be statistically significant in one of them just by chance.

Unfortunately, academic journals prefer to publish papers where variables are statistically significant as opposed to statistically insignificant. So journals end up publishing too many papers where some variable is irrelevant but was statistically significant just by chance. We know this because researchers have a difficult time trying to reproduce the results in many academic papers.

The *Wall Street Journal* reported that "Most results, including those that appear in top-flight peer reviewed journals, can't be reproduced."[1] The *Journal of the American Medical Association* reported that "In an examination of 49 medical studies, one third of the research was subsequently refuted by later work."[2] And Amy Cuddy, a social psychologist, had the second most watched TED talk titled "Your Body Language May Shape Who You Are." Unfortunately, her research results were not reproducible,[3] and she quietly left her tenure track position at Harvard.

---

[1] *Wall Street Journal*, 2 December 2011.

[2] Ioannidis, "Contradicted and Initially Stronger Effects in Highly Cited Clinical Research," *Journal of the American Medical Association*, 13 July 2005.

[3] Dominus, "When the Revolution Came for Amy Cuddy," *New York Times Magazine*, 18 October 2017.

12.10.6 *Correlation is not causation*

Over the past two decades, the rate of autism has been steadily rising in the United States. Over the past two decades, the annual per capita income in China has been steadily rising. If you run a regression of per capita income in China on U.S. autism rates, income in China will be statistically significant. But we know that these have nothing to do with each other.

If you run a regression of cumulative rainfall in Los Angeles on the population in Australia over the past century, rainfall will be statistically significant. But we know that rain in Los Angeles does not cause babies in Australia. Correlation is not causation.

Of course, sometimes we do not care whether there is causation or not. It is good enough to know that things are correlated. For example, how does Amazon know what kind of books I like to read or how does Netflix know what kind of movies I like to watch? Do they call up my friends and ask them? They know that people who like Harry Potter books will probably like Percy Jackson books. They know that people who like Jean-Claude Van Damme movies will probably like Jason Statham movies. There is no causation here, but it does not matter. Sometimes we don't care that correlation is not causation. If SAT scores and high school GPA are correlated with first-year performance in college, the information is valuable. There is clearly no causation here. People who buy cheap, generic automotive oil tend to be poor credit risks, while people who buy carbon monoxide monitors tend to be good credit risks. These correlations can provide useful information.

12.10.7 *Reverse causality*

In a regression, we assume the causality runs from the Xs to Y and not the other way around. If the causality runs in the reverse direction, or if it runs in both directions, OLS can give us biased results. In the real world, causality between the Xs and Y can often run in both directions. Higher education spending can lead to higher economic growth, and higher economic growth can lead to higher education spending. Higher income can lead to higher consumption, and higher consumption can lead to higher income. If we do not properly account for the reverse causation, our results will be biased and invalid.

12.10.8 *Extrapolating beyond the data*

We need to be careful not to extrapolate beyond the limits of the data. Extrapolation is generally less accurate than interpolation. When you are interpolating, you are estimating the value of a point between two known points. When you are extrapolating, you only have data on one side of the point. Extrapolation also becomes more and more inaccurate the further you get from the known data. We can estimate the relationship between height and weight for 35-year-olds fairly well. We have plenty of data on people in their 30s. But if you want to extrapolate this out to people over 100 or 200, you are likely to get into trouble.

A data analyst is on board a 747 passenger jet flying across the Pacific. The captain makes an announcement over the passenger address system "We have lost an engine, but there is no need to worry. We can fly on three engines. It will just take us an hour longer to reach Tokyo."

Thirty minutes later, the captain announces: "This is your captain speaking. We have lost another engine — but we will be fine. Our flight to Tokyo will just take an extra two hours."

A little bit later, the captain makes another announcement: "Unfortunately we are down to one engine now. We can still make it safely, but we will be landing in Tokyo three hours late."

"I sure hope we don't lose the last engine," says the data analyst, "Then we'll be up here forever."

12.10.9 *Please be careful*

"With great power comes great responsibility.[4]" Regression analysis is a very powerful tool. Like fire, knives, and cars, it can be used to make our world a much better place. But it can also do a lot of

[4]Benjamin Parker in the Marvel comic series Spiderman.

harm if it is used improperly. In particular, make sure you do not kill people with your regressions. In the mid-1990s, the American Heart Association was recommending hormone replacement therapy to older women to help prevent heart disease and osteoporosis. In 2002, estrogen therapy was exposed as a hazard to women's health. "Meanwhile, the question of how many women may have died prematurely or suffered strokes or breast cancer because they were taking a pill that their physicians had prescribed to protect them against heart disease lingers unanswered. A reasonable estimate would be tens of thousands."[5] It is important to do careful work.

12.11 Exercises

(1) Using U.S. state-level data, we ran an ordinary least squares regression on COVID death rates:

$$\begin{aligned}\text{COVIDDR} = 133.24 - &3.00\,\text{Vax} + 5.16\,\text{Obesity}\\ &+ 0.18\,\text{PopDensity}\\ &(1.10) \quad (2.23) \quad (0.03)\end{aligned}$$

Standard errors are in parentheses. $N = 50$. $R^2 = 0.49$

All the variables, vaccination rates, obesity rates, and population density are statistically significant. But which variable is the most economically significant? Calculate the beta star coefficients with the following information:

Variable	Mean	Standard Deviation
DeathPC	179.38	63.95
Vax	50.88	8.48
Obesity	31.43	3.82
PopDensity	202.65	266.24

(population density)

(2) Money demand should depend on income and the interest rate. Using U.S. quarterly data from 1959, we have the following

[5] Gary Taubes, "Do We Really Know What Makes Us Healthy," *The New York Times Magazine*, September 16, 2007.

regression output where *money* is real M2, *income* is real GDP, and the *interest rate* is the interest rate on 3 month Treasury Bills (secondary market). Standard errors are presented in parentheses:

$$\begin{aligned}\ln(\text{money}) = \underset{(0.157)}{0.926} + \underset{(0.017)}{0.763}\ln(\text{income}) - \underset{(0.0056)}{0.054}\ln(\text{interest rate})\\ N = 253 \quad R^2 = 0.94\end{aligned}$$

(a) Test the hypothesis that the elasticity of money demand with respect to income is 0.50. (reject)
(b) Test the hypothesis that the elasticity of money demand with respect to the interest rate is −0.50. (reject)

(3) According to Okun's law, there is a stable relationship between GDP and unemployment. We run the following regression using quarterly U.S. data from 1969:

$$\begin{aligned}\ln(\text{GDP}) = \underset{(0.4243)}{-45.493} + \underset{(0.0002)}{0.0275}\,\text{Year} - \underset{(0.1931)}{1.153}\,\text{Unemployment}\\ N = 212 \quad R^2 = 0.988\end{aligned}$$

Standard errors are presented in parentheses.

(a) What is the annual growth rate of real GDP? (2.75%)
(b) What happens to GDP when the unemployment rate rises by 1% point? (decreases by 1.153%)

(4) This is a regression of cumulative rainfall in Pasadena, California, on the population of Australia with annual data from 1906–2017:

$$\begin{aligned}\text{PopAus} = \underset{(211.9)}{1938.0} + \underset{(0.17)}{9.27}\,\text{CumRain}\\ R^2 = 0.96 \quad N = 112\end{aligned}$$

Standard errors are in parentheses. Test the hypothesis that rain in Pasadena causes increases in the population of Australia. Explain.

(5) Using state-level data, we run a regression of median household income on average SAT scores. Standard errors are in parentheses:

$$\begin{gathered}\text{SAT} = \underset{(72.7)}{1197.11} - \underset{(1.13)}{1.12}\,\text{Income}\\ R^2 = 0.01 \quad N = 51\end{gathered}$$

(a) Is there a relationship between household income and SAT scores? (no)

In some states, most high school students take the SAT. In other states, very few high school students take the SAT. An important variable may be the percent of high school students who take the SAT in each state:

$$\begin{gathered}\text{SAT} = \underset{(38.80)}{1107.94} + \underset{(0.64)}{1.57}\,\text{Income} - \underset{(0.23)}{2.65}\,\text{Percent}\\ R^2 = 0.74 \quad N = 51\end{gathered}$$

(b) Is there a relationship between household income and SAT scores now? Explain. (yes)

Appendix

Table A.1. Cumulative standard normal probabilities.

Z	0.00	0.01	0.02	0.03	0.04	0.05	0.06	0.07	0.08	0.09
(a) $P(-\infty < Z < z)$										
−3.0	0.00135	0.00131	0.00126	0.00122	0.00118	0.00114	0.00111	0.00107	0.00104	0.00100
−2.9	0.00187	0.00181	0.00175	0.00169	0.00164	0.00159	0.00154	0.00149	0.00144	0.00139
−2.8	0.00256	0.00248	0.00240	0.00233	0.00226	0.00219	0.00212	0.00205	0.00199	0.00193
−2.7	0.00347	0.00336	0.00326	0.00317	0.00307	0.00298	0.00289	0.00280	0.00272	0.00264
−2.6	0.00466	0.00453	0.00440	0.00427	0.00415	0.00402	0.00391	0.00379	0.00368	0.00357
−2.5	0.00621	0.00604	0.00587	0.00570	0.00554	0.00539	0.00523	0.00508	0.00494	0.00480
−2.4	0.00820	0.00798	0.00776	0.00755	0.00734	0.00714	0.00695	0.00676	0.00657	0.00639
−2.3	0.01072	0.01044	0.01017	0.00990	0.00964	0.00939	0.00914	0.00889	0.00866	0.00842
−2.2	0.01390	0.01355	0.01321	0.01287	0.01255	0.01222	0.01191	0.01160	0.01130	0.01101
−2.1	0.01786	0.01743	0.01700	0.01659	0.01618	0.01578	0.01539	0.01500	0.01463	0.01426
−2.0	0.02275	0.02222	0.02169	0.02118	0.02068	0.02018	0.01970	0.01923	0.01876	0.01831
−1.9	0.02872	0.02807	0.02743	0.02680	0.02619	0.02559	0.02500	0.02442	0.02385	0.02330
−1.8	0.03593	0.03515	0.03438	0.03362	0.03288	0.03216	0.03144	0.03074	0.03005	0.02938
−1.7	0.04457	0.04363	0.04272	0.04182	0.04093	0.04006	0.03920	0.03836	0.03754	0.03673
−1.6	0.05480	0.05370	0.05262	0.05155	0.05050	0.04947	0.04846	0.04746	0.04648	0.04551
−1.5	0.06681	0.06552	0.06426	0.06301	0.06178	0.06057	0.05938	0.05821	0.05705	0.05592
−1.4	0.08076	0.07927	0.07780	0.07636	0.07493	0.07353	0.07215	0.07078	0.06944	0.06811
−1.3	0.09680	0.09510	0.09342	0.09176	0.09012	0.08851	0.08691	0.08534	0.08379	0.08226
−1.2	0.11507	0.11314	0.11123	0.10935	0.10749	0.10565	0.10383	0.10204	0.10027	0.09853
−1.1	0.13567	0.13350	0.13136	0.12924	0.12714	0.12507	0.12302	0.12100	0.11900	0.11702
−1.0	0.15866	0.15625	0.15386	0.15151	0.14917	0.14686	0.14457	0.14231	0.14007	0.13786
−0.9	0.18406	0.18141	0.17879	0.17619	0.17361	0.17106	0.16853	0.16602	0.16354	0.16109
−0.8	0.21186	0.20897	0.20611	0.20327	0.20045	0.19766	0.19489	0.19215	0.18943	0.18673
−0.7	0.24196	0.23885	0.23576	0.23270	0.22965	0.22663	0.22363	0.22065	0.21770	0.21476
−0.6	0.27425	0.27093	0.26763	0.26435	0.26109	0.25785	0.25463	0.25143	0.24825	0.24510
−0.5	0.30854	0.30503	0.30153	0.29806	0.29460	0.29116	0.28774	0.28434	0.28096	0.27760
−0.4	0.34458	0.34090	0.33724	0.33360	0.32997	0.32636	0.32276	0.31918	0.31561	0.31207
−0.3	0.38209	0.37828	0.37448	0.37070	0.36693	0.36317	0.35942	0.35569	0.35197	0.34827
−0.2	0.42074	0.41683	0.41294	0.40905	0.40517	0.40129	0.39743	0.39358	0.38974	0.38591
−0.1	0.46017	0.45620	0.45224	0.44828	0.44433	0.44038	0.43644	0.43251	0.42858	0.42465
−0.0	0.50000	0.49601	0.49202	0.48803	0.48405	0.48006	0.47608	0.47210	0.46812	0.46414

(Continued)

Table A.1. (*Continued*)

Z	0.00	0.01	0.02	0.03	0.04	0.05	0.06	0.07	0.08	0.09
(b) $P(-\infty < Z < z)$										
0.0	0.50000	0.50399	0.50798	0.51197	0.51595	0.51994	0.52392	0.52790	0.53188	0.53586
0.1	0.53983	0.54380	0.54776	0.55172	0.55567	0.55962	0.56356	0.56749	0.57142	0.57535
0.2	0.57926	0.58317	0.58706	0.59095	0.59483	0.59871	0.60257	0.60642	0.61026	0.61409
0.3	0.61791	0.62172	0.62552	0.62930	0.63307	0.63683	0.64058	0.64431	0.64803	0.65173
0.4	0.65542	0.65910	0.66276	0.66640	0.67003	0.67364	0.67724	0.68082	0.68439	0.68793
0.5	0.69146	0.69497	0.69847	0.70194	0.70540	0.70884	0.71226	0.71566	0.71904	0.72240
0.6	0.72575	0.72907	0.73237	0.73565	0.73891	0.74215	0.74537	0.74857	0.75175	0.75490
0.7	0.75804	0.76115	0.76424	0.76730	0.77035	0.77337	0.77637	0.77935	0.78230	0.78524
0.8	0.78814	0.79103	0.79389	0.79673	0.79955	0.80234	0.80511	0.80785	0.81057	0.81327
0.9	0.81594	0.81859	0.82121	0.82381	0.82639	0.82894	0.83147	0.83398	0.83646	0.83891
1.0	0.84134	0.84375	0.84614	0.84849	0.85083	0.85314	0.85543	0.85769	0.85993	0.86214
1.1	0.86433	0.86650	0.86864	0.87076	0.87286	0.87493	0.87698	0.87900	0.88100	0.88298
1.2	0.88493	0.88686	0.88877	0.89065	0.89251	0.89435	0.89617	0.89796	0.89973	0.90147
1.3	0.90320	0.90490	0.90658	0.90824	0.90988	0.91149	0.91309	0.91466	0.91621	0.91774
1.4	0.91924	0.92073	0.92220	0.92364	0.92507	0.92647	0.92785	0.92922	0.93056	0.93189
1.5	0.93319	0.93448	0.93574	0.93699	0.93822	0.93943	0.94062	0.94179	0.94295	0.94408
1.6	0.94520	0.94630	0.94738	0.94845	0.94950	0.95053	0.95154	0.95254	0.95352	0.95449
1.7	0.95543	0.95637	0.95728	0.95818	0.95907	0.95994	0.96080	0.96164	0.96246	0.96327
1.8	0.96407	0.96485	0.96562	0.96638	0.96712	0.96784	0.96856	0.96926	0.96995	0.97062
1.9	0.97128	0.97193	0.97257	0.97320	0.97381	0.97441	0.97500	0.97558	0.97615	0.97670
2.0	0.97725	0.97778	0.97831	0.97882	0.97932	0.97982	0.98030	0.98077	0.98124	0.98169
2.1	0.98214	0.98257	0.98300	0.98341	0.98382	0.98422	0.98461	0.98500	0.98537	0.98574
2.2	0.98610	0.98645	0.98679	0.98713	0.98745	0.98778	0.98809	0.98840	0.98870	0.98899
2.3	0.98928	0.98956	0.98983	0.99010	0.99036	0.99061	0.99086	0.99111	0.99134	0.99158
2.4	0.99180	0.99202	0.99224	0.99245	0.99266	0.99286	0.99305	0.99324	0.99343	0.99361
2.5	0.99379	0.99396	0.99413	0.99430	0.99446	0.99461	0.99477	0.99492	0.99506	0.99520
2.6	0.99534	0.99547	0.99560	0.99573	0.99585	0.99598	0.99609	0.99621	0.99632	0.99643
2.7	0.99653	0.99664	0.99674	0.99683	0.99693	0.99702	0.99711	0.99720	0.99728	0.99736
2.8	0.99744	0.99752	0.99760	0.99767	0.99774	0.99781	0.99788	0.99795	0.99801	0.99807
2.9	0.99813	0.99819	0.99825	0.99831	0.99836	0.99841	0.99846	0.99851	0.99856	0.99861
3.0	0.99865	0.99869	0.99874	0.99878	0.99882	0.99886	0.99889	0.99893	0.99896	0.99900

Table A.2. Critical values of the chi-square (χ^2) distribution: Probability of right-hand tail.

DF	0.995	0.990	0.975	0.950	0.900	0.100	0.050	0.025	0.010	0.005
1	0.000039	0.00016	0.00098	0.0039	0.0158	2.706	3.841	5.024	6.635	7.879
2	0.0100	0.0201	0.0506	0.103	0.211	4.605	5.991	7.378	9.210	10.597
3	0.072	0.115	0.216	0.352	0.584	6.251	7.815	9.348	11.345	12.838
4	0.207	0.297	0.484	0.711	1.064	7.779	9.488	11.143	13.277	14.860
5	0.412	0.554	0.831	1.145	1.610	9.236	11.070	12.833	15.086	16.750
6	0.676	0.872	1.237	1.635	2.204	10.645	12.592	14.449	16.812	18.548
7	0.989	1.239	1.690	2.167	2.833	12.017	14.067	16.013	18.475	20.278
8	1.344	1.646	2.180	2.733	3.490	13.362	15.507	17.535	20.090	21.955
9	1.735	2.088	2.700	3.325	4.168	14.684	16.919	19.023	21.666	23.589
10	2.156	2.558	3.247	3.940	4.865	15.987	18.307	20.483	23.209	25.188
11	2.603	3.053	3.816	4.575	5.578	17.275	19.675	21.920	24.725	26.757
12	3.074	3.571	4.404	5.226	6.304	18.549	21.026	23.337	26.217	28.300
13	3.565	4.107	5.009	5.892	7.042	19.812	22.362	24.736	27.688	29.819
14	4.075	4.660	5.629	6.571	7.790	21.064	23.685	26.119	29.141	31.319
15	4.601	5.229	6.262	7.261	8.547	22.307	24.996	27.488	30.578	32.801

Table A.2. (*Continued*)

DF	0.995	0.990	0.975	0.950	0.900	0.100	0.050	0.025	0.010	0.005
16	5.142	5.812	6.908	7.962	9.312	23.542	26.296	28.845	32.000	34.267
17	5.697	6.408	7.564	8.672	10.085	24.769	27.587	30.191	33.409	35.718
18	6.265	7.015	8.231	9.390	10.865	25.989	28.869	31.526	34.805	37.156
19	6.844	7.633	8.907	10.117	11.651	27.204	30.144	32.852	36.191	38.582
20	7.434	8.260	9.591	10.851	12.443	28.412	31.410	34.170	37.566	39.997
21	8.034	8.897	10.283	11.591	13.240	29.615	32.671	35.479	38.932	41.401
22	8.643	9.542	10.982	12.338	14.041	30.813	33.924	36.781	40.289	42.796
23	9.260	10.196	11.689	13.091	14.848	32.007	35.172	38.076	41.638	44.181
24	9.886	10.856	12.401	13.848	15.659	33.196	36.415	39.364	42.980	45.559
25	10.520	11.524	13.120	14.611	16.473	34.382	37.652	40.646	44.314	46.928
26	11.160	12.198	13.844	15.379	17.292	35.563	38.885	41.923	45.642	48.290
27	11.808	12.879	14.573	16.151	18.114	36.741	40.113	43.195	46.963	49.645
28	12.461	13.565	15.308	16.928	18.939	37.916	41.337	44.461	48.278	50.993
29	13.121	14.256	16.047	17.708	19.768	39.087	42.557	45.722	49.588	52.336
30	13.787	14.953	16.791	18.493	20.599	40.256	43.773	46.979	50.892	53.672
40	20.707	22.164	24.433	26.509	29.051	51.805	55.758	59.342	63.691	66.766
50	27.991	29.707	32.357	34.764	37.689	63.167	67.505	71.420	76.154	79.490
60	35.534	37.485	40.482	43.188	46.459	74.397	79.082	83.298	88.379	91.952
70	43.275	45.442	48.758	51.739	55.329	85.527	90.531	95.023	100.425	104.215
80	51.172	53.540	57.153	60.391	64.278	96.578	101.879	106.629	112.329	116.321
90	59.196	61.754	65.647	69.126	73.291	107.565	113.145	118.136	124.116	128.299
100	67.328	70.065	74.222	77.929	82.358	118.498	124.342	129.561	135.807	140.169
200	152.241	156.432	162.728	168.279	174.835	226.021	233.994	241.058	249.445	255.264

Table A.3. Critical values of the Student's t–Distribution: Probability of right-hand tail.

DF	0.100	0.050	0.025	0.010	0.005
1	3.0777	6.3138	12.7062	31.8205	63.6567
2	1.8856	2.9200	4.3027	6.9646	9.9248
3	1.6377	2.3534	3.1824	4.5407	5.8409
4	1.5332	2.1318	2.7764	3.7469	4.6041
5	1.4759	2.0150	2.5706	3.3649	4.0321
6	1.4398	1.9432	2.4469	3.1427	3.7074
7	1.4149	1.8946	2.3646	2.9980	3.4995
8	1.3968	1.8595	2.3060	2.8965	3.3554
9	1.3830	1.8331	2.2622	2.8214	3.2498
10	1.3722	1.8125	2.2281	2.7638	3.1693
11	1.3634	1.7959	2.2010	2.7181	3.1058
12	1.3562	1.7823	2.1788	2.6810	3.0545
13	1.3502	1.7709	2.1604	2.6503	3.0123
14	1.3450	1.7613	2.1448	2.6245	2.9768
15	1.3406	1.7531	2.1314	2.6025	2.9467
16	1.3368	1.7459	2.1199	2.5835	2.9208
17	1.3334	1.7396	2.1098	2.5669	2.8982
18	1.3304	1.7341	2.1009	2.5524	2.8784
19	1.3277	1.7291	2.0930	2.5395	2.8609

Table A.3. (*Continued*)

DF	0.100	0.050	0.025	0.010	0.005
20	1.3253	1.7247	2.0860	2.5280	2.8453
21	1.3232	1.7207	2.0796	2.5176	2.8314
22	1.3212	1.7171	2.0739	2.5083	2.8188
23	1.3195	1.7139	2.0687	2.4999	2.8073
24	1.3178	1.7109	2.0639	2.4922	2.7969
25	1.3163	1.7081	2.0595	2.4851	2.7874
26	1.3150	1.7056	2.0555	2.4786	2.7787
27	1.3137	1.7033	2.0518	2.4727	2.7707
28	1.3125	1.7011	2.0484	2.4671	2.7633
29	1.3114	1.6991	2.0452	2.4620	2.7564
30	1.3104	1.6973	2.0423	2.4573	2.7500
35	1.3062	1.6896	2.0301	2.4377	2.7238
40	1.3031	1.6839	2.0211	2.4233	2.7045
45	1.3006	1.6794	2.0141	2.4121	2.6896
50	1.2987	1.6759	2.0086	2.4033	2.6778
55	1.2971	1.6730	2.0040	2.3961	2.6682
60	1.2958	1.6706	2.0003	2.3901	2.6603
65	1.2947	1.6686	1.9971	2.3851	2.6536
70	1.2938	1.6669	1.9944	2.3808	2.6479
75	1.2929	1.6654	1.9921	2.3771	2.6430
80	1.2922	1.6641	1.9901	2.3739	2.6387
85	1.2916	1.6630	1.9883	2.3710	2.6349
90	1.2910	1.6620	1.9867	2.3685	2.6316
95	1.2905	1.6611	1.9853	2.3662	2.6286
100	1.2901	1.6602	1.9840	2.3642	2.6259
110	1.2893	1.6588	1.9818	2.3607	2.6213
120	1.2886	1.6577	1.9799	2.3578	2.6174
130	1.2881	1.6567	1.9784	2.3554	2.6142
140	1.2876	1.6558	1.9771	2.3533	2.6114
150	1.2872	1.6551	1.9759	2.3515	2.6090
160	1.2869	1.6544	1.9749	2.3499	2.6069
170	1.2866	1.6539	1.9740	2.3485	2.6051
180	1.2863	1.6534	1.9732	2.3472	2.6034
190	1.2860	1.6529	1.9725	2.3461	2.6020
200	1.2858	1.6525	1.9719	2.3451	2.6006
300	1.2844	1.6499	1.9679	2.3388	2.5923
∞	1.2816	1.6449	1.9600	2.3263	2.5758

Table A.4. Fisher–Snedecor distribution.

10%	Numerator Degrees of Freedom 1	2	3	4	5	6	7	8	9	10	11	12	13	14
(a) 10% right-hand tail														
1	39.863	49.500	53.593	55.833	57.240	58.204	58.906	59.439	59.858	60.195	60.473	60.705	60.903	61.073
2	8.526	9.000	9.162	9.243	9.293	9.326	9.349	9.367	9.381	9.392	9.401	9.408	9.415	9.420
3	5.538	5.462	5.391	5.343	5.309	5.285	5.266	5.252	5.240	5.230	5.222	5.216	5.210	5.205
4	4.545	4.325	4.191	4.107	4.051	4.010	3.979	3.955	3.936	3.920	3.907	3.896	3.886	3.878
5	4.060	3.780	3.619	3.520	3.453	3.405	3.368	3.339	3.316	3.297	3.282	3.268	3.257	3.247
6	3.776	3.463	3.289	3.181	3.108	3.055	3.014	2.983	2.958	2.937	2.920	2.905	2.892	2.881
7	3.589	3.257	3.074	2.961	2.883	2.827	2.785	2.752	2.725	2.703	2.684	2.668	2.654	2.643
8	3.458	3.113	2.924	2.806	2.726	2.668	2.624	2.589	2.561	2.538	2.519	2.502	2.488	2.475
9	3.360	3.006	2.813	2.693	2.611	2.551	2.505	2.469	2.440	2.416	2.396	2.379	2.364	2.351
10	3.285	2.924	2.728	2.605	2.522	2.461	2.414	2.377	2.347	2.323	2.302	2.284	2.269	2.255
11	3.225	2.860	2.660	2.536	2.451	2.389	2.342	2.304	2.274	2.248	2.227	2.209	2.193	2.179
12	3.177	2.807	2.606	2.480	2.394	2.331	2.283	2.245	2.214	2.188	2.166	2.147	2.131	2.117
13	3.136	2.763	2.560	2.434	2.347	2.283	2.234	2.195	2.164	2.138	2.116	2.097	2.080	2.066
14	3.102	2.726	2.522	2.395	2.307	2.243	2.193	2.154	2.122	2.095	2.073	2.054	2.037	2.022
15	3.073	2.695	2.490	2.361	2.273	2.208	2.158	2.119	2.086	2.059	2.037	2.017	2.000	1.985
16	3.048	2.668	2.462	2.333	2.244	2.178	2.128	2.088	2.055	2.028	2.005	1.985	1.968	1.953
17	3.026	2.645	2.437	2.308	2.218	2.152	2.102	2.061	2.028	2.001	1.978	1.958	1.940	1.925
18	3.007	2.624	2.416	2.286	2.196	2.130	2.079	2.038	2.005	1.977	1.954	1.933	1.916	1.900
19	2.990	2.606	2.397	2.266	2.176	2.109	2.058	2.017	1.984	1.956	1.932	1.912	1.894	1.878
20	2.975	2.589	2.380	2.249	2.158	2.091	2.040	1.999	1.965	1.937	1.913	1.892	1.875	1.859
21	2.961	2.575	2.365	2.233	2.142	2.075	2.023	1.982	1.948	1.920	1.896	1.875	1.857	1.841
22	2.949	2.561	2.351	2.219	2.128	2.060	2.008	1.967	1.933	1.904	1.880	1.859	1.841	1.825
24	2.927	2.538	2.327	2.195	2.103	2.035	1.983	1.941	1.906	1.877	1.853	1.832	1.814	1.797
26	2.909	2.519	2.307	2.174	2.082	2.014	1.961	1.919	1.884	1.855	1.830	1.809	1.790	1.774
28	2.894	2.503	2.291	2.157	2.064	1.996	1.943	1.900	1.865	1.836	1.811	1.790	1.771	1.754
30	2.881	2.489	2.276	2.142	2.049	1.980	1.927	1.884	1.849	1.819	1.794	1.773	1.754	1.737
35	2.855	2.461	2.247	2.113	2.019	1.950	1.896	1.852	1.817	1.787	1.761	1.739	1.720	1.703
40	2.835	2.440	2.226	2.091	1.997	1.927	1.873	1.829	1.793	1.763	1.737	1.715	1.695	1.678
45	2.820	2.425	2.210	2.074	1.980	1.909	1.855	1.811	1.774	1.744	1.718	1.695	1.676	1.658
50	2.809	2.412	2.197	2.061	1.966	1.895	1.840	1.796	1.760	1.729	1.703	1.680	1.660	1.643
60	2.791	2.393	2.177	2.041	1.946	1.875	1.819	1.775	1.738	1.707	1.680	1.657	1.637	1.619
70	2.779	2.380	2.164	2.027	1.931	1.860	1.804	1.760	1.723	1.691	1.665	1.641	1.621	1.603
80	2.769	2.370	2.154	2.016	1.921	1.849	1.793	1.748	1.711	1.680	1.653	1.629	1.609	1.590
90	2.762	2.363	2.146	2.008	1.912	1.841	1.785	1.739	1.702	1.670	1.643	1.620	1.599	1.581
100	2.756	2.356	2.139	2.002	1.906	1.834	1.778	1.732	1.695	1.663	1.636	1.612	1.592	1.573
120	2.748	2.347	2.130	1.992	1.896	1.824	1.767	1.722	1.684	1.652	1.625	1.601	1.580	1.562
140	2.742	2.341	2.123	1.985	1.889	1.817	1.760	1.714	1.677	1.645	1.617	1.593	1.572	1.553
160	2.737	2.336	2.118	1.980	1.884	1.811	1.755	1.709	1.671	1.639	1.611	1.587	1.566	1.547
180	2.734	2.332	2.114	1.976	1.880	1.807	1.750	1.705	1.667	1.634	1.607	1.583	1.561	1.543
200	2.731	2.329	2.111	1.973	1.876	1.804	1.747	1.701	1.663	1.631	1.603	1.579	1.558	1.539
300	2.722	2.320	2.102	1.964	1.867	1.794	1.737	1.691	1.652	1.620	1.592	1.568	1.546	1.527
∞	2.706	2.303	2.084	1.945	1.847	1.774	1.717	1.670	1.632	1.599	1.570	1.546	1.524	1.505

Rows: Denominator Degrees of Freedom

Table A.4. (*Continued*)

10%	Numerator Degrees of Freedom													
Denominator Degrees of Freedom	15	16	17	18	19	20	22	24	26	28	30	35	40	45
1	61.220	61.350	61.464	61.566	61.658	61.740	61.883	62.002	62.103	62.190	62.265	62.416	62.529	62.617
2	9.425	9.429	9.433	9.436	9.439	9.441	9.446	9.450	9.453	9.456	9.458	9.463	9.466	9.469
3	5.200	5.196	5.193	5.190	5.187	5.184	5.180	5.176	5.173	5.170	5.168	5.163	5.160	5.157
4	3.870	3.864	3.858	3.853	3.849	3.844	3.837	3.831	3.826	3.821	3.817	3.810	3.804	3.799
5	3.238	3.230	3.223	3.217	3.212	3.207	3.198	3.191	3.184	3.179	3.174	3.165	3.157	3.152
6	2.871	2.863	2.855	2.848	2.842	2.836	2.827	2.818	2.811	2.805	2.800	2.789	2.781	2.775
7	2.632	2.623	2.615	2.607	2.601	2.595	2.584	2.575	2.568	2.561	2.555	2.544	2.535	2.528
8	2.464	2.455	2.446	2.438	2.431	2.425	2.413	2.404	2.396	2.389	2.383	2.371	2.361	2.354
9	2.340	2.329	2.320	2.312	2.305	2.298	2.287	2.277	2.268	2.261	2.255	2.242	2.232	2.224
10	2.244	2.233	2.224	2.215	2.208	2.201	2.189	2.178	2.170	2.162	2.155	2.142	2.132	2.124
11	2.167	2.156	2.147	2.138	2.130	2.123	2.111	2.100	2.091	2.083	2.076	2.062	2.052	2.043
12	2.105	2.094	2.084	2.075	2.067	2.060	2.047	2.036	2.027	2.019	2.011	1.997	1.986	1.977
13	2.053	2.042	2.032	2.023	2.014	2.007	1.994	1.983	1.973	1.965	1.958	1.943	1.931	1.923
14	2.010	1.998	1.988	1.978	1.970	1.962	1.949	1.938	1.928	1.919	1.912	1.897	1.885	1.876
15	1.972	1.961	1.950	1.941	1.932	1.924	1.911	1.899	1.889	1.880	1.873	1.857	1.845	1.836
16	1.940	1.928	1.917	1.908	1.899	1.891	1.877	1.866	1.855	1.847	1.839	1.823	1.811	1.801
17	1.912	1.900	1.889	1.879	1.870	1.862	1.848	1.836	1.826	1.817	1.809	1.793	1.781	1.771
18	1.887	1.875	1.864	1.854	1.845	1.837	1.823	1.810	1.800	1.791	1.783	1.766	1.754	1.744
19	1.865	1.852	1.841	1.831	1.822	1.814	1.800	1.787	1.777	1.767	1.759	1.743	1.730	1.720
20	1.845	1.833	1.821	1.811	1.802	1.794	1.779	1.767	1.756	1.746	1.738	1.721	1.708	1.698
21	1.827	1.815	1.803	1.793	1.784	1.776	1.761	1.748	1.737	1.728	1.719	1.702	1.689	1.678
22	1.811	1.798	1.787	1.777	1.768	1.759	1.744	1.731	1.720	1.711	1.702	1.685	1.671	1.661
24	1.783	1.770	1.759	1.748	1.739	1.730	1.715	1.702	1.691	1.681	1.672	1.654	1.641	1.630
26	1.760	1.747	1.735	1.724	1.715	1.706	1.690	1.677	1.666	1.656	1.647	1.629	1.615	1.604
28	1.740	1.726	1.715	1.704	1.694	1.685	1.669	1.656	1.644	1.634	1.625	1.607	1.592	1.581
30	1.722	1.709	1.697	1.686	1.676	1.667	1.651	1.638	1.626	1.616	1.606	1.588	1.573	1.562
35	1.688	1.674	1.662	1.651	1.641	1.632	1.615	1.601	1.589	1.579	1.569	1.550	1.535	1.523
40	1.662	1.649	1.636	1.625	1.615	1.605	1.588	1.574	1.562	1.551	1.541	1.521	1.506	1.493
45	1.643	1.629	1.616	1.605	1.594	1.585	1.568	1.553	1.540	1.529	1.519	1.499	1.483	1.470
50	1.627	1.613	1.600	1.588	1.578	1.568	1.551	1.536	1.523	1.512	1.502	1.481	1.465	1.452
60	1.603	1.589	1.576	1.564	1.553	1.543	1.526	1.511	1.498	1.486	1.476	1.454	1.437	1.424
70	1.587	1.572	1.559	1.547	1.536	1.526	1.508	1.493	1.479	1.467	1.457	1.435	1.418	1.404
80	1.574	1.559	1.546	1.534	1.523	1.513	1.495	1.479	1.465	1.453	1.443	1.420	1.403	1.388
90	1.564	1.550	1.536	1.524	1.513	1.503	1.484	1.468	1.455	1.442	1.432	1.409	1.391	1.377
100	1.557	1.542	1.528	1.516	1.505	1.494	1.476	1.460	1.446	1.434	1.423	1.400	1.382	1.367
120	1.545	1.530	1.516	1.504	1.493	1.482	1.463	1.447	1.433	1.421	1.409	1.386	1.368	1.353
140	1.537	1.522	1.508	1.495	1.484	1.473	1.454	1.438	1.424	1.411	1.400	1.376	1.357	1.342
160	1.530	1.515	1.502	1.489	1.477	1.467	1.448	1.431	1.417	1.404	1.393	1.369	1.350	1.334
180	1.526	1.510	1.497	1.484	1.472	1.462	1.443	1.426	1.411	1.399	1.387	1.363	1.344	1.328
200	1.522	1.507	1.493	1.480	1.468	1.458	1.438	1.422	1.407	1.394	1.383	1.358	1.339	1.323
300	1.510	1.495	1.481	1.468	1.456	1.445	1.426	1.409	1.394	1.381	1.369	1.344	1.325	1.308
∞	1.487	1.471	1.457	1.444	1.432	1.421	1.401	1.383	1.368	1.354	1.342	1.316	1.295	1.278

Table A.4. (*Continued*)

10%	Numerator Degrees of Freedom												
Denominator Degrees of Freedom	50	60	70	80	90	100	120	140	160	180	200	300	∞
1	62.688	62.794	62.870	62.927	62.972	63.007	63.061	63.099	63.127	63.150	63.167	63.221	63.328
2	9.471	9.475	9.477	9.479	9.480	9.481	9.483	9.484	9.485	9.486	9.486	9.488	9.491
3	5.155	5.151	5.149	5.147	5.145	5.144	5.143	5.141	5.140	5.140	5.139	5.137	5.134
4	3.795	3.790	3.786	3.782	3.780	3.778	3.775	3.773	3.772	3.770	3.769	3.767	3.761
5	3.147	3.140	3.135	3.132	3.129	3.126	3.123	3.120	3.118	3.117	3.116	3.112	3.105
6	2.770	2.762	2.756	2.752	2.749	2.746	2.742	2.739	2.737	2.736	2.734	2.730	2.722
7	2.523	2.514	2.508	2.504	2.500	2.497	2.493	2.490	2.487	2.486	2.484	2.480	2.471
8	2.348	2.339	2.333	2.328	2.324	2.321	2.316	2.313	2.310	2.308	2.307	2.302	2.293
9	2.218	2.208	2.202	2.196	2.192	2.189	2.184	2.181	2.178	2.176	2.174	2.169	2.159
10	2.117	2.107	2.100	2.095	2.090	2.087	2.082	2.078	2.075	2.073	2.071	2.066	2.055
11	2.036	2.026	2.019	2.013	2.009	2.005	2.000	1.996	1.993	1.991	1.989	1.983	1.972
12	1.970	1.960	1.952	1.946	1.942	1.938	1.932	1.928	1.925	1.923	1.921	1.915	1.904
13	1.915	1.904	1.896	1.890	1.886	1.882	1.876	1.872	1.869	1.866	1.864	1.858	1.846
14	1.869	1.857	1.849	1.843	1.838	1.834	1.828	1.824	1.820	1.818	1.816	1.810	1.797
15	1.828	1.817	1.808	1.802	1.797	1.793	1.787	1.782	1.779	1.776	1.774	1.768	1.755
16	1.793	1.782	1.773	1.766	1.761	1.757	1.751	1.746	1.743	1.740	1.738	1.731	1.718
17	1.763	1.751	1.742	1.735	1.730	1.726	1.719	1.714	1.711	1.708	1.706	1.699	1.686
18	1.736	1.723	1.714	1.707	1.702	1.698	1.691	1.686	1.683	1.680	1.678	1.671	1.657
19	1.711	1.699	1.690	1.683	1.677	1.673	1.666	1.661	1.657	1.654	1.652	1.645	1.631
20	1.690	1.677	1.667	1.660	1.655	1.650	1.643	1.638	1.635	1.632	1.629	1.622	1.607
21	1.670	1.657	1.647	1.640	1.634	1.630	1.623	1.618	1.614	1.611	1.608	1.601	1.586
22	1.652	1.639	1.629	1.622	1.616	1.611	1.604	1.599	1.595	1.592	1.590	1.582	1.567
24	1.621	1.607	1.597	1.590	1.584	1.579	1.571	1.566	1.562	1.559	1.556	1.549	1.533
26	1.594	1.581	1.570	1.562	1.556	1.551	1.544	1.538	1.534	1.531	1.528	1.520	1.504
28	1.572	1.558	1.547	1.539	1.533	1.528	1.520	1.514	1.510	1.506	1.504	1.495	1.478
30	1.552	1.538	1.527	1.519	1.512	1.507	1.499	1.493	1.489	1.485	1.482	1.474	1.456
35	1.513	1.497	1.486	1.478	1.471	1.465	1.457	1.451	1.446	1.442	1.439	1.430	1.411
40	1.483	1.467	1.455	1.447	1.439	1.434	1.425	1.418	1.413	1.410	1.406	1.397	1.377
45	1.460	1.443	1.431	1.422	1.415	1.409	1.399	1.393	1.388	1.384	1.380	1.370	1.349
50	1.441	1.424	1.412	1.402	1.395	1.388	1.379	1.372	1.367	1.362	1.359	1.349	1.327
60	1.413	1.395	1.382	1.372	1.364	1.358	1.348	1.340	1.335	1.330	1.326	1.315	1.291
70	1.392	1.374	1.361	1.350	1.342	1.335	1.325	1.317	1.311	1.306	1.302	1.291	1.265
80	1.377	1.358	1.344	1.334	1.325	1.318	1.307	1.299	1.293	1.288	1.284	1.271	1.245
90	1.365	1.346	1.332	1.321	1.312	1.304	1.293	1.285	1.278	1.273	1.269	1.256	1.228
100	1.355	1.336	1.321	1.310	1.301	1.293	1.282	1.273	1.267	1.261	1.257	1.244	1.214
120	1.340	1.320	1.305	1.294	1.284	1.277	1.265	1.256	1.249	1.243	1.239	1.224	1.193
140	1.329	1.309	1.294	1.282	1.272	1.264	1.252	1.243	1.235	1.230	1.225	1.210	1.176
160	1.321	1.301	1.285	1.273	1.263	1.255	1.242	1.233	1.225	1.219	1.214	1.199	1.163
180	1.315	1.294	1.279	1.266	1.256	1.248	1.235	1.225	1.217	1.211	1.206	1.190	1.153
200	1.310	1.289	1.273	1.261	1.250	1.242	1.228	1.218	1.211	1.204	1.199	1.183	1.144
300	1.295	1.273	1.256	1.243	1.233	1.224	1.209	1.199	1.190	1.184	1.178	1.160	1.115
∞	1.263	1.240	1.222	1.207	1.195	1.185	1.169	1.156	1.146	1.137	1.130	1.106	1.000

Table A.4. (*Continued*)

5%	Numerator Degrees of Freedom													
Denominator Degrees of Freedom	1	2	3	4	5	6	7	8	9	10	11	12	13	14
(b) 5% right-hand tail														
1	161.448	199.500	215.707	224.583	230.162	233.986	236.768	238.883	240.543	241.882	242.983	243.906	244.690	245.364
2	18.513	19.000	19.164	19.247	19.296	19.330	19.353	19.371	19.385	19.396	19.405	19.413	19.419	19.424
3	10.128	9.552	9.277	9.117	9.013	8.941	8.887	8.845	8.812	8.786	8.763	8.745	8.729	8.715
4	7.709	6.944	6.591	6.388	6.256	6.163	6.094	6.041	5.999	5.964	5.936	5.912	5.891	5.873
5	6.608	5.786	5.409	5.192	5.050	4.950	4.876	4.818	4.772	4.735	4.704	4.678	4.655	4.636
6	5.987	5.143	4.757	4.534	4.387	4.284	4.207	4.147	4.099	4.060	4.027	4.000	3.976	3.956
7	5.591	4.737	4.347	4.120	3.972	3.866	3.787	3.726	3.677	3.637	3.603	3.575	3.550	3.529
8	5.318	4.459	4.066	3.838	3.687	3.581	3.500	3.438	3.388	3.347	3.313	3.284	3.259	3.237
9	5.117	4.256	3.863	3.633	3.482	3.374	3.293	3.230	3.179	3.137	3.102	3.073	3.048	3.025
10	4.965	4.103	3.708	3.478	3.326	3.217	3.135	3.072	3.020	2.978	2.943	2.913	2.887	2.865
11	4.844	3.982	3.587	3.357	3.204	3.095	3.012	2.948	2.896	2.854	2.818	2.788	2.761	2.739
12	4.747	3.885	3.490	3.259	3.106	2.996	2.913	2.849	2.796	2.753	2.717	2.687	2.660	2.637
13	4.667	3.806	3.411	3.179	3.025	2.915	2.832	2.767	2.714	2.671	2.635	2.604	2.577	2.554
14	4.600	3.739	3.344	3.112	2.958	2.848	2.764	2.699	2.646	2.602	2.565	2.534	2.507	2.484
15	4.543	3.682	3.287	3.056	2.901	2.790	2.707	2.641	2.588	2.544	2.507	2.475	2.448	2.424
16	4.494	3.634	3.239	3.007	2.852	2.741	2.657	2.591	2.538	2.494	2.456	2.425	2.397	2.373
17	4.451	3.592	3.197	2.965	2.810	2.699	2.614	2.548	2.494	2.450	2.413	2.381	2.353	2.329
18	4.414	3.555	3.160	2.928	2.773	2.661	2.577	2.510	2.456	2.412	2.374	2.342	2.314	2.290
19	4.381	3.522	3.127	2.895	2.740	2.628	2.544	2.477	2.423	2.378	2.340	2.308	2.280	2.256
20	4.351	3.493	3.098	2.866	2.711	2.599	2.514	2.447	2.393	2.348	2.310	2.278	2.250	2.225
21	4.325	3.467	3.072	2.840	2.685	2.573	2.488	2.420	2.366	2.321	2.283	2.250	2.222	2.197
22	4.301	3.443	3.049	2.817	2.661	2.549	2.464	2.397	2.342	2.297	2.259	2.226	2.198	2.173
24	4.260	3.403	3.009	2.776	2.621	2.508	2.423	2.355	2.300	2.255	2.216	2.183	2.155	2.130
26	4.225	3.369	2.975	2.743	2.587	2.474	2.388	2.321	2.265	2.220	2.181	2.148	2.119	2.094
28	4.196	3.340	2.947	2.714	2.558	2.445	2.359	2.291	2.236	2.190	2.151	2.118	2.089	2.064
30	4.171	3.316	2.922	2.690	2.534	2.421	2.334	2.266	2.211	2.165	2.126	2.092	2.063	2.037
35	4.121	3.267	2.874	2.641	2.485	2.372	2.285	2.217	2.161	2.114	2.075	2.041	2.012	1.986
40	4.085	3.232	2.839	2.606	2.449	2.336	2.249	2.180	2.124	2.077	2.038	2.003	1.974	1.948
45	4.057	3.204	2.812	2.579	2.422	2.308	2.221	2.152	2.096	2.049	2.009	1.974	1.945	1.918
50	4.034	3.183	2.790	2.557	2.400	2.286	2.199	2.130	2.073	2.026	1.986	1.952	1.921	1.895
60	4.001	3.150	2.758	2.525	2.368	2.254	2.167	2.097	2.040	1.993	1.952	1.917	1.887	1.860
70	3.978	3.128	2.736	2.503	2.346	2.231	2.143	2.074	2.017	1.969	1.928	1.893	1.863	1.836
80	3.960	3.111	2.719	2.486	2.329	2.214	2.126	2.056	1.999	1.951	1.910	1.875	1.845	1.817
90	3.947	3.098	2.706	2.473	2.316	2.201	2.113	2.043	1.986	1.938	1.897	1.861	1.830	1.803
100	3.936	3.087	2.696	2.463	2.305	2.191	2.103	2.032	1.975	1.927	1.886	1.850	1.819	1.792
120	3.920	3.072	2.680	2.447	2.290	2.175	2.087	2.016	1.959	1.910	1.869	1.834	1.803	1.775
140	3.909	3.061	2.669	2.436	2.279	2.164	2.076	2.005	1.947	1.899	1.858	1.822	1.791	1.763
160	3.900	3.053	2.661	2.428	2.271	2.156	2.067	1.997	1.939	1.890	1.849	1.813	1.782	1.754
180	3.894	3.046	2.655	2.422	2.264	2.149	2.061	1.990	1.932	1.884	1.842	1.806	1.775	1.747
200	3.888	3.041	2.650	2.417	2.259	2.144	2.056	1.985	1.927	1.878	1.837	1.801	1.769	1.742
300	3.873	3.026	2.635	2.402	2.244	2.129	2.040	1.969	1.911	1.862	1.821	1.785	1.753	1.725
∞	3.841	2.996	2.605	2.372	2.214	2.099	2.010	1.938	1.880	1.831	1.789	1.752	1.720	1.692

Table A.4. (*Continued*)

5%	Numerator Degrees of Freedom													
Denominator Degrees of Freedom	15	16	17	18	19	20	22	24	26	28	30	35	40	45
1	245.950	246.464	246.918	247.323	247.686	248.013	248.579	249.052	249.453	249.797	250.095	250.693	251.143	251.494
2	19.429	19.433	19.437	19.440	19.443	19.446	19.450	19.454	19.457	19.460	19.462	19.467	19.471	19.474
3	8.703	8.692	8.683	8.675	8.667	8.660	8.648	8.639	8.630	8.623	8.617	8.604	8.594	8.587
4	5.858	5.844	5.832	5.821	5.811	5.803	5.787	5.774	5.763	5.754	5.746	5.729	5.717	5.707
5	4.619	4.604	4.590	4.579	4.568	4.558	4.541	4.527	4.515	4.505	4.496	4.478	4.464	4.453
6	3.938	3.922	3.908	3.896	3.884	3.874	3.856	3.841	3.829	3.818	3.808	3.789	3.774	3.763
7	3.511	3.494	3.480	3.467	3.455	3.445	3.426	3.410	3.397	3.386	3.376	3.356	3.340	3.328
8	3.218	3.202	3.187	3.173	3.161	3.150	3.131	3.115	3.102	3.090	3.079	3.059	3.043	3.030
9	3.006	2.989	2.974	2.960	2.948	2.936	2.917	2.900	2.886	2.874	2.864	2.842	2.826	2.813
10	2.845	2.828	2.812	2.798	2.785	2.774	2.754	2.737	2.723	2.710	2.700	2.678	2.661	2.648
11	2.719	2.701	2.685	2.671	2.658	2.646	2.626	2.609	2.594	2.582	2.570	2.548	2.531	2.517
12	2.617	2.599	2.583	2.568	2.555	2.544	2.523	2.505	2.491	2.478	2.466	2.443	2.426	2.412
13	2.533	2.515	2.499	2.484	2.471	2.459	2.438	2.420	2.405	2.392	2.380	2.357	2.339	2.325
14	2.463	2.445	2.428	2.413	2.400	2.388	2.367	2.349	2.333	2.320	2.308	2.284	2.266	2.252
15	2.403	2.385	2.368	2.353	2.340	2.328	2.306	2.288	2.272	2.259	2.247	2.223	2.204	2.190
16	2.352	2.333	2.317	2.302	2.288	2.276	2.254	2.235	2.220	2.206	2.194	2.169	2.151	2.136
17	2.308	2.289	2.272	2.257	2.243	2.230	2.208	2.190	2.174	2.160	2.148	2.123	2.104	2.089
18	2.269	2.250	2.233	2.217	2.203	2.191	2.168	2.150	2.134	2.119	2.107	2.082	2.063	2.048
19	2.234	2.215	2.198	2.182	2.168	2.155	2.133	2.114	2.098	2.084	2.071	2.046	2.026	2.011
20	2.203	2.184	2.167	2.151	2.137	2.124	2.102	2.082	2.066	2.052	2.039	2.013	1.994	1.978
21	2.176	2.156	2.139	2.123	2.109	2.096	2.073	2.054	2.037	2.023	2.010	1.984	1.965	1.949
22	2.151	2.131	2.114	2.098	2.084	2.071	2.048	2.028	2.012	1.997	1.984	1.958	1.938	1.922
24	2.108	2.088	2.070	2.054	2.040	2.027	2.003	1.984	1.967	1.952	1.939	1.912	1.892	1.876
26	2.072	2.052	2.034	2.018	2.003	1.990	1.966	1.946	1.929	1.914	1.901	1.874	1.853	1.837
28	2.041	2.021	2.003	1.987	1.972	1.959	1.935	1.915	1.897	1.882	1.869	1.841	1.820	1.803
30	2.015	1.995	1.976	1.960	1.945	1.932	1.908	1.887	1.870	1.854	1.841	1.813	1.792	1.775
35	1.963	1.942	1.924	1.907	1.892	1.878	1.854	1.833	1.815	1.799	1.786	1.757	1.735	1.718
40	1.924	1.904	1.885	1.868	1.853	1.839	1.814	1.793	1.775	1.759	1.744	1.715	1.693	1.675
45	1.895	1.874	1.855	1.838	1.823	1.808	1.783	1.762	1.743	1.727	1.713	1.683	1.660	1.642
50	1.871	1.850	1.831	1.814	1.798	1.784	1.759	1.737	1.718	1.702	1.687	1.657	1.634	1.615
60	1.836	1.815	1.796	1.778	1.763	1.748	1.722	1.700	1.681	1.664	1.649	1.618	1.594	1.575
70	1.812	1.790	1.771	1.753	1.737	1.722	1.696	1.674	1.654	1.637	1.622	1.591	1.566	1.546
80	1.793	1.772	1.752	1.734	1.718	1.703	1.677	1.654	1.634	1.617	1.602	1.570	1.545	1.525
90	1.779	1.757	1.737	1.720	1.703	1.688	1.662	1.639	1.619	1.601	1.586	1.554	1.528	1.508
100	1.768	1.746	1.726	1.708	1.691	1.676	1.650	1.627	1.607	1.589	1.573	1.541	1.515	1.494
120	1.750	1.728	1.709	1.690	1.674	1.659	1.632	1.608	1.588	1.570	1.554	1.521	1.495	1.474
140	1.738	1.716	1.696	1.678	1.661	1.646	1.619	1.595	1.575	1.557	1.541	1.507	1.481	1.459
160	1.729	1.707	1.687	1.669	1.652	1.637	1.609	1.586	1.565	1.547	1.531	1.497	1.470	1.448
180	1.722	1.700	1.680	1.661	1.645	1.629	1.602	1.578	1.557	1.539	1.523	1.489	1.462	1.440
200	1.717	1.694	1.674	1.656	1.639	1.623	1.596	1.572	1.551	1.533	1.516	1.482	1.455	1.433
300	1.700	1.677	1.657	1.638	1.621	1.606	1.578	1.554	1.533	1.514	1.497	1.463	1.435	1.412
∞	1.666	1.644	1.623	1.604	1.587	1.571	1.542	1.517	1.496	1.476	1.459	1.423	1.394	1.370

Table A.4. (*Continued*)

5%	Numerator Degrees of Freedom												
Denominator Degrees of Freedom	50	60	70	80	90	100	120	140	160	180	200	300	∞
1	251.774	252.196	252.497	252.724	252.900	253.041	253.253	253.404	253.518	253.606	253.677	253.889	254.314
2	19.476	19.479	19.481	19.483	19.485	19.486	19.487	19.489	19.489	19.490	19.491	19.492	19.496
3	8.581	8.572	8.566	8.561	8.557	8.554	8.549	8.546	8.544	8.542	8.540	8.536	8.526
4	5.699	5.688	5.679	5.673	5.668	5.664	5.658	5.654	5.651	5.648	5.646	5.640	5.628
5	4.444	4.431	4.422	4.415	4.409	4.405	4.398	4.394	4.390	4.387	4.385	4.378	4.365
6	3.754	3.740	3.730	3.722	3.716	3.712	3.705	3.700	3.696	3.693	3.690	3.683	3.669
7	3.319	3.304	3.294	3.286	3.280	3.275	3.267	3.262	3.258	3.255	3.252	3.245	3.230
8	3.020	3.005	2.994	2.986	2.980	2.975	2.967	2.961	2.957	2.954	2.951	2.943	2.928
9	2.803	2.787	2.776	2.768	2.761	2.756	2.748	2.742	2.737	2.734	2.731	2.723	2.707
10	2.637	2.621	2.610	2.601	2.594	2.588	2.580	2.574	2.570	2.566	2.563	2.555	2.538
11	2.507	2.490	2.478	2.469	2.462	2.457	2.448	2.442	2.437	2.434	2.431	2.422	2.404
12	2.401	2.384	2.372	2.363	2.356	2.350	2.341	2.335	2.330	2.326	2.323	2.314	2.296
13	2.314	2.297	2.284	2.275	2.267	2.261	2.252	2.246	2.241	2.237	2.234	2.225	2.206
14	2.241	2.223	2.210	2.201	2.193	2.187	2.178	2.171	2.166	2.162	2.159	2.150	2.131
15	2.178	2.160	2.147	2.137	2.130	2.123	2.114	2.107	2.102	2.098	2.095	2.085	2.066
16	2.124	2.106	2.093	2.083	2.075	2.068	2.059	2.052	2.047	2.043	2.039	2.030	2.010
17	2.077	2.058	2.045	2.035	2.027	2.020	2.011	2.004	1.998	1.994	1.991	1.981	1.960
18	2.035	2.017	2.003	1.993	1.985	1.978	1.968	1.961	1.956	1.951	1.948	1.938	1.917
19	1.999	1.980	1.966	1.955	1.947	1.940	1.930	1.923	1.917	1.913	1.910	1.899	1.878
20	1.966	1.946	1.932	1.922	1.913	1.907	1.896	1.889	1.883	1.879	1.875	1.865	1.843
21	1.936	1.916	1.902	1.891	1.883	1.876	1.866	1.858	1.853	1.848	1.845	1.834	1.812
22	1.909	1.889	1.875	1.864	1.856	1.849	1.838	1.830	1.825	1.820	1.817	1.806	1.783
24	1.863	1.842	1.828	1.816	1.808	1.800	1.790	1.782	1.776	1.771	1.768	1.756	1.733
26	1.823	1.803	1.788	1.776	1.767	1.760	1.749	1.741	1.735	1.730	1.726	1.714	1.691
28	1.790	1.769	1.754	1.742	1.733	1.725	1.714	1.706	1.699	1.694	1.691	1.679	1.654
30	1.761	1.740	1.724	1.712	1.703	1.695	1.683	1.675	1.669	1.664	1.660	1.647	1.622
35	1.703	1.681	1.665	1.652	1.643	1.635	1.623	1.614	1.607	1.602	1.598	1.585	1.558
40	1.660	1.637	1.621	1.608	1.597	1.589	1.577	1.567	1.560	1.555	1.551	1.537	1.509
45	1.626	1.603	1.586	1.573	1.562	1.554	1.541	1.531	1.524	1.518	1.513	1.499	1.470
50	1.599	1.576	1.558	1.544	1.534	1.525	1.511	1.502	1.494	1.488	1.484	1.469	1.438
60	1.559	1.534	1.516	1.502	1.491	1.481	1.467	1.457	1.449	1.443	1.438	1.422	1.389
70	1.530	1.505	1.486	1.471	1.459	1.450	1.435	1.424	1.416	1.410	1.404	1.388	1.353
80	1.508	1.482	1.463	1.448	1.436	1.426	1.411	1.399	1.391	1.384	1.379	1.361	1.325
90	1.491	1.465	1.445	1.429	1.417	1.407	1.391	1.380	1.371	1.364	1.358	1.340	1.302
100	1.477	1.450	1.430	1.415	1.402	1.392	1.376	1.364	1.355	1.348	1.342	1.323	1.283
120	1.457	1.429	1.408	1.392	1.379	1.369	1.352	1.340	1.330	1.322	1.316	1.297	1.254
140	1.442	1.414	1.393	1.376	1.363	1.352	1.335	1.322	1.312	1.304	1.298	1.277	1.232
160	1.430	1.402	1.381	1.364	1.350	1.339	1.321	1.308	1.298	1.290	1.283	1.262	1.214
180	1.422	1.393	1.371	1.354	1.340	1.329	1.311	1.297	1.287	1.279	1.272	1.250	1.200
200	1.415	1.386	1.364	1.346	1.332	1.321	1.302	1.289	1.278	1.270	1.263	1.240	1.189
300	1.393	1.363	1.341	1.323	1.308	1.296	1.277	1.262	1.251	1.241	1.234	1.210	1.150
∞	1.350	1.318	1.293	1.273	1.257	1.243	1.221	1.204	1.191	1.179	1.170	1.138	1.000

Table A.4. (*Continued*)

2.5%	Numerator Degrees of Freedom 1	2	3	4	5	6	7	8	9	10	11	12	13	14
(c) 2.5% right-hand tail														
Denominator Degrees of Freedom 1	647.789	799.500	864.163	899.583	921.848	937.111	948.217	956.656	963.285	968.627	973.025	976.708	979.837	982.528
2	38.506	39.000	39.165	39.248	39.298	39.331	39.355	39.373	39.387	39.398	39.407	39.415	39.421	39.427
3	17.443	16.044	15.439	15.101	14.885	14.735	14.624	14.540	14.473	14.419	14.374	14.337	14.304	14.277
4	12.218	10.649	9.979	9.605	9.364	9.197	9.074	8.980	8.905	8.844	8.794	8.751	8.715	8.684
5	10.007	8.434	7.764	7.388	7.146	6.978	6.853	6.757	6.681	6.619	6.568	6.525	6.488	6.456
6	8.813	7.260	6.599	6.227	5.988	5.820	5.695	5.600	5.523	5.461	5.410	5.366	5.329	5.297
7	8.073	6.542	5.890	5.523	5.285	5.119	4.995	4.899	4.823	4.761	4.709	4.666	4.628	4.596
8	7.571	6.059	5.416	5.053	4.817	4.652	4.529	4.433	4.357	4.295	4.243	4.200	4.162	4.130
9	7.209	5.715	5.078	4.718	4.484	4.320	4.197	4.102	4.026	3.964	3.912	3.868	3.831	3.798
10	6.937	5.456	4.826	4.468	4.236	4.072	3.950	3.855	3.779	3.717	3.665	3.621	3.583	3.550
11	6.724	5.256	4.630	4.275	4.044	3.881	3.759	3.664	3.588	3.526	3.474	3.430	3.392	3.359
12	6.554	5.096	4.474	4.121	3.891	3.728	3.607	3.512	3.436	3.374	3.321	3.277	3.239	3.206
13	6.414	4.965	4.347	3.996	3.767	3.604	3.483	3.388	3.312	3.250	3.197	3.153	3.115	3.082
14	6.298	4.857	4.242	3.892	3.663	3.501	3.380	3.285	3.209	3.147	3.095	3.050	3.012	2.979
15	6.200	4.765	4.153	3.804	3.576	3.415	3.293	3.199	3.123	3.060	3.008	2.963	2.925	2.891
16	6.115	4.687	4.077	3.729	3.502	3.341	3.219	3.125	3.049	2.986	2.934	2.889	2.851	2.817
17	6.042	4.619	4.011	3.665	3.438	3.277	3.156	3.061	2.985	2.922	2.870	2.825	2.786	2.753
18	5.978	4.560	3.954	3.608	3.382	3.221	3.100	3.005	2.929	2.866	2.814	2.769	2.730	2.696
19	5.922	4.508	3.903	3.559	3.333	3.172	3.051	2.956	2.880	2.817	2.765	2.720	2.681	2.647
20	5.871	4.461	3.859	3.515	3.289	3.128	3.007	2.913	2.837	2.774	2.721	2.676	2.637	2.603
21	5.827	4.420	3.819	3.475	3.250	3.090	2.969	2.874	2.798	2.735	2.682	2.637	2.598	2.564
22	5.786	4.383	3.783	3.440	3.215	3.055	2.934	2.839	2.763	2.700	2.647	2.602	2.563	2.528
24	5.717	4.319	3.721	3.379	3.155	2.995	2.874	2.779	2.703	2.640	2.586	2.541	2.502	2.468
26	5.659	4.265	3.670	3.329	3.105	2.945	2.824	2.729	2.653	2.590	2.536	2.491	2.451	2.417
28	5.610	4.221	3.626	3.286	3.063	2.903	2.782	2.687	2.611	2.547	2.494	2.448	2.409	2.374
30	5.568	4.182	3.589	3.250	3.026	2.867	2.746	2.651	2.575	2.511	2.458	2.412	2.372	2.338
35	5.485	4.106	3.517	3.179	2.956	2.796	2.676	2.581	2.504	2.440	2.387	2.341	2.301	2.266
40	5.424	4.051	3.463	3.126	2.904	2.744	2.624	2.529	2.452	2.388	2.334	2.288	2.248	2.213
45	5.377	4.009	3.422	3.086	2.864	2.705	2.584	2.489	2.412	2.348	2.294	2.248	2.208	2.172
50	5.340	3.975	3.390	3.054	2.833	2.674	2.553	2.458	2.381	2.317	2.263	2.216	2.176	2.140
60	5.286	3.925	3.343	3.008	2.786	2.627	2.507	2.412	2.334	2.270	2.216	2.169	2.129	2.093
70	5.247	3.890	3.309	2.975	2.754	2.595	2.474	2.379	2.302	2.237	2.183	2.136	2.095	2.059
80	5.218	3.864	3.284	2.950	2.730	2.571	2.450	2.355	2.277	2.213	2.158	2.111	2.071	2.035
90	5.196	3.844	3.265	2.932	2.711	2.552	2.432	2.336	2.259	2.194	2.140	2.092	2.051	2.015
100	5.179	3.828	3.250	2.917	2.696	2.537	2.417	2.321	2.244	2.179	2.124	2.077	2.036	2.000
120	5.152	3.805	3.227	2.894	2.674	2.515	2.395	2.299	2.222	2.157	2.102	2.055	2.014	1.977
140	5.134	3.788	3.211	2.879	2.658	2.500	2.379	2.284	2.206	2.141	2.086	2.039	1.998	1.961
160	5.120	3.775	3.199	2.867	2.647	2.488	2.368	2.272	2.194	2.129	2.074	2.027	1.986	1.949
180	5.109	3.766	3.189	2.858	2.638	2.479	2.359	2.263	2.185	2.120	2.065	2.018	1.976	1.940
200	5.100	3.758	3.182	2.850	2.630	2.472	2.351	2.256	2.178	2.113	2.058	2.010	1.969	1.932
300	5.075	3.735	3.160	2.829	2.609	2.451	2.330	2.234	2.156	2.091	2.036	1.988	1.947	1.910
∞	5.024	3.689	3.116	2.786	2.567	2.408	2.288	2.192	2.114	2.048	1.993	1.945	1.903	1.866

Table A.4. (*Continued*)

2.5%	Numerator Degrees of Freedom													
Denominator Degrees of Freedom	15	16	17	18	19	20	22	24	26	28	30	35	40	45
1	984.867	986.919	988.733	990.349	991.797	993.103	995.362	997.249	998.849	1000.222	1001.414	1003.803	1005.598	1006.997
2	39.431	39.435	39.439	39.442	39.445	39.448	39.452	39.456	39.459	39.462	39.465	39.469	39.473	39.476
3	14.253	14.232	14.213	14.196	14.181	14.167	14.144	14.124	14.107	14.093	14.081	14.055	14.037	14.022
4	8.657	8.633	8.611	8.592	8.575	8.560	8.533	8.511	8.492	8.476	8.461	8.433	8.411	8.394
5	6.428	6.403	6.381	6.362	6.344	6.329	6.301	6.278	6.258	6.242	6.227	6.197	6.175	6.158
6	5.269	5.244	5.222	5.202	5.184	5.168	5.141	5.117	5.097	5.080	5.065	5.035	5.012	4.995
7	4.568	4.543	4.521	4.501	4.483	4.467	4.439	4.415	4.395	4.378	4.362	4.332	4.309	4.291
8	4.101	4.076	4.054	4.034	4.016	3.999	3.971	3.947	3.927	3.909	3.894	3.863	3.840	3.821
9	3.769	3.744	3.722	3.701	3.683	3.667	3.638	3.614	3.594	3.576	3.560	3.529	3.505	3.487
10	3.522	3.496	3.474	3.453	3.435	3.419	3.390	3.365	3.345	3.327	3.311	3.279	3.255	3.237
11	3.330	3.304	3.282	3.261	3.243	3.226	3.197	3.173	3.152	3.133	3.118	3.086	3.061	3.042
12	3.177	3.152	3.129	3.108	3.090	3.073	3.043	3.019	2.998	2.979	2.963	2.931	2.906	2.887
13	3.053	3.027	3.004	2.983	2.965	2.948	2.918	2.893	2.872	2.853	2.837	2.805	2.780	2.760
14	2.949	2.923	2.900	2.879	2.861	2.844	2.814	2.789	2.767	2.749	2.732	2.699	2.674	2.654
15	2.862	2.836	2.813	2.792	2.773	2.756	2.726	2.701	2.679	2.660	2.644	2.610	2.585	2.565
16	2.788	2.761	2.738	2.717	2.698	2.681	2.651	2.625	2.603	2.584	2.568	2.534	2.509	2.488
17	2.723	2.697	2.673	2.652	2.633	2.616	2.585	2.560	2.538	2.519	2.502	2.468	2.442	2.422
18	2.667	2.640	2.617	2.596	2.576	2.559	2.529	2.503	2.481	2.461	2.445	2.410	2.384	2.364
19	2.617	2.591	2.567	2.546	2.526	2.509	2.478	2.452	2.430	2.411	2.394	2.359	2.333	2.312
20	2.573	2.547	2.523	2.501	2.482	2.464	2.434	2.408	2.385	2.366	2.349	2.314	2.287	2.266
21	2.534	2.507	2.483	2.462	2.442	2.425	2.394	2.368	2.345	2.325	2.308	2.273	2.246	2.225
22	2.498	2.472	2.448	2.426	2.407	2.389	2.358	2.331	2.309	2.289	2.272	2.237	2.210	2.188
24	2.437	2.411	2.386	2.365	2.345	2.327	2.296	2.269	2.246	2.226	2.209	2.173	2.146	2.124
26	2.387	2.360	2.335	2.314	2.294	2.276	2.244	2.217	2.194	2.174	2.157	2.120	2.093	2.071
28	2.344	2.317	2.292	2.270	2.251	2.232	2.201	2.174	2.150	2.130	2.112	2.076	2.048	2.025
30	2.307	2.280	2.255	2.233	2.213	2.195	2.163	2.136	2.112	2.092	2.074	2.037	2.009	1.986
35	2.235	2.207	2.183	2.160	2.140	2.122	2.089	2.062	2.038	2.017	1.999	1.961	1.932	1.909
40	2.182	2.154	2.129	2.107	2.086	2.068	2.035	2.007	1.983	1.962	1.943	1.905	1.875	1.852
45	2.141	2.113	2.088	2.066	2.045	2.026	1.993	1.965	1.940	1.919	1.900	1.861	1.831	1.807
50	2.109	2.081	2.056	2.033	2.012	1.993	1.960	1.931	1.907	1.885	1.866	1.827	1.796	1.772
60	2.061	2.033	2.008	1.985	1.964	1.944	1.911	1.882	1.857	1.835	1.815	1.775	1.744	1.719
70	2.028	1.999	1.974	1.950	1.929	1.910	1.876	1.847	1.821	1.799	1.779	1.739	1.707	1.681
80	2.003	1.974	1.948	1.925	1.904	1.884	1.850	1.820	1.795	1.772	1.752	1.711	1.679	1.653
90	1.983	1.955	1.929	1.905	1.884	1.864	1.830	1.800	1.774	1.752	1.731	1.690	1.657	1.631
100	1.968	1.939	1.913	1.890	1.868	1.849	1.814	1.784	1.758	1.735	1.715	1.673	1.640	1.614
120	1.945	1.916	1.890	1.866	1.845	1.825	1.790	1.760	1.733	1.710	1.690	1.647	1.614	1.587
140	1.929	1.900	1.873	1.850	1.828	1.808	1.773	1.743	1.716	1.693	1.672	1.629	1.596	1.568
160	1.917	1.887	1.861	1.837	1.816	1.796	1.760	1.730	1.703	1.680	1.659	1.616	1.582	1.554
180	1.907	1.878	1.852	1.828	1.806	1.786	1.750	1.720	1.693	1.669	1.649	1.605	1.571	1.543
200	1.900	1.870	1.844	1.820	1.798	1.778	1.742	1.712	1.685	1.661	1.640	1.597	1.562	1.534
300	1.877	1.848	1.821	1.797	1.775	1.755	1.719	1.688	1.661	1.637	1.616	1.571	1.536	1.507
∞	1.833	1.803	1.776	1.751	1.729	1.708	1.672	1.640	1.612	1.588	1.566	1.520	1.484	1.454

Table A.4. (*Continued*)

2.5%	Numerator Degrees of Freedom												
Denominator Degrees of Freedom	50	60	70	80	90	100	120	140	160	180	200	300	∞
1	1008.117	1009.800	1011.004	1011.908	1012.612	1013.175	1014.020	1014.625	1015.078	1015.431	1015.713	1016.561	1018.258
2	39.478	39.481	39.484	39.485	39.487	39.488	39.490	39.491	39.492	39.492	39.493	39.495	39.498
3	14.010	13.992	13.979	13.970	13.962	13.956	13.947	13.941	13.936	13.932	13.929	13.920	13.902
4	8.381	8.360	8.346	8.335	8.326	8.319	8.309	8.302	8.296	8.292	8.289	8.278	8.257
5	6.144	6.123	6.107	6.096	6.087	6.080	6.069	6.062	6.056	6.051	6.048	6.037	6.015
6	4.980	4.959	4.943	4.932	4.923	4.915	4.904	4.897	4.891	4.886	4.882	4.871	4.849
7	4.276	4.254	4.239	4.227	4.218	4.210	4.199	4.191	4.185	4.180	4.176	4.165	4.142
8	3.807	3.784	3.768	3.756	3.747	3.739	3.728	3.720	3.714	3.709	3.705	3.693	3.670
9	3.472	3.449	3.433	3.421	3.411	3.403	3.392	3.383	3.377	3.372	3.368	3.357	3.333
10	3.221	3.198	3.182	3.169	3.160	3.152	3.140	3.131	3.125	3.120	3.116	3.104	3.080
11	3.027	3.004	2.987	2.974	2.964	2.956	2.944	2.935	2.929	2.924	2.920	2.908	2.883
12	2.871	2.848	2.831	2.818	2.808	2.800	2.787	2.779	2.772	2.767	2.763	2.750	2.725
13	2.744	2.720	2.703	2.690	2.680	2.671	2.659	2.650	2.643	2.638	2.634	2.621	2.595
14	2.638	2.614	2.597	2.583	2.573	2.565	2.552	2.543	2.536	2.531	2.526	2.513	2.487
15	2.549	2.524	2.506	2.493	2.482	2.474	2.461	2.452	2.445	2.440	2.435	2.422	2.395
16	2.472	2.447	2.429	2.415	2.405	2.396	2.383	2.374	2.367	2.361	2.357	2.343	2.316
17	2.405	2.380	2.362	2.348	2.337	2.329	2.315	2.306	2.299	2.293	2.289	2.275	2.247
18	2.347	2.321	2.303	2.289	2.278	2.269	2.256	2.246	2.239	2.233	2.229	2.215	2.187
19	2.295	2.270	2.251	2.237	2.226	2.217	2.203	2.193	2.186	2.180	2.176	2.162	2.133
20	2.249	2.223	2.205	2.190	2.179	2.170	2.156	2.146	2.139	2.133	2.128	2.114	2.085
21	2.208	2.182	2.163	2.148	2.137	2.128	2.114	2.104	2.097	2.091	2.086	2.072	2.042
22	2.171	2.145	2.125	2.111	2.099	2.090	2.076	2.066	2.058	2.052	2.047	2.033	2.003
24	2.107	2.080	2.060	2.045	2.034	2.024	2.010	2.000	1.992	1.986	1.981	1.966	1.935
26	2.053	2.026	2.006	1.991	1.979	1.969	1.954	1.944	1.936	1.930	1.925	1.909	1.878
28	2.007	1.980	1.959	1.944	1.932	1.922	1.907	1.896	1.888	1.882	1.877	1.861	1.829
30	1.968	1.940	1.920	1.904	1.892	1.882	1.866	1.855	1.847	1.841	1.835	1.819	1.787
35	1.890	1.861	1.840	1.824	1.811	1.801	1.785	1.774	1.765	1.758	1.753	1.736	1.702
40	1.832	1.803	1.781	1.764	1.751	1.741	1.724	1.712	1.703	1.696	1.691	1.673	1.637
45	1.788	1.757	1.735	1.718	1.705	1.694	1.677	1.665	1.655	1.648	1.642	1.624	1.586
50	1.752	1.721	1.698	1.681	1.667	1.656	1.639	1.626	1.616	1.609	1.603	1.584	1.545
60	1.699	1.667	1.643	1.625	1.611	1.599	1.581	1.568	1.558	1.550	1.543	1.524	1.482
70	1.660	1.628	1.604	1.585	1.570	1.558	1.539	1.526	1.515	1.507	1.500	1.480	1.436
80	1.632	1.599	1.574	1.555	1.540	1.527	1.508	1.494	1.483	1.474	1.467	1.446	1.400
90	1.610	1.576	1.551	1.531	1.516	1.503	1.483	1.469	1.457	1.449	1.441	1.419	1.371
100	1.592	1.558	1.532	1.512	1.496	1.483	1.463	1.448	1.437	1.428	1.420	1.397	1.347
120	1.565	1.530	1.504	1.483	1.467	1.454	1.433	1.417	1.405	1.396	1.388	1.364	1.310
140	1.546	1.510	1.483	1.463	1.446	1.432	1.411	1.395	1.382	1.372	1.364	1.339	1.283
160	1.531	1.495	1.468	1.447	1.430	1.416	1.394	1.377	1.365	1.355	1.346	1.320	1.261
180	1.520	1.484	1.456	1.435	1.417	1.403	1.381	1.364	1.351	1.341	1.332	1.305	1.244
200	1.511	1.474	1.447	1.425	1.407	1.393	1.370	1.353	1.340	1.329	1.320	1.293	1.229
300	1.484	1.446	1.417	1.395	1.377	1.361	1.337	1.319	1.305	1.294	1.285	1.255	1.182
∞	1.428	1.388	1.357	1.333	1.313	1.296	1.268	1.247	1.231	1.217	1.205	1.166	1.000

Table A.4. (*Continued*)

1%	Numerator Degrees of Freedom 1	2	3	4	5	6	7	8	9	10	11	12	13	14
(d) 1% right-hand tail														
Denominator Degrees of Freedom 1	4052.181	4999.500	5403.352	5624.583	5763.650	5858.986	5928.356	5981.070	6022.473	6055.847	6083.317	6106.321	6125.865	6142.674
2	98.503	99.000	99.166	99.249	99.299	99.333	99.356	99.374	99.388	99.399	99.408	99.416	99.422	99.428
3	34.116	30.817	29.457	28.710	28.237	27.911	27.672	27.489	27.345	27.229	27.133	27.052	26.983	26.924
4	21.198	18.000	16.694	15.977	15.522	15.207	14.976	14.799	14.659	14.546	14.452	14.374	14.307	14.249
5	16.258	13.274	12.060	11.392	10.967	10.672	10.456	10.289	10.158	10.051	9.963	9.888	9.825	9.770
6	13.745	10.925	9.780	9.148	8.746	8.466	8.260	8.102	7.976	7.874	7.790	7.718	7.657	7.605
7	12.246	9.547	8.451	7.847	7.460	7.191	6.993	6.840	6.719	6.620	6.538	6.469	6.410	6.359
8	11.259	8.649	7.591	7.006	6.632	6.371	6.178	6.029	5.911	5.814	5.734	5.667	5.609	5.559
9	10.561	8.022	6.992	6.422	6.057	5.802	5.613	5.467	5.351	5.257	5.178	5.111	5.055	5.005
10	10.044	7.559	6.552	5.994	5.636	5.386	5.200	5.057	4.942	4.849	4.772	4.706	4.650	4.601
11	9.646	7.206	6.217	5.668	5.316	5.069	4.886	4.744	4.632	4.539	4.462	4.397	4.342	4.293
12	9.330	6.927	5.953	5.412	5.064	4.821	4.640	4.499	4.388	4.296	4.220	4.155	4.100	4.052
13	9.074	6.701	5.739	5.205	4.862	4.620	4.441	4.302	4.191	4.100	4.025	3.960	3.905	3.857
14	8.862	6.515	5.564	5.035	4.695	4.456	4.278	4.140	4.030	3.939	3.864	3.800	3.745	3.698
15	8.683	6.359	5.417	4.893	4.556	4.318	4.142	4.004	3.895	3.805	3.730	3.666	3.612	3.564
16	8.531	6.226	5.292	4.773	4.437	4.202	4.026	3.890	3.780	3.691	3.616	3.553	3.498	3.451
17	8.400	6.112	5.185	4.669	4.336	4.102	3.927	3.791	3.682	3.593	3.519	3.455	3.401	3.353
18	8.285	6.013	5.092	4.579	4.248	4.015	3.841	3.705	3.597	3.508	3.434	3.371	3.316	3.269
19	8.185	5.926	5.010	4.500	4.171	3.939	3.765	3.631	3.523	3.434	3.360	3.297	3.242	3.195
20	8.096	5.849	4.938	4.431	4.103	3.871	3.699	3.564	3.457	3.368	3.294	3.231	3.177	3.130
21	8.017	5.780	4.874	4.369	4.042	3.812	3.640	3.506	3.398	3.310	3.236	3.173	3.119	3.072
22	7.945	5.719	4.817	4.313	3.988	3.758	3.587	3.453	3.346	3.258	3.184	3.121	3.067	3.019
24	7.823	5.614	4.718	4.218	3.895	3.667	3.496	3.363	3.256	3.168	3.094	3.032	2.977	2.930
26	7.721	5.526	4.637	4.140	3.818	3.591	3.421	3.288	3.182	3.094	3.021	2.958	2.904	2.857
28	7.636	5.453	4.568	4.074	3.754	3.528	3.358	3.226	3.120	3.032	2.959	2.896	2.842	2.795
30	7.562	5.390	4.510	4.018	3.699	3.473	3.304	3.173	3.067	2.979	2.906	2.843	2.789	2.742
35	7.419	5.268	4.396	3.908	3.592	3.368	3.200	3.069	2.963	2.876	2.803	2.740	2.686	2.639
40	7.314	5.179	4.313	3.828	3.514	3.291	3.124	2.993	2.888	2.801	2.727	2.665	2.611	2.563
45	7.234	5.110	4.249	3.767	3.454	3.232	3.066	2.935	2.830	2.743	2.670	2.608	2.553	2.506
50	7.171	5.057	4.199	3.720	3.408	3.186	3.020	2.890	2.785	2.698	2.625	2.562	2.508	2.461
60	7.077	4.977	4.126	3.649	3.339	3.119	2.953	2.823	2.718	2.632	2.559	2.496	2.442	2.394
70	7.011	4.922	4.074	3.600	3.291	3.071	2.906	2.777	2.672	2.585	2.512	2.450	2.395	2.348
80	6.963	4.881	4.036	3.563	3.255	3.036	2.871	2.742	2.637	2.551	2.478	2.415	2.361	2.313
90	6.925	4.849	4.007	3.535	3.228	3.009	2.845	2.715	2.611	2.524	2.451	2.389	2.334	2.286
100	6.895	4.824	3.984	3.513	3.206	2.988	2.823	2.694	2.590	2.503	2.430	2.368	2.313	2.265
120	6.851	4.787	3.949	3.480	3.174	2.956	2.792	2.663	2.559	2.472	2.399	2.336	2.282	2.234
140	6.819	4.760	3.925	3.456	3.151	2.933	2.769	2.641	2.536	2.450	2.377	2.314	2.260	2.212
160	6.796	4.740	3.906	3.439	3.134	2.917	2.753	2.624	2.520	2.434	2.360	2.298	2.243	2.195
180	6.778	4.725	3.892	3.425	3.120	2.904	2.740	2.611	2.507	2.421	2.348	2.285	2.230	2.182
200	6.763	4.713	3.881	3.414	3.110	2.893	2.730	2.601	2.497	2.411	2.338	2.275	2.220	2.172
300	6.720	4.677	3.848	3.382	3.079	2.862	2.699	2.571	2.467	2.380	2.307	2.244	2.190	2.142
∞	6.635	4.605	3.782	3.319	3.017	2.802	2.639	2.511	2.407	2.321	2.248	2.185	2.130	2.082

Table A.4. (*Continued*)

1%	Numerator Degrees of Freedom													
Denominator Degrees of Freedom	15	16	17	18	19	20	22	24	26	28	30	35	40	45
1	6157.285	6170.101	6181.435	6191.529	6200.576	6208.730	6222.843	6234.631	6244.624	6253.203	6260.649	6275.568	6286.782	6295.519
2	99.433	99.437	99.440	99.444	99.447	99.449	99.454	99.458	99.461	99.463	99.466	99.471	99.474	99.477
3	26.872	26.827	26.787	26.751	26.719	26.690	26.640	26.598	26.562	26.531	26.505	26.451	26.411	26.379
4	14.198	14.154	14.115	14.080	14.048	14.020	13.970	13.929	13.894	13.864	13.838	13.785	13.745	13.714
5	9.722	9.680	9.643	9.610	9.580	9.553	9.506	9.466	9.433	9.404	9.379	9.329	9.291	9.262
6	7.559	7.519	7.483	7.451	7.422	7.396	7.351	7.313	7.280	7.253	7.229	7.180	7.143	7.115
7	6.314	6.275	6.240	6.209	6.181	6.155	6.111	6.074	6.043	6.016	5.992	5.944	5.908	5.880
8	5.515	5.477	5.442	5.412	5.384	5.359	5.316	5.279	5.248	5.221	5.198	5.151	5.116	5.088
9	4.962	4.924	4.890	4.860	4.833	4.808	4.765	4.729	4.698	4.672	4.649	4.602	4.567	4.539
10	4.558	4.520	4.487	4.457	4.430	4.405	4.363	4.327	4.296	4.270	4.247	4.200	4.165	4.138
11	4.251	4.213	4.180	4.150	4.123	4.099	4.057	4.021	3.990	3.964	3.941	3.895	3.860	3.832
12	4.010	3.972	3.939	3.909	3.883	3.858	3.816	3.780	3.750	3.724	3.701	3.654	3.619	3.592
13	3.815	3.778	3.745	3.716	3.689	3.665	3.622	3.587	3.556	3.530	3.507	3.461	3.425	3.398
14	3.656	3.619	3.586	3.556	3.529	3.505	3.463	3.427	3.397	3.371	3.348	3.301	3.266	3.238
15	3.522	3.485	3.452	3.423	3.396	3.372	3.330	3.294	3.264	3.237	3.214	3.167	3.132	3.104
16	3.409	3.372	3.339	3.310	3.283	3.259	3.216	3.181	3.150	3.124	3.101	3.054	3.018	2.990
17	3.312	3.275	3.242	3.212	3.186	3.162	3.119	3.084	3.053	3.026	3.003	2.956	2.920	2.892
18	3.227	3.190	3.158	3.128	3.101	3.077	3.035	2.999	2.968	2.942	2.919	2.871	2.835	2.807
19	3.153	3.116	3.084	3.054	3.027	3.003	2.961	2.925	2.894	2.868	2.844	2.797	2.761	2.732
20	3.088	3.051	3.018	2.989	2.962	2.938	2.895	2.859	2.829	2.802	2.778	2.731	2.695	2.666
21	3.030	2.993	2.960	2.931	2.904	2.880	2.837	2.801	2.770	2.743	2.720	2.672	2.636	2.607
22	2.978	2.941	2.908	2.879	2.852	2.827	2.785	2.749	2.718	2.691	2.667	2.620	2.583	2.554
24	2.889	2.852	2.819	2.789	2.762	2.738	2.695	2.659	2.628	2.601	2.577	2.529	2.492	2.463
26	2.815	2.778	2.745	2.715	2.688	2.664	2.621	2.585	2.554	2.526	2.503	2.454	2.417	2.388
28	2.753	2.716	2.683	2.653	2.626	2.602	2.559	2.522	2.491	2.464	2.440	2.391	2.354	2.324
30	2.700	2.663	2.630	2.600	2.573	2.549	2.506	2.469	2.437	2.410	2.386	2.337	2.299	2.269
35	2.597	2.560	2.527	2.497	2.470	2.445	2.401	2.364	2.333	2.305	2.281	2.231	2.193	2.162
40	2.522	2.484	2.451	2.421	2.394	2.369	2.325	2.288	2.256	2.228	2.203	2.153	2.114	2.083
45	2.464	2.427	2.393	2.363	2.336	2.311	2.267	2.230	2.197	2.169	2.144	2.093	2.054	2.023
50	2.419	2.382	2.348	2.318	2.290	2.265	2.221	2.183	2.151	2.123	2.098	2.046	2.007	1.975
60	2.352	2.315	2.281	2.251	2.223	2.198	2.153	2.115	2.083	2.054	2.028	1.976	1.936	1.904
70	2.306	2.268	2.234	2.204	2.176	2.150	2.106	2.067	2.034	2.005	1.980	1.927	1.886	1.853
80	2.271	2.233	2.199	2.169	2.141	2.115	2.070	2.032	1.999	1.969	1.944	1.890	1.849	1.816
90	2.244	2.206	2.172	2.142	2.114	2.088	2.043	2.004	1.971	1.942	1.916	1.862	1.820	1.787
100	2.223	2.185	2.151	2.120	2.092	2.067	2.021	1.983	1.949	1.919	1.893	1.839	1.797	1.763
120	2.192	2.154	2.119	2.089	2.060	2.035	1.989	1.950	1.916	1.886	1.860	1.806	1.763	1.728
140	2.169	2.131	2.097	2.066	2.038	2.012	1.966	1.927	1.893	1.863	1.836	1.781	1.738	1.704
160	2.153	2.114	2.080	2.049	2.021	1.995	1.949	1.910	1.875	1.845	1.819	1.763	1.720	1.685
180	2.140	2.102	2.067	2.036	2.008	1.982	1.936	1.896	1.862	1.832	1.805	1.749	1.706	1.671
200	2.129	2.091	2.057	2.026	1.997	1.971	1.925	1.886	1.851	1.821	1.794	1.738	1.694	1.659
300	2.099	2.061	2.026	1.995	1.966	1.940	1.894	1.854	1.819	1.789	1.761	1.705	1.660	1.624
∞	2.039	2.000	1.965	1.934	1.905	1.878	1.831	1.791	1.755	1.724	1.696	1.638	1.592	1.555

Table A.4. (*Continued*)

1%	Numerator Degrees of Freedom												
Denominator Degrees of Freedom	50	60	70	80	90	100	120	140	160	180	200	300	∞
1	6302.517	6313.030	6320.550	6326.197	6330.592	6334.110	6339.391	6343.166	6345.999	6348.203	6349.967	6355.262	6365.864
2	99.479	99.482	99.485	99.487	99.488	99.489	99.491	99.492	99.493	99.494	99.494	99.496	99.499
3	26.354	26.316	26.289	26.269	26.253	26.240	26.221	26.207	26.197	26.189	26.183	26.164	26.125
4	13.690	13.652	13.625	13.605	13.590	13.577	13.558	13.545	13.534	13.527	13.520	13.501	13.463
5	9.238	9.202	9.176	9.157	9.142	9.130	9.112	9.099	9.089	9.081	9.075	9.057	9.020
6	7.091	7.057	7.032	7.013	6.998	6.987	6.969	6.956	6.947	6.940	6.934	6.916	6.880
7	5.858	5.824	5.799	5.781	5.766	5.755	5.737	5.725	5.715	5.708	5.702	5.685	5.650
8	5.065	5.032	5.007	4.989	4.975	4.963	4.946	4.934	4.924	4.917	4.911	4.894	4.859
9	4.517	4.483	4.459	4.441	4.426	4.415	4.398	4.385	4.376	4.369	4.363	4.346	4.311
10	4.115	4.082	4.058	4.039	4.025	4.014	3.996	3.984	3.975	3.968	3.962	3.944	3.909
11	3.810	3.776	3.752	3.734	3.719	3.708	3.690	3.678	3.669	3.661	3.656	3.638	3.602
12	3.569	3.535	3.511	3.493	3.478	3.467	3.449	3.437	3.428	3.420	3.414	3.397	3.361
13	3.375	3.341	3.317	3.298	3.284	3.272	3.255	3.242	3.233	3.225	3.219	3.202	3.165
14	3.215	3.181	3.157	3.138	3.124	3.112	3.094	3.082	3.072	3.064	3.059	3.040	3.004
15	3.081	3.047	3.022	3.004	2.989	2.977	2.959	2.947	2.937	2.930	2.923	2.905	2.868
16	2.967	2.933	2.908	2.889	2.875	2.863	2.845	2.832	2.822	2.815	2.808	2.790	2.753
17	2.869	2.835	2.810	2.791	2.776	2.764	2.746	2.733	2.723	2.715	2.709	2.691	2.653
18	2.784	2.749	2.724	2.705	2.690	2.678	2.660	2.647	2.637	2.629	2.623	2.604	2.566
19	2.709	2.674	2.649	2.630	2.614	2.602	2.584	2.571	2.561	2.553	2.547	2.528	2.489
20	2.643	2.608	2.582	2.563	2.548	2.535	2.517	2.503	2.493	2.485	2.479	2.460	2.421
21	2.584	2.548	2.523	2.503	2.488	2.475	2.457	2.443	2.433	2.425	2.419	2.400	2.360
22	2.531	2.495	2.469	2.450	2.434	2.422	2.403	2.389	2.379	2.371	2.365	2.345	2.305
24	2.440	2.403	2.377	2.357	2.342	2.329	2.310	2.296	2.286	2.278	2.271	2.251	2.211
26	2.364	2.327	2.301	2.281	2.265	2.252	2.233	2.219	2.208	2.200	2.193	2.173	2.131
28	2.300	2.263	2.236	2.216	2.200	2.187	2.167	2.153	2.142	2.134	2.127	2.106	2.064
30	2.245	2.208	2.181	2.160	2.144	2.131	2.111	2.096	2.085	2.077	2.070	2.049	2.006
35	2.137	2.099	2.072	2.050	2.034	2.020	2.000	1.985	1.973	1.965	1.957	1.936	1.891
40	2.058	2.019	1.991	1.969	1.952	1.938	1.917	1.902	1.890	1.881	1.874	1.851	1.805
45	1.997	1.958	1.929	1.907	1.889	1.875	1.853	1.838	1.826	1.816	1.809	1.786	1.737
50	1.949	1.909	1.880	1.857	1.839	1.825	1.803	1.786	1.774	1.765	1.757	1.733	1.683
60	1.877	1.836	1.806	1.783	1.764	1.749	1.726	1.710	1.697	1.687	1.678	1.653	1.601
70	1.826	1.785	1.754	1.730	1.711	1.695	1.672	1.654	1.641	1.630	1.622	1.596	1.540
80	1.788	1.746	1.714	1.690	1.671	1.655	1.630	1.613	1.599	1.588	1.579	1.552	1.494
90	1.759	1.716	1.684	1.659	1.639	1.623	1.598	1.580	1.566	1.555	1.546	1.518	1.457
100	1.735	1.692	1.659	1.634	1.614	1.598	1.572	1.554	1.539	1.528	1.518	1.490	1.427
120	1.700	1.656	1.623	1.597	1.576	1.559	1.533	1.514	1.499	1.487	1.477	1.447	1.381
140	1.675	1.630	1.596	1.570	1.549	1.532	1.505	1.485	1.469	1.457	1.447	1.416	1.346
160	1.656	1.610	1.576	1.550	1.528	1.511	1.483	1.463	1.447	1.434	1.424	1.392	1.319
180	1.641	1.595	1.561	1.534	1.512	1.494	1.466	1.446	1.429	1.416	1.406	1.373	1.297
200	1.629	1.583	1.548	1.521	1.499	1.481	1.453	1.432	1.415	1.402	1.391	1.357	1.279
300	1.594	1.547	1.511	1.483	1.460	1.441	1.411	1.389	1.372	1.358	1.346	1.309	1.220
∞	1.523	1.473	1.435	1.404	1.379	1.358	1.325	1.299	1.278	1.261	1.247	1.200	1.000

Index

www.ingramcontent.com/pod-product-compliance
Lightning Source LLC
LaVergne TN
LVHW052030200926
848481LV00005B/1632
* 9 7 8 9 8 1 1 2 8 7 9 2 3 *